MATERIAL APPROACHES
TO ROMAN MAGIC

Occult Objects and Supernatural Substances

MATERIAL APPROACHES TO ROMAN MAGIC

OCCULT OBJECTS AND SUPERNATURAL SUBSTANCES

Edited by

Adam Parker and Stuart Mckie

TRAC THEMES IN ROMAN ARCHAEOLOGY
VOLUME 2

Series Editor: Sergio González Sánchez

OXBOW | books
Oxford & Philadelphia

Published in the United Kingdom in 2018 by
OXBOW BOOKS
The Old Music Hall, 106–108 Cowley Road, Oxford OX4 1JE

and in the United States by
OXBOW BOOKS
1950 Lawrence Road, Havertown, PA 19083

Hardcover Edition: ISBN 978-1-78570-881-7
Digital Edition: ISBN 978-1-78570-882-4 (epub)

A CIP record for this book is available from the British Library

Library of Congress Control Number: 2018935376

For a complete list of Oxbow titles, please contact:

UNITED KINGDOM
Oxbow Books
Telephone (01865) 241249, Fax (01865) 794449
Email: oxbow@oxbowbooks.com
www.oxbowbooks.com

UNITED STATES OF AMERICA
Oxbow Books
Telephone (800) 791-9354, Fax (610) 853-9146
Email: queries@casemateacademic.com
www.casemateacademic.com/oxbow

Oxbow Books is part of the Casemate Group

Front cover: Anthropomorphic amber amulet, from Colchester. COLEM: 1986.66.693.1 ©Colchester Museums.

Printed and bound in Great Britain by Marston Book Services Ltd, Oxfordshire

Contents

Series Foreword

Sergio Gonzalez Sanchez

The Theoretical Roman Archaeology Conference (TRAC) and its Standing Committee are committed to evolving hand in hand with the demands of an ever-developing archaeological community searching for new ways of approaching theory in Roman archaeology. New times and new trends require new ways of sharing knowledge within academia and with the public. Honouring this commitment, we have recently launched two new publication platforms of the highest quality: the brand new *Theoretical Roman Archaeology Journal* (an online, open-access journal hosted by the Open Humanities Library) and the *TRAC Themes in Roman Archaeology* series, the second volume of which you have in your hands right now.

This series intends to offer an attractive venue for publication of research monographs or thematically-coherent edited volumes showing a strong engagement with theory in Roman archaeology. The first volume of this series, edited by Alexandra Guglielmi and myself, was dedicated to the analysis of different theoretical approaches to Roman–'barbarian' interactions in the Northern frontiers of the Roman Empire and beyond. The response to that first volume was extremely positive and encouraging, and reassured the TRAC team of the benefit and importance of producing thematic approaches to specific topics within

Roman archaeology. Roman magic, or the beliefs and experiences of those who practised it in Roman times, are better reflected upon through the material evidence available, examples of which are compiled in the different case-studies presented on these pages. We feel this second volume of the series is a perfect follow up to the first volume and we are convinced it will meet everyone's expectations.

I am honoured to have acted as the series editor for this second volume, and I am certainly delighted with the result. The release of this magnificent volume would not have been possible without the professionalism and commitment of many people. Thus, thanks are owed to the team at Oxbow Books whose support and patience made its release possible; to the authors whose papers are collected here for sharing their research and knowledge on the topic, making it accessible for all audiences; to the reviewers whose expertise and advice have elevated the quality of this volume. Last but most definitely not least, to the volume editors, Adam Parker and Stuart McKie, the real gears behind this project, for your constant efforts to make this volume a true reference on the topic and for making my job way too easy. I hope you as a reader enjoy these pages as much as we have enjoyed producing them. May this series sustain its success based on high quality theoretical research for many years to come.

University of Leicester
11 November 2017

Introduction: Materials, Approaches, Substances, and Objects

Stuart McKie and Adam Parker

The core of this book comes from a panel held at the *Theoretical Roman Archaeology Conference* (*TRAC*) 2015 entitled *Charmed I'm Sure: Roman Magic – Old Theory, New Approaches*, which was organised by Adam Parker. One of the most exciting features of that panel was the coming together of university academics, postgraduate students, professional archaeologists and museum curators in the pooling of ideas and approaches to Roman magic. This volume has maintained that variety and energy, with papers from five of the original contributors plus further articles from authors working in the same wide range of professions. Our aim with this collection of papers is to further develop some of the ideas presented at *TRAC* 2015, particularly the focus on materiality and embodied experience of magic in the Roman world. At the core of this volume is the contention that fine-grained artefact analysis has great potential to offer new ways to understand ancient magic practices.

In this introduction we will set out the aims of the present volume, and the problems and gaps in existing scholarship that it intends to address. The study of ancient magic is a dynamic, growing field, and there are considerable opportunities to drive the agenda in new directions. In particular the material, embodied experiences of particularly Roman magical practices have been relatively neglected, and thus a volume of this nature is sorely needed. With TRAC's long pedigree of being a forum for exciting new approaches to established scholarship, it seems appropriate that this collection of papers should be published under its aegis. The editors would like to take this opportunity to thank past and present members of the TRAC Standing Committee, especially Darrell Rohl, Sergio González Sánchez and Matthew Mandich, for their tireless efforts in helping them to prepare this volume for publication.

Special thanks also go to Véronique Dasen, not just for her paper but also for her thoughtful comments on the text of the whole volume.

Lie of the Land

There are two main issues that this volume seeks to address: (1) the relative lack of attention paid to the material evidence for magical beliefs and practice in the Roman world and (2) the relatively poor penetration of recent theoretical discussions into the study of Roman magic, especially around ideas of materiality and embodied experience.

The theoretical study of magic in the ancient world, certainly since its re-emergence on the scene in the 1980s, includes both conceptualist ideas, which have outlined, defined and engaged with broad areas of Greek, Hellenistic and Egyptian magic (Luck 1985 and 2000; Graf 1997; Janowitz 2001; Styers 2004) as well as attempts to outline the functional aspects of magic and the methodologies through which it may be used (Versnel 1991; Flint *et al.* 1999; Thomassen 1999). The focus of most of these works has predominantly been on the more abundant Greek and Graeco-Egyptian material. The emergence of studies into Roman magic contributing towards these grand ideas is a relatively recent phenomenon, certainly until very recently with the emergence of specific works on Roman magic (Kropp 2008; Gordon and Marco Simón 2010).

The study of Roman magical theory and thought has become entrenched in the study of Classics and literature (Otto 2013: 308ff), with artefactual studies often given only a cursory or secondary role in the interpretation of Roman magic. Andrew Wilburn's (2012) *Materia Magica* is the only modern monograph that has attempted to tackle contextualised material culture studies of Roman magic as a standalone phenomenon. The narrow range of chronological focus to which his book explicitly applies deliberately excludes, at least in part, the wider study of magic in historical archaeology with the aim of delving deeper into the concerns of the Roman world. Whilst there are certainly important connections with Ancient Greek and Egyptian material culture, as well as that of the Post-Roman periods, Roman magic is much underrepresented amongst the excellent range of scholarship into ancient magic, as noted by Bremmer (2015: 8) in the introduction to the edited volume *Materiality of Magic* (the most recent volume to attempt an analysis of ancient magic from the perspective of material culture). Roman magic is not completely absent from scholarship, especially given the recent surge of work into this particular field in the wake of the seminal *Magical Practice in the Latin West* (Gordon and Marco Simón 2010). Recent work includes Bailliot and Symmons 2012; Chadwick 2012 and 2015; Wilburn 2012 and 2015; Bailliot 2015; Boschung and Bremmer 2015 (itself including at least four papers explicitly approaching the material evidence for magic in the Roman world); McKie 2016; Parker 2016; Quercia and Cazzulo 2016 to name but a few. However, the range remains sufficiently small to provide a clear justification for further promoting the investigation of Roman magic on its own merit.

Within the wider field of historical archaeology there has been a recent upsurge in interest in the materiality of magic, best exemplified by the recent publication of edited volumes on the topic. The Historical Archaeology volume on *Manifestations of Magic: The Archaeology and Material Culture of Folk Religion* (Fennell and Manning 2014) and the collection of papers from the 2012 *Theoretical Archaeology Group* session entitled *The Materiality of Magic: An Artefactual Investigation into Ritual Practices and Popular Belief* (Houlbrook and Armitage 2015) both seek to demonstrate the range and potential of the material culture of magic within historical archaeology. The issue with these, in relation to the study of Roman archaeology at least, is the minimal use of Roman small finds within their research areas. Frequently we are forced to retroject the interpretations made for Medieval, Post-Medieval, Early Modern and even Contemporary social and cultural groups in order to begin to understand the material manifestations of magic in the Roman world. There is a wide-ranging uniqueness in the material culture of Roman magic which needs further attention. Both of the above volumes represent important modern contributions to a research agenda set out by Ralph Merrifield in his ground-breaking 1987 publication *The Archaeology of Ritual and Magic*: a monograph to which the Fennel and Manning volume is rightly dedicated. Merrifield worried that the study of magic and ritual in archaeology would become associated with a 'loony fringe'

of post-processual thought (Merrifield 1987: 3). The recent magical revival, heralding new investigations into material culture as part of 'the material turn' of magic (Bremmer 2015: 9) is working to re-appropriate this study.

Defining an Issue

The elephant in the room, for both the veteran and uninitiated of this subject, is the question 'what is magic?' The short answer is that, as a scholarly community, we have not agreed on a single answer to that question. Indeed, there are multiple answers depending upon a particular reading of previous works in the subjects of religious studies, anthropology, and sociology. There are multiple definitions about what magic is and is not, how it functions, how it relates to religion, and what practices may or may not be defined as magical.

Explicitly, for the purposes of this collection of papers on the subject of magic we have opted not to provide a single, rigid definition for our contributors to use and adhere to; this is because of the multi-disciplinary nature of this volume and the unique backgrounds and knowledge of our contributors. If we, as a community, cannot decide upon a single definition (for examples of modern definitions see: Merrifield 1987: 6; Tambiah 1990: 7; Faraone 2001: 16; Manning 2014: 1; Chadwick 2015: 37; Stein and Stein 2016: 140) it would be socially crass and intellectually limiting to force our contributors to conform to a boundary that we have arbitrarily supplied. Rather than failing to answer the question, we see this approach as the only logical way to provide the necessary space for this range of material approaches to Roman magic to be brought into world.

However, we do not use the word 'magic' lightly and without the due care and attention that it deserves. Thus, a short historiography of magic, both in the ancient world and in scholarship is necessary, if only to signpost the development of the study of magic and how it relates to this volume. Etymologically, 'magic' has its roots in the Old Persian *magus* (Graf 1997: 20; Pasi 2006: 1134) coming into Greek in the late sixth to the early fifth century B.C., where it refers to a group of people: the Magians. The meaning of the word morphed throughout the following centuries but continues to be related to a group of ritual specialists, closely associated with religious practices (Hdt. 1.132.1–3; Xen. *Cyr.* 8.3.11; Pseudo-Plato, *Alc.* 122; Strabo, *Geog.* 15.3.14; Polybius, *Hist. Fishing Near Scylla*; App. *B Civ.* 2.21.151). By the time the word entered the Latin language and was used by the writers of the early centuries A.D., 'magic' had come to refer to a wide range of ritual practices (Vitr. *De arch.* 7.1; Plin. *HN* 18.90) but was frequently used pejoratively in connection with practices related to human sacrifice, divination, and necromancy (Pliny. *HN* 30.3; 30.5). As a fluid, catch-all term for a huge range of illicit practices, 'magic' became the paradigm of dangerous un-Roman behaviour in the imperial period, especially associated with foreigners (Tac. *Ann.* 2.23) and old witches (Luc. 6.577). However, in contemporary and later Greek texts, the term could still be used positively, even by practitioners as a marker of identity (for example *PGM*:1.127; 1.331; 4.210; 4.243; 4.2082; 4.2290; 4.2319; 4.2450; 4.2454; 63.5). Although important for the scholarly understanding and usage of the term, this emic Roman discussion of magic is not the same as the modern discourse on the subject, which has understandably taken a very different line (for further discussion on the ancient usages of the term see Dickie 2001 and Rives 2010).

The works of Tylor (1867; 1881), Frazer (1900), Evans-Pritchard (1933), and Malinowski (1948) remain hugely influential on the study of ancient magic, and provided the foundation upon which modern studies are based, but they have proved unsuccessful in creating a united front. In material terms, whatever it is that modern scholarship considers to be either 'magical' or 'religious' is categorised as such because of our interpretations of intrinsic differences in how these ancient social practices are considered to have functioned, both practically and supernaturally (Versnel 1991; Luck 2000: 209) and whether or not aspects of this complex relationship are visible in the literary evidence or the archaeological record. Alternatives to such attempts at categorisation include the complete removal of this debate from the academic discussion in which it is taking place. To take one very recent example, Quercia and Cazzulo (2016: 33, 40) consider the non-normative ritual elements of 'deviant' burials in Roman Northern Italy as 'magical' but do not enter into an etymological discussion on the nature of the term or into the theoretical implications of using it. For them, magic remains undefined and it is left to the reader to interpret the consequences of this definition.

Addressing where the boundaries of magic and religion might lie, Luck (1985: 4) characterised four different scholarly positions on the relationship of magic to religion: that magic becomes religion; that religion attempts to reconcile personal power once magic has failed; that religion and magic have common roots; that magic is a degenerate form of religion. Three of the four place religion 'higher' than magic, implying that religion is something to be aspired to and magic is somehow unsophisticated or underdeveloped in an evolutionary sense. These positions do provide a sense of conceptual difference between magic and religion. In the entry for 'magic' in the *Oxford Classical Dictionary*, Versnel refines these distinctions between religion and magic down to their most basic, arguing that the essential difference between the two is magic's 'manipulative, coercive or performative strategy, as compared with the pursuit of concrete goals' (2012: 884). Both Versnel's distilled definition and Luck's more extensive characterisation accept that both religion and magic could exist within the same conceptual framework. Both are closely related and available, in a functional way, for use by those who wished to partake. The co-existence of magic and religion in the Roman world, by its very nature, suggests that there were appropriate times to choose one over the other, or that they may have been accessed by different social groups reacting to different stimuli. Several pieces of modern academic discourse reject these direct relational interpretations of the relationship between magic and religion and instead promote a general, yet complex, relationship between the two; one that is not easily codified and is much more ephemeral than previously considered (Merrifield 1987: 6–9; Johns 1982; Bailliot 2015: 94; Bremmer 2015: 11; Chadwick 2015: 37–8). Amongst these latter positions, the subject of magic may be defined, but is done so with broad brushstrokes and with a central concern for the specific contexts in which magical beliefs and practices might be found. Indeed, the editors of this volume currently sit on different sides of this theoretical argument: McKie has previously approached curse tablets from the position that magic is complex and uncodified (2016: 23), whereas Parker has approached jet *gorgoneia* from the position that magic can be functionally defined (2016: 109–10). We see value in both approaches. Defining the concept of magic is, by the effort of doing so, inherently restricting to the range of material culture which might be regarded as such. Importantly, the uncritical use of such a definition may be dangerously anachronistic to the material study of the ancient world.

Aims of the Volume

Turning to the present volume, there are two main aims with which we have set out. Firstly, there is a conscious intent to continue the investigation of magical beliefs and practices as they were specifically manifested in the Roman world. In terms of chronology and geography, the majority of papers are set in Italy and the western provinces between the first and fourth centuries A.D. (although Wilburn's case study from Egypt and Sagiv's gemstones from Israel are notable exceptions). Part of the reason for this relatively restricted focus, as has already been established, is the lack of scholarly attention it has received to date. However, there are firm methodological grounds for focusing on specific times and regions, in that doing so draws out the importance of context to the rituals under consideration. Recent debates on Roman culture in general have emphasised that the ways in which people acted in the past were fundamentally influenced by the social, cultural, economic, and physical environments in which they were embedded. The burgeoning field of sensory studies in antiquity has provided fertile ground for discussion, and has greatly advanced our understanding of life in the Roman world (Hamilakis 2014; Toner 2014; Betts 2017). In terms of Roman religion, the *Lived Ancient*

Religion and *Religious Individualization* projects directed by Rüpke at the University of Erfurt have refocused the scholarly discussions away from institutions and '*polis*' worship onto the actions of individuals, situated within social contexts firmly located in time and space (Rüpke 2012; Rüpke and Spickermann 2012; Rüpke 2013; Rüpke and Woolf 2013; Rüpke 2015; Rüpke and Raja 2015; Rüpke 2016). Approaching magical practices in these context-focussed ways can reveal more of the lived experience of the individuals who performed them in their daily lives, but can also illuminate broader questions on the nature of a particular society as it changed over space and time. In the case of the Roman world, the four centuries of the imperial period saw massive shifts in all aspects of life for people across the Mediterranean and northern Europe, including in the ways in which they communicated with the supernatural. Much work has been done on how these changes effected the beliefs and practices conventionally called religion, but there is much scope for exploring those called magic.

The specific focus on Roman magic is not intended to claim that it was a stand-alone phenomenon, divorced from what came before. The inheritance of Greek understandings of relationships with the supernatural world in Rome has long been recognised, and it would be impossible to ignore it here, not to mention the debt that Roman magic owed to other cultures based in North Africa and the Near East. Papers by Sánchez Natalías, Wilburn, Whitmore, Sagiv, and McKie engage directly with some of this heritage, but nevertheless all their arguments point out the important changes that occurred as these ritual practices found their way into the Roman world. At the other end of the Empire, papers by Garland and Davis both explore possible influences from Iron Age practices in the magical rituals of Roman Britain. If anything, it is this range of cultural influence that sets magic in the Roman imperial period apart from the rituals of the preceding centuries, with practitioners making use of virtually limitless permutations in the potential forms of their actions. This could be seen as a symptom of the almost unprecedented levels of interconnectivity between regions and peoples during the Roman imperial period, as ideas, goods, and individuals moved around the Mediterranean with much greater freedom than had been possible before (Morley 2015: 54).

The second of the two main aims of the present volume is to champion the role of material culture as evidence for ancient magical practices. As has already been discussed, the study of ancient magic has been dominated by analysis of texts, and is often strictly linguistic in approach. This has been to the relative detriment of the huge wealth of relevant objects that have survived in the archaeological record. Consideration for material objects is conspicuous in its absence: it takes only a cursory scan through the spell books and recipes of the *PGM* to see how absolutely essential ink, papyrus, metal, stone, wood, leaves, blood, bone, hair and a host of other materials, substances, and objects were to the performance and understandings of ancient magical rituals. It is crucial that scholars give them due appreciation if they intend to create fully-rounded interpretations. However, our aim with this volume is not to simply illustrate existing scholarship with attractive images of objects, but is instead to call for a realignment of scholarly understandings of ancient magical practices that puts material culture at the absolute centre, on an equal footing with written texts. As has already been mentioned, we are not the first to make this call, with Bremmer (2015: 9) already explicitly connecting *The Materiality of Magic* to the wider 'material turn' in scholarship. Dasen and Spieser (2014) have also explored the role of objects and images as modes of transmission for magical knowledge and practice. However, there is still much work to be done, not least in the continued working through of some of the more nuanced theoretical implications of these movements.

This is not necessarily the place for a detailed historiography of 'materiality' or other object-centred approaches, which have been traced back through the structuralist and post-processualist movements of the twentieth century, into the philosophy of late-nineteenth century thinkers such as Marx and Husserl. Plenty of such tracts already exist (Miller 2005; Tilley 2006; Hicks 2010 to name but three), and the debates surrounding these theories and approaches are too contentious and amorphous to be condensed into this introduction. Even some of the most significant scholars in the field have noted the elaborate and potentially bewildering state of the debate at times (Ingold, quoted in Hicks 2010: 79–80), and it can indeed be off-putting for newcomers to the field. Nevertheless, it is important to set out a broad background, so that the papers that follow can be put into their proper theoretical context.

At its absolute core, materiality is an analysis of things: tangible, substantial, even fleshy objects that exist in the real world. It is concerned with how and why things are made, the materials that constitute them, the technology required to produce them, and the manners in which things relate to people, places, ideas, memories, social structures and so on (Tilley *et al.* 2006: 4). The field of material culture studies, which had its genesis in the dialogue between archaeology, anthropology and a number of social sciences, has grown out of a central concern for the place of things in human society, based most recently on the theories of Bourdieu (1977), Giddens (1984) and Latour (2005). Scholars working in these areas have argued that material objects have a central role in the construction, maintenance, interpretation and re-interpretation of all aspects of human society. They act as signifiers of ethnic, class and gender identity (Hodder 1982), they induce psychological and emotional effects such as anger, fear, joy and lust (Gell 1998), and they are instrumental in legitimising, reproducing and challenging social inequalities. As can be seen, the emphasis of material culture studies has been on the relationships between people and objects, or on the ways in which objects influence relationships between people, and a number of scholars have argued forcefully that this is as it should be (Meskell 2005: 4; Joyce 2015: 185). Others have been critical of this (Hicks 2010: 69), and there has been a reactionary movement back towards considering the objects themselves through the idea of object agency, by which things are understood to be able to act within society, independently of human intentions (Kopytoff 1986; Latour 2005; Knappett and Malafouris 2008). Archaeologists have made substantial contributions to all of these debates, not least prehistoric archaeologists such as Tilley and Hodder, but those that study the Roman period were mostly absent during the 'high period' of material culture studies in the 1990s. This has begun to change in recent years, especially through the application of sensory approaches to Roman archaeology that has already been mentioned.

The potential benefits that could be gained by an application of material-focused approaches to the study of Roman magic are vast, as the papers in this volume aim to show. Curse tablets, phallic amulets, inscribed gemstones and other magical objects were all ascribed with agency by those who used them, in that these objects were believed to have the ability to influence the real world, for better or for worse. As will be seen throughout the various contributions collected here, magical objects could have significant impacts on the social lives of those who used them. These things could protect children, attract a lover, attack business rivals or safely conduct the dead to the underworld. The substances with which they were made were also given significance, not just exotic or rare materials such as amber or spices, but mundane substances such as lead and wax. The importance of these materials was intimately connected to context; the times, places, and ways in which they were used mattered a great deal for their efficacy.

Outline of Papers

The papers in this volume offer a wealth of different perspectives on the themes outlined in this introduction, and there are strong continuities across them all. Although it is certainly possible to dip into certain chapters, the editors hope that the reader will recognise the value of the volume as a cohesive whole.

The chapters have been arranged according to loose thematic groupings, although the interrelated themes of materiality and lived experience are visible across all the contributions. The opening four papers, by Sánchez Natalías, Whitmore, Derrick, and Sagiv, deal with specific object types used in magical practices across the Roman

world in the imperial period (curse tablets, phallic objects, unguentaria and gemstones respectively). All four of these authors have gone beyond simple catalogues, however, to demonstrate the central importance of material objects to the understanding and practice of magic for people in the Roman world. They have also shown concern for not thinking about Roman magical practices in a vacuum, and Whitmore in particular embraces a cross-cultural methodology. Present in the arguments of a number of these contributions, especially those by Derrick, Sánchez Natalías, and Sagiv, is the relationship between the objects they study and the literary testimonies that survive from the ancient world. The individual papers address these interrelationships in different ways: Sagiv discusses the mythological backgrounds to images found on magical gemstones, Derrick discusses the place of perfumes and cosmetics in the presentation of elite women in Roman literature, and Sánchez Natalías explores the metaphors of materiality in curse texts. By giving centre-stage to the objects, rather than the texts, these papers are united in bucking the trends that have become established in scholarship on Roman magic, and provide fresh insights that will help move on some occasionally stale research agendas. They all demonstrate that, in the future, scholars ignore materiality in Roman magic at their own peril.

The second group of papers, those by Parker, Davis and Garland, explores the influences of Roman magical practices, with their own influences from further east, on the regions of western Europe that fell under Roman control in the early imperial period, exemplified in these cases by Britain. Building on similar methodologies to the papers in the previous group, Parker's and Davis' contributions use single object types – *tintinnabula* and amber artefacts respectively– to explore how magical beliefs and practices may have been adopted and adapted in new provincial contexts. Both of these papers also demonstrate the wealth of information that is available to scholars on ancient magic in museum catalogues and archaeological grey literature. There is much to be gained by tapping into these largely overlooked resources, and these papers show the value of opening and maintaining channels of communication between museum professionals and university academics. In looking at a single burial from early-Roman *Camulodunum*, Garland's paper takes the focus down onto perhaps the smallest scale possible: the level of specific individuals. In his fine-grained analysis of the assemblage of grave goods in the Stanway Doctor's Burial, Garland not only explores the intersections between 'Roman' and 'Native' beliefs and practices, but also between 'magic' and 'medicine', all of which have been controversial contact points in previous scholarship.

The final group of papers, comprising those by Wilburn and McKie, demonstrate even more clearly the importance of context. Although this is a strong current running through the whole volume, these two papers show that the objects used in Roman magical practices were not important alone, but relied on specific temporal and physical contexts for their efficacy. Wilburn shows how important the home was as a locus for magical practices, especially in terms of defending the family from malign forces. Consideration for this extended from the physical fabric of houses themselves to the actions of residents, guests and even passers-by. McKie investigates the role of the human body in Roman magical practices, concluding that context is paramount. Actions, movements and gestures could be interpreted very differently depending not only on the places in which they were performed, but also on the specific bodies with which they were performed. The age, class and gender of those involved had significant effects both on what certain actions were thought to achieve and also how they were perceived by wider society.

At the end of the volume Dasen provides an overview of the central themes of this volume and draws on the object-focussed approach set out in this introduction to address a range of new issues relating to amulets, the history of the body and personal agency in changing social and religious contexts.

Department of Classics and Ancient History,
University of Manchester
Department of Classical Studies, The Open University

Bibliography

Ancient Sources

Appian (Translated by H. White 1899). *The Civil Wars.* London: Macmillan.
Herodotus (Translated by A.D. Godley 1920). *The Histories.* Cambridge, MA: Harvard University Press.
Pliny the Elder (Translated by J. Bostock 1855). *Natural History.* London: Taylor and Francis.
Polybius (Translated by E.S. Shuckburgh 1889 (1962 Reprint)). *The Histories.* London and New York: Macmillan.
Pseudo-Plato (Translated by W.R.M. Lamb 1955). *Alcibiades I.* Cambridge, MA: Harvard University Press.
Strabo (Translated by H.L. Jones 1932). *Geography.* Cambridge, MA: Harvard University Press.
Tacitus (Translated by C. Moore and J. Jackson 1931). *Annals.* Cambridge, MA: Harvard University Press.
Vitruvius (Translated by M.H. Morgan 1914). Cambridge, MA: Harvard University Press.
Xenophon (Translated by W. Miller 1914) *Cryopaedia.* Cambridge, MA: Harvard University Press.

Modern Sources

Bailliot, M. 2015. Roman magic figurines from the western provinces of the Roman Empire. *Britannia* 46: 93–110.
Bailliot. M. and Symmons, R. 2012. Note from the Roman palace at Fishbourne (Sussex): A Roman magic lead figurine? *Britannia* 43: 249–60.
Betts, E. (ed.) 2017. *Senses of Empire: Multisensory Approaches to Roman Culture.* London and New York: Routledge.
Betz, H.D. (ed.) 1992. *The Greek Magical Papyri in Translation (Including the Demotic Spells).* 2nd edition. Chicago, IL and London: University of Chicago Press.
Bremmer, J.N. 2015. Preface: the materiality of magic. In D. Boschung and J.N. Bremmer (eds) *The Materiality of Magic.* Paderborn: Wilhelm Fink: 7–20.
Boschung, D. and Bremmer, J. (eds) 2015. *The Materiality of Magic.* Paderborn: Wilhelm Fink.
Bourdieu, P. 1977. *An Outline of a Theory of Practice* (Translated by R. Nice). Cambridge: Cambridge University Press.
Chadwick, A. 2012. Routine magic, mundane ritual: towards a unified notion of depositional practice. *Oxford Journal of Archaeology* 31: 283–315.
Chadwick, A. 2015. Doorways, ditches and dead dogs: excavating and recording material manifestations of practical magic amongst later prehistoric and Romano-British communities. In C. Houlbrook and N. Armitage (eds) *The Materiality of Magic: An Artefactual Investigation into Ritual Practices and Popular Belief.* Oxford: Oxbow Books: 37–64.
Dasen, V. and Spieser J.-M. (eds) 2014. *Les savoirs magiques et leur transmission de l'Antiquité à la Renaissance* (Micrologus 60). Florence: Sismel.
Dickie, M. 2001. *Magic and Magicians in the Greco-Roman World.* London and New York: Routledge.
Evans-Pritchard, E.E. 1933. The intellectualist (English) interpretation of magic. *Bulletin of the Faculty of Arts, University of Egypt* 1: 283–311.
Faraone, C.A. 2001. *Ancient Greek Love Magic.* Cambridge, MA, London: Harvard University Press.
Fennell, C. and Manning, M.C. 2014. Manifestations of magic: the archaeology and material culture of folk religion. *Historical Archaeology* 48: 1–200.
Flint, V., Gordon, R., Luck, G., and Ogden, D. 1999. *Witchcraft and Magic in Europe: Volume 2 Ancient Greece and Rome.* London: Athlone.
Frazer, J. 1900. *The Golden Bough: A Study in Magic and Religion.* 2nd edition. London: Macmillan.
Gell, A. 1998. *Art and Agency: A New Anthropological Theory.* Oxford: Oxford University Press.
Giddens, A. 1984. *The Constitution of Society: Outline of the Theory of Structuration.* Cambridge: Polity.
Gordon, R. and Marco Simón, F. (eds) 2010. *Magical Practice in the Latin West: Papers from the International Conference Held at the University of Zaragoza, 30 Sept. –1 Oct. 2005.* Leiden: Brill.
Graf, F. 1997. Magic in the Ancient World (Translated by F. Philip). Cambridge, MA, London: Harvard University Press.
Hamilakis, Y. 2014. *Archaeology and the Senses: Human Experience, Memory and Affect.* Cambridge: Cambridge University Press.
Hicks, D. 2010. The material-cultural turn: event and effect. In D. Hicks and M. Beaudry (eds) *The Oxford Handbook of Material Culture Studies.* Oxford: Oxford University Press: 25–98.

Hodder, I. 1982. *Symbols in Action*. Cambridge: Cambridge University Press.

Houlbrook, C. and Armitage, N. (eds) 2015. *The Materiality of Magic: An Artefactual Investigation into Ritual Practices and Popular Belief*. Oxford: Oxbow Books.

Janowitz, N. 2001. *Magic in the Roman World: Pagans, Jews and Christians*. London, New York: Routledge.

Johns, C. 1982. *Sex or Symbol? Erotic Images of Greece and Rome*. London: British Museum Press.

Joyce, R. 2015. Transforming archaeology, transforming materiality. *Archaeological Papers of the American Anthropological Association* 26: 181–91.

Kropp, A. 2008. *Magische Sprachverwendung in vulgärlateinischen Fluchtafeln (defixiones)*. Tübingen: G. Narr.

Knappett, C. and Malafouris, L. (eds) 2008. *Material Agency: Towards a Non-Anthropocentric Approach*. New York: Springer.

Kopytoff, I. 1986. The cultural biography of things: commoditization as a process. In A. Appadurai (ed.) *The Social Life of Things*. Cambridge: Cambridge University Press: 64–91.

Latour, B. 2005. *Reassembling the Social: An Introduction to Actor-Network Theory*. Oxford: Oxford University Press.

Luck, G. 1985. *Arcana Mundi: Magic and the Occult in the Greek and Roman Worlds*. Baltimore, ML, London: Johns Hopkins University Press.

Luck, G. 2000. *Ancient Pathways and Hidden Pursuits: Religion, Morals and Magic in the Ancient World*. Ann Arbor, MI: University of Michigan Press.

Malinowski, B. 1948. *Magic, Science and Religion, and Other Essays*. New York: Anchor Books.

Manning, M.C. 2014. Magic, religion, and ritual in historical archaeology. *Historical Archaeology* 48: 1–9.

McKie, S. 2016. Distraught, drained, devoured, or damned? The importance of individual creativity in Roman cursing. In M.J. Mandich, T. J. Derrick, S. González-Sánchez, G. Savani and E. Zampieri (eds) *TRAC 2015: Proceedings of the Twenty-Fifth Annual Theoretical Roman Archaeology Conference*. Oxford: Oxbow Books:15–27.

Merrifield, R. 1987. *The Archaeology of Ritual and Magic*. London: BT Batsford.

Meskell, L. 2005. Introduction: object orientations. In L. Meskell (ed.) *Archaeologies of Materiality*. Oxford: Blackwell: 1–17.

Miller, D. 2005. Materiality: an introduction. In D. Miller (ed) *Materiality*. Durham, NC and London: Duke University Press: 1–50.

Morley, N. 2015. Globalisation and the Roman economy. In M. Pitts and M. Versluys (eds) *Globalisation and the Roman World: World History, Connectivity and Material Culture*. Cambridge: Cambridge University Press: 49–68.

Otto, B.-C. 2013. Towards historicizing 'magic' in antiquity. *Numen* 60: 308–47.

Parker, A. 2016. Staring at death: The jet *gorgoneia* of Roman Britain. In S. Hoss and A. Whitmore (eds) *Small Finds and Ancient Social Practices in the Northwest Provinces of the Roman Empire*. Oxford: Oxbow Books: 98–113.

Pasi, M. 2006. Magic. In K. Von Stuckrad (ed.) *The Brill Dictionary of Religion: Volume III, M-R*. Leiden and Boston: Brill: 1134–40.

Quercia, A. and Cazzulo, M. 2016. Fear of the dead? 'Deviant' burials in Roman Northern Italy. In M.J. Mandich, T.J. Derrick, S. González-Sánchez, G. Savani and E. Zampieri (eds) *TRAC 2015: Proceedings of the Twenty-Fifth Annual Theoretical Roman Archaeology Conference*. Oxford: Oxbow Books: 28–42.

Rives, J. 2010. Magus and its cognates in classical Latin. In R. Gordon and F. Marco Simón (eds) *Magical Practice in the Latin West: Papers from the International Conference Held at the University of Zaragoza, 30 Sept.–1 Oct. 2005*. Leiden: Brill: 53–77.

Rüpke, J. 2012. *Lived Ancient Religion: Questioning 'Cults' and 'Polis Religion'. Presentation of a New Research Program*. Available: http://www.uni-erfurt.de/fileadmin/public-docs/Max-Weber-Kolleg/6-pdfs/projekte/2012-Ruepke_Lived_anc_rel.pdf [Accessed: 18/07/17]

Rüpke, J. (ed.) 2013. *The Individual in the Religions of the Ancient Mediterranean*. Oxford: Oxford University Press.

Rüpke, J. 2015. Religious agency, identity, and communication: reflections on history and theory of religion. *Religion* 45: 344–66.

Rüpke, J. 2016. *On Roman Religion: Lived Religion and the Individual in Ancient Rome*. Ithaca, NY and London: Cornell University Press.

Rüpke, J. and Raja, R. 2015. Appropriating religion: methodological issues in testing the 'lived ancient religion' approach. *Religion in the Roman Empire* 1: 11–19.

Rüpke, J. and Spickermann, W. (eds) 2012. *Reflections on Religious Individuality: Greco-Roman and Judaeo-Christian Texts and Practices*. Berlin: Walter de Gruyter.

Rüpke, J. and Woolf, G. (eds) 2013. *Religious Dimensions of the Self in the Second Century CE*. Tubingen: Mohr Siebeck.

Stein, R. L. and Stein, P. L. 2016. *The Anthropology of Religion, Magic and Witchcraft*. 3rd edition. London, New York: Routledge.

Styers, R. 2004. *Making Magic: Religion, Magic and Science in the Modern World*. Oxford: Oxford University Press.

Tambiah, S.J. 1990. *Magic, Science, Religion, and the Scope of Rationality*. Cambridge: Cambridge University Press.

Tilley, C. 2006. Theoretical perspectives. In C. Tilley, W. Keane, S. Küchler, M. Rowlands, P. and Spyer. 2006 (eds) *Handbook of Material Culture*. London: SAGE Publications: 7–11.

Tilley, C., Keane, W., Küchler, S., Rowlands, M., and Spyer, P. 2006. Introduction. In C. Tilley, W. Keane, S. Küchler, M. Rowlands, P. and Spyer. 2006 (eds) *Handbook of Material Culture*. London: SAGE Publications: 1–6.

Toner, J. (ed.) 2014. *A Cultural History of the Senses in Antiquity*. London: Bloomsbury.

Thomassen, E. 1999. Is magic a subclass of ritual? In D.R. Jordan, H. Montgomery and E. Thomassen (eds) *The World of Ancient Magic: Papers from the First International Eitrem Seminar at the Norwegian Institute at Athens 4–8 May 1997*. Bergen: Norwegian Institute at Athens: 55–66.

Tylor, E.B. 1867. *Primitive Culture: Researches into the Development of Mythology, Philosophy, Religion, Language, Art, and Custom*. London: John Murray.

Tylor, E.B. 1881. *Anthropology: An Introduction to the Study of Man and Civilizations*. London: Macmillan.

Versnel, H.S. 1991. Some reflections on the relationship magic-religion. *Numen* 38: 177–95.

Versnel, H.S. 2012. Magic. In S. Hornblower, A. Spawforth and E. Eidinow (eds) *The Oxford Classical Dictionary*. 4th edition. Oxford: Oxford University Press: 884–885.

Wilburn, A.T. 2012. *Materia Magica: The Archaeology of Magic in Roman Egypt, Cyprus and Spain*. Ann Arbor, MI: University of Michigan Press.

Wilburn, A.T. 2015. Inscribed ostrich eggs at Berenike and materiality in ritual performance. *Religion in the Roman Empire* 1: 263–85.

Abbreviations

PGM = *Papyri Grecae Magicae* (see Betz 1992).

The Medium Matters:
Materiality and Metaphor in Some Latin Curse Tablets

Celia Sánchez Natalías

Introduction

Though 'materiality' has been around for well over a century (Knappett 2013: 4702), it has only been in recent years that the term has transfixed the archaeological community and has arrived to other areas of study, such as ancient magic. While I am persuaded by Bremmer's (2015: 12) provocative argument that our interest in ancient materiality is linked to trends in our own consumerist society, the increasing focus on the power and agency of objects also provides a needed opportunity to re-examine long-held assumptions about the relative importance of text over material that have, in my opinion, hindered our understanding of magical practices. As Knappett's (2013: 4702) definition of materiality underscores, 'the on-going dynamic of human-artefactual relations' is central to these practices and we need to 'downplay the duality between mind and matter.' As we shall see in the following pages, in the realm of magic, mind and intention become inextricably linked to matter.

Materiality, therefore, addresses the relationship between objects and living beings, a multidirectional and dynamic connection that plays an exceedingly important role in the sphere of magic. In this field, the human-artefactual relationship is expressed through the creation and/or the treatment of things as agents (Gordon 2015: 136). Thus, materiality can be analysed in at least two different directions: first, from the perspective of an apparently innocuous object that, thanks to the transference of agency from the practitioner, becomes itself a powerful agent encoded with a completely new significance (i.e. a simple lead tablet that develops into a *defixio*; or a piece of stone that becomes an amulet). The second direction comes from the victims' perspective: in other words, his/her reaction to uncovering a magical object (= an agent) nearby. A classic example is the deterioration of health that Germanicus

suffered when human remains, spells and lead tablets inscribed with his name were discovered at his home (Tac. *Ann.* 2.69). Another good, though less well known, example is the relief and immediate healing of Libanius when a mutilated chameleon was found in his lecture room, which finally offered an explanation for his mysterious muteness and immobility (1.243–250). As these two examples show, discovering a magical object can have drastic effects, either for good or bad. As Bremmer suggests, the use and even simply the existence of objects like amulets, *defixiones*, antidotes, gems, or magical books were 'agents that influenced the lives of those around them as long as they were part of their social or magical imagination' (Bremmer 2015: 12).

Of all these objects with the potential to shape and mould lives and experiences, this article examines the corpus of curse tablets (also known as *defixiones*) from the Roman West in an attempt to analyse the materiality of magic by stressing the significance of the physicality of objects. In other words, I place special focus on the connection between a particular spell and the material on which it was inscribed to throw into relief how different media used in Roman magic concretely demonstrated (sometimes through loquacious metaphors) a specific materiality: the relationship between a spell and its victim. With this purpose in mind, and after addressing the definition of a *defixio*, I tackle a series of questions surrounding different media and analyse the importance of the physical object in creating a connection between a curse and its target.

Defining Curse Tablets

We owe the standard definition of a *defixio* to Jordan (1985: 151), who describes them as 'inscribed pieces of lead, usually in the form of small, thin sheets, intended to influence, by supernatural means, the actions or welfare of persons or animals against their will.' The same author revisited this definition some years later, adding that there is 'no reason to exclude tablets on material other than lead' (2001: 5–6). And indeed, there are, as we shall see, other media employed including papyrus, marble, and terracotta. The use of these various materials was by no means meaningless, but rather was always directly linked to the aim of successfully carrying out the ritual. Taking lead for granted, then, is a dangerous misstep.

Another common perception surrounding *defixiones* deserves brief mention, namely that they are thought of as private texts. Some of the reasons these texts are considered private do make good sense in light of legal proscriptions against the act of cursing that were in place by the fifth century B.C. (*XII Tables*, VIII A). In addition, curses are comprised of secret content, were intended for a restrictive audience (supernatural beings), and they were often deposited in isolated and inaccessible places meant, in part, to avoid the possibility of someone interfering with a spell. Judged from this perspective, *defixiones* do indeed fall under the larger umbrella of private inscriptions (Beltrán 2015a: 90, 105).

It is necessary, however, to highlight another fundamental aspect of these texts that marks a key difference between *defixiones* and some other types of private texts, namely their 'expiration date'. While the majority of private inscriptions communicate something ephemeral and fleeting (Beltrán 2015a: 89), curse tablets are meant to endure by creating a lasting bond with their victims (Piccaluga 2010: 13–14, 16). Given that writing itself, according to the logic of ancient magic, was considered potentially dangerous (Poccetti 2002: 15; Faraone and Kropp 2010 on the verb *vertere* and a text's *ordinatio*), the connection established by a *defixio* was thought to endure simply through the inscription of the victim's name. In some cases, the expiration of the curse could coincide with the positive resolution of a problem (like the return of the stolen property, as in *Tab. Sulis* 32); in other cases, however, the curse seems likely to endure forever, since the *defigens* demands something impossible (such as in *Tab. Sulis* 100, where the victim is asked to sell a bushel of cloud and a bushel of smoke in exchange for forgiveness). Furthermore, the lasting nature of the bond created by a *defixio* is at times made explicit through certain formulas, like those that ask the gods to prolong the spell's power until the victim's death ('*(ad) diem mortis*' *AE* 1991, 1167; or '*quandius vita vixerit*' *DTM* 5), or renewing expressions such as '*rediviva*' (*RIB* I, 306) that seek to perpetuate the power of the curse.

Explicit comparisons between the act of writing and a spell's durability, however, are omitted in the majority of texts, quite possibly because the author of a given curse was well aware of the long-lasting nature of spells.

This is perhaps the defining characteristic of a *defixio*: the practitioner – whether or not a professional – imbued the object with a nearly inexhaustible agency. As Gordon has maintained (2015: 139), the resulting agency was 'a social construction in which practitioners, patients, victims and witnesses all have an interest'. As Gordon goes on to suggest, this agency was usually recognised *a posteriori* when a victim manifested symptoms of an illness that was thought to have a magical origin (2015: 139).

To take Gordon's insight a bit further, it seems likely to me that this agency would have already been anticipated by the author of a text before any sign of a curse's efficacy surfaced. As the *Greek Magical Papyri* (*PGM*) make clear, the spell could be reinforced with the recitation of formulas meant to increase either its potency (*PGM* 4.332 and ff.) or longevity (*PGM* 7.453ff.). Accordingly, it seems reasonable to suppose that a practitioner was well aware of this transference and also mindful of the best ways of increasing his *defixio*'s potency.

All of these attempts to increase and prolong a curse's power complicate the association of *defixiones* with the larger corpus of private texts, which are often considered ephemeral in nature. Perhaps the case of *defixiones* shows how such a distinction between public and private epigraphy can be unhelpful. Like in public inscriptions, curse tablets were meant to endure and last, at the very least, until the *defigens* obtained the desired outcome. When studying *defixiones*, therefore, the traditional public/private distinction does not quite fit.

The Medium Matters: Materiality and Metaphor in Some Latin Curse Tablets

'Certes l'aspect de ces modestes documents importe beaucoup moins que leur contenu. Il n'est cependant, en plus d'un cas, nullement négligeable.' With these words dating from 1933 (31), Auguste Audollent – though somewhat dismissive himself – signalled the lack of attention that specialists paid the media used in the creation of curse tablets. This gap in the scholarship has recently been addressed in works like Bevilacqua's 2010 volume, as well as in some articles which focus on curse tablets from Athens (Curbera 2015) or *defixiones* from the Roman West (Sánchez Natalías 2011). The latter corpus, comprised of texts written in Latin, Oscan, Etruscan, Phoenician and Celtic, contains over 600 items that will serve as a basis for this paper. We will analyse them following the structure that I have previously put forth (Sánchez Natalías 2011), which distinguishes between specific media (i.e. materials normally employed in writing) and atypical media (i.e. materials not usually inscribed with curses), and also between perishable and durable media.

In the following paragraphs, we will examine some of the various materials used in the manufacture of curse tablets, while comparing archaeological evidence with written sources (mostly the *PGM*) when useful. We will pay particular attention to the media whose link to the targets was reinforced through the employment of analogies or metaphors.

Specific Media

By 'specific media', I mean objects one of whose primary functions was to serve as writing media, and which were created deliberately for that purpose. For obvious reasons (preservation, weather, etc.), perishable materials have left their traces for the most part in the *PGM*, where papyrus is specially recommended for love spells of attraction (which constitute curses as well, as Faraone 2001 41–54 explains). Interestingly enough, according to the *PGM* (5.304–305), in a curse levelled against an enemy or a woman, either papyrus or lead could be used, which shows that in certain circumstances both materials were considered equally effective.

Regarding specific and durable media, we can distinguish between stone and metal. Although the *PGM* contains no instance of the first, there are three surviving artefacts, all of which date to the imperial period. Two of these texts are plaques, one of slate from Pompeii and a marble one from *Emerita Augusta* (Elefante 1985; *CIL* 2.462), while the third was inscribed on the backside of a funerary altar (*CIL* 6. 20905). The use of such media here should be understood as a reflection of monumental epigraphy, which was reaching its heights in the period in question (if we take the so-called 'epigraphic habit' into account (Beltrán 2015b)). In addition, the employment of these materials may reflect the *defigentes'* desire to display their curses publicly. If so, this would bring further infamy upon adversaries. This type of invective would certainly place these *defixiones* among public inscriptions, functioning as a type of anti-encomium. Open display, however, also reveals some potential setbacks that the *defigens* could encounter, such as the high cost of the materials used as well as potential legal backlash for taking part in illegal magical practices. Fully aware of these possible legal perils, these three *defigentes* attempted to navigate potential dangers through mechanisms like 'anonymity' and/or the camouflage of curses as poems, epitaphs, or votive inscriptions (further discussion in Sánchez Natalías 2016: 74–6).

Even if it is well known that among the different media for writing a curse lead reigns supreme, it is worth stressing that there is literary and archaeological evidence for the use of other metals, such as tin and copper. The *PGM*, for instance, recommends the use of tin tablets for agonistic and love curses among other things (*PGM* 4.2212 and 7.459). Although tin is not commonly employed, metallurgical analysis of the 130 curse tablets discovered in the sacred spring of the sanctuary of Sulis Minerva in Bath (ancient *Aquae Sulis*) has shown that pure tin was used at least in two cases (and another six contain more than 90% tin). Given that tin visually resembles lead and that the curses from Bath were written by 'amateur' *defigentes*, perhaps the metals were confused and hence used indiscriminately. As for copper, Jerome in a controversial passage (*Life of Hilarion,* 21) claims that this metal (*aeris Cyprii lamina*) was used for a love charm in Gaza. Again, the archaeological record backs up the literary sources: two *defixiones*, found in the fountain of Anna Perenna in Rome and dated to Late Antiquity, were inscribed on pure hammered copper tablets and deposited within lamps in the place of the wick (Blänsdorf 2012a and 2012b). Although it is not clear why the magical practitioner chose this metal given the fragmentation of the text and the absence of parallels in the *PGM*, it seems quite possible that the redness of the copper evoked the flame of the lamp. Ultimately, and as we shall see with this paper's final example, this would have allowed for a very appropriate association between the target, light and life.

Before looking at lead, it merits mention that, as far as I know, neither silver nor gold curse tablets have been found. There are no literary or archaeological sources that attest the use of them for such a 'dark' purpose. On the contrary, these precious metals are often employed in the production of amulets, such as a probably Roman-period golden *lamella* from Carthage (*DT* 262) engraved with magical signs and the term '*mareamar*', which at one point was thought to be a *defixio*, until Kotansky's re-examination (Kotansky 1994: 374, no. 63).

It is a well-documented fact that in Antiquity lead was one of the most ubiquitous writing materials, because it was common, cheap and easy to inscribe (Poccetti 1999: 545–61). According to Faraone (2012: 117), this metal became popular in the late fifth to fourth centuries B.C. in Athens because it was a by-product of the purification of silver. Despite that, at first, the connection between lead and the practice of cursing was incidental in the long term it became inextricable. As Graf (1995: 129–30) has pointed out, magical practices embraced this metal, imbuing it with several connotations that turned it into the perfect medium for cursing. Linked to Saturn, lead was cold and heavy just like a corpse. Even Aristotle (*apud* Plin., *HN* 11.114, 275) suggested that if a person's skin had a leaden hue, he was going to die. Given this existing nexus of connotations, lead's harmful properties were thought to be transferred to a curse's victim through his/her name (which was considered intricately connected to the person), due to the magical notion of *similia similibus* or persuasive analogy, which is that like provokes like.

The transference of these properties from material to victim is already attested in the *PGM*, which in one case (7.925–926) recommends 'a metal lead tablet from a yoke for mules' for two restraining spells, where the thought may be that just as the lead controls the animals, so it should subjugate the *defigens*' enemies. Other recipes tell readers to 'take lead from a cold-water pipe and make a lamella' (*PGM* 7. 397–398) or to use 'a sheet of lead from a cold-water channel' (*PGM* 7.432), or even 'hammered out while cold' (*PGM* 36.1–2), since it was believed that lead would symbolically freeze the victim. But the connotations of lead were not only used in line with a Roman culture of common sense: at times, they were elaborated in the form of loquacious metaphors.In this regard, Tilley (1999: 16) has argued: 'metaphor is not so much a matter of language in general, and literary use of language in particular, but a matter of thought.' Metaphors can help us to connect concrete and abstract thoughts, shaping ideas that otherwise would appear disconnected from reality, and that is what our *defigentes* (or the professionals who were assisting them) tried to accomplish through lead-based metaphor.

Interestingly enough, the same concepts documented in the *PGM* about the coldness of lead are attested in some Greek curse tablets from Athens, whose objective was to freeze the victim to the point of becoming inanimate (*DTA* 105 and 107). Nevertheless, while references to the idea of coldness do surface in some Latin curse tablets (such as *DTM* 2 or *AE* 2011, 378), these texts do not exploit this physical aspect of lead, alluding instead to other features of this metal, such as its weight and density.Accordingly, one *defixio,* discovered in the amphitheatre at Petronell (ancient *Carnuntum*) and dated to the second or third century A.D., reads, '... quom]od<o>i[l]<l>e(!) plu<m>bus(!) po<n>dus h<a>bet sic et/ [E]ud<e>mus h<a>beat v[o]s iratos ...': 'Just as this lead has weight, in this way may Eudemus have you [the gods], angry [with him]' (*AE* 1929, 228). The text, with its somewhat strained repetition of *habere,* clearly connects the weight of the tablet to the level of the gods' anger against the victim: as the tablet cannot lose its weight, so Eudemus cannot escape the ire of the gods.

In addition to referring simply to the properties of lead, there are other occasions in which parallels are drawn between the use of lead in the ritual and the desired outcome for the victim. These metaphorical references principally draw their comparisons from the act of deposition in specific places. In the case of *defixiones*, there are four main types of deposition: in sanctuaries, aquatic settings (rivers, fountains, wells, etc.), necropoleis, and finally sites close to a victim (a house or place of work). The act of depositing a tablet was considered a fundamental stage in the ritual since the spell could take effect only after this final step was complete. A first-century A.D. text found at Montfo (*Gallia Narbonensis*) bears this out. The tablet opens with an interesting analogy, '*Quomodo hoc plumbu(m) non paret et decadet, sic decadat aetas, membra, vita, bos, gran ⌐u⌐ (m), mer(x), eorum qui mihi malu(m) dolum fecerunt ...*' (*AE* 1981, 621). This analogy compares the way the lead will fall into the well with the desired outcome, both the physical and economic

downfall of the victim. In other words, the act of deposition itself demonstrates what ought to be done. And while the law of gravity ensures that any item dropped into a well will eventually reach the bottom, the weight of the lead remains important here: the tablet would fall quickly and directly, perhaps indicating that the victim should also suffer a sharp and unavoidable turn in fate. Unsurprisingly, this curse was discovered among other offerings at the bottom of a well, a sacred place for communication with the gods according to Celtic belief (see Bacou and Bacou 1975: 17–22). Its discovery in such a place clearly indicates that the text itself was carefully planned, that is to say that the author was thinking in advance about the ritual performance that was going to be carried out. Deposition was no afterthought.

Two texts found at the sanctuary of Isis and Magna Mater in Mainz provide further examples of how the manipulation of lead during the deposition of a tablet is reflected in the text of the curse. In this sanctuary, which has been dated to the first through third centuries A.D., 24 *defixiones* were discovered in the back of the building. In that area two altars were built where the curse tablets were put alongside other typical offerings (Witteyer 2005: 116; Blänsdorf 2012c: 1–6, 39–40). Of this larger ensemble, two *defixiones* will hold our attention for the time being. Both of the texts compare the way that the lead tablets were melted in a sacred fire to the way in which the *defigens* wanted the limbs of the victim to turn into liquid: '... sic illorum/ membra liquescan(t)/ quatmodum hoc plum-/bum liquesce t...' and '... qu[omo]di hoc liquescet/ (...) [sic co] llum membra/ me[du]lla ...' (*DTM* 11 and 12; McKie 2016: 24). In a similar way to the previously mentioned case of Montfo, this deposition actively enacted what the *defigens* wanted to happen: the lead tablets, which represented the victims themselves, would have melted in the sacred fire, and so the victims mentioned in the text would themselves subsequently dissolve bit by bit.

The third and final example engraved on lead that I would like to examine also comes from the sanctuary of Isis and Magna Mater in Mainz, although it does not mention the deposition of the tablet. The curse, certainly the most finely elaborated of the Mainz corpus, was inscribed on a perfectly square lead tablet and written in beautiful capital letters. It was directed against a women called Prima Aemilia, a lady (maybe still in her youth) who is compared to the tablet itself: '... ⌐q⌐ qu)omo(do) haec carta/ nu ⌐m⌐ quam florescet/ sic illa nu ⌐m⌐ quam/ quicquam florescat ...' (*DTM* 15). As pointed out by the editor, the use of the verb *floresco* ought to be taken as a poeticism, referring to the *defigens*' desire to deprive *Prima Aemilia* of her prosperity. But which type of prosperity? Given that the victim was a woman, we can conjecture that one of the purposes of the curse was to make the victim infertile: since lead is associated with death and coldness, the medium of the curse provides a good illustration of what Prima Aemilia should be reduced to. And indeed, infertility is an expressed outcome in some curse tablets (Varone 1998; *Tab. Sul.* 10).

Whatever the case may be, all the examples discussed above clearly show how the textual metaphor attested in these curse tablets depends on the physicality of lead and/ or a specific ritual deposition to make sense. In addition to the well-known analogy between the coldness of the metal and the hoped for cadaverous frigidity of the target, the magical practitioner used its heaviness to speak about the anger of the deities against *Eudemus*. In other cases, the metaphor involved a carefully planned procedure, since the *defigentes* knew exactly how to deposit the tablet to complete the practice of cursing. At the bottom of the well or melted by the sacrificial fire, their words would reach the invoked deities without interference, and so the victims of their curses would suffer the expected turn in fate.

Atypical Media

Now I would like to turn to atypical media, in other words, all those objects that were used for writing a curse, although they were originally created for other purposes. Sometimes, we can think of these as recycled or appropriated items, which were imbued with a new significance by the magical practitioner (whether professional or not).

Within this group, the *PGM* prescribes different sorts of perishable materials for love spells of attraction, such as the wings of a living bat (*PGM* 12.376–377). This perishable medium is quite apt, since the spell seeks to plague its victim with insomnia 'until she consents': the bat, after all, is the nocturnal animal *par excellence* and hence well linked to unwanted wakefulness.

When it comes to durable materials, the *PGM* recommends the use of sea shells and magnetite as surfaces on which to write love spells of attraction (*PGM* 7.467 and ff.; 4.1723–1724, respectively). The choice of neither object is casual, since shells are common symbols of Venus and magnetite was well known for its properties of attraction (as stated by Plin. *HN*, 36.127), which will bring the beloved person to the *defigens*' arms in no time. Unfortunately, the archaeological record does not preserve any of these items discussed in the *PGM*, where indeed a large variety of atypical media used in aggressive magic is discussed.

Among these items we find quotidian objects that have been (used or) reused, such as tiles, clay jars, a pendant and a pewter plate etc.. As is the case with some of these objects (Sánchez Natalías 2011: 86–7), the brief and elliptical nature of the inscription, which at times is little more than a list of names, precludes any in depth analysis of the relationship between a curse and its medium. Perhaps practitioners resorted to these items since they were believed to possess the *ousia* (substance) for which certain spells call. Generally, the *PGM* considers things like pieces of fabric, hairs or finger and toenails that belong to the victim

to comprise *ousia*. Since these items hailed from the victim, they were believed to reinforce even further the bond between a victim and curse. Hence, they were often put inside of a lead tablet to increase a spell's power (for some good examples see Bevilacqua *et al.* 2012: 236). While this theory offers one compelling reason that everyday objects (perhaps purloined?) were used in the creation of these curses, the lack of any surviving organic material and the above-mentioned brevity of the texts defy any absolute conclusion (further discussion in Sánchez Natalías 2011: 87; *Tab. Sulis* 18 and 30).

Fortunately, other, more elaborate *defixiones* provide us with additional clues. A second century A.D. piece discovered in a necropolis just off the Via Appia in Rome, for example, makes explicit the relationship between an atypical medium and its curse. The object in question is a (sort of 'mass produced') terracotta votive that depicts the busts of two adults and a child (Mancini 1923: 37–9) and presumably represents a family. Thus, we can state that this votive was never created with a magical purpose, but rather re-appropriated by the *defigens*, and so it will fit into the category of curses written on 'atypical' media discussed here. That said, and despite the fact that this object is not a 'typical' magical figurine, it has been generally grouped with the figurines rather than *defixiones* simply because of the anthropomorphic shape (Faraone 1991: no. 21; McKie, this volume). Recently, however, scholars have been eager to warn against any rigid divide between these figurines and *defixiones*, since both groups of objects have the same function, were made with the same purposes and only differ in shape (Ogden 2009: 245). For these various reasons, I have included this curse in the present discussion.

The object boasts two inscriptions: the first is a so called *ante cocturam* stamp that was applied to the piece in the workshop where it was produced. The second inscription, which was etched into the object after the terracotta had been fired (hence, *post cocturam*), is what will hold our attention here. The inscription, whose text and meaning have been contested, begins with the formula, '*Quomodo isti non cumbe(re) inter se ...*' after which follows another fragmentary formula and a series of names, undoubtedly those of the intended victims. If *cumbe(re) inter se* can be taken as a synonym of the compound *concumbo*, the inscription could contain a sexual connotation (see *OLD*). Following this hypothesis, it would be possible to understand that the magical practitioner established an analogy between the figurines on the votive and the victims of the *defixio*. As the sculpted group is by definition rigid and cannot move, so it appears that the *defigens* asks for his victims to become as brittle and immobile as a piece of terracotta so as to avoid any sexual relationship.

Another *defixio* deserving attention comes from an unknown archaeological context, though the piece, according to its first editor, must have come from Rome or thereabouts before making its way into the Museo delle Terme di Diocleziano in the 1930s (Muzzioli 1939: 42–3). What makes this text stand out (and currently unparalleled) is the fact that it was painted on the internal surface of cinerary urn. Dated to the fourth or fifth century A.D., the curse asks the Holy Angels to see to it that 'just as this spirit enclosed within [this urn] is held and constrained and as it does not see light and does not have any reprieve, in this way may the spirit, the mind and the body of *Collecticius* whom Agnella bore remain, burn, and melt forever' (... *quomodo (ha)ec anima intus in-/ clusa tenetur et angust{i}atur/ et non v ̔i ̔ de(t) neque lum ̔e ̔ n{e} ne<que> aliquem/ refrigerium non (h)abet sicut anima/ mentes corp ̔u ̔s Collecticii quem peperit Agnella// teneatur ardeat destabescat usque ...* (*AE* 1941, 138)). As this text suggests, the desired outcome for the victim of the curse is compared to the remains of a previously deceased individual who was placed in the very urn that serves as the medium for the curse. Hence, the curse makes use of both the urn as well as the ashes, which serve as the subject of the comparison for the *defigens*' magical desires.

While some *PGM* recipes call for the use of skulls or bones, this way of reusing a cinerary urn is unique in the Roman West. There may be, however, a partial parallel from the fountain of Anna Perenna at Rome, where recent excavations have uncovered (amongst other objects) a series of lead cylindrical containers which contained *defixiones* and magical figurines (Piranomonte 2016). As I have argued elsewhere (Sánchez Natalías 2011: 87–9), these containers likely represent cinerary urns in miniature and they would employ the same logic and tropes that are made explicit in the painted curse from Museo delle Terme di Diocleziano.

The final example that I would like to discuss of 'atypical media' is dated to the first century A.D. and like the abovementioned cinerary urn comes from an unknown archaeological context, though it is thought to have come from Rome where it later became a part of the Museo Kircheriano (Vallarino 2010: 66). Also, like the previous example, this text was painted, but this time on a lamp. Unfortunately, the lamp is now missing and we do not know its formal characteristics, though the text has been recorded (*CIL* 15. 6265). The use of a lamp as the medium for a curse is unparalleled in the Roman West, though there is a parallel that comes from fourth-century B.C. Athens, which contains a list of six names written from right to left. As Thompson noted (1958: 159), this direction of writing places the Athenian lamp squarely in the context of aggressive magic, since this technique is employed in many Greek curse tablets. Accordingly, the names on the Athenian lamp provide the names of a series of victims.

Mastrocinque (2007) has connected this Athenian lamp to several lamps discovered in the abovementioned fountain of Anna Perenna. Inside of at least three of these lamps (there are 74 in total), *defixiones* were put in the place normally occupied by a wick (Blänsdorf 2012a; 2012b;

2012d and Mastrocinque 2007: 96). Mastrocinque has fruitfully emphasised the symbolism surrounding light in various strands of ancient thought (Christian, Roman, etc.) and has usefully collected literary sources that connect light and mankind. He reaches the surprising, though compelling, conclusion that in the realm of magic 'the offering of a lamp could substitute for the offering of a man' (2007: 96). He has, however, overlooked an object that makes his conclusions all the more secure, namely the lamp mentioned at the beginning of the previous paragraph. It reads, '*Helenus · su ̔u ̔m · nomen · {e}i ̔n ̔feris/ mandat · stipem · strenam · lumen/ su ̔u ̔m · secum · defert · ne quis · eum / solvat · nisi · nos · qui · fecimus*'. The curse draws an analogy between the lamp's light and the life of the victim. A person's light, like their name, serves as a metonymy for their life and being. By mentioning all three together, the *defigentes* are strongly emphasising the damnation of the victim. We can even speculate that during the ritual deposition of this curse, the lamp would have been lit and then extinguished to reinforce the spoken and written word of the spell.

Again, and regardless of the type of material employed for cursing, both the literary and archaeological examples discussed in the last section demonstrate how the analogies established between curses and targets draw heavily on media to work. The use and/or reuse of these objects show that the practitioners planned every detail of the ritual, and this planning allowed them to establish creative and durable links between matter and victim. The materiality of that connection could take different forms, at times appealing to the *ousia* (substance), to the physical features of the objects, or to the ideas that these items represented. Indeed, in the eyes of the *defigens*, the very rigidity of a sculpture, confinedness of a urn and obscurity of an extinguished lamp could help them imagine dire scenarios for their targets.

Conclusions

As highlighted in the introduction, materiality can be defined as the complex and multidirectional relationship between an object and living beings. In this environment, the object, in this case a *defixio*, sets into motion a nexus of relations that involves at least three subjects. Once the relationship between the object and the magical practitioner was established, the invoked power(s) and the victim(s) of the curse were thought to be (almost) immediately affected. Obviously, the types of bonds that a *defixio* had with these beings were different in terms of duration and character: the practitioner would endow the object with his or her human agency from manufacturing to depositing the artefact. From this point on, the evoked powers and then the victim(s) are compelled to undertake a relationship with the *defixio*, whose agency manifests itself in still different ways. The invoked powers are compelled to respond as quickly as possible before being freed from their duty. For the victims, on the other hand, the relationship will continue in the form of illness and symptoms until the resolution of the situation or maybe even their death. Thus, the agency would be perceived in terms of duty by the invoked power(s), while it would take the form of symptoms and pathologies in the eyes of the victims.

The present contribution has sought to provide an analysis of the relationships that *defixiones* were believed to set into motion with a special focus on how the physicality of the object was evoked to strengthen the curse's efficacy. In this regard, *defixiones* stand apart from many other genres of epigraphy. With this objective in mind, I have laid particular emphasis on the media of *defixiones* from the Roman West, classifying the different examples attested. Although lead was by far the most common and widely used medium, practitioners were presented with an array of options ranging from materials often used for writing (papyrus, marble, etc.) to objects seldom used (or reused) as a surface to be inscribed (parts of living animals, magnetite, shells, and everyday objects). It should be stressed that, as is the case with religious rituals, magical practices followed a specific protocol in which no step could be omitted. The choice of material, then, was never random, since it was one of the keys for a successful ritual.

In light of the evidence analysed, we can state that materiality and metaphor were concepts that operated simultaneously during the process of manufacture of the pieces. As we have seen, some of the texts discussed above evoke the physical features of the media used, at times through metaphorical language, to reinforce a very specific materiality: their relationship with the targets. It seems clear that, in these curses, metaphors were used at least with three different purposes: 1) to reinforce the link between victim and spell; 2) to allow the author of the text express his desires in a more detailed and creative way; and 3) to 'help' the readers of the curses (supernatural entities) to accomplish their mission(s). In many cases, metaphors were drawn from the properties of the materials employed, binding (even more) target and *defixio*. The practitioners were well aware of the interrelation between these two and that is why stressing their link could be only aide in the 'happy' ending of a spell.

Acknowledgements

I would like to thank Prof. Francisco Marco Simón and Prof. Christopher A. Faraone for their suggestions and notes. My gratitude is likewise due to Dr Ben Jerue for the translation from Spanish into English and extremely helpful comments on this text, whose contents are my sole responsibility. Also special thanks to the editors, Stuart McKie and Adam Parker, who invited me to join this volume and (together with the anonymous referees) improved this paper through their questions and advice.

Bibliography

Ancient Sources

Libanius (Translated by P. Petit 1978). *Discours. Autobiographie.* Paris: Les Belles Lettres.
Pliny the Elder (Translated by A. Ernout 1968). *Naturalis Historia.* Paris: Les Belles Lettres.
Tacitus (Translated by P. Wuilleumier 1978). *Annales.* Paris: Les Belles Lettres.

Modern Sources

Audollent, A. 1904. *Defixionum Tabellae. Quotquot innotuerunt tam in graecis orientis quem in totius occidentis partibus praeter atticas.* Paris: Fontemoing.
Audollent, A. 1933. Les inscriptions de la Fontaine aux mille amphores à Carthage. *Cinquième congrès international d'archéologie classique, Alger 14–16 avril 1930.* Argel: Société Historique: 119–38.
Beltrán, F. 2015a. Latin Epigraphy: the main types of inscriptions. In C. Bruun and J. Edmondson (eds) *The Oxford Handbook of Roman Inscriptions.* Oxford, New York: Oxford University Press: 89–108.
Beltrán, F. 2015b. The Epigraphic habit in the Roman world. In C. Bruun and J. Edmondson (eds) *The Oxford Handbook of Roman Inscriptions.* Oxford, New York: Oxford University Press: 131–48.
Betz, H.D. (ed) 1992. *The Greek Magical Papyri in Translation (Including the Demotic Spells).* 2nd edition. Chicago, IL, London: University of Chicago Press.
Bevilacqua, G. 2010. *Scrittura e Magia. Un repertorio di oggetti iscritti della magia greco-romana.* Rome: Quasar.
Bevilacqua, G. Colacchichi, O. and Giuliani, M.R. 2012. Tracce di *ousia* in una *defixio* dalla Via Ostiense: un lavoro multidisciplinare. In M. Piranomonte and F. Marco Simón (eds) *Contesti Magici. Contextos mágicos.* Atti del convegno internazionale Roma, Palazzo Massimo, 4–6 novembre 2009. Rome: De Luca Editori d'Arte: 229–36.
Blänsdorf, J. 2012a. Maledizione con invocazione di Abraxas. In R. Friggeri, M.G. Granino Cecere and G.L. Gregori (eds) *Terme di Diocleziano. La collezione epigrafica.* Rome: Electa: 630.
Blänsdorf, J. 2012b. Tra paganesimo e cristianesimo: invocazione alle Ninfe e a Cristo. In R. Friggeri, M.G. Granino Cecere and G.L. Gregori (eds) *Terme di Diocleziano. La collezione epigrafica.* Rome: Electa: 629.
Blänsdorf, J. 2012c. *Die defixionum tabellae des Mainzer Isis- und Mater Magna-Heiligtums. Defixionum Tabellae Mogontiacenses (DTM)* (Mainzer Archäologische Schriften 9). Mainz: Generaldirektion Kulturelles Erbe.
Blänsdorf, J. 2012d. Tre maledizioni contro *Victor.* In R. Friggeri, M.G. Granino Cecere and G.L. Gregori (eds) *Terme di Diocleziano. La collezione epigrafica.* Rome: Electa: 631.
Bremmer, J.N. 2015. Preface: the materiality of magic. In D. Boschung and J.N. Bremmer (eds) *The Materiality of Magic.* Paderborn: Wilhlem Fink: 7–19.
Collingwood, R.G. and Wright, R.P. (eds) 1965. *Roman Inscriptions of Britain: I, Inscriptions on Stone.* Oxford: Clarendon Press.
Curbera, J. 2015. From the magician's workshop: notes on the materiality of Greek curse tablets. In D. Boschung and J.N.

Bremmer (eds) *The Materiality of Magic*. Paderborn: Wilhlem Fink: 97–122.

Elefante, M. 1985. Un caso di *defixio* nella necropoli pompeiana di Porta Nocera? *Parola del Passato* 225: 431–43.

Faraone, C. 1991. Binding and burying the forces of evil: The defensive use of 'voodoo-dolls' in Ancient Greece. *Classical Antiquity* 2: 165–220.

Faraone, C. 2001. *Ancient Greek Love Magic*. Cambridge, MA: Harvard University Press.

Faraone, C. 2012. The problem of dense concentrations of data for cartographers (and chronographers) of ancient Mediterranean magic: Some illustrative cases from the east. In M. Piranomonte and F. Marco Simón (eds) *Contesti Magici. Contextos mágicos*. Atti del convegno internazionale Roma, Palazzo Massimo, 4–6 novembre 2009. Rome: De Luca Editori d'Arte: 115–22.

Faraone, C. and Kropp, A. 2010. Inversion, adversion and perversion as strategies in Latin curse-tablets. In R. Gordon and F. Marco (eds) *Magical Practice in the Latin West*. Papers from the International Conference held at the University of Zaragoza 30 Sept–1 Oct 2005 (Religions in the Roman World 168). Leiden: Brill: 381–98.

Gordon, R. 2015. From substance to text: three materialities of 'magic' in the Roman imperial period. In D. Boschung and J.N. Bremmer (eds) *The Materiality of Magic*. Paderborn: Wilhelm Fink: 133–76.

Graf, F. 1995. *La magia nel mondo antico*. Rome: Il Mulino.

Jordan, D.R. 1985. A survey of Greek *defixiones* not included in the special *corpora*. *Greek Roman and Byzantine Studies* 26: 151–97.

Jordan, D.R. 2001. New Greek curse tablets. *Greek Roman and Byzantine Studies* 41: 5–46.

Knappett, C. 2013. Materiality in archaeological theory. In C. Smith (ed.) *Encyclopedia of Global Archaeology*. New York: Springer Reference: 4700–8.

Kotansky, R. 1994. Greek magical amulets. *The Inscribed Gold, Silver, Copper, and Bronze Lamellae. Part I: Published Texts of Known Provenance* (Papyrologica Coloniensia 22/1). Opladen: Westdeutscher Verlag.

Mancini, G. 1923. Scavi sotto la basilica di S. Sebastiano sull'Appia Antica. *Notizie e Scavi di Antichità*: 1–79.

Mastrocinque, A. 2007. Late antique lamps with *defixiones*. *Greek, Roman and Byzantine Studies* 47: 87–99.

McKie, S. 2016. Distraught, drained, devoured, or damned? The importance of individual creativity in Roman cursing. In M. Mandich, T. Derrick, S. González Sánchez, G. Savani and E. Zampieri (eds) *TRAC 2015: Proceedings of the 25th Annual Theoretical Roman Archaeology Conference 2015*. Oxford: Oxbow: 15–27.

Muzzioli, G. 1939. Urna inscritta del Museo delle Terme. *Studi e Materiali di Storia delle Religioni* 15: 42–50.

Ogden, D. 2009. *Magic, Witchcraft and Ghosts in the Greek and Roman World*. Oxford: Oxford University Press.

Piccaluga, G. 2010. Tecnica grafica e liturgia magica nelle *tabellae defixionum*. *Studi e Materiali di Storia delle Religioni* 76(1): 13–20.

Piranomonte, M. 2016. The discovery of the fountain of Anna Perenna and its importance on the study of ancient magic. In G. Bąkowska-Czerner, A. Roccati and A. Świerzowska (eds) *The Wisdom of Thoth: Magical Texts in Ancient Mediterranean Civilizations*. Oxford: Archaeopress: 71–85.

Poccetti, P. 1999. Il metallo come supporto di iscrizioni nell'Italia antica: aree, lingue e tipologie testuali. In F. Villar and F. Beltrán (eds) *Pueblos, lenguas y escrituras en la Hispania prerromana. Actas del VII Coloquio sobre lenguas y culturas paleohispánicas*. Salamanca: Universidad de Salamanca: 545–61.

Poccetti, P. 2000. Manipolazione della realtà e manipolazione della lingua: alcuni aspetti de testi magici dell'Antichità. In R. Morresi (ed) *Linguaggio-linguaggi. Invenzione-scoperta*. Atti del Convegno Macerata-Fermi, 22–23 ottobre 1999. Rome: Il Calamo: 11–59.

Sánchez Natalías, C. 2011. Escribiendo una *defixio*: los textos de maldición a través de sus soportes. *Acta Classica Universitatis Scientiarum Debreceniensis* 47: 79–93.

Sánchez Natalías, C. 2013. *El contenido de las defixiones en el Occidente del Imperio Romano*. PhD Thesis. Zaragoza-Verona.

Sánchez Natalías, C. 2016. Epigrafía pública y *defixiones*: paradigmas (y paradojas) del Occidente Latino. *Acta Classica Universitatis Scientiarum Debreceniensis* 52: 69–77.

Thompson, H.A. 1958. Activities in the Athenian agora: 1957. *Hesperia* 27: 145–60.

Tilley, C. 1999. *Metaphor and Material Culture*. Oxford: Blackwell.

Tomlin, R.S.O. 1988. The curse tablets. In B. Cunliffe (ed) *The Temple of Sulis Minerva at Bath, 2: The Finds from the Sacred Spring*. Monograph Series 16. Oxford: Oxford University Committee for Archaeology: 59–269.

Vallarino, G. 2010. Una tipologia di oggetti magici iscritti: una proposta di classificazione. In G. Bevilacqua (ed.), *Scrittura e Magia. Un repertorio di oggetti iscritti della magia greco-romana*. Rome: Quasar: 21–81.

Varone, A. 1998. *Tabella defixionis* di piombo composta da due tavolette. In P.G. Guzzo (coord), *Pompei oltre la vita. Nuove testimonianze dalle necropoli. XIII Settimana per i Beni Culturali e Ambientali*. Pompei: Soprintendenza Archeologica di Pompei: 100–1.

Witteyer, M. 2005. Curse tablets and voodoo dolls from Mainz. The archaeological evidence for magical practices in the sanctuary of Isis and Magna Mater. *Mene* 5: 105–24.

Wünsch, R. 1897. *Defixionum Tabellae Atticae. Inscriptiones Graecae III, pt. 3*. Berlin.

Abbreviations

AE = *L'Année Épigraphique*, Paris 1888.

CIL = *Corpus Inscriptionum Latinarum*. Berlin.

DT = *Defixionum Tabellae* (see Audollent 1904).

DTA = *Defixionum Tabellae Atticae* (see Wünsch 1897).

DTM = *Defixionum Tabellae Mogontiacenses* (see Blänsdorf 2012c).

OLD = *Oxford Latin Dictionary*. Oxford.

PGM = *Papyri Grecae Magicae* (see Betz 1992).

RIB = *Roman Inscriptions of Britain* (see Collingwood and Wright 1965).

Tab. Sulis = *Tabellae Sulis* (see Tomlin 1988).

Phallic Magic: A Cross Cultural Approach to Roman Phallic Small Finds

Alissa Whitmore

The archaeological record of the Roman world has preserved phallic images from a wide variety of materials, contexts, dates, and locations. The human penis – sometimes flaccid, other times erect, and occasionally depicted with legs, arms, wings, and additional phalli – featured on pendants, hairpins, rings, wind-chimes (*tintinnabula*), seal boxes, and votive offerings (Johns 1989: 57–8, 63–6; Swift 2017: 166–71; Whitmore 2017; see also Parker this volume). Phalli that are depicted without the rest of the body are generally interpreted as examples of apotropaic magic, which protected people and places from the evil eye (Johns 1989: 63–8; Clarke 2003: 95–114; Parker 2015; Whitmore 2017). Like other types of Roman magic, these depictions were used by individuals for personal gain, but protective magic and amulets differ from curse tablets and aggressive magic in that they worked publicly, not privately (Wilburn 2016: 15, 19). Roman magic often drew upon religious traditions to increase its efficacy and legitimacy (Wilburn 2016: 17–8), and this is evident with phallic protective magic. These images and objects are related to fertility deities, particularly Fascinus (Plin. *HN* 28.39), and phallic pendants sometimes incorporated fertility symbols, such as horns, bulls, the moon, and the *manus fica* gesture (a fist with the thumb between the fingers; Crummy 1983: 139; Greep 1994: 82–3; Plouviez 2005: 161; Nicolay 2007: 229; Peña 2008: 334).

This paper examines Roman phallic pendants as magical objects that people wore or used to achieve an individual benefit, and endeavours to reach a fuller understanding of who used them, how the magic was believed to work, and which functions and abilities these objects had. Since only a few ancient texts indirectly reference phallic amulets (see Whitmore 2017: 47–50, and below), I incorporate interpretations of wider phallic iconography, information from burial contexts, and offer a detailed comparison between ancient Roman and modern Thai phallic pendants. The latter is a relatively uncommon methodology in classical archaeology, but one useful for examining topics that are not well documented in texts (cf. Greene 2012: 106). In looking at Thai phallic pendants, I focus on the same questions as in the Roman world – who uses these objects, for which purposes, and how do they work – and since Thai amulets are still used today, it is possible to offer nuanced answers. I use this understanding of Thai amulets to generate questions about Roman pendant use, which are then evaluated for plausibility using evidence from ancient texts, burials, and iconography. This line of inquiry reveals that phallic pendants, which are relatively rare in both cultures, share a primary function of protecting children, but Roman and Thai amulets are magically empowered and used in different ways, which relate to the differing dangers against which these objects protect. The Thai comparison also allows for a more critical appraisal of the possible fertility aspects of Roman phallic amulets and their occasional association with adult men and women.

Before discussing cross-cultural analogy further, it is useful to reflect upon the extent of the Roman phallic iconographic tradition, examples of which are geographically and temporally dispersed throughout the Roman world. Phalli have been found carved into the walls and roads of Pompeii and Leptis Magna (Johns 1989: 64–5, figs 3, 77, and 123), onto bridges and aqueducts in Merida (Del Hoyo and Vázquez Hoys 1996: 448–9), and on a variety of military structures in Britain (Parker 2017). Phallic pendants have been found throughout Europe and into the Middle East, from contexts dating from the first century B.C. to the fourth century A.D. (Whitmore 2017: 50–4). Broadly speaking, the evidence suggests that a phallic iconographic tradition was present in much of the Roman world during this period.

This does not, however, mean that everyone within the sphere of Roman influence used phallic objects or considered them in the same way. Certain phallic pendant types appear more often in different time periods or regions (Parker 2015: 139; Whitmore forthcoming), but the cultural or functional significance of these variations is not yet clear. Phallic iconography is generally considered a Roman import into the provinces (Parker 2015: 139), but current evidence does not reveal how their meanings and functions may have differed among provincial peoples. Given the geographic breadth of the Empire, and the centuries of Roman influence, change and variation in phallic iconography and related beliefs is expected, but at present, we simply do not know the nuances. As a result, in this paper I draw upon evidence from a variety of dates and contexts to reconstruct the Roman phallic pendant tradition broadly. While this might produce a somewhat idealised, over-simplified understanding of this practice, this is a necessary baseline so that this belief system can be compared with that of the Thai, and through this comparison, variations can be identified and further explored.

Cross Cultural Analogy and Classical Archaeology

While prehistoric archaeologists have long used comparisons with modern cultures to help interpret the archaeological record of past societies, classical archaeologists have often been less inclined to do so (Terrenato 2002: 1108–9; Webster 2008: 103–4) though there are notable exceptions. Lisa Nevett incorporates ethnographic comparisons of female seclusion in Islamic cultures to interpret ancient Greek household architecture and female segregation (1994; 1999: 30–1, 72–3). Elizabeth Greene compares the writings of the Romano-Batavian Sulpicia Lepidina with the American Elizabeth Custer to better understand the lives of officers' wives and women living in military communities on the Roman frontier (2012). Scholars of Graeco-Roman slavery have more widely adopted comparative approaches to examine the social identities and spaces associated with slaves (see Webster 2008: 106–11 and Borbonus 2015: 327). But cultural comparisons, in general, remain an under-used method for classical archaeologists.

Several scholars offer explanations for why this may be so. Cross-cultural analogy is more strongly associated with New Archaeology, a set of methodologies and theories that prehistoric and anthropological archaeologists developed in the 1970s. Generally, these approaches were not widely embraced by classical archaeologists (Terrenato 2002: 1108), with the exception of researchers who studied provincial, colonised, or non-literate peoples (Webster 2008: 104–5). Supporters highlight cross-cultural comparisons as a way to give voice to past peoples and the archaeological record (Peregrine 2001: 1), but the abundance of classical

texts – in spite of authorial bias and limited focus – can make cultural comparisons seem unnecessary to classical scholars (Webster 2008: 105). The rare use of analogy can also be attributed to the role and importance granted to the Greeks and Romans in shaping modern western culture, which led to the privileging of these societies over others. As a result, comparing the Graeco-Roman world with other cultures can be seen to challenge the uniqueness of classical societies, as well as the uniqueness of the West, which may have unconsciously biased European and North American scholars against such comparisons (Terrenato 2002: 1109; Webster 2008: 104).

The use of cross-cultural analogy is not without complications and critiques. A common problem with early cross-cultural analogies was that they uncritically projected present behaviours into the past, ignoring important differences between cultures and changes over time (Greene 2012: 106). Too closely equating past and present cultures can lead to the presumed existence of a behaviour that was not present in the past (Borbonus 2015: 340–1), or mask an ancient cultural feature that is no longer present today (Peregrine 2001: 2–3; Hodder 2012: 14). In focusing on the similarities between cultures, scholars can become blind to important differences (Borbonus 2015: 340–1), and wrongly anticipate further similarities between societies when only a few surface parallels might exist (Hodder 2012: 12–13). Most importantly, scholars using analogy must be conservative with their interpretations, since without statistical analyses of a large sample of cultures, or the demonstration of a near universal association between specific behaviours and material remains, conclusions drawn from analogies can subjective, uncontrolled, and unreliable (Peregrine 2001: 9–10; Hodder 2012: 19).

With acknowledgement and awareness of these issues, however, cross-cultural analogy holds promise as one of many tools at an archaeologist's disposal, and even more so for classical archaeologists, who can interrogate presumed similarities between cultures with evidence from texts and other sources. To avoid unwarranted conclusions related to equating a past and present culture, I use analogy as a starting place to open up new avenues to further explore and query phallic pendant use (cf. Greene 2012: 106). Since I compare only two cultures qualitatively, my analogy is subjective in nature, but I have taken steps to strengthen its reliability.

Selecting a suitable culture for comparison is crucial when using cross-cultural analogy. No two societies will offer a perfect one-to-one correlation, since no two cultures are identical, but a comparison is stronger when there are many similarities between two cultures, and in particular, similarities relating to the behaviour, activity, or object under investigation (Nevett 1994: 104–5). The existence of many known similarities makes it more likely – though never certain – that other similarities related to this activity or object might exist (Hodder 2012: 16–9). For Roman phallic pendants, a desirable comparison is with a culture that has similar objects used in the same way; i.e. small pendants that clearly depict a penis and can be worn by humans.

Phallic pendants are known from historic Italy, the European Upper Paleolithic, Neolithic Greece, Phoenicia, and modern Thailand. Italian pendants would make for a desirable analogy, given the link between Roman and Italian cultures. Such an analogy, called a direct historical analogy, is often considered stronger since the two societies being compared are historically and culturally related, and some continuity in behaviours might be possible (Peregrine 2001: 2; Hodder 2012: 18). But while eighteenth and nineteenth century scholars and travellers compared Roman phallic pendants to Italian amulets, these objects, called *cornos*, were a small horn made of gold or coral, and today, their red plastic appearance resembles a pepper. Italian *cornos* may indeed represent a sanitised depiction of a phallus (Dumas 1843: 181; Berry 1968: 252–3), but they do not clearly portray a penis. As such, in spite of a cultural connection, Italian *cornos* are missing a key characteristic of Roman phallic pendants, and thus, are not an ideal comparison.

Cross-cultural analogies are typically drawn between present or recent historical groups and a past culture, and information from the better documented, more recent society is used to interpret the archaeological record of the lesser known ancient one. Since my analogy is intended to provoke further questions about the use of Roman phallic pendants, this comparison requires a culture with a well-documented set of phallic pendant beliefs and practices. This makes prehistoric phallic pendants from the European Upper Palaeolithic (27,000–23,000 B.C.) and the Greek Neolithic (6,500–5,300 B.C.) poorly suited for comparison, since the absence of written records obscures the use of these relatively rare objects, whose identification as phalli is somewhat ambiguous (Hansen 2001: 39–43; Nanoglou 2010: 217–9). Likewise, detailed knowledge on the use of Phoenician pendants (seventh to sixth century B.C.; Barnett and Mendelson 1987: 42, 111; Regev 2013: 105–6) is also complicated by the limited survival of Phoenician and Punic texts. Since our understanding of Roman phallic pendants is already challenging due to their rare mention in written sources, drawing an analogy with an earlier culture, whose use of these objects is even more poorly understood, would only compound this problem.

In contrast, Thai phallic pendants offer an attractive and robust comparison. These pendants are still in use today and scholars, art dealers, and tourists have written about them. While these pendants will be discussed in greater detail below, it is useful here to note some of the basic similarities that Thai pendants share with their Roman equivalents. Their appearance is clearly phallic, and while there is a great deal of variation, some Thai pendants also incorporate anthropomorphic elements – such as arms, legs, and multiple

phalli – reminiscent of Roman examples. Thai pendants also share the same primary functions as Roman phallic pendants: they are suspended from the body to offer magical protection to the wearer.

Just because these similarities exist, however, does not mean that Roman and Thai cultures, magical beliefs, and phallic pendant practices are identical. Indeed, I will highlight a number of key differences between the pendants in these cultures. Nor do I seek to interpret the Roman material record as if it belonged to the Thai. Instead, I use this comparison, and the similarities and differences that it reveals, to generate ideas about how Roman pendants *might have been* used. Then, using evidence from Roman texts, burials, and iconography, I evaluate the suitability of these ideas for the Roman world. This approach allows us to sidestep the textual record's silence on phallic pendants to gain a more complete understanding of the place these objects held within Roman magical thought.

Thai Phallic Pendants

Amulets, or objects which have sacred or supernatural power (Tambiah 1984: 193), are popular in modern Thailand, and phallic amulets (*palad khik*) are just one of many types. The term *palad khik* includes several different phallic objects used in magical rites in Thailand, ranging from small wearable amulets to roughly life-size carved phalli to enormous sculpted examples that are metres tall. The following discussion focuses primarily on the small Thai phallic pendants.

Palad khik pendants, made of bone, stone, metal, or wood, are typically 3–5cm long, though occasionally, life-size examples are worn (Figure 3.1; Textor 1973: 141; Friedman 1997: 178, fig. 9). These amulets clearly depict a phallus with a detailed glans and sometimes have magical or sacred formulas written in Old Khmer or Pali, an early Buddhist language (Friedman 1977: 173; Chinalai 2004).

Figure 3.1 Wooden palad khik hanging in a market stall, Bangkok, Thailand (photo: Ursula Wall).

Figure 3.2 Bronze palad khik, blessed at the Wat Lahanrai temple (purchased online and photographed by author).

Neither language is commonly spoken or written anymore, and they function as sacred scripts read by scholars, students, and religious officials. Some *palad khik* have anthropomorphic characteristics (Figure 3.2), including phallic heads, arms, or legs, and others have monkeys or women riding on top of the phallus (Friedman 1977: 174).

Where Thai amulets are worn on the body depends upon their associations. Buddha amulets, which represent purity and morality, are worn around the neck, while love charms depicting people with exaggerated genitalia are linked to immorality and pollution and are worn around the waist. Phallic amulets are of ambiguous, middle-lower morality (Yee 1996: 5–6), and are typically worn tied around the waist or carried in a pocket (Friedman 1977: 171–2).

Palad khik are most strongly associated with pre-pubescent male children, and these amulets protect them from physical harm, including animal bites (Textor 1973: 141–2). Phallic pendants can also divert the attacks of malicious spirits who might try make the child ill or injure his genitals and future virility, and this function may relate to one translation of *palad khik* to mean 'surrogate', with the amulet – worn to the side of the body, away from the boy's genitals – providing an alternate target for such spiritual attacks (Friedman 1977: 173). An alternative explanation for the supernatural protective power of the *palad khik* is that it depicts an erect adult penis, confusing spirits into mistaking a vulnerable boy for an adult man, with whom the spirits would be less likely to interfere (Sanders 2012: 11).

While children are the original and most socially appropriate users of *palad khik*, adult men sometimes wear these amulets as well. Anthropologists studying in Thailand during the 1950s and 1960s noted that men wore these amulets in secret around their waist, where they were sometimes associated with sorcery and aggressive magic (Textor 1973: 142; Terwiel 1975: 91–92). Individuals writing later, however, document men's open and proud collection and use of *palad khik*, which could miraculously save these individuals from car accidents and gunfire (Friedman 1977: 177–8; Chinalai 2004; cf. Sanders 2012: 12). When used by adults, these amulets are also sometimes granted additional abilities. Merchants use larger, life-size carved phalli in rituals to attract customers and prosperity (Ngamkham 2005), and some vendors grant smaller phallic pendants this same ability, blessing their wares with their *palad khik* before returning it to their waist, pocket, or neck (Chinalai 2004). These amulets can also bring popularity, including with the opposite sex (Friedman 1977: 177; Ngamkham 2005), and enhance men's virility and sexual potency (Whittaker 2015: 60, 76).

A few sources document adult women using *palad khik*, though this is less common and sometimes associated with unusual individuals, such as a beauty queen who wore one in her hair (Ngamkham 2005). Some believe that prostitutes carry these amulets for protection, since they would be particularly vulnerable to magical attacks due to their close interactions with clients or pimps who could steal their hair or bodily fluids (Yee 1996: 9). Women might wear or carry a *palad khik* in their purse, where it offers them protection, good luck, and popularity (Friedman 1977: 178; Sanders 2012: 11). Whittaker, who studied upper class couples at Bangkok infertility clinics, mentions that men and women can wear a type of *palad khik* to enhance their fertility (2015: x, 10, 76). This function may be another ability that has spread to these amulets from other Thai phallic objects. Couples experiencing fertility difficulties can ask for assistance at the shrine of the goddess San Jao Mae Thap Thim, located near Bangkok's Nai Lert Hotel, and the proper offering to this goddess is a large wooden phallus (Whittaker 2015: 89–92). For those struggling to conceive, a phallic pendant may be just another tool to conquer their infertility.

Palad khik users believe that their origins are in Hinduism, which grants these objects greater cultural legitimacy (Sanders 2012: 22). Some legends say they are shrunken *lingam* statues that depict the god Shiva's phallus, which were brought to Thailand and later inscribed with Buddhist spells (Friedman 1977: 172, 176; Whittaker 2015: 76). *Palad khik* gain their supernatural power in several ways. Like other Thai amulets, they are blessed by monks or spiritual leaders, and the power and abilities of these individuals are transferred to the amulets (Textor 1973: 142; Friedman 1977: 176–7). Inscribed magical words can also increase a pendant's effectiveness (Friedman 1977: 173). The phallus' association with aggressive force (Terwiel 1975: 78, 92), and the belief that sexual or immoral objects can repel malevolent forces (Friedman 1977: 171), might also augment the *palad khik*'s magic. Some Thais believe that anomalous individuals possess strength, power, and sexual prowess, and they are often featured on amulets (Tambiah 1984: 225). This belief in the magical power of the unusual might also extend to anthropomorphic *palad khik*, and the inclusion of multiple phalli on a single pendant is believed to augment its effectiveness (Friedman 1977: 178).

The popularity and significance of these amulets today is debated. *Palad khik* can still be found in markets and amulet catalogues (Chinalai 2004), though those depicting monks or the Buddha receive much more space (Sanders 2012: 4). These amulets are rarely the focus of academic scholarship, but they are mentioned in some recent studies (Yee 1996). Whittaker, who did fieldwork during 2007–2008, noted that it was common for Thai men to wear *palad khik*, though educated, urban middle class men would generally not admit this in public (2015: 60; cf. Friedman 1977: 173). This tension surrounding *palad khik*, especially for urban elite, relates to larger cultural concerns about modernity and globalisation, and in Thai English-language media, these amulets are typically portrayed as humorous curiosities, rural superstition, or embarrassing examples of 'low culture' (Sanders 2012: 8–9).

Roman Phallic Pendants

Iconography and texts suggest that Roman phallic pendants, as well as related phallic mounts, rings, earrings, and hairpins, were used to protect against the evil eye. Phalli, alone or accompanied by other apotropaic figures, appear on wall carvings and sculptures battling eyes (Johns 1989: 66–8, 93–4; Parker and Ross 2016). A few texts seem to indirectly reference phallic pendants offering protection (Plin. *HN* 28.39; Varro, *Ling.* 7.96–97), and the Latin term *fascinum*, which the Romans used for both fascination and phallic objects, has been attributed to phallic pendants in light of this connection (Adams 1990: 63–4; Whitmore 2017: 48–9).

Ancient texts most often link children with phallic pendants. Pliny the Elder offers the most explicit reference in the first century A.D., noting that the god Fascinus, whose name is related to *fascinum*, protected children from bewitchments (*HN* 28.39). Varro's first century B.C. passage, which mentions shameful and deformed pendants protecting children when worn at the neck (*Ling.* 7.96–97), has also been interpreted as a reference to phallic pendants (Whitmore 2017: 48–50).

Phallic pendants from burial contexts can also offer insights into their use. Grave goods do not offer a straightforward reflection of the identity of the deceased, as it was the living, rather than the dead, who selected and buried these items (Eckardt 2014: 60). Some objects may have been the possessions of the deceased, and can convey information about how the items were used in life, but others may be related to funerary rites, beliefs about the afterlife, or were used to construct a new identity for the deceased (Cool 2011: 298–9; Wilburn 2016: 48–9; Swift 2017: 70). While grave goods most accurately convey information about the identity of the buried person as a deceased individual, this

identity is connected to the one that they had, or would have had, in life. The burials of female children with over-sized jewellery may offer an example of the latter, and these objects have been interpreted as the dowry that they never were able to use (Cool 2011: 310–11). A culture's funerary practices can reflect, as well as help create and reinforce, their ideas about social identities more broadly (Moore 2016: 322). Grave goods convey culturally acceptable, if idealised, associations between objects and social groups.

While grave goods do not always reflect objects that an individual used in life (Swift 2017: 164), the evidence seems particularly strong for children and Roman phallic pendants. Here, the textual and burial evidence converge to suggest that these amulets were associated with children in life and death. Phallic pendants are infrequent finds in Roman burial contexts, particularly those with skeletal remains that can be anthropologically analysed, but when they do appear, they are most often found with children. Over a dozen graves in Europe (France, Britain, Germany, Italy, and Hungary), dating from the first century B.C. to the fourth century A.D., had child occupants buried with phallic pendants (Lassányi and Bechtold 2006; Bel 2012: 208; Whitmore 2017: 51). Several were found at the neck of the deceased, suggesting that these amulets were worn at burial, likely in the same way as in life (Varro, *Ling.* 7.96–97), making it more probable that these pendants were personal possessions, rather than funerary rituals (cf. Swift 2017: 164–5).

While Thai phallic pendants are supposed to be used by children, adult men and occasionally women wear or carry them as well. It is worth exploring whether phallic pendants were also more widely used in the Roman world. There are no texts that connect women with phallic pendants, but phallic hairpins and earrings were likely used by females (Allason-Jones 1989: 50; Hall and Wardle 2005: 178; Whitmore 2017: 52). Most examples come from unstratified contexts, so it is impossible to determine whether these phallic objects were used by female children or adults. In the western part of the Roman Empire, there are no definitive examples of adult women buried with phallic pendants. On the eastern edge of the Empire, however, these amulets have been found in a handful of first to third century graves associated with women (Whitmore forthcoming), and further east, a second to third century burial of a 45–55 year-old woman in Gorny Altai had two phallic pendants (Figure 3.3; Bogdanov and Sljusarenko 2007).

The god Fascinus protected not only children but also generals (Plin. *HN* 28.39), linking phallic protection with military men, and phallic carvings (Parker 2017) and pendants have been found on military sites (Crummy 1983: 139; Bishop 1988: 98; Philpott 1991: 161; Parker 2015: 144). No iconographic depictions show soldiers with phallic pendants, but it is possible that they may have worn them on belts (Eckardt 2014: 161). The Roman connection between phallic pendants and the military presents a contrast with

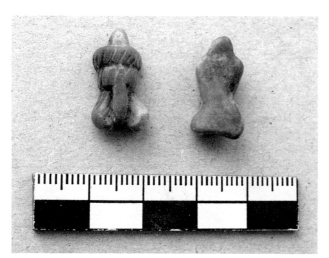

Figure 3.3 Roman phallic pendants buried with a 45–55 year old woman at Gorny Altai, second to third century, showing front (left) and back (right) of pendants (© E.S. Bogdanov; Bogdanov and Sljusarenko 2007).

Thai culture; while some Thai men use phallic pendants, and many types of amulets are popular with the Thai military, phallic pendants are not among these (cf. Tambiah 1984: 197, 278, 287).

While children were associated with Roman phallic pendants in life and death, adult men are almost never buried with these objects (Whitmore 2017: 52–3), even in cemeteries adjacent to military forts. Silver phallic pendants were found in four graves in a cemetery near the Krefeld-Gellep fort, but all belonged to children (Pirling and Siepen 2006: 33). Of the 13 graves with phallic objects from a cemetery near the Viminacium military camp, six burials have identified skeletal remains. All belonged to children, buried with bone and bronze phallic pendants and amber and carnelian phallic beads (Spasidj-Durid2008: 122–39, 147–9).

The absence of phallic pendants in adult male graves does not definitively mean that soldiers never wore them in life. Adults in the Roman period typically had few grave goods, perhaps suggesting that the living did not believe the deceased required many possessions (Cool 2011: 309). Soldiers are also rarely buried in armour or with weapons, and many cemeteries around forts typically have little *militaria* (Anderson 2009: 78–81). While phallic pendants continued to protect children in death (cf. Wilburn 2016: 48–9), they are rarely part of adult graves, soldier or civilian. Assemblages which might more likely reflect use of the amulets in life, such as the first century A.D. artefacts found with ambushed soldiers at the Oberesch site of Kalkriese Hill and the victims of the eruption at Herculaneum (cf. Swift 2011: 203–4), do not strongly associate phallic pendants with individual adults either. While the deceased soldiers at Kalkriese were looted for weapons and armour, over 5000 small finds were recovered, including fittings from military belts and aprons (Rost and Wilbers-Rost 2010: 123). Only

two phallic pendants were found, however, one of which was in direct association with an animal, rather than a soldier (Harnecker 2008: 17; and see below). Only a few Herculaneum victims were found with phallic amulets: two were in jewellery boxes associated with groups of people, one of whom was an adult man, and another was found with the body of a young woman (Scatozza Höricht 1989: 92–5; Whitmore 2015: 61 n. 16, 62 n. 29).

Since phallic amulets are not associated with adult men in mortuary contexts, the only evidence that ties these objects to military men is Pliny's reference to Fascinus protecting the general and the association of phallic carvings and pendants with military contexts. While phallic carvings are indeed built into the fabric of military forts and related structures (Parker 2017), we must be cautious of presuming that pendants found in and near military forts necessarily belonged to soldiers, since children would have also been present in these spaces (Allison 2013; Eckardt 2014: 72–3; cf. Swift 2011: 214). Upon returning to Pliny's reference, however, the phallic god Fascinus protected the military general by hanging under his triumphal chariot (*HN* 28.39). Texts and burials suggest that children wore phallic pendants around the neck (Whitmore 2017: 54), but these objects may have provided *indirect* protection to military men by hanging from their mounts (or triumphal chariots), rather than on the men themselves.

Phallic Decorations, Transport Animals, and the Evil Eye

No phallic pendants have been found associated with chariots or other vehicles, though a linchpin found in Surrey may have a phallic terminal (Bird 1997). Phallic ornaments, however, have been found in direct association with the skeletons of at least two equids. Three phallic studs or mounts (Figure 3.4), lunate and pelta studs, a bell,

Figure 3.4 Three Roman phallic mounts interred with a horse at Beuningen, first to third century, showing the front of the bronze mounts and the front and back (right) of the bone mount (left) (© Museum Het Valkhof, Nijmegen (Provinciaal Depot voor Bodemvondsten)).

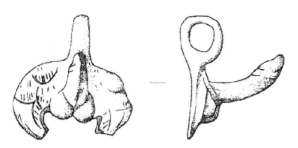

Figure 3.5 Roman ithyphallic lunate pendant found on the harness from Celles, third century. H 3.7cm, W 3.6cm (image after Massart 2000, fig. 13).

and a lunate pendant were found near the head of a first to third century horse at Beuningen, whose large size has led to its identification as a military mount (Zwart 1998). At the Oberesch site of the Kalkriese Hill, where the Roman army was ambushed in the first century A.D., a copper alloy fist and phallus amulet (L: 3.8cm, W: 5.7cm), a tear-drop pendant, beads, and a bronze bell were found near the spine and scapula of a mule. Strips of leather were still attached to the pendant's suspension loop and the bell's handle, which were likely the remains of the harness or connective element (Wilbers-Rost *et al.* 2007: 95–7; Harnecker 2008: 17, no. 258; Rost and Wilbers-Rost 2010).

Fist and phallus pendants with attached strap fittings have been found at Eauze (Arramond *et al.* 1986: 23) and Nijmegen (Nicolay 2007: 204, fig. 19, 203.1), and these may have decorated horse or vehicle harnesses (Bishop 1988: 98). In a third century Celles tumulus, a leather horse harness was found with three lanceolate pendants,

two of which may have stylised phalli, and an ithyphallic pendant (Figure 3.5; H: 3.7cm, W: 3.6cm), which was on a thicker, worn piece that likely went around the animal's neck (Massart 2000: 511, 518–20).

This ithyphallic pendant is stylistically similar to two others found in human burials, both without evidence of horse gear, but whose contexts suggest that they were not worn by the deceased. A third–fourth century burial of a 10-year-old child at Arras produced one phallic amulet that is similar in size (Figure 3.6; H: 4.0cm, W: 3.5cm) to the Celles pendant. The Arras example, however, was attached to a bronze bell by an iron chain, forming a small *tintinnabulum* (Jelski 1984: 264, 267–8). The other pendant came from a third century burial of an adult man at Guilden Morden and is larger than the others (Figure 3.7; H: 5.7cm, W: 5.5cm). This pendant's suspension ring bears traces of rust, perhaps suggesting it was once joined to the iron chain and bronze and iron rods with which it was found (Fox and Lethbridge 1926: 58–60). Whether this assemblage is definitively part of a single artefact, and what type of object this may have been, is uncertain.

These three phallic pendants – roughly similar in size though found in different contexts – are useful when considering pendant typologies. Most phallic pendants were found without contextual information, so determining whether they were used by humans or animals can be challenging. Since many pendant types, including phallic amulets, are found in both military and domestic contexts, Allison suggests that only pendants that are at least 8cm long, or recovered with other harness elements, should be assigned exclusively to horses, and that smaller pendants were likely used by either humans or animals (2013: 86–8). Phallic pendants from child mortuary contexts are between

Figure 3.6 Roman ithyphallic lunate pendant buried with 10 year old at Arras, third to fourth century (© Miriam Redouane/Service Archéologique d'Arras, with permission of Alain Jacques, Director of the Service).

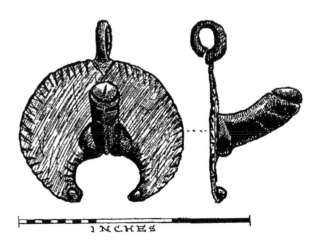

Figure 3.7 Roman ithyphallic lunate pendant buried with an adult man at Guilden Morden, third century. University of Cambridge Museum of Archaeology and Anthropology (no. 1924.1286 A; image after Fox and Lethbridge 1926, fig. 6).

1–6cm in their largest dimension, while most of the pendants found with animals or harness elements are between 4–6cm, with the Nijmegen example alone reaching 8cm in length (Nicolay 2007: 204, fig. 19, 203.1). This suggests that while some horse pendants will fall short of Allison's suggested minimum length of 8cm, smaller phallic pendants (1–2cm) were rarely, if ever, used on animals. The Celles harness pendant – which is less than 4cm long – illustrates that smaller pendants were used on animals and confirms Allison's suggested overlap in the sizes of human and horse phallic pendants.

Phallic pendants from child mortuary contexts vary stylistically, and include simple horizontal or vertical phalli with testes, anthropomorphic phalli with wings or horns, phallic bone roundels, ithyphallic lunate pendants, flaccid phalli, and fist and phallus amulets (Whitmore 2017: 51), a type which is also often associated with the military (Parker 2015: 135). While Nicolay lists many types of horse phallic pendants (2007: 202–4, fig. 6.9; pls. 91–2), most of these examples lack contexts tying them to animals and several were plausibly associated with people (2007: 204). If we consider only pendants found with equids or their harnesses, they appear in two broad types, both of which have parallels to children's amulets. The Celles horse harness has an ithyphallic lunate pendant, a type also found in child burials (Whitmore 2017: 51). The Oberesch mule had a fist and phallus pendant, but its type differs from those with the Hérault and Catterick infants. The Hérault pendant is a simple gold fist and phallus pendant, with testes and a suspension ring in the centre (Bel 2012: fig. 11). Between the fist and phallus on the Catterick pendants, there is a central scallop shell (Parker 2015). In contrast, the Oberesch pendant has a central, flaccid phallus and testes, with a wide suspension loop (Harnecker 2008: 17; pl. 17.258). This type of pendant is often identified as belonging to cavalry horses or transport animals (Arramond *et al.* 1986: 22–3; Bishop 1988: 98, figs. 48–9; Nicolay 2007: fig. 5.19, pl. 89), though at least one has been found in a human burial (May 1930: 275–276, pl. 85).

Based on the pendant types found in child burials and those associated with animals or harnesses, some tentative observations can be made. While phallic pendants between 3–6cm are associated with both children and animals, those that are 1–2cm have only been found with children, while those larger than 6cm are more likely to have been used with animals. Many different types of phallic pendants are associated with children, but only ithyphallic lunate and fist and phallus variations have been recovered directly with animals or harness elements. Both types combine multiple protective motifs (the phallus, *lunula*, and *manus fica*) to create a powerful amulet, and both are found with children as well, though there are stylistic variations between the fist and phallus amulets associated with children and animals.

Phalli Guarding Horses, Cars, and Buildings

Phallic harness pendants can be attributed to the ancient belief that animals could be cursed, especially horses. Circus curses feature horses and charioteers being bound, getting into accidents, and being chopped into bits (Gager 1992: 44–6, 53–9; Jordan 2002), and this danger seems to have extended to military mounts. The third to fourth century solider Apsyrtus wrote about horse afflictions and cures, and he relates a spell to cast the evil eye from a horse (*CHG* II. M979). The spell used an incantation and an amulet (περιαπτομένου, *'periaptomenoy'*) to remove the evil eye (βασκοσένη, *'baskosyne'*). The precise nature of the amulet is unclear, though elsewhere, Apsyrtus' horse amulets (περίαπτα, *'periapta'*) were scraps of paper or metal with written spells. These spells were spoken aloud and the amulet was attached to either the horse's halter or afflicted part (McCabe 2007: 146–52).

Letters to Roman cavalrymen stationed in Egypt during the second century also attest to military horses being susceptible to the evil eye. One individual began a letter by wishing his brother good health and that his horse stays safe from the evil eye (μετὰ τοῦ ἀβασκάντου σοῦ ἵππου; *O. Flor.* 15), and a father began and ended a letter to his son using the same phrase (*O. Flor.* 18; Bagnall 1976: 54–5, 58–9). This same wish for a horse's protection appears on yet another contemporary but poorly preserved letter (*O. Amst.* 18; Bagnall 1976: 55; Elliot 2016: 4). The word ἀβασκάντος (*'abaskantos'*) is found in numerous first to third century letters from Greek-speaking Egypt, referring sometimes to adults but most often to children (Elliot 2016: 1–4; *BGU* 3.811; *P. Brem.* 20.18; *P. Oxy.* 6.930, 14.1666, 46.3312, 46.3313). These papyri may suggest that children and horses in Egypt were deemed particularly susceptible to the evil eye, and the association of phallic pendants in child burials and on animal harnesses elsewhere may suggest the same.

While these animals were valuable and likely worthy of protection themselves, amulets also presumably offered indirect protection to riders in the Roman world, who both depended on the mounts and could be cursed themselves. Similarly, the Roman *tintinnabula* that hung in buildings and the carvings found on shops, storehouses, bridges, and roads did not simply protect and offer good luck to these structures, but the people who used them (Clarke 2014: 524–5; Parker 2017). This type of indirect protection also appears in modern Thai society, where phallic statues in homes and businesses offer good luck (Chinalai 2004) and phallic amulets hang in cars and on key chains to protect drivers from accidents (Friedman 1977: 174, 177–8).

How Did Roman Phallic Pendants Work?

For most Thai people, the *palad khik* has protective power simply because it does, and they prefer older amulets that have already been proven to work. The *palad khik*'s primary source of external power is the monk who blessed the amulet, and to a lesser degree, any inscriptions carved or written on it. Phallic pendants may also gain power from the sexual, immoral, or aggressive associations of the phallus in Thai culture (Terwiel 1975: 78, 91–2; Friedman 1977: 171, 173–6), and examples carved from unusual materials – such as a coffin or a tree struck by lightning – are particularly powerful (Friedman 1977: 177; Chinalai 2004). Most Thai amulets can be recharged with additional blessings, propitiated with offerings, and invoked with sacred formulas to transfer their power to the user (Tambiah 1984: 196), and some of these practices are documented with market vendors and phallic amulets. These merchants, who use *palad khik* to increase sales, sometimes make offerings of incense, flowers, or food to their phallic amulets and carvings, and touch them to items they wish to sell (Chinalai 2004).

No sources discuss the creation of Roman phallic pendants. In the ancient world, *Greek Magical Papyri* included spells to create amulets and experts would have been needed to carve spells onto lamellae and gems, but other amulets could have been made without specialised knowledge or training (Bohak 2015: 90–1). Like Thai amulets, most Roman phallic pendants, particularly those in metal or glass paste, were likely purchased already made and empowered (cf. Wilburn 2016: 36–7). Unlike *palad khik*, Roman phallic amulets lack inscriptions, and if they had painted spells, these are no longer visible. Some phallic carvings have inscriptions (Parker 2017: 121), and a few attest to the power of the phallus, including a wall carving and statuette (or amulet?) that picture a phallus and label it lucky (Johns 1989: 65 fig. 47; MOL MFI87[156]A<16>), and a lintel that describes the phallus as a tool against envy (*RIB* 983). Scholars suggest that the power of Roman phallic pendants was rooted in their depiction of the phallus, but why does the phallus have this ability?

Phallic pendants might have gained supernatural power through their connection to phallic deities. Pliny described the god Fascinus guarding babies and generals and being attended by the Vestals. Fascinus, the subject in this clause, likely refers to the god himself or perhaps his effigy. But next, Pliny wrote that Fascinus protected triumphal chariots by hanging underneath them (*HN* 28.39). By this, Pliny presumably did not mean that the god spent time under chariots, but instead, a representation of him was there, likely a phallic pendant. Here, the phallic deity Fascinus is equated with a phallic object that is equal in protective power to the god it signified. Thus, all phallic representations might gain power through their association with Fascinus.

The author Alexandre Dumas offers another explanation for phallic protective power, which is best categorised as a classical myth created in nineteenth century Naples. Explaining the connection between the evil eye and the phallus, Dumas tells about the birth of the god Priapus. Venus tried to keep her pregnancy with Bacchus' child a secret, but Juno found out, became jealous, and sought to curse the child. Disguising herself as a midwife, Juno attended the labour, but just as she was about to cast the evil eye on Priapus emerging from the womb, she was distracted by the child's abnormally large penis. This offered just enough time for Bacchus to arrive and save the child (Dumas 1843: 26–9). While a great story, this myth cannot be found in classical sources. However, its underlying idea – that an unusual phallus can distract malevolent forces and protect against the evil eye – has been offered as an explanation for the depiction of socially marginalised, macrophallic men on mosaic floors (Clarke 1996). It is worth evaluating whether ancient sources support an interpretation of phallic amulets functioning in a similar way.

Merrifield suggests that protective amulets had a magical power of their own, separate from the gods, and that phallic representations were 'lightning conductors, capable of diverting harmlessly to themselves the malign influence of the evil eye' (1969: 177). Plutarch described the evil eye as a harmful manifestation of jealousy: if someone became envious upon seeing another, their eyes can focus this jealousy into a supernatural attack. This was particularly dangerous since these attacks could be unintentional, and children were most the most vulnerable (Plut. *Quaest. conv.* 5.7.680c–683b). This same passage notes that amulets can protect against the evil eye, especially those that are unusual in appearance (ἀτοπίαν), because they distract the one casting the evil eye, partially shielding the victim (Plut. *Quaest. conv.* 5.7.681f–682a). Magical theory supports this idea: objects used in magic are often purposefully made to look unusual or strange, which makes them more powerful (Wilburn 2016: 13). While Plutarch did not say that these unusual amulets are phallic, several factors suggest that this might be so.

Phallic amulets that feature wings, legs, and multiple phalli strike modern viewers as particularly unusual images. If they were similarly unusual in appearance to the Romans, these amulets might be well suited to capture attention and avert the evil eye. Aside from myths of metamorphoses and monsters, texts offer no explanation for anthropomorphic phalli. Scholars have suggested that the incorporation of various animal features might make the phallus into its own being, capable of attacking the evil eye (Turnbull 1978: 204–5; Johns 1989: 68–70).

A simple phallic pendant depicting only genitals, however, would not be particularly unusual (Plut. *Quaest. conv.* 5.7.681f–682a), nor shameful or deformed (*turpicula*; Varro, *Ling.* 7.96–97) in the Roman mindset (Whitmore 2017: 49–50). Pendants depicting erect phalli might reference the large erections of Priapus or other comic figures, whose genitals conflict with the classical ideal of a small penis, making them both unbecoming (*atopia*) and hilarious, with laughter able to dispel the evil eye (Clarke 2014: 525–6). Cicero (*Off.* 1.35) offers another explanation. Writing on propriety and nature, he said that people should hide their body parts that perform natural functions, since while the functions themselves were not shameful (*turpe*), to speak of them publicly was indecent (*obscenum*). More specifically, Cicero noted that begetting children was virtuous, but speaking of it was indecent. So, a visible phallus might be shameful or indecent, particularly if worn near the face, a location that would make a 'normal' phallus unusual. The visibility of amulets is critical to their efficacy in Plutarch; they have to be seen to distract the evil eye. At least some phallic amulets were worn around the neck by children (Varro, *Ling.* 7.96–97; Whitmore 2017: 54), so it may have been the act of wearing of a penis at one's neck in public that made this object indecent and unusual, and thus, powerful.

The ancients may have used any, all, or none of these magical theories to explain phallic pendants. There was likely no over-arching idea or single explanation regarding the effectiveness of amulets, and some may simply have been known to work, even though no one knew why (Bohak 2005: 91). Like Thai amulets, Roman phallic pendants provided an alternative target that attracted malicious spirits and the evil eye away from the victim. A key difference, however, is in their visibility. Plutarch's connection between distraction and the evil eye suggests that for amulets to work, they had to be seen, while most Thai amulets, including phallic ones, are typically worn under clothing. The Thai practice of wearing amulets under clothes may relate to recent stigma associating them with lack of education and modernity (cf. Tambiah 1984: 197; Sanders 2012: 8; Whittaker 2015: 10, 60), but the differential visibility between Roman and Thai amulets might also relate to the threats they protected against. Thai amulets primarily guard against supernatural attacks and protect the body from physical harm caused by animals, accidents, and humans. None of these threats necessarily require the amulets to be seen. For the Romans, however, phallic amulets protected against supernatural attacks and the evil eye, a threat which every human potentially posed, making highly visible phallic protection necessary.

The hidden nature of Thai phallic amulets also relates to their morally ambiguous status in this culture. Phallic pendants are traditionally worn around the waist because Thais view both the amulets and this part of the body as less moral and pure; these amulets should not be worn around the neck because that is a sacred part of the body (Yee 1996: 5). While their morally ambiguous status relegates phallic amulets to the waist, in part, they have the power to repel spirits *because* they depict this sexual, morally ambiguous organ (Friedman 1977: 171). Cicero, Varro, and Plutarch together suggest that the Romans also believed that, in certain contexts, the phallus could be obscene, but unlike the

Thai, phallic apotropaic protection was magnified through its visibility. The power of Roman phallic amulets came not only from supernatural deities, but also their ability to shock, surprise, and distract viewers, presumably because they were seeing a phallus (and sometimes, a very unusual one) where they did not expect one.

This may suggest that, to be effective, phallic depictions were rather uncommon in the Roman world. If there was a phallus on every street corner or person's neck, they would lose their ability to surprise viewers, and thus, their potency and protective abilities. It is possible that scholars, museums, and historical collecting practices have exaggerated the importance and ubiquity of these objects due to their provocative appearance. Small finds studies may offer some support for this. Swift's study includes over 1000 finger rings from across the Roman Empire, and only 10 had phallic motifs (2017: 167–9). A study of 151 horse pendants from Pompeii only lists 3 phallic pendants (Ortisi 2015: 48), and a volume on jewellery from Herculaneum records 191 amulets and pendants, only 26 were phallic (Scatozza Höricht 1989). Out of the thousands of Roman artefacts recovered in Colchester, only nine phallic pendants or mounts were recorded in Crummy's study (1983: 139–40).

Phallic pendants are similarly rare in burial contexts, including those of children. In the hundreds of Romano-British burials examined by Philpott, only six had phallic pendants (1991: 161–2). In a publication of 64 tombs in Pompeii's Porta Nocera necropolis, one child had a phallic pendant and another had an amulet of the ithyphallic god Bes (Brives 2013: 1260–2). 57 children under the age of 10 were buried during the Roman period in the Necropolis of Sainte Barbe, but only two had phallic pendants (Moliner *et al.* 2003: 92, 309, 334). Of the 215 children buried at Krefeld Gellep, 108 had grave goods, but only four of these had phallic pendants (Pirling and Siepen 2006: 28, 33). While phallic pendants are found in child burials, their absence in many suggests that their inclusion was not considered a necessary burial rite for children. While this evidence best speaks to mortuary practices – and it is distinctly possible that a child's amulets might have been given to another when they died (Bohak 2015: 88) – many children may not have been buried with a phallic pendant because they did not have one in life.

Roman Phallic Pendants and Fertility Magic

Since phallic pendants depict the male sexual anatomy, it is worth considering whether they had a fertility or virility component. In Thai society, men and women can wear phallic amulets to overcome impotence or conceive (Whittaker 2015: 76), and these pendants also protect the future sexual potency of boys (Friedman 1977: 173). While Roman phallic imagery was not pornographic, have we been too quick to take sex out of our interpretations of these objects?

Phalli had a place in Roman fertility magic. The fifth century A.D. Christian theologian Augustine described the festival of Liber, which included a phallic procession through the country and city, and at Lavinium, the crowning of a phallic statue in the forum, activities which brought fertility and drove bewitchments (*fascinatio*) from the land (*De civ. D.* 7.21). Priapus, the fertility god with an oversized, omnipresent erection, also brought fertility to the land (Johns 1989: 50–2), and priapic statues were placed in cities, temples, gardens, and vineyards, where they punished those who attempt to cast spells (βασκαίνοντάς, '*baskainontas*') against the crops or possessions of others (Diod. Sic. 4.6.1). The protective capabilities of these phallic deities and representations are tied to, and perhaps stem from, their fertility powers (Johns 1989: 62).

Just as bewitchments and the evil eye could harm the fertility of crops, they could also cause impotence in men (Porphyrio's Commentary on Hor. *Epod.* 8.18; Ov. *Am.* 3.7.27–36, 73–84). The Graeco-Roman world had many remedies for impotence and fertility issues, and some magical cures involved phalli. Consuming a hyena's genitals with honey was a male aphrodisiac, and to prevent miscarriage, a woman should wear around her neck a gazelle's skin containing a stag's penis and a hyena's breast and hair (Plin. *HN.* 28.98–99). Phallic ex-votos have been found at sanctuaries, which were offered in the hopes that the deities would cure the afflicted part and restore virility (Johns 1989: 57–9; Schörner 2015). The *Priapea*, poems told as if by Priapic statues, also featured men and prostitutes promising gifts (in one case, wooden phalli) for successful sexual encounters and curing penile injuries (34, 37, 40, 59; Richlin 1992: 126).

Since phallic gods, statues, and animal parts were associated with agricultural and human fertility, which could be harmed by the evil eye, people might have used phallic amulets to increase or protect their fertility. Scholars have noted that phallic pendants might have had fertility or virility aspects (Turnbull 1978: 199; Philpott 1991: 161; Johns and Wise 2003: 275; Peña 2008: 333). Horned phallic amulets included the fertility and virility symbols of the *lunula* and bull (Plouviez 2005: 161; Crummy 1983: 139). The *manus fica* on fist and phallus pendants referenced sex (Nicolay 2007: 229), and the scallop shells, evoking Venus, on the Catterick pendants might have added a fertility component (Parker 2015: 141–3). Antler phallic roundels may have had ties to Cernunnos, an antlered fertility and virility god (Greep 1994: 83). While fertility was not the primary function of phallic amulets, these fertility and virility symbols strengthened the phallus' apotropaic power or perhaps added a secondary fertility function.

Since the evil eye and magical attacks could result in impotence, it is tempting to consider whether phallic pendants – particularly those with erect phalli – might have

protected against this in the Roman world (Whitmore 2017: 58–9). While phallic amulets inherently referenced men, and erect pendants alluded to sex, there is little evidence that adult men wore them. In addition, ancient texts list cures for impotence, including some amulets (Petron. *Sat.* 131), but phallic pendants were never mentioned among these. There is little to suggest that women's phallic ornaments had a strong fertility function, and several earrings depict the phallus attacking an eye (PAS: NMS-B9A004), firmly rooting them in apotropaic imagery.

Fertility or virility would not seem to be an active concern for children, but for the Thai, phallic pendants not only protect boys from danger, but also preserve their future virility (Friedman 1977: 173). Could Roman phallic pendants similarly have protected a children's adult fertility? Numerous curses throughout the Roman Empire threatened infertility, the loss of a child, or the happiness of children (Moga 2014: 25–9). An early third century funerary epitaph from Aphrodisias included the curse: 'may the offspring of his children die and may another (offspring) not come to life for ever' (Moga 2014: 27). In his summary of Graeco-Roman beliefs, Ogden suggests that plants and humans were particularly vulnerable to the evil eye while they were young and still developing (2009: 224; Plut. *Quaest. conv.* 5.7.680c–683b). Since phallic deities and other depictions had associations with both apotropaic protection and fertility, and children were the most vulnerable to the evil eye and the most frequent users of phallic pendants, it is plausible that phallic amulets, in shielding them from such magical attacks, not only preserved their lives but also acted to ensure their future sexual potency and fertility.

Aggressive Roman Phallic Magic?

While *palad khik* are much more strongly associated with protective magic, occasionally they are associated with black magic practitioners (Ngamkham 2005), and one anthropologist likens them to magical tattoos of ejaculating phalli that are inked onto the thighs of those wishing to wield malicious magic (Terwiel 1975: 91–2). Is there an aspect of Roman phallic pendants that might have related to aggressive magic? Roman protective iconography included powerful, aggressive phalli, including those that fought the evil eye by stabbing, sawing them in two, and ejaculating at them (Johns 1989: 66–8, 93–4; Clarke 2003: 108–9; Ogden 2009: 225; Parker and Ross 2016; Parker 2017: 117–8, 122). The *Priapea* offer another example, with tales of Priapic statues threatening to use their phalli as weapons to rape garden thieves (Richlin 1992: 120–2).

Some phallic pendants also had aspects that referenced force or aggression. The *manus fica* gesture found on Roman fist and phallus pendants was a sexual one, but it was also a fist, a symbol of strength (Parker 2015: 135), and the incorporation of bull's horns may have functioned in the same way (Crummy 1983: 139). Scholars suggest that such potentially aggressive aspects of these charms would have attracted military personnel (Turnbull 1978: 204; Plouviez 2005: 163), and indeed, phallic pendants were found in military contexts, though it is possible that they adorned buildings, animals, and children in these spaces more often than men.

But did Roman phallic pendants have ties to black magic? In the Roman world, sorcerers were both envious of other sorcerers and the target of their jealousy (Ogden 2009: 224), and a declamation by Libanius mentions a sorcerer who claimed that his abilities made him the target those casting the evil eye (*baskaiontas;* 41.27). However, ancient texts offer no indication that sorcerers used phallic pendants to protect themselves, and while erotic magic sometimes included phallic ingredients, there is nothing to suggest that sorcerers drew upon phalli to kindle or augment magic intended to harm. While protective phalli were depicted aggressively at times, Roman phallic pendants did not seem to have a malicious magical function, and since they were more strongly associated with children, it seems unlikely that they were used in this way.

Conclusions

By adopting a comparative approach with Thai phallic pendants, this paper seeks to expand current knowledge on who used Roman phallic pendants, for what, and how the ancients may have understood this magic to work. One of the most useful lessons to come from this comparison is the reminder that people use objects in ways other than how they are 'supposed' to. While children are the original and most proper users of small *palad khik* to obtain apotropaic protection, in practice, some adults also use them for a variety of purposes. In the ancient world, Roman phallic pendants were strongly associated with children in life and death, but the Thai examples offer a starting place to explore the rare cases where Roman phallic amulets were found in the burials of adults, which perhaps offer evidence for these individuals using phallic pendants for protection in life. In looking closer at the military association of phallic pendants, it seems probable that soldiers used these objects differently than children, hanging the amulets not on themselves but on their mounts and transport animals, where they protected beasts, humans, and goods alike. Archaeological contexts may indicate that children were associated with a wider stylistic variety of phallic pendants than animals, but both groups were associated with amulets which combine apotropaic elements – the fist and phallus and ithyphallic lunate pendants – underlining the necessity of strong magical protection for children and equids alike.

Roman and Thai pendants share a primary purpose of apotropaic protection, but function in different ways. Thai phallic amulets are worn secretly to protect against spirits and physical dangers, and they are empowered by religious officials and magical inscriptions. Roman pendants were worn visibly and offered protection through the power of phallic gods and the culturally acknowledged ability of surprising, improper, or hilarious phalli to disrupt the evil eye. Assuredly, not everyone in the Roman world shared this belief, as the relative scarcity of phallic pendants and images might suggest. Indeed, their infrequent appearance may have made these objects more effective, since they would have been more surprising to viewers and disruptive of the evil eye. The absence of phallic pendants where they might be expected also reinforces the fact that these objects and images were just one of many techniques that the ancients used to protect themselves. Other amulets also provided apotropaic protection, and so could a variety of other behaviours, such as spitting (Plin. *HN.* 28.35), which left no archaeological trace.

John Clarke offers an anecdote from 1970s Sicily, in which local men, upon seeing a hearse drive by, touched their testicles and explained that 'fertility (male fertility, obviously) drives away death' (2003: 97). These men did not require an amulet, since their own (adult) genitals had the power to protect them, a belief that is also held in Thai culture (Sanders 2012: 11), and perhaps in Roman culture as well. This connection between fertility and protection would have been recognised in the Roman world, where fertility gods protected people and the lands. By averting the evil eye, phallic pendants helped to ensure the survival of children and animals, and perhaps their (future) fertility, in a physically and spiritually dangerous world.

Acknowledgements

My thanks to Douglas Sanders for sharing his research and answering questions about Thai *palad khik*, Stefanie Hoss and Adam Parker, and the staff of the Perry Public Library. Photo permissions were kindly granted by Ursula Wall, Evgeniy Bogdanov, Miriam Redouane and Alain Jacques (Service Archéologique d'Arras), the Museum Het Valkhof, Renate Thomas (*Kölner Jahrbuch*), and Catherine Hills (*Proceedings Cambridge Antiquarian Society*). This paper was greatly improved by comments from the editors and anonymous reviewers. Any errors are mine alone.

Bibliography

Ancient Sources

Augustine (Translated by R.W. Dyson 1998) *The City of God against the Pagans.* New York: Cambridge University Press.

Cicero (Translated by W. Miller 1913). *De Officiis.* New York: Macmillan.

Diodorus Siculus (Translated by C.H. Oldfather 1967). *Diodorus of Sicily,* vol. 2. Cambridge, MA: Harvard University Press.

Libanius (Translated by D. Ogden 2009). *Magic, Witchcraft, and Ghosts in the Greek and Roman Worlds. A Sourcebook.* New York: Oxford University Press.

Ovid (Translated by G. Showerman 1914) *Heroides and Amores.* New York: Macmillan.

Petronius (Translated by M. Heseltine 1913). *Petronius.* New York: Macmillan.

Pliny the Elder (Translated by W.H.S. Jones 1963). *Natural History,* vol. 8. Cambridge, MA: Harvard University Press.

Plutarch (Translated by D. Ogden 2009). *Magic, Witchcraft, and Ghosts in the Greek and Roman Worlds. A Sourcebook.* New York: Oxford University Press.

Porphyrio (Ed. A. Holder 1894). *Pomponi Porfyrionis Commentum in Horatium Flaccum.* Ad Aeni Pontem, Sumptibus et Typis Wagneri.

Priapea (Translated by R.W. Hooper 1999). *The Priapus Poems. Erotic Epigrams from Ancient Rome.* Urbana, IL: University of Illinois Press.

Varro (Translated by R.G. Kent 1938). *On the Latin Language,* vol. 1. Cambridge, MA: Harvard University Press.

Documentary Sources

BGU III (1903) *Aegyptische Urkunden aus den Königlichen Museen zu Berlin, Griechishe Urkunden.* Berlin: Weidmannsche Buchhandlung.

CHG II (Ed. E. Oder and C. Hoppe 1927). *Corpus Hippiatricorum Graecorum, vol. II: Hippiatrica Parisina, Hippiatrica Cantabrigiensia, Additamenta Londinesia, Excerpta Lugdunensia.* Stuttgart.

O. Amst. (Ed. R.S. Bagnall, P.J. Sijpesteijn, and K.A. Worp 1976). *Ostraka in Amsterdam Collections (O. Amst.).* Zutphen: Terra Publishing.

O. Flor. (Translated by R.S. Bagnall 1976). *The Florida Ostraka (O. Florida).* Durham: Duke University.

P. Brem. (Ed. U. Wilcken 1936). *Die Bremer Papyri.* Berlin: Walter de Gryter U. Co.

P. Oxy. 6 (Ed. B.P. Grenfell and A.S. Hunt 1908). *The Oxyrhynchus Papyri,* vol. 6. London: Egyptian Exploration Society.

P. Oxy. 14 (Ed. B.P. Grenfell and A.S. Hunt 1920). *The Oxyrhynchus Papyri,* vol. 14. London: Egyptian Exploration Society.

P. Oxy. 46 (Ed. J.R. Rea 1978). *The Oxyrhynchus Papyri,* vol. 46. London: Egyptian Exploration Society.

Modern Sources

Adams, J.N. 1990. *The Latin Sexual Vocabulary.* Ann Arbor, MI: John Hopkins University Press.

Allason-Jones, L. 1989. *Ear-rings in Roman Britain.* British Archaeological Report 201. Oxford: British Archaeological Reports.

Allison, P.M. 2013. *People and Spaces in Roman Military Bases.* Cambridge: Cambridge University Press.

Anderson, L.M. 2009. *The Roman Military Community as Expressed in its Burial Customs during the First to Third Centuries CE.* PhD thesis. Brown University.

Arramond, J.-C., Guilbaut, J.-E., Masson, M., and Roux, J.-C. 1986. *Eauze. Témoins archéologiques de l'antique cité des Elusates.* Soreze: Association pour la Promotion de l'Archéology en Midi-Pyrénées.

Bagnall, R.S. 1976. *The Florida Ostraka (O. Florida). Documents from the Roman Army in Upper Egypt.* Durham, NC: Duke University Press.

Barnett, R.D. and C. Mendelson. 1987. *Tharros: A Catalogue of Material in the British Museum from Phoenician and other Tombs at Tharros, Sardinia.* London: British Museum Publications.

Bel, V. 2012. Les dépôts de mobilier dans les tombes d'enfants et d'adolescents en Gaule Narbonnaise au Haut-Empire. In A. Hermary and C. Dubois (eds) *L'Enfant et la Mort dans l'Antiquité. III. Le Matériel Associé aux Tombes d'Enfants.* Paris: Centre Camille Jullian: 193–216.

Berry, V. 1968. Neapolitan charms against the evil eye. *Folklore* 79(4): 250–256.

Bird, J. 1997. A Romano-British linch-pin head from Chelsham. *Surrey Archaeological Collections* 84: 187–9.

Bishop. M.C. 1988. Cavalry equipment of the Roman army in the first century A.D. In J.C. Coulston (ed.) *Military Equipment and the Identity of Roman Soldiers.* British Archaeological Report International Series 394. Oxford: British Archaeological Reports: 67–195.

Bogdanov, E.S. and Sljusarenko, I.Y. 2007. Egyptian faience amulets from Gorny Altai. *Archaeology, Ethnology, and Anthropology of Eurasia* 4(32): 77–80.

Bohak, G. 2015. Amulets. In R. Raja and J. Rüpke (eds) *A Companion to the Archaeology of Religion in the Ancient World.* Malden: Wiley Blackwell: 83–95.

Borbonus, D. 2015. Roman columbarium tombs and slave identities. In L.W. Marshall (ed.) *The Archaeology of Slavery: A Comparative Approach to Captivity and Coercion.* Carbondale, IL: Southern Illinois University Press: 326–46.

Brives, A.-L. 2013. Métal et petit mobilier en contexte funéraire. In W. van Andringa, H. Duday, S. Lepetz, D. Joly and T. Lind (eds) *Mourir à Pompéi. Fouille d'un Quartier Funéraire de la Nécropole Romaine de Porta Nocera (2003–2007).* Rome: École Française de Rome: 1247–64.

Chinalai, L.J. 2004. The facts about *Palad-Khik* – true and phallus. San Francisco, CA: *San Francisco Tribal & Textile Arts Show Catalog,* February 2004: 18–25.

Clarke, J. 1996. Hypersexual black men in Augustan baths: ideal somatotypes and apotropaic magic. In N.B. Kampen (ed.) *Sexuality in Ancient Art.* New York: Cambridge University Press: 184–98.

Clarke, J. 2003. *Roman Sex: 100 B.C. to A.D. 250.* New York: Harry N. Abrams.

Clarke, J. 2014. Sexuality and visual representation. In T.K. Hubbard (ed.) *A Companion to Greek and Roman Sexualities.* Malden: Wiley Blackwell: 509–33.

Cool, H.E.M. 2011. Funerary contexts. In L. Allason-Jones (ed.) *Artefacts in Roman Britain: Their Purpose and Use.* Cambridge: Cambridge University Press: 293–313.

Crummy, N. 1983. *The Roman Small Finds from the Excavations in Colchester 1971–1979.* Colchester: Colchester Archaeological Trust.

Del Hoyo, J. and A.M. Vázquez Hoys. 1996. Clasificación functional y formal de amuletos fálicos en Hispania. *Espacio, Tiempo y Forma, Serie II, Historia Antigua* 9: 441–66.

Dumas, A. 1843. *Le Corricolo*. Vol. 2. Brussels: Société Belge de Librairie.

Eckardt, H. 2014. *Objects and Identities: Roman Britain and the North-Western Provinces*. Oxford: Oxford University Press.

Elliot, J.H. 2016. *Beware the Evil Eye. Volume 2: Greece and Rome*. Eugene, OR: Cascade Books.

Fox, C. and Lethbridge, T.C. 1926. The La Tène and Romano-British cemetery, Guilden Morden. *Proceedings of the Cambridge Antiquarian Society* 27: 49–63.

Friedman, B. 1977. Thai phallic amulets. *Journal of the Siam Society* 65: 171–8.

Gager. J.G. 1992. *Curse Tablets and Binding Spells from the Ancient World*. New York: Oxford University Press.

Greene, E. 2012. Sulpicia Lepidina and Elizabeth Custer: a cross-cultural analogy for the social role of women on a military frontier. In M. Duggan, F. McIntosh, and D.J. Rohl (eds) *TRAC 2011: Proceedings of the 21st Annual Theoretical Roman Archaeology Conference*. Oxford: Oxbow Books: 105–14.

Greep, S. 1994. Antler roundel pendants from Britain and the north-western Roman provinces. *Britannia* 25: 79–97.

Hall, J., and A. Wardle. 2005. Dedicated followers of fashion? Decorative bone hairpins from Roman London. In N. Crummy (ed.) *Image, Craft, and the Classical World*. Montagnac: Éditions Monique Mergoil: 173–80.

Hansen, S. 2001. Neolithic sculpture. Some remarks on an old problem. In P.F. Biehl and F. Bertemes (eds) *The Archaeology of Cult and Religion*. Budapest: Archaeolingua: 37–52.

Harnecker, J. 2008. *Kalkriese 4. Katalog der Römischen Funde vom Oberesch. Die Schnitte 1 bis 22*. Mainz: Philipp von Zabern.

Hodder, I. 2012. *The Present Past. An Introduction to Anthropology for Archaeologists*. Barnsley: Pen and Sword Archaeology.

Jelski, G. 1984. Pendentifs phalliques clochettes et peltae dans les tombes d'enfants de Gaule Belgique. Une découverte à Arras. *Revue du Nord* 66(260): 261–80.

Johns, C. 1989. *Sex or Symbol? Erotic Images of Greece and Rome*. London: British Museum Press.

Johns, C. and Wise, P.J. 2003. A Roman gold phallic pendant from Braintree, Essex. *Britannia* 34: 274–6.

Jordan, D. 2002. A curse on charioteers and horses at Rome. *Zeitschrift für Papyrologie und Epigraphik* 141: 141–7.

Lassányi, G. and Bechtold, E. 2006. Recent excavations in the cemetery along the Aranyhegyi Stream. *Aquincumi Füzetek* 12: 73–8.

Massart, C. 2000. Éléments de char et de harnachement das les tumulus Tongres du IIIᵉ s. Les deux harnachements du tumulus de Celles (Waremme), Belgique. *Kölner Jahrbuch* 33: 509–22.

May, T. 1930. *Catalogue of the Roman Pottery in the Colchester and Essex Museum*. Cambridge: Cambridge University Press.

McCabe, A. 2007. *A Byzantine Encyclopaedia of Horse Medicine: the Sources, Compilation, and Transmission of the* Hippiatrica. New York: Oxford University Press.

Merrifield, R. 1969. *Roman London*. New York: Frederick A. Praeger.

Moga, I. 2014. This shall fall upon their children's children! Some considerations regarding funerary curse formulas in Roman imperial Anatolia. *Istorie* 60: 21–30.

Moliner, M., Mellinand, P., Naggiar, L. Richier, A. and Villemeur, I. 2003. *La Nécropole de Sainte-Barbe à Marseille (IVe s.av. J.-C. – IIe s.ap. J.-C.)*. Aix-en-Provence: Centre C. Jullian.

Moore, A. 2016. The life course. In M. Millett, L. Revell and A. Moore (eds) *The Oxford Handbook of Roman Britain*. Oxford: Oxford University Press: 321–40.

Nanoglou, S. 2010. The representation of phalli in Neolithic Thessaly, Greece. *Documenta Praehistorica* 37: 215–25.

Nevett, L. 1994. Separation or seclusion? Towards an archaeological approach to investigating women in the Greek household in the 5th–3rd centuries B.C. In M.P. Pearson and C. Richards (eds) *Architecture and Order: Approaches to Social Space*. New York: Routledge: 95–112.

Nevett, L. 1999. *House and Society in the Ancient Greek World*. New York: Cambridge University Press.

Ngamkham, W. 2005. A charm for all seasons. *Bangkok Post*. 21 August 2005. Available: http://squaresiam.blogspot. co.uk/2005/04/charm-for-all-seasons.html [Accessed: 01/11/17]

Nicolay, J. 2007. *Armed Batavians. Use and Significance of Weaponry and Horse Gear from Non-Military Contexts in the Rhine Delta (50 B.C. to A.D. 450)*. Amsterdam: Amsterdam University Press.

Ogden, D. 2009. *Magic, Witchcraft, and Ghosts in the Greek and Roman Worlds*. 2nd edition. New York: Oxford University Press.

Ortisi, S. 2015. *Militärische Ausrüstung und Pferdegeschirr aus den Vesuvstädten*. Rome: Deutsches Archäologisches Institut Rom.

Parker, A. 2015. The fist-and-phallus pendants from Roman Catterick. *Britannia* 46: 135–49.

Parker, A. 2017. Protecting the troops? Phallic carvings in the north of Roman Britain. In A. Parker (ed.) *Ad Vallum: Papers on the Roman Army and Frontiers in Celebration of Dr. Brian Dobson*. British Archaeological Report 631. Oxford: British Archaeological Reports: 117–30.

Parker, A. and Ross, C. 2016. A new phallic carving from Roman Catterick. *Britannia* 47: 271–9.

Peña, Á. G. 2008. Amuleto fálico Romano hallado en la Puebla del Río (Sevilla). *SPAL Revista de Prehistoria y Arqueología de la Universidad de Sevilla* 17: 329–34.

Peregrine, P.N. 2001. Cross-cultural comparative approaches in archaeology. *Annual Review of Anthropology* 30: 1–18.

Philpott, R. 1991. *Burial Practices in Roman Britain: a Survey of Grave Treatment and Furnishing, AD 43–410*. British Archaeological Report 219. Oxford: British Archaeological Reports.

Pirling, R. and M. Siepen. 2006. *Die Funde aus den Römischen Gräbern von Krefeld-Gellep*. Stuttgart: Franz Steiner.

Plouviez, J. 2005. Whose good luck? Roman phallic ornaments from Suffolk. In N. Crummy (ed.) *Image, Craft, and the Classical World*. Montagnac: Éditions Monique Mergoil: 157–64.

Regev, D. 2013. Egyptian stone objects from Miqne-Ekron: Canaanite-Phoenician trade in Egyptian cult-objects and their Mediterranean distribution. In L. Bombardieri, A. D'Agostino, G. Guarducci, V. Orsi and S. Valentini (eds) *SOMA 2012. Identity and Connectivity*, vol. 1. British Archaeological Report International Series 2581(I). Oxford: Archaeopress: 103–10.

Richlin, A. 1992. *The Garden of Priapus: Sexuality and Aggression in Roman Humor*. Revised edition. New York: Oxford University Press.

Rost, A. and Wilbers-Rost, S. 2010. Weapons at the battlefield of Kalkriese. *Gladius: Estudios sobre Armas Antiguas, Arte Militar y Vida Cultural en Oriente y Occidente* 30: 117–36.

Sanders, D. 2012. *Palad Khik: A Phallic Amulet Tradition Moves from Simple Protection to Magical Exuberance.* Unpublished paper presented to the Siam Society, Bangkok. 30 April 2012.

Scatozza Höricht, L.A. 1989. *I Monili di Ercolano.* Rome: L'Erma di Bretschneider.

Schörner, G. 2015. Anatomical ex votos. In R. Raja and J. Rüpke (eds) *A Companion to the Archaeology of Religion in the Ancient World.* Malden: Wiley Blackwell: 397–411.

Spasidj-Durid, D. 2008. Falicki Motivi iz Viminacijuma. *Journal of the Serbian Archaeological Society* 24: 121–74.

Swift, E. 2011. Personal ornament. In L. Allason-Jones (ed.) *Artefacts in Roman Britain: Their Purpose and Use.* Cambridge: Cambridge University Press: 194–218.

Swift, E. 2017. *Roman Artefacts and Society: Design, Behaviour, and Experience.* New York: Oxford University Press.

Tambiah, S.J. 1984. *The Buddhist Saints of the Forest and the Cult of Amulets.* New York: Cambridge University Press.

Terrenato, N. 2002. The innocents and the sceptics: *Antiquity* and Classical archaeology. *Antiquity* 76: 1104–11.

Terwiel, B.J. 1975. *Monks and Magic: an Analysis of Religious Ceremonies in Central Thailand.* Lund: Curzon Press.

Textor, R.B. 1973. *Roster of the Gods: an Ethnography of the Supernatural in a Thai Village.* New Haven, CO: Human Relations Area Files. Available: http://hraf.yale.edu/ [Accessed: 27/02/15]

Turnbull, P. 1978. The phallus in the art of Roman Britain. *Bulletin of the Institute of Archaeology, University of London* 15: 199–206.

Webster, J. 2008. Less beloved. Roman archaeology, slavery and the failure to compare. *Archaeological Dialogues* 15(2): 103–23.

Whitmore, A. 2017. Fascinating *fascina*: apotropaic magic and how to wear a penis. In M. Cifarelli and L. Gawlinski (eds) *What Shall I Say of Clothes? Theoretical and Methodological Approaches to the Study of Dress in Antiquity.* Boston, MA: American Institute of Archaeology: 47–65.

Whitmore, A. forthcoming. The opposite of sex? Flaccid phallic pendants in the Roman provinces. In R. Collins and T. Ivleva (eds) *Un-Roman Sex: Gender, Sexuality, and Lovemaking in the Roman Provinces and Frontiers.* London: Routledge.

Whittaker, A. 2015. *Thai in Vitro. Gender, Culture and Assisted Reproduction.* New York: Berghahn.

Wilbers-Rost, S., H.-P. Uerpmann, M. Uerpmann, B. Grosskopf, and E. Tolksdorf-Lienemann (eds). 2007. *Kalkriese 3. Interdisziplinäre untersuchungen auf dem Oberesch in Kalkriese. Archäologische Befunde und Naturwissenschaftliche Begleituntersuchungen.* Mainz: Philipp von Zabern.

Wilburn, A.T. 2012. *Materia Magica: the Archaeology of Magic in Roman Egypt, Cyprus, and Spain.* Ann Arbor, MI: University of Michigan Press.

Yee, S. 1996. Material interests and morality in the trade of Thai talismans. *Southeast Asian Journal of Social Science* 24(2): 1–21.

Zwart, A.J.M. 1998. A bridled horse burial from Beuningen (NL). *Journal of Military Equipment Studies* 9: 77–84.

Abbreviations

PAS = Portable Antiquities Scheme. Available: https://finds.org.uk/database [Accessed: 07/02/17]

MOL = Museum of London. *Collections Online.* Available: https://www.museumoflondon.org.uk/collections [Accessed: 27/09/17]

RIB = S. Vanderbilt & University of Oxford. *Roman Inscriptions of Britain Online.* Available: https://romaninscriptionsofbritain.org/inscriptions/searchnumber [Accessed: 27/09/17]

4

Little Bottles of Power: Roman Glass Unguentaria in Magic, Ritual, and Poisoning

Thomas Derrick

The subject of this chapter is a group of items seemingly common in Roman period contexts throughout the Roman world: glass unguentaria. The vessels are often considered relatively mundane, and their presence to be a routine part of the glass assemblage from an archaeological site. The name unguentaria – a useful heuristic term invented by antiquarians – stems from an identification of their use with the *unguenta* of Latin literature, a fat-based perfume. These small vessels may actually have served several purposes, possibilities include: perfumes, medicaments, cosmetics, food extracts, herbs/spices, medical specimens, 'potions', magical concoctions, bodily fluids, and anything else that comes in a small volume and considered of a suitable worth for someone to preserve. The scant iconography relating to these bottles points strongly to their use in the realms of human beautification. To date, chemical residue analysis has done little to disprove their use in the containing of *unguenta* and *medicamenta* (e.g. Ribechini *et al.* 2008), nor has mainstream archaeological interpretation or their presentation in museum environments.

This chapter, however, explores the role of the glass unguentarium in Roman society in an altogether more holistic way, with a specific and pointed focus on 'atypical' contexts and sources that might point towards more nuanced understandings of their use. Rather, through seeing them as vehicles for 'performative belief', which sees them as a material trace of the secret wishes of the consumer and the arcane knowledge of the producer (who need not be different parties), we can begin to move past potentially reductive identifications. The below discussion uses examples from Imperial period Italy and Roman-occupied Britain, but the conclusions it reaches are applicable to other provinces and suggests that more work/interpretive plurality is warranted. It is furthermore hoped that the contrasting relationships between the archaeological record and the availability of

relevant ancient texts in Italy and Britain will be mutually beneficial. That said, the literary material has to be dealt with critically as it is, by its nature, limited in world-view, geographical focus, and therefore explanatory power. Ancient text is not a skeleton key for understanding the deposition of the artefacts, but insights about ancient behaviours should not be dismissed out of hand.

This chapter situates itself within a recent trend for the increase in prominence of studies of magic and ritual in archaeology (e.g. Boschung and Bremmer 2015; Houlbrook and Armitage 2015). Ralph Merrifield's influential *Archaeology of Ritual and Magic* represented a sea-change in archaeological interpretation. Merrifield's assertion that 'Ritual and magic were formerly part of everyday life, but by association with fantasy fiction and occultism they have now acquired an aura of sensationalism that has discouraged investigation' (1987: xiii–xiv) still holds true today. Site excavators of historic periods were (and are) encouraged to think more critically about the material traces of these activities in the archaeological record beyond a focus on those discovered in a 'manifestly religious or mortuary context' (1987: xiii).

Studies of Greek and Roman magic, however, have been more traditionally rooted in the disciplines of Classics and Ancient History with only occasional and uncritical recourse to archaeological/artefactual information (Bremmer 2015, 7–9). Chadwick (2013), however, has renewed arguments for an approach to magic and ritual in the archaeological record that is altogether more encompassing and inclusive in which these practices are considered rather more mundane and part of wider societal practices (see also Wilburn 2013). Studies of magic were also subject to the wider 'material turn', and thus the 'cultural turn', which arguably began in the 1980s as a natural consequence of the rise of the modern consumer society (Bremmer 2015: 8–9). However, we should not consider a scholarly focus on materiality a product of modern social habitus – material and materiality were clearly important elements of ancient magic and ritual (Bremmer 2015: 8–9). This work is situated in this ideological framework, to date studies of all of the types of substances listed above have been almost exclusively relegated to literary ones which do not engage with the abundant physical evidence. The work of De Tommaso on, what he terms, '*ampullae vitrae*' (1990) represents an important deviation, as does Luigi Taborelli's various works on ceramic and glass unguentaria (1992; 2002), but this work is qualitative and does not use polyfunctional interpretative approach offered here. The publication and presentation of unguentaria in excavation catalogues or museum environments has not traditionally engaged in the linking of the vessels to practices outside of perfume, medicines, and cosmetics. This chapter aims to redress this.

If the traditional disciplines cannot sufficiently decide upon the vessels' function in simple functional (and non-magical/ritual) terms – i.e. these are used in personal beautification/hygiene/medicine – then we cannot hope to understand their role in magic, ritual, and poisoning. This tension was previously rooted in a disciplinary fondness for – and publishing tendency towards – typology (cf. Stig Sørensen 2015) and finds classification by material. The field has significantly changed in the last decade or more, however, and deliberate efforts are made to avoid these tendencies. Even within the post-processual methodologies of discussing artefacts in terms of their broad social uses (adornment, medicine/hygiene, alimentation, etc.), the vast range of functional possibilities for these vessels defies strict classification. Although, as the below discussion hopefully proves, there is much cause for optimism.

The following sub-sections comprise thematic discussions of behaviours and potential motivations involved in the use and understanding of these substances: 1) Exoticism and efficacy; 2) Power and femininity; 3) Physical modification, containing, and miniaturising; 4) Death, liminality, and the chthonic. However, this separation is my own and artificial, as the sections have a significant amount of overlap. Archaeological case studies are given alongside the discussion in a way that is hopefully helpful and not akin to what Kyriakidis terms interpretative 'overreaching' (Kyriakidis 2007: 2; Houlbrook and Armitage 2015: 7–9).

Exoticism and Efficacy

A key *topos* in the study of literary depictions of perfumes, cosmetics, and related compounds is the use of exotic substances. This likely arose for clear reasons: 1) The literary sources use eastern aromatics as a by-word for luxurious excess and danger; 2) Eastern trade is discussed within the frameworks of large scale economic trade and connections between the Mediterranean littoral and the East; 3) The ideological investment in focusing on the cosmopolitan and 'modern' nature of ancient Rome. The monetary scale of the Mediterranean trade with the East in the Roman period has often been discussed, but it is the social impact of this trade which remains understudied and theorised. The actual nature and scale of this relationship is, however, not important for the present discussion, but rather the way in which the performative qualities of the source of rare or exotic substances could be called forth for magical and/or medicinal efficacy.

In Roman literature, dangerous substances – magical or toxic – were often described through the land from which they came, and vice-versa. There are explicit, noted connections to poisons from Egypt, North-Africa, and Pontus (Jones-Lewis 2012), and the aromatics from Meroitic Kush and India were often characterised through reference to luxurious excess and magic (Pollard 2013). Pollard has argued that the 'othering' of these regions and the goods that came from them (chiefly by Pliny the Elder) can be explained through world historical analysis (2013: 1–5), and that the fear of them came through increased anxieties about the scale and social impact of such a trade, along with characteristic Roman moralising and pro-Italian chauvinism (On Italo-centrism: Beagon 2007; Jones-Lewis 2012: 51–2). These anxieties manifested in the characterising of these substances as belonging in occult or repugnant behaviours.

In the work of Pliny, poisons came from places where Rome had first-hand prominent military campaigns, and in the case of Pontus and Egypt the link between their final leaders (Mithridates VI and Cleopatra VII) and their use of poison was intrinsically linked to their characterisation by various Roman authors (Jones-Lewis 2012). The lands beyond the Empire which Rome had only trade relations with were therefore mystified and mythologised as a result. Ancient authors and modern authors often mention the trade in cinnamon and cassia, which were commonly used spices in aromatic and medicinal preparations in the Graeco-Roman world. The smell and sight of cinnamon is undeniable, a wonderful spicy and lingering smell and a deep russet-brown colour. These qualities coupled with the fact that consumers knew that these substances came from India – and Pliny the Elder's story that they are the phoenix's nesting material (*HN* 10.2) – made them a common literary trope in Roman literature. Once again, the performative power of not only an exotic and mythical creature but also a liminal and far-flung land is emphasised.

These literary snippets are often cautionary digressions from much larger discussions which detail cosmetic, adornment, or medicinal preparations. Within the descriptions of these substances, however, there is not much of a practical difference between the quotidian substances and the nature of poisons, potions, and magical concoctions (Richlin 1995; Olson 2009). These substances have much in common, and in Latin many of the words to describe them are the same and the meaning can only be inferred from context and comparison (Horstmanshoff 1999; Johnson 2016: 127–8). It is the intent of the concoction, or the 'performative belief', in its manufacture which denotes its social importance.

Exotic and efficacious ingredients need not necessarily be from far flung provinces or beyond, simply rare, or evocative/non-quotidian items could still be used in a similar way. An example of this type of exoticism would be the use of bear fat for curing hair loss suggested by a woman named Cleopatra in a lost work entitled *Cosmetics,* cited by Galen and others (Plant 2004: 136–44). While wearing our 'rationalist hat' – informed by modern science and an understanding of active ingredients – we know that it is very unlikely that the fat of a bear when included in a paste could help one regrow hair. Although the simple application here of wishful-thinking, performative belief or sympathetic magic suggests that as bears are particularly hairy there could be some sort of animism happening through the physical qualities of the bear. The concept of *similia similibus curantur* 'like cures like' can also be seen in the use of 'young' ingredients (such as the first antlers of a stag) in rejuvenating face creams (Johnson 2016: 64–5). The degree to which the consumer could distinguish ursine from other mammalian fats, remains to be argued, but it is the fable which is most intriguing here.

In the Greek Magical Papyri, the 'Powerful spell of the Bear which accomplishes anything' (*PGM* 4. 1331–89) involves the wearing of a bear hair diadem and the smearing of the lips with donkey, she-goat, and bull fat, spiced with Ethiopian cumin. Elsewhere, the 'Bear-charm which accomplishes everything' (*PGM* 4. 1275–1322) involves an offering which includes, myrrh, cassia, pepper, and saffron among others, along with the brain of a black ram. Although these spells seem to draw on the power of the bear as an astronomical constellation (Betz 1986: 62, fn. 173), the use of bear hair and the use of the fat of black and dappled animals in the first spell, and the use of a black ram brain (itself with a high fat content) in the second, bring a specific animalistic materiality. The combination of these properties and the central role of exotic aromatics in these two spells points to a clear equivocation between the exotic and wild and the magically/medicinally efficacious.

If we consider the, now infamous, stories of western 'snake oil' salesmen, a trope in many movies and television programmes of the twentieth century, we can begin to maybe understand this relationship in more detail. 'Snake oil' had its roots in traditional Chinese medicine but it was not until 1917 when Clark Stanley's Snake Oil Liniment was tested and found not to include any snake extract (or anything not found in other similar chili pepper based liniments; Nickell 1998), that they were debunked. The actual source of the substances within did not really matter, it was what the

'doctor' or 'pharmacist' made the consumer believe was in there and what the preparation could do which is important.

Much ink has been spilt, based on a few literary passages, about the collection of gladiator sweat for female medicinal use (Plin. *HN* 15.4.19). Gladiator imagery is known on unguentaria in the form of the helmet shaped 'dropper' flasks of the third century A.D. likely produced at Cologne (Isings 1957: 113, type 95c). However, there are few types of Roman artefacts that are not occasionally decorated with gladiatorial scenes, and these rare dropper flasks are to be considered artistic 'one-offs' with limited circulation. Contemporary related forms include pigs and sandaled feet and extreme caution should be afforded to their symbolism, the relationship between a figurative container and the contents has never been convincingly argued, furthermore, the vast majority of unguentaria are devoid of any decoration. However, gladiator equivocation (in verbal/textual media if not physical) could quite possibly be used to suggest that preparations were particularly good at treating physical aches, cuts, and bruises, all things to which the seasoned fighter was accustomed. In this example, the actual collection of gladiator sweat, or the endorsement of gladiators is not important, it is the performative personage of the gladiator as powerful and exotic symbol that is important.

The Flavian Basilica at Silchester

We need not dismiss the power of the placebo effect through a rationalist lens, and it is likely a helpful way of examining the way that these preparations 'worked' and were regarded in the Roman world. Much of the above discussion focuses around the literary evidence, but how can that help us decode the material record? I will now discuss an archaeological example from an entirely different context from the world of the Italian authorial elite. It is an example from Roman Britain and I wish to use the lens of exoticism and efficacy to examine and attempt to decode it, while avoiding over-interpretation.

The Flavian timber basilica at Silchester represents an interesting case. The publication of the Forum-Basilica by Fulford and Timby (2000) is notable for the number of unguentaria present at the site (Figure 4.1 and Figure 4.2). Unguentaria are a common, but rarely predominant, part of the typical Romano-British glass assemblage. Ten catalogue entries, from at least six vessels, however, were discovered from Period 5 contexts – nine from the South Hall (Allen 2000, nos. 43, 44, and 46, unillustrated: 45a–b, 45d, 45f–h) and one from the Entrance Hall (no. 45i). The one from the Entrance Hall was in the floor surface close to Feature F445, a central post-hole in a supposed tiled floor perhaps designed to support a door or a wooden superstructure.

There are several speculative possibilities for the source of the vessels used in both the makeup levels and construction levels of the floor. The Basilica, an official civic building,

Figure 4.1 Snake-thread gladiator helmet flask in colourless glass, 3rd century A.D. manufactured in Cologne. British Museum. H 102mm, RD 50mm (© Carole Raddato via Wikimedia Commons [CC BY-SA 2.0]).

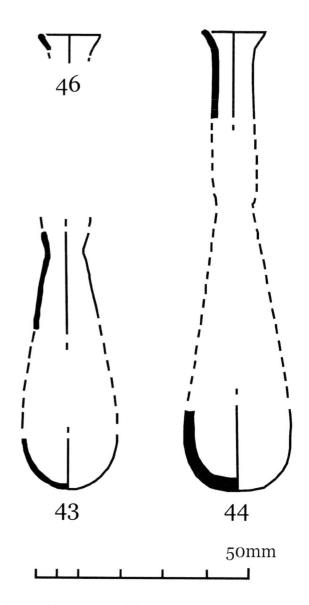

Figure 4.2 First century tubular unguentaria with constrictions and flared rims from Silchester Basilica (after Allen 2000: fig. 147).

was undoubtedly an important building in Flavian Silchester and its construction came in a period of increasing and widespread urbanism in Roman Britain. It is possible that prior to the erection of the building that the unguentaria were used in some sort of preparatory ceremony, possibly of sanctification. We know, for example, that the military standards were anointed with perfumes (Faure 2012) and it is possible that the vessels were used in some sort of similar process. Their deposition in the floor may well have come as debris from this activity, in the way that empty vessels were thought to be deposited in graves after they fulfilled their role in the funerary feast or preparation of the corpse.

A cursory interpretation could also be that these vessels were filled with a substance or group of substances and were subsequently imbedded in the floor for possible ritual/ magical reasons during the construction. However, they are fragmented, and given the thorough nature of the work on the glass from the site, were therefore broken before they were deposited – complete vessels would not survive in a floor construction layer. Deposition of artefacts in a seemingly votive and/or ritually/magically interpreted

context is a common occurrence in Roman Britain and the western Empire at large (Kiernan 2009; Chadwick 2013; Baillot 2015). In Roman Britain ritual deposition is clearly a common occurrence on pre-invasion Late Iron Age contexts, and we need not necessarily see the case at Silchester as a typically Roman activity using a typical Roman item of material culture, but a continuation of 'native' rituals using newly available material culture.

Beyond the social and construction context of this example is the socio-technical context of the manufacture and consumption of unguentaria in the province. Our earliest evidence for glassworking in Roman Britain dates between A.D. 50–60 (beads), and the first blown vessels that were produced in the late A.D. 60s in London were unguentaria (and stirring rods) and cups (Wardle *et al.* 2015: 97–9). There was a clear demand for them in the province at this period and it is the Flavian period up until the late second century A.D. when unguentaria were most common in Roman Britain (Derrick 2018). This deposition comes at a period when these vessels were fiercely popular and were somewhat part of a 'craze', possibly related to the increasing importance of the Romano-British elite after the tumult of the Boudican Revolt. Increasing competitive social stratification could be the reason for the increase of unguentaria dating to this period, as the phenomenon is particularly noticeable at sites with Late Iron Age origins which continued in use in the Roman period (Derrick 2018). The construction of the Silchester Basilica is a monumental example of this social change, as the building itself was to be used in the administration of the town.

As well as unguentaria and their contents being part of a 'craze' and intimately involved in the construction of identity in a period of dynamic change in Roman Britain, arguably, one may also see them as refuse/debris of some form of ritual (the nature of which is unknowable) which uses an item of material culture that is new to the province and therefore evocative – this is even without taking in to account the pre-deposition contents of the bottles. Cosmetic grinders and palettes are common in Iron-Age as well as Roman-period Britain (Jackson 2010), and these bottles may well have fitted in to existing behaviours, but small bottles for preserving these substances are a post-Claudian invasion phenomenon. Exploring the thinking pattern of exoticism/novelty and religious/supernatural efficacy behind a possible sanctification ritual of a Roman public building offers an interesting interpretation.

Power and Femininity

An important social element of the use of these substances, particularly in secretive behaviours, is the role of women in their use. As already suggested above the substances which are the subject of this paper are intrinsically linked to the more routine substances like perfumes, cosmetics, and medicaments. If an individual did not employ someone to do their make-up or own a slave to do it for them, it is likely that they prepared these at home. Indeed, the fragmentary *Medicamina Faciei Femineae* by Ovid is an explicit instructional text to do just that, with the express aim of improving female beauty and thus romantic success.

Women producing, mixing, altering, and consuming perfumes, cosmetics, medicines (and therefore perhaps also poisons and magical substances) behind closed doors, aroused the suspicions of elite male writers about the secret behaviours they were engaged with, and potentially, the resulting power they held (Johnson 2016: 1–40). With recourse to mythology one can consider the evocative *exemplum* of Medea – from poison *locus* Pontus (Jones-Lewis 2012: 52) – but there are several historical examples in Roman historiography which follow this *topos* (Horstmanshoff 1999). The next insinuation is that they were producing bewitching substances, and if individuals died then commonly the first accusation to be made was that the woman/women involved – or judged to be involved – were involved in poisoning or witchcraft. The trope of the manipulative and baneful stepmother for example, and the citron-based antidotes against their harmful herbal preparations, receives a treatment in Virgil's *Georgics* (2.109–135) – although some consider this part an interpolation (Johnson 2016: 39, fn. 27). Ovid in the *Medicamina* expressly warns his female audience about using and creating botanical potions, including the famous *hippomanes*, for magical purposes, and against magic:

> Thus it is more likely that passion drives us rather than powerful herbs, which the sorceress' hand plucks with a frightful art. Do not place your trust in grasses or a mix of juices, try not the baneful venom of a mare on heat. Snakes are not split down the middle by Marsian spells, the wave is not reversed and returned to its own source. And though someone may have set aside Temesaean bronze, the Moon will never be shaken from her chariot. (Ov. *Medic.* 35–42)

As previously mentioned, one can hardly tell the story of Cleopatra without a discussion of poisons and magical activities – how else could historians explain how the divine Julius Caesar was taken in? If you combine the eastern exoticism through which she was characterised – Egypt was a land of perfumes, medicines, and magic – and the fact that she was a powerful woman, this portrayal acts as a negative example of stereotypical female behaviour in the light of male neuroses (Jones-Lewis 2012: 56–7). Moreover, the tales told of the less popular Julio-Claudian women either point to them as ruthless poisoners (Livia, Agrippina the Younger) or wanton adulterers (Julia the Elder) (Pomeroy 1995; Horstmanshoff 1999). The use of perfumes and cosmetics was considered a normative, if dangerous and profligate, part of life for women of all social classes (Olson 2009). However, when men engage in these activities (particularly the wearing of perfumes and cosmetics) they are the subject of harsher opinions, and this falls in to wider societal debates about effeminacy and gender boundaries and norms in elite society. The authorial absolution of guilt for the murder of L. Plotius Plancus under the Triumvirate in 43 B.C. (Pliny, *HN* 13.25), because his hiding spot was revealed by his perfume, when seen in this context coupled with his personal distain for the widespread use of perfumes and related substances in society, is perhaps unsurprising. Archaeologically, however, Martin-Kilcher (1998) has demonstrated in her survey of the graves from Ornavasso San Bernando that although unguentaria are more frequently found in female graves, the differential is not as large as the literature might suggest. They are frequently considered a female object (Allison 2013; 2015) but this need not necessarily be the case, and there are problems with relying too heavily on the construction of identity in death and their use in life. Archaeologically speaking we should not rely on the vessels to characterise ancient femininity or vice-versa, but these items were clearly actively involved in the construction of polyvalent identities which included gendered ones.

Poison and Archaeological Visibility

Much of the above discussion is necessarily literary, but we can use the ancient texts to tentatively frame the ways in which we might interpret archaeological deposits. Summaries of, for example, all the examples of poisonings in the work of Tacitus (Horstmanshoff 1999) cannot credibly inform the connection between the quotidian archaeological record and imperial history. The archaeological visibility of poison and poison containers is problematic. There has not, to date, been a container found that is definitively a poison bottle dating to the Roman period. Taborelli has tentatively suggested that unguentaria and other glass bottles would have had paper labels (1992; 2002), but there is no pictorial or archaeological evidence to support this. As previously mentioned unguentaria in the shape of plants, animals, and fragmentary and whole humans, are unlikely to have a direct connection to their contents, and are in any case very rare. Archaeobotanical evidence pointing towards the cultivation and harvesting of poisonous and medicinal plants probably gives us one of the few glimpses in to this behaviour.

However, there is an interesting iconographic example that may suggest a certain amount. In part of the 'Heraklitos Mosaic' (Fathy 2017) in the collections of the Vatican Museum there is clearly an unguentarium strategically placed behind the two theatrical masks in the foreground (Taborelli 1992; Figure 4.3). The contents of the transparent vessel are decidedly very dark and even black, there are two identifications possible. The first is that it depicts black kohl, a type of eye cosmetic, and the second is that it depicts a vessel of poison. Whatever substance is in the vessel it appears great care was taken in securing the end of it with leather or some sort of cloth and string. One vessel, from Pompeii, was chemically identified to contain goethite, which Ciarallo has suggested was involved in theatrical cosmetics rather than in female adornment (2012: 357). That different substances were solely for actors seems unlikely, and it seems probably that minerals like goethite and other oxides had multiple applications in compound substances. It seems more likely that the vessel here is symbolic of poison/intoxicant/medicament and the role that they played in theatrical tragedy and death more broadly, given the iconographic context of the pavement. If this identification is correct, it at least goes to show that the standard containers were used, and at least some of our archaeologically discovered material may have also been used for this purpose.

Figure 4.3 Detail from the 'Heraklitos Mosaic' or 'the unswept floor' with a transparent unguentarium with dark contents, sealed with textile/leather/bark and string. Hadrianic, Aventine Hill, Rome. Museo Gregoriano Profano, Vatican City (from Taborelli 1992, fig. 1).

When considered as part of the whole large pavement, the masks pictured are just two of six on the bottom side above the author's Heraklitos' signature, and they are surrounded with other items of Dionysian paraphernalia (Fathy 2017: 17–18). The other outer panels are covered in hyper-realistic images of luxury food waste and detritus, in the Hellenistic trompe-l'œil 'asàrotos òikos' motif as described by Pliny (HN 36.60.25). Fathy (2017) has argued that together they form an 'elitist' carpe diem motif that stems from the cultural anxieties of the Roman elite in the period of the Second Sophistic. The fragmented Nilotic scenes, and their links to the myth of Isis and Osiris, are fragmentary but should be considered as wholly related. The theatrical masks at the bottom (including the potential poison/drug bottle), are indicative of conspicuous consumption and elite life but also the vicissitudes of the theatrical life cycle and the proximity of death. In the Late Antique period, there is a clear link between the so-called 'pipette bottles' and artefacts pertaining to Dionysian and other mystery cults (see below, p.41), and it is in this chthonic context that the unguentarium from this pavement should be regarded. Memento mori are common in Roman decorative schemes (particularly in dining areas), and it is perhaps the dark bottle here that was designed to remind the pavement's audience of the rapidity of death and the transformative effects of strong human-made medicines which, in the Roman period, could cure or kill depending on the dose and the skill and intent of the doctor, herbalist, or the purchaser (Horstmanshoff 1999).

Physical Modification, Containing, and Miniaturising

The material alteration and manipulation of symbolic or functional items was integral to Roman magical practice. Understanding the role of materiality of unguentaria and their contents, with reference to other related artefacts which are more clearly related to magic and ritual behaviours, adds crucial nuance to our understanding of their cultural role. The pre-deposition physical manipulation and damage of items of metal and other substances is clear in the archaeological record, and this is often interpreted as evidence of ritual activity or the performativity of ritual. This, however, is not possible with glass in the same way, but one way that glass unguentaria were physically modified is through fire, and they are a common pyre good. Although the contents of unguentaria could have practical roles in funerary ritual – as ointments for the preparation of the corpse and for the feeding of the flames – there may be a symbolic physical aspect to their use in this area.

Miniature votive objects are common finds at Roman period sites (Kiernan 2009). Miniature vessels, human body parts, or objects/animals have often been identified as being worn as amulets or deposited in religious/ritual contexts. The deposition of miniature items has frequently been interpreted as the amplification of power and symbolism. The so-called 'bucket pendants' found at the Roman cemetery in Brougham in Carlisle (Figure 4.4), for example are amulets that may well have contained powders, incense, or some other small object(s) with magical or ritual significance (Cool 2004). They have been used as evidence of mobility in the Roman world (Eckardt 2014: 35–45) but here it is their materiality that I wish to draw attention to. A link can be drawn between these and the so-called 'Amulet Cases'

(Figure 4.5) which are small gold canister pendants which could contain spells, phylacteries, or other items of *materia magica* (Kotansky 1994: 17). Although these items are not in themselves miniatures they are sealed metal cylinders like the much larger *cistae* and *pyxides*, and the wearing of them as an amulet is likely closely related to their role as a secretive small container.

Although there are not miniature forms of unguentaria that are used in this sense, they are in themselves a small container. The adding of different reagents in to one container, each with their own physical and symbolic properties, may well be involved in a similar thinking pattern. An interesting analogy to what may be happening with unguentaria in extraordinary (ritual?) contexts is to consider the medieval and post-medieval so-called 'Witch Bottles' discussed in detail by Merrifield (1987: 163–183). The creation of these bottles involved the combination of sharp items with disposable parts of the human body and bodily fluids (hair, nail clippings, blood, urine) within a pottery flagon or glass bottle, which was then sealed and buried under the walls of an individual's property as an anti-witchcraft device (Figure 4.6). Although we have nothing as evocative and visceral as this happening with glass unguentaria, there are clues that they have acted in a similar capacity, in terms of protecting a structure in the example of Silchester's Flavian Basilica (although the containers were not buried whole), and in terms of stopping the actions of the occult in the burial from the Bologna Train Station discussed below (see below, p.40).

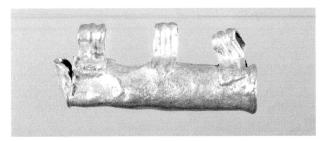

Figure 4.5 Gold 'amulet case' from Eaton Constantine, Shropshire (PAS:HESH-21275B; ©Portable Antiquities Scheme [CC BY SA 2.0]).

Figure 4.6 Stoneware 'witch-bottle' from Ipswich c. A.D. 1700, containing a fork, human hair, glass fragments, pieces of felt with pins, iron nails, wooden spills, and brass studs (from Merrifield 1987, figs 56–7).

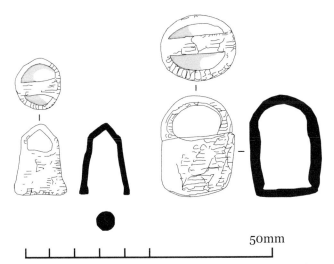

50mm

Figure 4.4 Iron bucket pendants from Brougham, Cumbria (from Eckardt 2014, 35 fig. 2.2; after Cool 2004: fig. 4.115, 3 and fig. 4.267, M5).

Death, Liminality, and the Chthonic

Unguentaria are items of material culture that operate in a liminal space in Roman culture, between life and death. At sites that are big enough to have distinct trade districts (as at Rome) there is a growing body of evidence that there is a close association between the allied trades of perfumer, glassblower, and funeral directors, the *pollinctores* – a word that stems from the Latin for powder (*pollen*) and their physical role in the preparation of the corpse (Hope 2000; 2009: 71; Derrick 2013).

In archaeological terms unguentaria are very commonly found in burial contexts. This is usually why there are large collections in museums, particularly on the continent, where elaborate tombs and particularly the material-culture rich Gallo-Roman burials in Gaul predominate. They are much rarer in Roman burials in Britain for example but burials at the large centres in the province (London, St Albans, and York) still yield many vessels. However, it is important to note that the Victorian practice of extra-urban railway infrastructure is behind the large unguentaria assemblage from York (Figure 4.7) – although it still seems that from habitation contexts the citizens of Roman York still commonly used these items (Derrick 2018). Perfumes had a functional role in embalming and corpse preparation as well as cremation and indeed the evidence suggests that they were an important part of the funerary processes at many sites such as at Lyon (Robin, Silvino, and Garnier 2012) and at York, where the vessels themselves were directly part of cremation rites they are deformed from a degree of warping to unrecognisable blobs. The status of unguentaria as a frequent grave good, based on biblical interpretations of Roman and Greek funerals, led them to be labelled 'lachrymatories', vessels for tear collection (Anderson-Stojanovic 1987). This interpretation is now outdated but the suggested role as a literal manifestation of the grief of the mourners, and the emotions involved in the funerary ritual, points towards the sort of more evocative interpretations this chapter advocates.

Modern archaeological/ancient historical practice has largely defined the role the vessels played in Roman society, but their actual use and symbolic meaning is likely more nuanced. Unguentaria, as stated before, are often linked to the construction of female identity in the burial. This seems completely possible, but the relationship is likely more complex than their use as either practical objects or connected to everyday items that are linked to a specific or group identity. The below examples certainly challenge this orthodoxy.

In their recent paper on deviant burials in Roman northern Italy, Quercia and Cazzulo included a peculiar burial of a young woman from the train station excavations in Bologna (2016: 31–3; Figure 4.8). The grave contained the lower half of her body and a glass unguentarium had been placed within a human-cut cavity in the pelvis. Quercia and Cazzulo suggest that the young woman in grave 244 – dated from the first to third centuries A.D. – had her upper body removed for some form of necromantic ritual and the unguentarium was placed in the pelvis after these events.

Whatever the motivations were behind this burial rite, it is clearly odd. The bulk of Quercia and Cazzulo's discussion focuses on the ways in which individuals in burials could be physically and symbolically contained – mutilation of the corpse, nailed down with fabrics or wooden frames, or pinned down with stones or large amphorae. The severing of the upper body of the woman in grave 244 is a clear continuation of this behaviour, but arguably so was the unguentarium. It is almost certain that the vessel once contained some sort of substance designed to stop the lower body rising from the grave, or uniting with her upper half. The function of the ceramic jug and coin in the burial is less

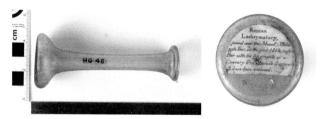

Figure 4.7 A second to third century 'candlestick' unguentarium likely from the York Railway Excavations. Text reads: 'Roman Lachrymatory, found near the Mount, Micklegate Bar, in the year 1814, together with the fragments of a cinerary urn [in] which it appears to have been enclosed.' YORYM: HG48, in the Yorkshire Museum (image by the author).

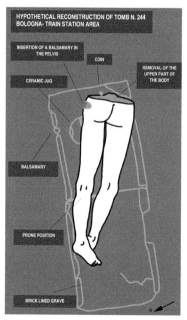

Figure 4.8 Tomb no. 244 from the Bologna train station excavations (from Quercia and Cazzulo 2016: fig. 3, no.2, after Cornelio-Cassai and Cavallari 2010: 102).

clear. This striking example has certainly made the author rethink many of the deposition contexts of these vessels.

A particularly unusual ampoule – a vessel which is physically sealed with the contents inside, to be broken when used – was discovered by Flinders Petrie at Hawara in the Fayyum, Egypt. For reasons of politeness befitting of the day it was described as a 'curious glass bottle with long neck and bilobed body' (Petrie 1911: 20, pl. xvi, n. 5; Walker and Bierbrier 1997: 206). It came from a funerary group also containing a rag on a stick, small lead baskets with handles, a glass stirring rod, a sandal, and lamp and pottery stands. The identity of the associated deceased is not known. The 100 × 30mm phallus-shaped glass unguentarium (Figure 4.9) was formed in a similar fashion to a globular/conical vessel which had been worked while the material was hot to form an indentation in the reservoir and a sealed tip. Ampoules have been identified from elsewhere in the Empire, particularly the sealed 'dove' and sphere vessels thought to be manufactured in the Canton of Ticino in southern Switzerland (Biaggio Simona 1991), but are almost exclusively broken when discovered. The only example to the contrary is the sealed dove bottle from the necropolis at Rovasenda, currently on display at the Musei di Antichità, Torino (Carducci 1968: Tav. 20). These vessels are designed to be broken, and were likely used in the funerary process or as donatives to the dead.

Phalluses were one of the main apotropaic devices used in Roman society (as well as a fertility symbol). It does not seem likely that this form was accidental. The combination here, however, of apotropaic symbol and vessel potentially containing a magical mix of substances highlights the link between them both and the liminal space between life and death that the unguentarium as a type of vessel inhabited. The actual biological function of the human penis, and the un-repeatable action of creation, is mirrored by an equally permanent dispensing of fluid. It seems clear in this context that this vessel is purposefully shaped thus and its creative shape points to a more complex and nuanced relationship between human agency and emotion and the material

traces of magical thinking and performative belief. Phallus artefacts are uncommon in burials and when they are deposited in this way they are frequently linked to children (Whitmore, this volume), the Rovasenda dove was buried with a young woman, and it is likely that we should see this artefact in this context (Carducci 1968: Tav. 20).

Established unguentaria typologies place 'pipette' bottles as a late third or fourth century form (summarised by Cool 2002: 134), and an extension of practical use from the vessels discussed above. However, these forms are exceptionally rare when compared to unguentaria of the first and second century, and even vessels of the third century. They are considerably larger than the earlier vessels ranging from 100mm to over 500mm in length. It seems unlikely that they always served the same functional purpose as said earlier vessels. They appear almost exclusively in funerary contexts from lead lined coffins from throughout the Empire, but particularly at sites that would be considered metropolitan by Roman standards.

Cool (2002) has convincingly linked these vessels to a use in Bacchic ritual due to the sheer number of the vessels that appear in burials with deliberate artefactual reference and allusions to Bacchus/Dionysus and Sabazios. Based on the funerary suites, Cool suggests that those that were buried with 'pipette bottles' were wealthy, likely adult, and may be female (Figure 4.10). They seemed to be worshippers or cult adherents to gods and goddesses that promised life after death (2002: 145). This is evidenced by the inscribed items and explicitly religious items as well as the repeated use of jet jewellery. If these are in the graves of initiates, it also explains why they are adults. They were frequently found in plaster burials and these have also been linked to life after death, and Brettell's (2015) work on the remains of aromatic resins in these burials may well be linked to the symbolic use of the unguentaria. The unguentarium from the Heraklitos Mosaic discussed above (Figure 4.3), whatever

Figure 4.9 Phallus shaped unguentarium from Hawara, Egypt (UC22498 © Courtesy of the Petrie Museum of Egyptian Archaeology, UCL).

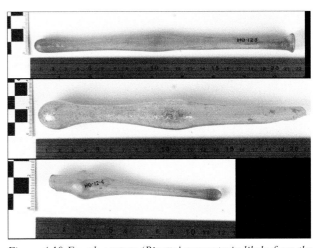

Figure 4.10 Fourth century 'Pipette' unguentaria likely from the York Railway Excavations. YORYM: HG123, HG119, HG23.4 respectively, all in the Yorkshire Museum (image by the author).

its contents, is depicted as part of Bacchic paraphernalia, and its parallels to the 'pipette bottles' and saviour cults seems relevant.

At Chelmsford and Spitalfields, these fourth century bottles have been found with jet objects. Jet was considered to have magical powers in antiquity, and Allason-Jones (1996: 16–17) has argued that some jet hairpins could be linked to the worship of either Christ or Bacchus. These bottles are found in association with jet objects also in sites on the continent (Cool 2002: 143). It is interesting to note that the child buried with these bottles at Marseilles in the fifth century was buried within the apse of the abbey of St Victoire (Cool 2002: 145–6), it is likely that these bottles has a role in many religious and magical practices in this period.

Amusingly, various traditions have arisen about the contents of these bottles: German scholars thought they were medicinal, French scholars thought they contained wine, Italian tradition held them as the vessel for the blood of Christian martyrs. Leaving British glass specialists as having 'never been sufficiently imaginative to develop their own story about them' (Cool 2002: 146).

The linkage of these vessels with ritual and mystery religions is owing to their rare preservation and their burial contexts. It seems likely that the more common 'utilitarian' unguentaria of the first to third centuries A.D. fulfilled a similar role in contemporary funerary ritual, these vessels may have had a practical (scenting/fire feeding) or symbolic (of personal/group identity) role in the funerary process but we should not rule out their use in magical, religious, or ritual behaviour.

Conclusions

In conclusion, this chapter has argued for more nuanced understanding of the role of unguentaria in antiquity, it has focused more on the secretive and occult elements of their use in magic, ritual, and poisoning. However, a similar or more encompassing paper could and should be written on the evidence for their use in pigments, medicine, and food preparation, but in any case, all of the substances used in these vessels likely had shared ingredients and we should focus on what unites them rather than impose modern distinctions.

What unites the allied uses for these vessels is that they were all produced by those that had specialist or learned knowledge of what they were creating (or were imitating those that did) and consumed by those that believed that the contents could have an outcome on an aspect of their existence, either in life or death. This model is harder to argue for substances such food extracts and pigments, but the skilful use of the former involves a belief that one can make food taste better and the latter that you can create evocative art. In the latter case, there is such a close link between pigments and cosmetics that it is very hard to distinguish between them archaeologically, because they are essentially the same and it is in the method of application where they differ (but even then, not markedly).

The concepts of magic and medicine are closely related, and this paper sheds light on these clearly related areas of life in the Roman world. In a modern context these two concepts could not operate in more different spheres. Modern linguistic characterisation has led to artificial intra-disciplinary boundaries, and this was a common theme in a conference session held at TRAC 2017 in Durham entitled '*Take two of these for what ails you" – Material approaches to Medicine and Magic'*, and the resultant discussions. Increasingly it is becoming clear that the mechanisms through which the curative effects of an artificially pragmatic Roman medicine, the mysterious spells and curses of Roman magic, and the interventions of petitioned deities, are entirely intertwined.

The discussion and examples presented above suggest that these vessels could be used in several ways and their contents could be mythologised by those that produced and consumed them, and those that sought to comment on this behaviour. An underpinning motivation behind the use of these related substances, is a belief that the substances in them could change your situation or the situation of another, and that by buying, applying, keeping, or burying these substances you were acting out these beliefs. This is not to say that their actual identifiable or analysable contents does not matter, but they do not present the whole nuanced belief-infused picture. Through believing in and evoking the efficacy of the exotic or the rare, the arcane, the secretive, the power of chthonic divinities, or any number of other powerful spheres, one could channel these beliefs (coupled with their motivations) in to their creative use of unguentaria – as archaeologists, our challenge is having now pointed towards these behaviours, to try and start seeing them more commonly in archaeological deposits.

School of Archaeology and Ancient History,
University of Leicester

Acknowledgements

My sincerest thanks go to the volume editors for the initial inspiration for this paper, for guidance in its formulation, and patience in waiting for its delivery. The anonymous peer reviewer provided very useful feedback including vital reframing of the material from Silchester and York. I thank my PhD supervisor Prof. Penelope Allison for her conversation and guidance which informed many parts of the text. The speakers and contributors present at *'"Take two of these for what ails you" – Material approaches to Medicine and Magic'* at TRAC 2017 in Durham provided hugely useful sounding boards and sensible insight, I am thankful, too, for the patient ears and wry observations of friends and colleagues. All mistakes and misinterpretations are mine.

Bibliography

Ancient Sources

Ovid (Translated by M. Johnson 2016). *Medicamina Faciei Femineae* in *Ovid on Cosmetics*. London: Penguin Books.

Pliny the Elder (Translated by H. Rackham 1958–1961). *Natural History. I–V & IX*. London: William Heinemann.

Pliny the Elder (Translated by W.H.S. Jones 1961–1963). *Natural History. VI–VIII*. London: William Heinemann.

Pliny the Elder (Translated by G.P. Goold 1962). *Natural History. X*. London: William Heinemann.

Virgil (Translated by P. Fallon 2006). *Georgics*. Oxford: Oxford World's Classics.

Modern Sources

Allen, D. 2000. The glass. In M. Fulford and J. Timby (eds) *Late Iron Age and Roman Silchester: Excavations on the Site of the Forum-Basilica 1977, 1980–86*. London: Society for the Promotion of Roman Studies: 312–19.

Allison, P.M. 2013. *People and Spaces in Roman Military Bases*. Cambridge: Cambridge University Press.

Allison, P.M. 2015. Characterizing Roman artifacts for investigating gendered practices in contexts without sexed bodies. *American Journal of Archaeology* 119(1): 103–23.

Anderson-Stojanović, V.R. 1987. The chronology and function of ceramic unguentaria. *American Journal of Archaeology* 91(1): 105–22.

Bailliot, M. 2015. Roman magic figurines from the western provinces of the Roman Empire: an archaeological survey. *Britannia* 46: 93–110.

Beagon, M. 2007. Situating nature's wonders in Pliny's Natural History. In E. Bispham and G. Rowe (eds) *Vita Vigilia Est: Essays in Honour of Barbara Levick*. London: Institute of Classical Studies: 19–40.

Betz, H.D. 1986. (ed.) *The Greek Magical Papyri in Translation Including the Demotic Spells*. Chicago, IL: University of Chicago Press.

Biaggio Simona, S. 1991. *I Vetri Romani: Provenienti dalle terre dell'attuale Cantone Ticino I–II*. Locarno: Armando Dadò.

Boschung, D. and Bremmer, J.N. 2015 (eds) *The Materiality of Magic*. Morphomata 20. Paderborn: Wilhelm Fink.

Bremmer, J.N. 2015. Preface: The materiality of magic. In D. Boschung and J.N. Bremmer (eds) *The Materiality of Magic*. Morphomata 20. Paderborn: Wilhelm Fink: 7–19.

Carducci, C. 1968. *Arte Romana in Piemonte*. Torino: Istituto Bancario San Paolo di Torino.

Chadwick, A. 2013. Routine magic, mundane ritual: towards a unified notion of depositional practice. *Oxford Journal of Archaeology* 31(3): 283–315.

Ciarallo, A.M. 2012. L'uso del Vetro a Pompei. Analisi del contenuto di alcuni unguentari pompeia. In L.A. Scatozza Höricht (ed.) *L'Instrumentum Vitreum di Pompei*. Rome: Aracne Editrice: 343–72.

Cool, H.E.M. 2002. Bottles for Bacchus. In M. Aldhouse-Green and P. Webster (eds) *Artefacts and Archaeology: Aspects of the Celtic and Roman World*. Cardiff: University of Wales Press: 132–51.

Cool, H.E.M. 2004. *The Roman Cemetery at Brougham, Cumbria: Excavations 1966–67*. London: Society for the Promotion of Roman Studies.

De Tommaso, G. 1990. *Ampullae Vitreae: Contenitore in Vetro di Unguenti e Sostanze Aromatiche dell'Italia Romana (I sec. a.C. – III sec. d.C.)*. Rome: Giorgio Bretschneider.

Derrick, T.J. 2013. *Containers and their Contents: The Case for a Holistic Reappraisal of the Roman Perfume Industry in Italy 70 B.C.–200 A.D.* MPhil Thesis: University of Bristol.

Derrick, T.J. 2018. *The Socio-cultural Implications of the Consumption of Unguentaria and their Contents in Roman Britain*. PhD Thesis, University of Leicester.

Eckardt, H. 2014. *Objects and Identities: Roman Britain and the North-Western Provinces*. Oxford: Oxford University Press.

Flinders Petrie, W.M. 1911. *Roman Portraits and Memphis (IV)*. London: British School of Archaeology in Egypt, University College.

Fathy, E. 2017. The asàrotos òikos mosaic as an elite status symbol. *Potestas* 10: 5–30.

Faure, P. 2012. Usages et images des huiles et parfums dans l'armée Romaine Impériale. In D. Frère and L. Hugot (eds) *Les huiles parfumées en Méditerranée occidentale et en Gaule VIIIe siècle av. – VIIIe siècle apr. J.–C.* Rennes: Universitaires de Rennes: 291–306.

Isings, C. 1957. *Roman Glass from Dated Finds*. Groningen: J.B. Wolters.

Hope, V.M. 2000. The treatment of the corpse in Ancient Rome. In V.M. Hope and E. Marshall (eds) *Death and Disease in the Ancient City*. London: Routledge: 104–27.

Hope, V.M. 2009. *Roman Death: Dying and the Dead in Ancient Rome*. London: Continuum.

Horstmanshoff, M. 1999. Ancient medicine between hope and fear: medicament, magic and poison in the Roman Empire. *European Review* 7(1): 37–51.

Houlbrook, C. and Armitage, N. 2015a (eds). *The Materiality of Magic: An Artefactual Investigation into Ritual Practices and Popular Beliefs*. Oxford: Oxbow Books.

Houlbrook, C. and Armitage, N. 2015b Introduction: the materiality of the materiality of magic. In C. Houlbrook and N. Armitage (eds) *The Materiality of Magic: An Artefactual Investigation into Ritual Practices and Popular Beliefs*. Oxford: Oxbow Books: 1–13.

Jackson, R. 2010. *Cosmetic Sets of Late Iron Age and Roman Britain*. London: British Museum.

Johnson, M. 2016. *Ovid on Cosmetics: Medicamina Faciei Femineae and Related Texts*. London: Bloomsbury.

Jones-Lewis, M.A. 2012. Poison: nature's argument for the Roman Empire in Pliny the Elder's Naturalis Historia. *Classical World* 106(1): 51–74.

Kiernan, P. 2009. *Miniature Votive Offerings in the North-West Provinces of the Roman Empire*. Mainz/Ruhpolding: Franz Philipp Rutzen.

Kotansky, R. 1994. *Greek Magical Amulets: The Inscribed Gold, Silver, Copper, and Bronze Lamellae – Part I – Published Texts of Known Provenance*. Opladen: Westdeutscher.

Kyriakidis, E. 2007. In search of ritual. In E. Kyriakidis (ed.) *The Archaeology of Ritual*. Los Angeles, CA: Cotsen Institute of Archaeology: 1–8.

Martin-Kilcher, S. 1998. Gräber der späten Republik und der frühen Kaiserzeit am Lago Maggiore: Tradition und Romanisierung. In P. Fasold, T. Fischer, H. von Hesberg, and M. Witteyer (eds) *Bestattungssitte und kulturelle Identität: Grabanlagen und Grabbeigaben der frühen römischen Kaiserzeit in Italien und den Nordwest-Provinzen*. Cologne/Bonn: Rheinland-Verlag/R. Habelt: 191–252.

Merrifield, R. 1987. *The Archaeology of Ritual and Magic*. London: Guild.

Nickell, J. 1998. Peddling Snake Oil. *Skeptical Briefs/Skeptical Inquirer* 8(4). Available: https://www.csicop.org/sb/show/peddling_snake_oil [Accessed: 18/11/17].

Olson, K. 2009. Cosmetics in Roman antiquity: substance, remedy, poison. *Classical World* 102.3: 291–310.

Pollard, E.A. 2013. Indian spices and Roman 'magic' in imperial and late antique Indomediterranea. *Journal of World History* 24(1): 1–23.

Plant, I.M. 2004. (ed.) *Women Writers of Ancient Greece and Rome: An Anthology*. London: Equinox.

Pomeroy, S.B. 1995. *Goddesses, Whores, Wives, and Slaves: Women in Classical Antiquity*. New York: Schocken Books.

Ribechini, E., Modugno, F., Colombini, M.P., and Evershed, R.P. 2008. Gas chromatographic and mass spectrometric investigations of organic residues from Roman glass unguentaria. *Journal of Chromatography A* 1183: 158–69.

Richlin, A. 1995. Making up a woman: the face of Roman gender. In W. Doniger and H. Eilberg-Schwartz (eds) *Off with Her Head: The Denial of Women's Identity in Myth, Religion, and Culture*. Berkeley, CA: University of California Press: 185–213.

Robin, L., Silvino, T., and Garnier, N., 2012. Les « balsamaires » en contexte funéraire à Lyon/Lugdunum (1e–IIe S. apr. J.-C.). In D. Frère and L. Hugot (eds) *Les huiles parfumées en Méditerranée occidentale et en Gaule VIIIe siècle av. – VIIIe siècle apr. J. –C.* Rennes: Universitaires de Rennes: 179–89.

Stig Sørensen, M.L. 2015. 'Paradigm lost': on the state of typology within archaeological theory. In K. Kristiansen, L. Šmejda and J. Turek (eds) *Paradigm Found: Archaeological Theory Present, Past and Future*. Oxford: Oxbow Books: 84–94.

Taborelli, L. 1992. Sulle 'Ampullae Vitreae': Spunti per l'approfondimento della loro problematica nell'ottica del rapport tra contenitore e contenuto. *Archeologia Classica* 46: 309–28.

Taborelli, L. 2002. Per l'Interpretazione del Bollo sui Contenitori Vitrei. *Athenaeum* 90: 539–47.

Walker, S. and Bierbrier, M. 1997. *Ancient Faces: Mummy Portraits from Roman Egypt*. London: British Museum Press.

Wardle, A., Freestone, I., McKenzie, M., and Shepherd, J. 2015. *Glass Working on the Margins of Roman London: Excavations at 35 Basinghall Street, City of London, 2005*. London: MOLA.

Wilburn, A.T. 2013. *Materia Magica: The Archaeology of Magic in Roman Egypt, Cyprus, and Spain*. Ann Arbor, MI: University of Michigan Press.

Abbreviations

PGM = *Papyri Grecae Magica* (see Betz 1986)
PAS = Portable Antiquities Scheme

Victory of Good over Evil?
Amuletic Animal Images on Roman Engraved Gems

Idit Sagiv

Introduction

Engraved gems are precious or semi-precious stones with images featuring on them. During the Greek and Roman periods, they were used as seals, jewellery, and amulets. Various images were carved on the gems, such as gods, mythological themes, famous sculptures, astrological signs, and portraits. The depictions on these gems were meaningful and often symbolic. Many of the images are no longer familiar to us, and research, based on ancient literature sources, is required in order to interpret their meanings.

This article focuses on the important role of engraved gems as amulets. The definition of amulet gems according to *The Campbell Bonner Magical Gems Databas*e is that of gems that were used as amulets, but do not belong to the category of magical gems in the narrow sense. Magical gems as a modern category are defined by three constituent features: magical names (*voces magicea, logoi*), magical signs (*characteres*), and unique iconographic schemes (e.g. Chnoubis, or the Anguipede scheme) which usually appear on both faces of the gems, as well as by three formal features, the use of specific stones, shapes and of engraving, not in mirror writing as for seals (Nagy 2011: 75, 2012: 72; Dasen and Nagy in press). Magical gems were mounted primarily in rings and constituted an independent category in the glyptic art of the Roman Imperial Period (Nagy 2011: 76, 2012: 72). By contrast, 'ordinary' gems usually bear an inscription, but sometimes can be regarded as amuletic when their iconographical schemes are mentioned in the ancient sources.

Engraved gems were thought by the Romans to have extraordinary properties such as protecting against disease, encouraging love or ensuring victory. According to Pliny the Elder (*HN* 37.139–143), it was believed that through their wearing it was possible to ward off evil forces or specific demons, to counter poison, as well as promoting any good cause. Amulets were usually worn, perhaps sewn into clothing, worn on a string around the neck, or somewhere else. According to Plutarch (*Quaes. conv.*: 5.7.681), some amuletic devices that could be gems served to neutralise the 'evil eye' through the use of alien images that supposedly trapped the harmful gaze and thus distanced the negative forces from the gem wearer. Gems used for this purpose were therefore considered apotropaic.

It was believed that an invisible demon dwelt within each gem, and that a secret relationship existed between the gems and the stars because of their similar sparkle. Thus was born the ancient relationship between the gems and the belief that attributed a magical, protective and astrological character to them (DAGR 1896: v. 2.2, 1460). Over time carved images of gods, priests, etc. began to appear on the gems in order to enhance the magic power. Whenever an individual needed the help of a god he would turn to the aid of his gem, which he always kept close to him and which became an emblem of his personality (DAGR 1896: v. 2.2, 1460). A gem could constitute an image or an icon allowing one direct access to the Divine or it could be amuletic, whose power is innate or implicit. Certain gemstones, including jasper and agate, were ascribed the power to cure disease, as well as being talismanic and possessing protective qualities. Pliny provides a long list of precious and semi-precious stones that were believed to possess such qualities, such as amethyst, said to prevent intoxication (probably due to its purple-red colour resembling wine); emerald, considered to be detoxifying when carved with the image of an eagle; and diamond, which acted as both a cure for insanity and false fears and protecting against the harmful effects of toxins (Plin. *HN* 36, 37.169; Dioscorides, *De materia medica*: no. 20, 5.126.I; Damigeron, *De virtutibus lapidum*: 18; Les lapidaire grecs 1985: lapidaire orphique 21).

Pliny refers to such beliefs with scepticism and ridicule but nonetheless attributes healing properties to some of the stones (Thorndike 1964, vol. 1: 80–1) when they are crushed to powder and drunk or when worn as amulets (Plin. *HN*37.12, 37, 39, 55). Pliny also repeats the belief specified in Theophrastus and Mucianus, according to which certain stones assist fertility (Plin. *HN*37.25, 39).

Although there is no evidence of a belief in the existence of magical gems in Ancient Greece, Homer already mentions some evidence of the Greek belief in magic attested by the Circe episode in the Odyssey and by the healing of the young Odysseus' wound with the aid of an incantation (Hom. *Od.* 10.203ff; 19.457. cf Bonner 1950: 3, n. 8). In the fifth and fourth centuries B.C. magical activities and artefacts are mentioned in the literature and the existence of amulets is even implied on vase paintings (Bonner 1950: 3–6; Nagy 2012: 71–106). At the end of the Classical period and during the Hellenistic period magical rings are mentioned in the written sources (Ar. *Plut.* 883–885); and during the Roman period the use of gems as amulets started to become widespread (Bonner 1950: 6–7).

In this article I present a group of Roman engraved gems (intaglios) featuring depictions of animals as the bearers of various amuletic meanings, comprising part of the collection of the Israel Museum, Jerusalem, which had never been published prior to this study. The work is based on a study that included photography, description, technical aspects, iconographic and stylistic analysis and, finally, dating of the gems. The dating of these gems was performed stylistically according to the sorting method developed by Marianne Maaskant-Kleibrink (1978) since nearly all the studied items lack a secure archaeological context.[1] In order to explore their interpretations and context, they were compared to other known gems that had already been published.

Heracles Battling the Nemean Lion

The first is a second to third century A.D. red jasper intaglio (Figure 5.1), which features Heracles' first labour: that of killing the Nemean lion. The muscular naked hero is shown strangling the predator bare-handed, his club upright in the background. The lion places its left front paw on Heracles' foot, while its right front paw, with its tail twirling around it, rests on the ground. The gem is a Roman copy of a Hellenistic gem from 200 B.C. Red jasper, which was particularly prevalent in the second to third century A.D. onwards (Richter 1956: 61; Sena Chiesa 1966: 60; Maaskant-Kleibrink 1978: 251–85; Guiraud 1996: 95), was valued as an amulet, believed to have occult virtues and attributed with magical qualities (Middleton 1891: 145; Walters 1926: lv; Bonner 1950: 8–9), as well as the ability to cure diseases (Plin. *HN*37.169–170). The red colour resembled blood in all its contexts: energy, dynamism, strength and even life itself (Andrews 1990: 37; Mastrocinque 2011).

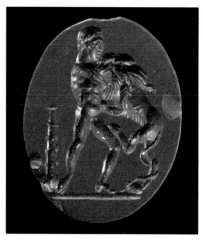

Figure. 5.1 Heracles battling the Nemean lion, red jasper, 21 × 15 mm, second to third century A.D., The Israel Museum, Jerusalem, Clark Collection (YMCA) purchased by Carmen and Louis Warschaw Fund for Archaeological Acquisition. IMJ90.24.403 (© The Israel Museum, Jerusalem, by Michael Smelansky).

Medical references in the essay 'On stones' confirm an early interest of Classical medicine in stones (Theophrastus, *De Lapidibus*). By the end of the first century A.D. this had become fully developed, as can be seen in the *Materia Medica*, a pharmacology essay by Dioscorides of Anazarbus from Cilicia in southern Asia Minor. The fifth book of *Materia Medica* deals mainly with the medicinal properties of gems (Dioscorides, *De materia medica*). The stones, even when not decorated, were believed to have some innate curative or other power. For example, hematite was recommended for healing eye diseases, sapphire against scorpion stings and all types of jasper were recommended as amulets that allowed a swift labour for women.

Ancient medicine had three main strands: Hippocratic or secular, ritual and magical (Nagy 2012: 71). Material evidence of the interaction between ancient magic and medicine is multifaceted, as exemplified by Dasen (2011; 2014). On the one hand, magical gems often refer to medical practices, while on the other hand, medical instruments may display divine or magical devices ensuring the success of the practitioner. There is evidence that pills and ointments bore images of divine or magical characters, with the figure of Heracles, for example, being prevalent on Graeco-Roman surgical tools (Dasen 2011: 69). His presence is explained by several factors: the glory attributed to his prowess and stamina; his talent and ability to repel evil (*alexikakos*); and finally, the genealogy of Hippocrates. It was believed that Hippocrates was a descendant of Asclepius through his father and of Heracles through his mother. An apocryphal letter to Abraxas compares Hippocrates, who fought 'wild' diseases, to Heracles, who defeated dangerous animals (Hippocrates, *Letter II* (9.314-5 L. = E. Littré, *Oeuvres complètes d'Hippocrate*, Paris, 10 vols, 1839–1861); see also Plin. *HN* 7.123; J. Jouanna, *Hippocrate*, Paris, 1992,

32–3, cf. Dasen 2011: 69, n. 2). Heracles' image on medical instruments was believed to 'tame' pain, just as he had tamed wild animals, and to increase the endurance and resilience of the patient (Dasen 2011: 69). The connection between Heracles and Hippocrates intensifies the efficacy of the depiction of the hero on healing amulets.

This scene of Heracles fighting the Nemean lion was considered to have healing power: in the sixth century A.D., a Greek physician named Alexander of Tralles gave the following instructions to those of his patients suffering from colic: 'On a Median stone engrave Heracles standing upright and throttling a lion. Set it in a gold ring and give it to the patient to wear' (Alexander of Tralles, *Therapeutica*: 2.579, cf. Bonner 1950: 62. See also Michel 2001: 248–9; Faraone 2011: 52, n. 28; Nagy 2012: 79, n. 25). The precise identification of the 'Median stone' mentioned in the text is uncertain, but according to Faraone it may have been a form of hematite or magnetite. Alexander's prescription, however, matches the depiction that appears in a common series of opaque red stone amulets (almost always red jasper): Heracles' struggle with the lion. For example, such a depiction of Heracles standing upright and battling the Nemean lion appears on a red jasper gem kept in the Cabinet des médailles, Paris (Mastrocinque 2014: 150, no. 398). Alexander points out that an amulet of this kind has two important components: a special stone and a special image; but most of the existing gems of this type include an additional component – an inscription of the Greek letter *kappa* three times on the reverse of the gem (Faraone 2011: 53), the K may be the initial of κωλική (*kolike*), 'colic' (Mastrocinque 2014: 150). Variants of this type include other inscriptions, like the gem kept in the Rijksmuseum van Oudheden, Leiden (Figure 5.2) which bears a magic formula that alludes to colic and contains three Ks: κολοκερ κολοφο (*koloker kolopho*).²

Another red jasper from the Cabinet des médailles, Paris, substantiates that these gems were indeed used in the treatment of the intestinal disease centuries before Alexander of Tralles wrote his prescription, for around the image of Heracles and the lion appears an inscription that translates as: 'Withdraw colic! The divine one pursues you' (Faraone 2011: 53, pl. 8; Mastrocinque 2014: 152, no. 403). On this gem the inscription of *kappa* letters (with pentagram) appears at the foot of the fighting couple, while on the other side of the gem appears a tri-form Hecate with the magical names Iao above and Abrasax below, which is another common magical image. The purpose of the depiction of Heracles' famous labour on this gem in Paris is easily interpreted: the image of the dangerous lion being strangled by a powerful hero is designed to scare away the intestinal disease and chase it far away from the wearer. This particular inscription has been found only on this gem to date, and is part of a far more ancient Greek tradition of protective incantations. It is more probable that on most of these kinds

Figure 5.2 Heracles battling the Nemean lion, red jasper, first to second century A.D., GS-01115, Rijksmuseum van Oudheden, Leiden (© Rijksmuseum van Oudheden, Leiden).

of gems the lion with its sharp claws represented the sharp stomach pains of the intestinal disease, which by a process of evincive magic was intended to be strangled and eliminated just as Heracles had strangled the lion (Faraone 2011: 53).

A number of scholars have suggested that the definition of magical gems is problematic due to its reductive nature (Nagy 2002: 153–79; 2012: 106;), and owing to its assumption that only inscribed ones can be regarded as such (Hamburger 1968: 3–4). Nagy has suggested that it would be more appropriate to regard magical gems as 'Hellenised' versions of amulets (Nagy 2002: 153–6, 169–70; 2012: 84–7, 106). We know from ancient sources like the *Lithika*, and the magical papyri, that there existed a much larger range of gems with magical properties, for example with regard to healing diseases (Nagy 2002: 153–79; 2011; 2012: 85–7; Dasen 2014: 178, n. 1). Bonner cites several specimens of uninscribed gems along with their inscribed counterparts, and points out that the lack of an inscription may not always invalidate their magical use. Further, he points out that certain gems, which bear no inscription of a magical character, may, nevertheless, have been worn as amulets (Bonner 1950: 14, cf. Hamburger 1968: 3). Faraone has noted that if we use Alexander's two criteria for a colic amulet, gems that present the correct medium (a red stone) and the correct image (Heracles and the lion) could presumably serve as amulets, although according to modern scholarship they are merely ornaments, because they lack the triple *kappas* on the reverse side (Faraone 2011: 53). However, according to Faraone, the image of Heracles and the lion was very old, imported from the East and thought to have inherent powers of its own; and furthermore 'the text is clearly the last to arrive of the three important features of magical gems' (Faraone 2011: 57. On the intimate relation of Heracles to the stomach, see Dasen 2008; 2014 and in the concluding chapter of this volume).

Combination Gem (Gryllos)

The second gem is a second century A.D. carnelian intaglio (Figure 5.3) which bears a representation of a horse's head with a wheat sheaf in its mouth, a bearded man (probably a Silenus mask), a ram's head(?), a cornucopia and a caduceus or palm branch(?) on rooster legs.[3]

Some of the apotropaic gems noted above are called 'combination gems', the simplest forms of which are composed of two or more human heads or a combination of human and animal heads. The human heads that are usually depicted are those of Silenus, satyrs and masks, while the animals that appear most frequently are eagles, roosters and peacocks. A more complex form of these kinds of gems includes the addition of elements such as the cornucopia, a wheat sheaf, wreath, thyrsus and caduceus. On a red jasper gem from Emory University Museum, Atlanta, a caduceus is depicted as well as an elephant's trunk (Lapatin 2011: 88–90, pls. 1–7). The elephant was closely linked with the victory of Dionysus/Bacchus, which is why its head and trunk were often combined within those 'combination gem' depictions whose imagery was largely bacchic (Henig 1980a: 333). The 'combination gems' are also called *'grylloi'*, following Pliny, who noted a fourth-century B.C. painting that featured a so-called *'gryllos'* figure in a ridiculous costume, and thereafter this kind of ridiculous painting was termed a *'gryllos'* (Plin. *HN* 35.37–114). 'Combination gems' began to appear in the fourth century B.C. and continued until the third century A.D.

The carnelian gem from Jerusalem constitutes a specific type of *'gryllos'* resembling a *hippalectryon*, consisting of integrated heads, a bearded man (generally identified as Silenus), a ram and a horse with rooster legs. This strange hybrid is a creature whose head and front legs are those of a horse, while its tail, wings and hind legs are those of a rooster. Lapatin mentions that the *hippalectrya* appear on Athenian vase paintings (Hafner 1940, cf. Lapatin 2011: 89, n. 5) and especially in Hellenistic and Roman wall paintings and other decorative arts (Sauron 1990: 36, note 7, 41, n. 47). Aristophanes mentions a *hippalectryon* as a symbol painted on ships, adopted from those depicted on Persian rugs (Ar. *Ran.* 930–938). Horace, in the introduction to *Ars Poetica*, describes a strange painting reminiscent of the *hippalectryon* (Horace, *Ars P.* 1–5). Another example of a 'combination gem' that is a specific type of *'gryllos'* resembling a *hippalectryon*, is that of a red jasper gem from the Rijksmuseum van Oudheden, Leiden (Figure 5.4). It features a Silenus mask, a ram with ears of wheat in its mouth on rooster legs but with a head of a rooster and not a horse. It seems that red jasper, carnelian and sard were the stones most commonly used for 'combination gems', as noted in studies linking the use of red stones to magical gems (Lapatin 2011: 89). As noted earlier, according to Plutarch those outlandish amulets served as a protection against

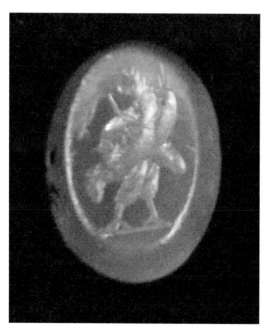

Figure 5.3 Combination gem (gryllos), carnelian, second century A.D., The Israel Museum, Jerusalem. Clark Collection (YMCA) purchased by Carmen and Louis Warschaw Fund for Archaeological Acquisition. IMJ90.24.404 (© The Israel Museum, Jerusalem).

Figure 5.4 Combination gem (gryllos), red jasper, second to third century A.D., GS-01089, Rijksmuseum van Oudheden, Leiden (© Rijksmuseum van Oudheden, Leiden).

malice through their strange appearance that supposedly attracted the harmful gaze of the 'evil eye', and thus exerted less pressure upon its victim (Plut. *Quaest. conviv.*: 5.7.681. see also Henig 1974: 101). As Blanchet observes, however, it is very probable that the composite figures of the *'grylloi'* had a prophylactic value, and there can be no doubt that many of the elements composing them relate to fertility and wealth (Blanchet 1921: 50. see also Henig 1974: 101).

A Predatory Animal Attacking its Prey

Other depictions of apotropaic animals include an image of a predatory animal killing its prey or devouring it, usually interpreted as an allegory of triumph over death (Henig 1977: 356), such as on a second-century A.D. yellow jasper gem portraying a lion attacking a deer, leaping upon its neck, with a six-pointed star above them (Figure 5.5).[4] The lion was considered a symbol of triumph in general and of victory over death in particular.

Several animals were accorded magical powers that could affect people in either a positive or a negative way. It was accepted that certain animals carved on gems could confer desirable traits upon their owners, such as courage, strength and fertility. These beliefs are supported in the ancient literary sources: for example, an image of the proud and brave lion appears in various of Plato's dialogues and is especially mentioned in the *Republic* (4.441 B) as a metaphor of courage. Another yellow jasper engraved gem from the Israel Museum (Figure 5.6), dating to the second to third century A.D., depicts a lion leaping upon the back of a goat, with both rearing up on their hind legs.[5]

Yellow jasper, which was called 'the gemstone with the colour of the lion's pelt', was ascribed with both amuletic and magical qualities (Henig 1980b: 331; 1994: 168, cat. 358, 175, cat. 381).[6] Yellow jasper was indeed often used for depictions of lions in general and the motif of the lion killing or eating its prey in particular, as on gems from the Aquileia collection (Sena Chiesa 1966: nos. 1142, 1145–7, 1153–4) and from Caesarea (Hamburger 1968: nos. 108–9). According to Henig, these gems, made of yellow jasper and engraved with this motif, were designed to protect the wearer due both to the substance of which they were made and to the depicted motif, a scene that has a chthonic significance but also a promise for the eternal afterworld of paradise and a celestial function (Henig 1977: 356–8). The fifth gem from Jerusalem, which dates to the first century A.D., made of agate and inlaid in a gold ring, shows a lion treading on a supine human, with one paw on his throat (Figure 5.7).[7]

Gems with depictions of a lion treading on another animal or a man were apparently used as amulets to protect their owners from harm (Bonner 1950: 36). Such gems could also have functioned as *memento mori*, a reminder that death can suddenly come upon each of us, just like the leap of a wild lion (Henig 1984a: 408, fig. 14, pl. lvii).

Gems Featuring a Rooster with a Mouse

Two gems from the Israel Museum feature a rooster with a mouse: the first red jasper one, which dates to the second century A.D. (Figure 5.8), portrays a rooster preying upon a mouse; and the second one, made of carnelian (Figure 5.9), bears a representation of a mouse riding a rooster and whipping it and dates to the third century A.D.[8] A pair of

Figure 5.5 Lion attacking a deer, yellow jasper, 12.5 × 10.5 × 2.5mm, second century A.D., The Israel Museum, Jerusalem. Bezalel Collection. IMJ77.31.976 (© The Israel Museum, Jerusalem, by Vladimir Naikhin).

Figure 5.6 Lion attacking a goat, yellow jasper, 15 × 11.5 × 3mm, second to third century A.D., The Israel Museum, Jerusalem, Bequest of Mr Adolphe Doreen, Paris. IMJ70.62.115 (© The Israel Museum, Jerusalem, by Pnina Arad).

Figure 5.7 Lion treading on a supine human, agate, 12 × 9mm, first century A.D., The Israel Museum, Jerusalem, The Harry Stern Collection, bequeathed by Dr Kurt Stern, London. In memory of his parents and his brother who perished at Sobibor. IMJ76.42.2426 (© The Israel Museum, Jerusalem).

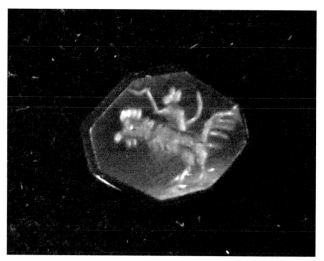

Figure 5.9 Mouse riding on a rooster, carnelian, 12.5 × 10 × 3.5mm, third century A.D., The Israel Museum, Jerusalem. Bequest of Mr Adolphe Doreen, Paris. IMJ70.62.363 (© The Israel Museum, Jerusalem).

Figure 5.8 Rooster preying upon a mouse, red jasper, 13 × 9.5 × 3mm, second century A.D., The Israel Museum, Jerusalem. Bequest of Mr Adolphe Doreen, Paris. IMJ70.62.330 (© The Israel Museum, Jerusalem).

gems from the Sa'd collection of Gadara in Transjordan (today near the Jordanian town of Um-Qais) bear a similar iconography and date (Henig and Whiting 1987: pls. 382–3).

The rooster was associated with daybreak, with light (Orth 1913: cols. 2532–3; Bonner 1950: 125–7; Gray 1951: 969), while a mouse, in contrast, was considered a chthonic creature (Ael. *NA* 12.5). Consequently, this depiction of a rooster preying upon a mouse was perceived as the victory of good over evil and of life overcoming darkness (Henig 1997: 47). The second gem, bearing a representation of a mouse riding a rooster, is considered as apotropaic since, as previously discussed, according to Plutarch whatever is curious was thought to attract and neutralise the baleful stare of the 'evil eye' away from the wearer (Plut. *Quaest. conviv.* 5.7.681. see also Henig 1977: 47). Similar gems featuring a

mouse riding a chariot drawn by a pair of roosters are found in the Sa'd collection and in Lippold's catalogue (Lippold 1923: Taf. xcvi, 12; Henig and Whiting 1987: pls. 380–1). Some of the gems bearing curious depictions probably had additional cryptic meanings: mice, for example, being considered chthonic creatures, could therefore indicate the power of life and productivity, in coming from the realm of Demeter, and perhaps even implying the mysteries of Eleusis and hence rebirth, as noted by Henig. In addition, these gems could also have been used as love charms: the mice are both nocturnal and domestic, and therefore could remind the gem wearer of his beloved whom he would meet in his home at night (Henig 1997: 47–8); the rooster has phallic associations and is linked to love and fertility deities (Baird 1981–82: 81–2, 85; Spier 2010: 246–7, figs. 3 and 4; Ael. *NA* 17.46; 4.29).

An Elephant Emerging from a Sea-Shell

A gem of nicolo (Figure 5.10), which is a Roman sardonyx with a bluish-white top layer and dark-blue/black bottom layer, kept at the Israel Museum and dated to the second century A.D.,[9] shows an elephant emerging from a sea-shell.

There are other similar Roman gems depicting a shell from which springs an animal: for example, a gem from the Fitzwilliam Museum in Cambridge, which also dates to the second century A.D. and features a shell with a rooster springing from it and catching a mouse (Henig 1994: 165, cat. 349); as well as one from France depicting a dog leaping from a sea-shell (Guiraud 1996: 139, no. 94).

The motif of an elephant emerging from a shell is a familiar one. This theme appears on engraved gems in various collections, while other objects, like a torch, a palm branch or a sheaf of wheat, are occasionally added

Figure 5.10 Elephant emerging from a sea-shell, nicolo, second century A.D., The Israel Museum, Jerusalem. Bequest of Mr Adolphe Doreen, Paris. IMJ70.62.371.(© The Israel Museum, Jerusalem).

Figure 5.11 Eros galloping on a lion, red jasper, 14 × 11 × 3mm, second to third century A.D., The Israel Museum, Jerusalem, Bequest of Mr Adolphe Doreen, Paris. IMJ70.62.344 (© The Israel Museum, Jerusalem).

to the elephant. All of these gems have been dated to the imperial period, the end of the first century to the beginning of the third century A.D. (Henig 1984b: 243–7, fig. 1a). Such depictions of the elephant and shell probably served an apotropaic function similar to that of 'combination gems' (Henig 1984b: 244). Furthermore, both shells and elephants had a symbolic significance in Antiquity. The sea-shell represented the *uterus* from which arises life, and therefore constituted a powerful symbol of fertility and rebirth. An elephant emerging from a sea-shell presents an apt symbol of rebirth, due both to its renowned longevity and to its being favoured by the sun god (Henig 1974: 102; 1984b: 244, 246). The '*Caelestia Animalia*' mentioned in an inscription dated A.D. 216 from Banasa in Mauretania are thought to have been elephants (Scullard 1974: 254–9, cf. Henig 1984b: 244, n. 8).

Gems Portraying Eros

Other gems in the collection of the Israel Museum were intended to encourage love. Indeed, depictions of Eros riding an animal appear on several such gems in the collection. These gems needed to be given to the other person, either overtly or in secret, or worn by the owner of the object. If a gem depicting Eros – in a ring or an amulet – was worn by someone seeking to attract a lover, it is probable that the intention was for it to affect the target due to the latter's belief in the god Eros, and not merely through its amuletic or magical power. Nonetheless, sometimes people would rub or even kiss an amulet or an image on a ring (Marshman 2017: 142–6). An amber ring carved with the bust of Minerva from Carlisle had clearly been rubbed by its owner.[10]

The figure of Eros is rarely simply a decorative motif (Platt 2007: 89). Hesiod indicates in the Theogony (Hes.

Theog. 116–29) that Eros was one of the primordial forces of nature, represented along with Chaos, Gea and Tartaros as one of the most ancient deities that existed at the genesis of the cosmos. His role was to arrange the elements that constituted the universe. He brought harmony to the chaos and enabled life to evolve. The power of Eros, the god of love, was regarded as immense, as illustrated in the anthropomorphic myths associated with him (Boardman 1978: 20).

The first of these gems is a red jasper intaglio (Figure 5.11) that dates to the second to third century A.D.,[11] on which Eros is depicted galloping on a rampant lion, holding a whip in his hands.

This motif is quite common on engraved gems from the Roman period and appears in slight variations (Walters 1926: no. 1486, pl. 20; nos. 2852–4, pl. 30; Brandt 1972: fig. 2288; Maaskant-Kleibrink 1978: fig. 1160a). The motif is also mentioned in the written sources, and Pliny refers to a statue of cupids playing with a lioness as if it was not a fierce predator (Plin. *HN* 36.41); and an epigram from the *Greek Anthology* tells of a signet ring bearing the motif of a lion harnessed to a chariot driven by Eros:

> I see upon the signet-ring Love, whom none can escape, driving a chariot drawn by mighty lions. One hand menaces their necks with the whip, the other guides the reins; about him is shed abundant bloom of grace. I shudder as I look on the destroyer of men, for he who can tame wild beasts will not show the least mercy to mortals (*Anthologia Graeca*: 9.221)

The second gem from the collection of those intended to evoke love is a carnelian intaglio, dating to the first century A.D.,[12] which bears a representation of Eros riding a dolphin and holding a trident in his hand (Figure 5.12).

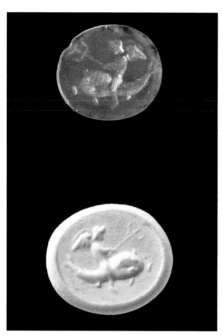

Figure 5.13 Eros riding a dolphin, plasma, first century A.D., GS-00510, Rijksmuseum van Oudheden, Leiden (© Rijksmuseum van Oudheden, Leiden).

Figure 5.12 Eros riding a dolphin, carnelian, 11.5 × 10 × 2mm, second century A.D., The Israel Museum, Jerusalem. Bequest of Mr Adolphe Doreen, Paris. IMJ70.62.393 (© The Israel Museum, Jerusalem, by Pnina Arad)..

Representations of Eros with a dolphin on engraved gems can be found from the fifth century B.C. onwards (Boardman 1970: pl. 691). Very similar in iconography and date is a plasma gem in the Rijksmuseum van Oudheden, Leiden (Figure 5.13).

Dolphins are the companions of Venus, who is sometimes portrayed as *Venus Marina*, accompanied by Erotes on dolphins, as on a famous fresco from Pompeii from the first century A.D. For the love goddess, as Hesiod tells us, was born from the foam of the sea (Hes. *Theog.* 188–202). Hence, the goddess too is deeply associated with dolphins and other marine creatures (Stebbins 1929: 83–4). The ancient sources also mention dolphins as servants of Venus (Gell. *NA* 7.8; Stuveras 1969: 159, n. 2, fig. 42). It was the presence of Eros during the birth of Venus (Hes. *Theog.* 201) that also connects him to the sea. The representation of Eros on a dolphin indicates that the young god is, among other things, his mother's servant and representative (LIMC 1981: 940). The connection between Eros and the dolphin can be summarised as signifying the control that the god exerts over the sea, as an epigram from the *Anthologia Graeca* tells us:

> ... [A]nd it is not without reason that he (Love) holds in his hands a dolphin and a flower, for in one hand he holds the earth, in the other – the sea (*Anthologia Graeca*: 16.207).

The third gem of this type is a red jasper intaglio (Figure 5.14) that dates to the second century A.D., featuring Eros riding a chariot led by two parrots.

Figure 5.14 Eros riding a chariot led by two parrots, red jasper, 13 × 11 × 2.5mm, second century A.D., The Israel Museum, Jerusalem. Bequest of Mr. Adolphe Doreen, Paris. IMJ70.62.362 (© The Israel Museum, Jerusalem, by Pnina Arad).

Depictions of Eros in a chariot led by animals are common throughout the Roman world. This motif is also common on intaglios, on which Eros can be seen riding in different types of chariots led by all sorts of animals, including lions and other feline species as well as deer, goats and horses (Walters 1926: fig. 1484; Zwierlein-Diehl 1970: fig. 448, pl. 79). Many of the animals harnessed to the chariot have a Dionysian context. These include parrots, which were considered a symbol of Dionysus because of their Indian origin, linking them to the god's journey to India (Middleton 1991: 66).

Other animals are also portrayed in a chariot race, as for example various species of fowl such as cocks or swans

(Walters 1926: fig. 1484), and even butterflies, as portrayed on an intaglio from the Royal Coin Cabinet, the Hague and now in the Rijksmuseum van Oudheden, Leiden (Maaskant-Kleibrink 1978: fig. 210a). The butterfly is of course a symbolic manifestation of Psyche, whose relationship with Eros as depicted on intaglios offered a prolific source of iconography for ancient Greek love magic, exemplified in various spells and erotic incantations found in the magical papyri (*PGM* 4.376–81; 4.1724–31, cf. Faraone 1999: 53; Platt 2006: 250; Platt 2007: 95). In the harnessing of animals to a chariot and controlling them we again encounter Eros, the dominant god. He not only controls wild beasts but, indeed, every possible animal, demonstrating his strong character, with which he also dominates the souls of men.

Conclusions

To conclude, many engraved gems of the Roman period were used as amulets and were ascribed with talismanic qualities due to the carved image on them, to their material and to their colour. Images of animals on gems, sometimes acting as attributes of various deities, were ascribed with qualities such as ensuring divine protection, attracting good fortune and wealth, victory of good over evil and life overcoming death, victory in battle, healing diseases, fertility, the promise of afterlife and even rebirth. An important group of apotropaic intaglios called 'combination gems' (or *'grylloi'*), was presumably a distinguished one, with depictions designed to avert evil influences. Several animals were accorded magical powers that could affect people in either a positive or a negative way. It was accepted that certain animals carved on gems could confer desirable traits upon their owners, such as courage, strength and fertility. Gems bearing representations of animals could also have been used to encourage and evoke love.

Nowadays it is difficult to identify the positive aspects attributed to engraved gems, and magical gems are regarded only as those that present specific magical iconography. However, we know from ancient sources like the *Lithika*, and the magical papyri, that there existed a much larger range of gems with magical properties, for example with regard to healing diseases. Such amuletic gems, like those we have just seen, were believed to possess the power to influence the course of events and the lives of human beings.

History of Art Department, Classical Section,
Tel-Aviv University

Notes

1   Maaskant-Kleibrink sorted the gems according to style and engraving technique rather than workshop, since it was clear that they had been executed in different provinces. In addition, the material and the shape of the stones themselves have helped in establishing the correct date, or at least an approximate one, since different materials were typical to different periods. These features were highly dependent on changes in 'fashion' and related to the different shapes for finger-rings (Maaskant-Kleibrink 1978: 59–61).

2   See Mastrocinque 2014: 150, n. 509 regarding the inscription and similar examples.

3   It probably represents a decline in quality at the expense of greater mass production, as demonstrated by the Snettisham Jeweller's Hoard, which also contains a seal-box suggesting sealing had not gone out of use.

4   This gem is carved in the 'Small Grooves Style' and therefore dated to the second century A.D. (Maaskant-Kleibrink 1978: 251–2).

5   This gem can be dated to the second–third century A.D. since it is made of yellow jasper which was popular in the late Roman period.

6   While magic involves actively incanting spells and performing rituals, an amulet is passive, normally protective.

7   This gem can be dated to the first century A.D. because the gold ring is Type II (see: Henig 2007, fig. 1, 9–12).

8   Gem no. 70.62.330 is engraved in the 'Small Grooves Style' and therefore dated to the second century A.D. (Maaskant-Kleibrink 1978: 251–2). In addition, red jasper was particularly prevalent in the second century A.D. (Maaskant-Kleibrink 1978: 251–85; Guiraud 1996: 95). Gem no. 70.62.363 is cut in an octagonal form and dates accordingly to the third century A.D. (M. Henig, 2011, pers. comm.). See also Goldman 2014: 164.

9   Gem no. 70.62.371 is made in the 'Small Grooves Style' and hence dated to the second century A.D. (Maaskant-Kleibrink 1978: 251–2). In addition, nicolo intaglios were chosen with especial frequency by second-century gem engravers (Maaskant-Kleibrink 1978: 251–85; Henig 1984b: 244).

10 I am indebted to Revd. Professor Martin Henig for this helpful information.

11 As noted above, red jasper was particularly prevalent in the second-third century A.D. (Richter 1956: 61; Maaskant-Kleibrink 1978: 251–85; Guiraud 1996: 95).

12 Gem no. 70.62.393 is carved in the 'Imperial Cap-with-Rim Style' and hence dated to the first century A.D. (Maaskant-Kleibrink 1978: 302).

Bibliography

Ancient Sources

Aelian (Translated by A.F. Scholfield 1958–1959). *De natura animalium*. Cambridge, MA: Harvard University Press.

Alexander of Tralles (Ed. T. Puschmann *Alexander von Tralles*, vol 1. 1878; vol 2. 1879). *Therapeutica*. Vienna (reprint. 1963 Amsterdam: A.M. Hakkert).

Anthologia Graeca (Translated by W.R. Paton 1956 (1918)). Cambridge, MA: Harvard University Press.

Aristophanes (Translated by J. Henderson 1998–2007. *Frogs*. Cambridge, MA: Harvard University Press.

Aristophanes (Translated by J. Henderson 2002). *Wealth (The Plutus)*. Cambridge, MA: Harvard University Press.

Damigeron (Translated by P. Tahil, J. Radcliffe (ed) 2005). *The Virtues of Stones: De virtutibus lapidum*. Seattle, WA: Ars Obscura Press.

Dioscorides (Translated by L.Y. Beck 2005). *De materia medica.* Hildesheim and New York: Olms-Weidmann.

Gellius, Aulus (Translated by J.C. Rolfe 1946). *Noctes atticae.* Cambridge, MA: Harvard University Press.

Hesiod (Translated by G.W. Most 2006–2007). *Theogonia.* Cambridge, MA: Harvard University Press.

Hippocrates (Translated by É. Littré 1839–1961). *Oeuvres complètes d'Hippocrate.* Paris: J.B. Baillière.

Homer (Translated by A.T. Murray 1995). *Odyssey.* Cambridge, MA: Harvard University Press.

Horace (Translated by H.R. Fairclough 1978 (1926)). *Satires, Epistles and Ars Poetica.* Cambridge, MA: Harvard University Press.

Les lapidaires grecs: Lapidaire Orphique; Kérygmes lapidaires d'Orphée; Socrate et Denys; Lapidaire nautique; Damigéron-Evax (Translated by R. Halleux and J. Schamp (eds) 1985). Paris: Belles Lettres.

Plato (Translated by P. Shorey 1935). *Republic.* Cambridge, MA: Harvard University Press.

Pliny the Elder (Translated by D.E. Eichholz 1962). *Natural History.* Cambridge, MA: Harvard University Press.

Plutarch (Translated by P.A. Clement and H.B. Hoffleit 1969). *Moralia, vol. VIII, Quaestiones convivales.* Cambridge, MA: Harvard University Press.

Theophrastus (Translated by D.E. Eichholz 1965). *De Lapidibus (On Stones).* Oxford: Clarendon Press.

Modern Sources

Andrews, C. 1990. *Ancient Egyptian Jewellery.* London: British Museum.

Baird, L.Y. 1981–1982. Priapus Gallinaceus: The role of the cock in fertility and eroticism in Classical Antiquity and the Middle Ages. *Studies in Iconography* 7–8: 81–111.

Blanchet, J.A. 1921. Recherches sur les 'Grylles', à propos d'une pierre gravée, trouvée en Alsace. *Revue des Études Anciennes.* Annales de la Faculté des lettres de Bordeaux 1921 (23). no. 1.

Boardman, J. 1970. *Greek Gems and Finger Rings.* London: Thames and Hudson.

Bonner, C. 1950. *Studies in Magical Amulets: Chiefly Graeco-Egyptian.* Ann Arbor, MI: University of Michigan Press.

Brandt, E. 1972. *Antike Gemmen in deutschen Sammlungen, Bd. I: Staatliche Münzsammlung München.* München : Prestel.

Dasen, V. 2008. Le secret d'Omphale, *Revue archéologique,* 2008, 265–81.

Dasen, V. 2011. Magic and medicine: gems and the power of seals. In N. Adams and C. Entwistle (eds) *Gems of Heaven: Recent Research on Engraved Gemstones in Late Antiquity.* British Museum Research Publication 117. London: British Museum Press: 69–74.

Dasen, V. 2014. Healing images. Gems and medicine. *Oxford Journal of Archaeology* 33(2): 177–91.

V. Dasen and Nagy, Á. M. in press. 'Magical gems'. In D. Frankfurter (ed) *A Guide to the Study of Ancient Magic,* Leiden, Brill.

Faraone, C.A. 1999. *Ancient Greece Love Magic.* Cambridge, MA: Harvard University Press.

Faraone, C.A. 2011. Text, image and medium: The evolution of Graeco-Roman magical gemstones. In N. Adams and

C. Entwistle (eds) *Gems of Heaven: Recent Research on Engraved Gemstones in Late Antiquity.* British Museum research publication 117. London: British Museum Press: 50–61.

Goldman, A.L. 2014. The octagonal gemstones from Gordion: observations and interpretations. *Anatolian Studies* 64: 163–97.

Gray, L.H. 1951. s.v. 'Cock'. In J. Hastings (ed). *Encyclopedia of Religion and Ethics,* VIII. New York: 694–8.

Guiraud, H. 1996. *Intailles et camées romains.* Paris: collection Antiqua.

Hafner, G. 1940. Neue Mischwesen des 4. Jahrhunderts. *Wiener Jahreshefte* 32.

Hamburger, A. 1968. Gems from Caesarea Maritima. *'Atiqot* 8: 1–31.

Henig, M. 1977. Death and the maiden: funerary symbolism in daily life. In J. Munby and M. Henig (eds) *Roman Life and Art in Britain: a Celebration in Honour of the Eightieth Birthday of Jocelyn Toynbee.* British Archaeological Report 41. Oxford: British Archaeological Reports: 347–66.

Henig, M. 1974. *A Corpus of Roman Engraved Gemstones from British Sites.* British Archaeological Report 8. Oxford: British Archaeological Reports.

Henig, M. 1980a. A new combination-gem. *Antiquaries Journal* 60: 332–3.

Henig, M. 1980b. An intaglio and sealing from Blackfriars, London. *Antiquaries Journal* 60: 331.

Henig, M. 1984a. A bronze key handle from Brampton, Norfolk. *Antiquaries Journal* 64: 407–8.

Henig, M. 1984b. The elephant and the sea-shell. *Oxford Journal of Archaeology* 3: 243–7.

Henig, M. 1994. *Classical Gems: Ancient and Modern Intaglios and Cameos in the Fitzwilliam Museum.* Cambridge: Cambridge University Press.

Henig, M. 1997. The meaning of animal images on Greek and Roman gems. In M.A. Brouset (ed.) *La glyptique des mondes classiques – mélanges en hommage à Marie-Louise Vollenweider.* Paris: Bibliothèque National de France: 45–53.

Henig, M. and Whiting M. 1987. *Engraved Gems from Gadara in Jordan: The Sa'd Collection of Intaglios and Cameos.* Monograph 6. Oxford: Oxford University Committee for Archaeology, Institute of Archaeology.

Jouanna, J. 1992. *Hippocrate.* Paris: Fayard.

Lapatin, K. 2011. Grylloi. In N. Adams and C. Entwistle (eds) *Gems of Heaven: Recent Research on Engraved Gemstones in Late Antiquity.* British Museum Research Publication 117. London: British Museum Press: 88–98.

Lippold, G. 1923. *Gemmen und Kameen des Altertums und der Neuzeit,* Stuttgart: J. Hoffmann.

Maaskant-Kleibrink, M. 1978. *Catalogue of the Engraved Gems in the Royal Coin Cabinet, The Hague: The Greek, Etruscan and Roman Collections.* Hague: Government Publications Office.

Marshman, I. 2017. All that glitters: Roman signet rings, the senses and the self. In E.M. Betts (ed.) *Senses of the Empire: Multisensory Approaches to Roman Culture.* London, New York: Routledge: 137–46.

Mastrocinque, A. 2011. The colours of magical gems. In N. Adams and C. Entwistle (eds) *Gems of Heaven: Recent Research on Engraved Gemstones in Late Antiquity.* British Museum Research Publication 117. London: British Museum Press: 62–8.

Mastrocinque, A. 2014. *Les intailles magiques du département des Monnaies, Médailles et Antiques.* Paris: Édition de la Bibliothèque nationale de France.

Michel, S. 2001. *Die magischen Gemmen im Britischen Museum,* London: The British Museum Press.

Middleton, J.H. 1891. *The Engraved Gems of Classical Times with a Catalogue of the Gems in the Fitzwilliam Museum.* Cambridge: Cambridge University Press.

Middleton, S.E.H. 1991. *Engraved Gems from Dalmatia.* Oxford: Oxford University Committee for Archaeology, Institute of Archaeology.

Nagy, A.M. 2002. Gemmae magicae selectae. Sept notes sur l'interprétation des gemmes magiques. In A. Mastrocinque (ed.) *Atti dell'incontro di studio 'Gemme gnostiche e cultura ellenistica', Verona, 22–23 Ottobre 1999.* Bologna: 153–79.

Nagy, A.M. 2011. Magical gems and classical archaeology. In N. Adams and C. Entwistle (eds) *Gems of Heaven: Recent Research on Engraved Gemstones in Late Antiquity.* British Museum Research Publication 117. London: British Museum Press: 75–81.

Nagy, A.M. 2012. Daktylios pharmakites. Magical healing gems and rings in the Graeco-Roman world. In I. Csepregi and C. Burnett (eds) *Ritual Healing. Magic Ritual and Medical Therapy from Antiquity Until the Early Modern Period.* Firenze: Micrologus Library: 71–106.

Orth, E. 1913. s.v. 'Huhn'. In A.F. Pauly and G. Wissowa (eds) *Pauly's Realencyclopädie der classischen Altertumswissenschaft,* Bd. 8(2). Stuttgart: cols. 2519–36.

Platt, V. 2006. Making an impression: replication and the ontology of the Graeco-Roman seal stone. *Art History* 29(2): 233–57.

Platt, V. 2007. Burning butterflies: seals, symbols and the soul in Antiquity. In L. Gilmour (ed.) *Pagans and Christians – from Antiquity to the Middle Ages: Papers in Honour of Martin Henig, Presented on the Occasion of his 65th Birthday.* British Archaeological Reports International Series 1610. Oxford: Archaeopress: 89–99.

Richter, G.M.A. 1956. *Catalogue of Engraved Gems: Greek, Etruscan and Roman, in the Metropolitan Museum of Art.* Roma: 'L'Erma' di Bretschneider.

Sauron, G. 1990. Les monstres, au coeur des conflits esthétiques à Rome au Ier siècle avant J.-C. *Revue de l'Art* 90: 35–45.

Scullard, H.H. 1974. *The Elephant in the Greek and Roman World.* Cambridge: Thames and Hudson.

Sena Chiesa, G. 1966. *Gemme del Museo Nazionale di Aquileia.* Aquileia: Associazione nazionale per aquileia.

Spier, J. 2010. Most fowl: Athena, Ares, and Hermes depicted as birds on engraved gems. *PALLAS (Revue d'études antiques)* 83: 245–250.

Stebbins, E.B. 1929. *The Dolphin in the Literature and Art of Greece and Rome.* Menasha, WI: George Banta Publishing.

Stuveras, R. 1969. *Le putto dans l'art romain.* Bruxelles: Latomus.

Thorndike, L. 1964. *A History of Magic and Experimental Science.* New York: Columbia University Press.

Walters, H.B. 1926. *Catalogue of the Engraved Gems and Cameos, Greek, Etruscan and Roman in the British Museum.* London: British Museum.

Zwierlein-Diehl, E. 1970. *Antike Gemmen in deutschen Sammlungen,* Bd. 2: Staatliche Museen Preußischer Kulturbesitz Antikenabteilung, Berlin. Munich: Prestel.

Abbreviations

DAGR 1896 = Babelon, E. 1896. s.v. Gemmae. In C. Daremberg and E. Saglio (eds) *Dictionnaire des antiquités grecques et romaines* Vol. 2(2). Paris: Hachette Livre: 1460–88.

LIMC 1981 = Hermary, A., Cassimatis, H. and R. Vollkommer. 1981. s.v. Eros. In *Lexicon Iconographicum Mythologiae Classicae* Vol. III. Zürich und München: Artemis: 850–942.

PGM = Papyri Grecae Magicae. Preisendanz, K. 1928–31. *Papyri Graecae Magicae. Die Griechischen Zauberpapyri,* 2 vols. Leipzig. Re-ed. Heinrichs, A. 1973–74. Stuttgart.

'The Bells! The Bells!' Approaching *Tintinnabula* in Roman Britain and Beyond

Adam Parker

Tintinnabula are one of the most sensational representations of sexuality in Roman art, both fantastical and shocking to the modern viewer. The metal figures of *tintinnabula* incorporate phallic elements at their core, either on their own as zoomorphic phallic beasts or as an anatomical aspect of a human or divine figure. The phalli are always ithyphallic (that is, erect) and frequently presented in a polyphallic form; there may also be multiple phalli connected, often in bizarre ways, to the central figure. With a number of bells suspended from chains beneath the main figural aspect, they acted as wind chimes or mobiles (Johns 1982: 67–8) and were designed to be suspended around a building. Beyond their eye-watering visual narrative lies an important apotropaic device of which we understand comparatively little. A visitor to the British Museum, one of the only places to see these objects first hand in Britain, will find several *tintinnabula* on display but none of these have a secure British provenance. Yet in Roman Britain we find hundreds of bells which would not be out of place suspended from a polyphallic figure and so I take this province as a case-study. This paper seeks to raise and discuss a number of questions relating to this topic, namely: why do we think these wind chimes were apotropaic or magical? What is the evidence for *tintinnabula* or comparable practices in Roman Britain? Where and how were *tintinnabula* used? The following paper will approach this topic by outlining the ancient literary and modern archaeological evidence relevant to this subject. There is a clear paucity of modern scholarship on *tintinnabula* in the Roman world; through a broadly speculative approach in the following sections I aim to begin raising the pertinent questions about the supernatural functionality and subsequent spatial use of these objects in order to reflect on their material and apotropaic implications.

Before we continue I shall introduce a few of the eponymous forms of *tintinnabula*, all of which featured prominently in the ground-breaking 1982 publication by Catherine Johns, *Sex or Symbol? Erotic Images of Greece and Rome* and are, perhaps, the typically encountered examples of *tintinnabula* in other literature. The first is a winged, zoomorphic phallic beast depicted as a macrophallic (an overtly and unfeasibly large phallus) and curving ithyphallic phallus which sports a pair of feline hind legs in addition to a snaking tail which itself terminates in a phallus. A secondary and smaller phallus extends from between its legs in an otherwise anatomically (or perhaps that should be 'mammalian'?) correct place. Rather than having a head proper, the head of the beast is the glans. Simple linked chains extend from the tips of each wing and from beneath the glans, the secondary phallus and one foot, and all of these terminate in a domed bell (Johns 1982: pl. 13; Figure 6.1). So far so fantastical. The second well-known *tintinnabulum* is less graphic and much more stylised. This latter example depicts a dwarven gladiator fighting a tiger which happens to also be his penis; the base of the animal extends from his groin in a long shaft and turns up to face him with teeth bared (Johns 1982: pl. 14). The gladiator figure also has five bells strung beneath him, one from his elbow, one from either foot, one from his testes and one from the back of the tiger/ penis. The gladiator and tiger are both well detailed – the heads and faces of both are clear and dynamic, his robes are shown clearly, and he holds a knife and a comb-like object in his hands. The third of the *tintinnabula* worthy of mention in an introduction to the type is something entirely different again. In this final example the main figure (Figure 6.2), Mercury, is bent sideways over to his right to glance back above his shoulder and also carries a money-bag in his right hand. He is depicted with a macrophallic appendage longer than his arm, projecting from his body in a Priapic fashion, but his winged-helm has a further four phalli extending from it – two upwards and one to either side.

Figure 6.2 Copper alloy tintinnabulum depicting a figure of an ithyphallic Mercury wearing a quad-phallic hat. In the Museo Archaeologico Nazionale di Napoli (© Marie-Lan Nguyen via Wikimedia Commons [CC-BY Attribution 2.5]).

Figure 6.1 Copper alloy tintinnabulum depicting a zoomorphic phallus. In the British Museum (BM 1856, 1226.1086; © Trustees of the British Museum [CC BY-NC-SA 4.0]).

These three *tintinnabula* serve to demonstrate the variability of the type: the central figure is phallic in some capacity, indeed it is ithyphallic, but may be joined by additional phalli or zoomorphic elements. In all cases the bells hang down from the figure, supported integrally about its body. Generally speaking, the exact nature of the figure and number and arrangements of the bells of *tintinnabula* is hugely variable with a macrophallus featuring prominently, but not exclusively, in the known examples; a conical (phallo-form?) bell with a human face from Merida, Spain (Blazquez 1985, figs. 1–2) is one such exception.

An object can be described as apotropaic if it is designed to ward off evil. Phalli and bells are discussed using this term in the following sections, particularly in relationship to magical practice. In seeking to prevent confusion through the uncritical use of such a term, a brief outline of my position on these subjects is called for. Whether phalli and bells may be definitively described as 'magic' ultimately depends upon the individual reader's understanding and application of the historic semantic argument regarding what is, is not, or

may be 'magical' and defining whether or not this concept is appropriate as a tool for discussing the material culture of the ancient world. The author follows an approach to Roman magic which accepts that it can be defined in terms of its functional difference to the allied concept of religion (Parker 2016: 109–10); largely following the approach first set out by Merrifield (1987: 6) and incorporating the functional terminology described by Versnel (1991) to suggest a positive case for the use and application of the term 'magic'. One must appreciate that more explicitly 'anti-magical' approaches are available (recently, for example, Otto 2013), at least in terms of their semantic position, that offer an alternative perspective on the subject (see the introduction to this volume for further discussion about the possible definitions of magic). The author accepts that the material presented in this paper is 'magical' in its theoretical sense and has done so implicitly in this case in order to prevent the explicit compartmentalisation of the material culture. Phalli are depicted as somewhat overt in their intended function by providing protection against (by distracting or mitigating the effects of) the evil eye and do so in a functionally instrumentive way that requires no divine invocations or ritual interactions. The evidence in the following suggests that bells and other noise-making objects may serve a contextualised magico-religious ritual function, though the nature and extent of this is somewhat unclear.

The 'magical' association with phalli primarily refers to the occasions when male genitals are divorced from the rest of the body and there are several references to the manifestation of this contemporary practice in the classical sources (cf. Whitmore, this volume). The use of the phallic symbol as a pendant may be mentioned in Varro's *De Lingua Latina* (7.97): 'Perhaps it is from this that a certain indecent object that is hung on the necks of boys, to prevent harm from coming to them, is called *scaevola*, on account of the fact that the *scaeva* is good. It is named from *scaeva*, that is *sinistra* 'left', because those things which are *sinistra...* are considered to be good auspices.' A votive phallus has a role in a Bacchic sacrifice in Aristophanes (*Ach.* 241), required to be 'held aloft' by Xanthias, a slave. The image of the god Fascinus (as a phallus) is attached, according to Pliny (*HN* 28.7), beneath the chariot of a general during a Triumph.

In the Roman world, the phallus is also widely depicted as an enemy of the evil eye (Turnbull 1978: 199–200). The evil eye is the embodiment of bad luck and is both feared and respected. In Virgil's *Eclogues* (3.1.103) the shepherds Damoetas and Menalcas are lamenting the state of their stock and Menalcas asks 'What eye is it that has fascinated my tender lambs?' (*nescio quis teneros oculus mihi fascinate agnos*). On the power of eyes and gazing, Pliny the Elder (*HN* 7.2) speaks of the ability of certain African 'enchanters' who have 'the power of fascination with the eyes and can even kill those on whom they fix their gaze for any length of time, especially if their look denotes anger; the age of puberty is said to be particularly obnoxious to the malign influence of such persons.' Plutarch (*Quaest. conv.* 5.7.2) also mentions the role of the eye in falling in love and curing disease. From these three examples we learn that the eye was believed to have supernatural effects and these can be both positive and negative and, in the quote from Pliny, that there are social groups who may be more or less affected by the negative influence of the eye. Equally the supernatural effects may be produced from a real, human eye, as well as from the concept of the supernatural eye. In order to disable or avert the eye, it may be conceptually 'attacked' and there are, subsequently, a number of depictions of the evil eye in the Roman world showing it under attack from its enemies. The most common of these shows the Eye under attack from all sides (the 'all suffering eye') of which the phallus is a main component: a mosaic from the 'House of the Evil Eye' at Antioch is attacked by macrophallic dwarf (Clarke 2009); a carved stone relief from Leptis Magna depicts a zoomorphic phallus ejaculating into the eye whilst a scorpion attacks it (Johns 1982: fig. 77); a gold earring from Norfolk includes two individual phalli pointing

Composite image. Not to scale.

Figure 6.3 Gold disc (earring?) from Keswick, Norfolk, depicting the 'all-suffering eye' surrounded by its enemies. Clockwise from the top, the images surrounding the eye are: phallus, crab, phallus, snake, scorpion, arrow, bow and arrow, winged horse/lion (PAS: NMS-B9A004; © Portable Antiquities Scheme [CC By-Attribution 2.0]).

towards the eye alongside a plethora of other apotropaic icons (Figure 6.3; Worrell and Pearce 2014: no. 20, fig. 20).

An alternative form of this visual narrative depicts only the phallus attacking an evil eye. The scene is depicted on stone phallic carvings in Britain and there are at least four examples of this here: two at Chesters (Coulston and Phillips: nos. 404 and 407), and one each from Maryport (Bailey and Haverfield 1915: 158, no. 86; *RIB* 872) and South Kesteven (PAS: LIN-CFA375; Parker 2017a). The phallus may be solely pointing towards the eye, touching it directly, or ejaculating towards it. A recently-excavated example from Catterick depicts an ejaculating phallus on its own, which may have been associated with an eye on a different stone (Parker and Ross 2016). Elsewhere in the Empire the battle between phalli and the eye can be seen on other media, for example a first century B.C. terracotta figure depicts two humanoid phalluses sawing an evil eye in half (Johns 1982: fig. 51). The issue of this narrative was best described by Johns (1982: 66): 'It is often completely ambiguous in cases where both eyes and phallus are represented, whether the phallus is supposed to be overpowering the evil eye, or whether the Eye motif is itself performing an apotropaic function.' As a further case in point, a second century gold figurine depicting Phthonos, the Greek personification of Envy was depicted with a large, stylised phallus. Phthonos is an alternate personification of the qualities of the evil eye according to Dasen (2015: 184, pl. 9). The effect of the phalli attacking the evil eye is to nullify its negative influences or, to put it another way, to provide an apotropaic effect. The invocation of a supernatural power in the above examples is instrumental through the repeated use of this single image. The apotropaic qualities of the phalli did not require any kind of supplication to their divine power; they existed *in situ* on buildings and worn by people, forever attempting to deflect the gaze of the evil eye. By any definition of the subject, this is magic in action.

It should be noted, though, that the number of phalli as singular objects or icons vastly outweighs the number in which they are depicting attacking the evil eye. The range of material culture in which a phallus is depicted is particularly extensive, facilitated somewhat by the ease in creating a phallic shape when it is divorced from the rest of the body. In Romano-British contexts they can be found on: pendants in gold (PAS: SWYOR-E56143; ESS-0CDDC1), copper alloy (PAS: LIN-9DF6E7; SF-5B3285), bone (PAS: SF-EE7435), amber (Johns 1982: pl. 10), chalk (Museum of London, MF187[156],16); mounts (PAS: DUR-F4D1F7; LEIC-B156DD; NLM-126D42); gold finger rings (Johns 1982: pl. 10); a copper alloy hair pin (PAS: DUR-6FDBA2); harness pendants (Bishop 1988: types 8l, 8o, 10a–10l) and strap fittings (PAS: LVPL1746); fist-and-phallus type pendants in bone (Crummy 1983: nos. 4258–9) and copper alloy (Parker 2015); antler roundels (Greep 1994: 81–2; fig. 3); seal boxes (Andrews 2012: 102–3); ceramic beakers of Nene Valley Colour Coated Ware (Webster 1989: 9); ceramic figurines (e.g. Turner 1999: 193, no. 8, fig. 125), and stone carvings (Parker 2017b). Objects which connect phallic imagery to other zoomorphic elements are also particularly relevant here. In the latter case a bear-like predator biting the base of a phallus, which is nearly as big as it is, springs to mind (PAS: DENO-82D537) as do phallic-nosed bull pendants (e.g. Plouviez 2005: figs. 1.7–8).

Considering the entire corpus of material evidence for phalli in the Roman world, the vast majority of these images depict the phallus as erect rather than flaccid. Whilst flaccid types do exist there is some evidence to suggest that they cease to be popular by the end of the first century A.D. (Johns 1982: 62; Deschler-Erb and Božič 2002). Speaking generally, the flaccid phallic objects do not represent the same range of zoomorphic and/or anthropomorphic features that are prevalent in the myriad erect manifestations of this image. In any case there are no flaccid *tintinnabula* known to archaeology.

The phallic elements of the *tintinnabula* have their own intrinsic efficacy, but it is an important characteristic of the type that polyphallism is not uncommon. The multiplication of the same protective image within a single, fantastical and composite figure might be seen as having an enhanced effect upon its supernatural properties. It may have deliberately intended to move the narrative away from simple, anatomical, human considerations and into the world of the supernatural or the mythological as a further efficacious enhancer. The use of multiple bells in a single example may also represent an attempt of multiplication or enhancement. No studies are available which account for the pitch or tone of a set of such bells, but a simple visual inspection reveals differing sizes of the bells (see Figure 6.1), thus producing different notes when rung. The sound produced by a Roman wind chime,

assuming at least two and possibly up to five individual notes, is a complex, randomised and constantly changing sound. The sound of the notes ringing is combined with the organic chaos of their order and the potential for continuous play. The randomisation of the notes played is due entirely to the pre-requisite for wind or, perhaps, a door or curtain (see below) moving the bells and both are events which are difficult to control. The wind is a natural force of the environment: its predictability related only to geographic locations (i.e. exposed coastal locations may be windier than the centre of an urban environment) and seasonal changes. It may be possible to control the passage of the wind in a domestic environment, specifically though architectural features such as narrowed windows or corridors (either deliberately or accidentally) in such a way to maximise its effect on a wind chime. It is, perhaps, worthy of note that one of the most frequent zoomorphic additions to the fantastical *tintinnabula* figurines is a pair of wings. Wings are designed to harness the natural power of the wind and air, allowing flight, movement, migration – the link between apotropaic protection and the ability to fly is unclear, but it does show a conceptual link between the elements and the methods which nature has used to overcome them.

Nina Crummy directly relates 'noise-making objects' with an apotropaic function both as ritual elements of religious activities (during the worship of Isis and Bacchus), as votive deposits in religious sites, and as grave goods (Crummy 2010: 53–4). She also mentions the use of the word *tinnitus* in Ovid associated with the religious ceremonies of Cybele (Ov. *Fast.* 4.184; Crummy 2010: 53–4.). *Tinnitus* is a 'ringing or jingling' sound and variations of this and the verb *tintino* 'to ring' are prevalent elsewhere in Classical texts and, unsurprisingly, not just for religious and ritual purposes. The word is shown to have additional meanings. Ammianus Marcellinus uses the word *tintinnabula* to refer to the 'ringing of bells' as a metaphorical distraction to the Emperor Julian (17.11). In Plautus (*Truc.* 4.3), Callicles' servant is threatened with being sent to the *tintinnaculos,* the 'men who go clink, clink' – a reference to torturers using fetters or tying bells to inmates to prevent them running away. In *Pseudolus* (1.3) Plautus again references bells as part of a professional toolkit: *Lanius inde accersam duo cum tintinnabulis* ('I'll fetch two sacrificers, with their bells'), but in this instance they are associated with a ritual sacrifice. The actual wearing of bells in Classical literature is primarily associated with livestock (Petron. *Sat.* 47; Apul. *Met.* 10.18) and shows that they served a practical function in being used to identify the movement of an animal – perhaps in this context Plautus' sacrificers may have been bringing an animal wearing a bell. This last literary reference reinforces the relationship between bells, animals and ritual practices; all of which are prominent features of these phallic wind chimes.

In the Greek Magical Papyri, there are few references to the use of bells in the ritual spells, which may be surprising considering their relevance to ritual performance. In *PGM* 4.3255–74 the practitioner is required to write a *vox magica* in the shape of bell (interestingly, in association with a drawing of an animal: an ass), and a ringing noise needs to be made in 4.88–93 though it is not explicit on the medium by which this is achieved. The comparative rarity of bells and other noise-making tools in the spell-books of Graeco-Roman Egypt is, perhaps, supplanted by the need to make noise with the body and usually with the mouth. In addition to the requirement for spoken parts in a huge number of the spells, other noises are required on occasion: hissing (*PGM* 4.475–829), popping (13.1–343), bellowing (13.734–1077), and laughter (13.343–646). Fourteen 'sacred' sounds are also listed as the companions of Mene (an epithet of Selene, the moon goddess (Betz 1992, 336)) in a prayer: 'and the first companion of your name is silence, the second a popping sound, the third groaning, the fourth hissing, the fifth a cry of joy, the sixth moaning, the seventh barking, the eighth bellowing, the ninth neighing, the tenth a musical sound, the eleventh a sounding wind, the twelfth a wind-creating sound, the thirteenth a coercive sound, the fourteenth a coercive emanation from perfection' (*PGM* 7.756–94). The eleventh and twelfth sounds require 'wind', and the former of these could refer (albeit tenuously) directly to the function of a *tintinnabulum*.

It is interesting that in the above text 'laughter' is described as one of the 'sacred' sounds. In Clarke's chapter on 'The displays of erotica and the erotics of display in public buildings' (1998: ch. 7) he argues that the construction of sexual scenes in a suburban Pompeiian bath-house are designed as a form of entertainment by highlighting non-conformist, deviant or unusual sexual scenes (1998: 239–40). In an earlier paper focussing on the depictions of African men in bath-house mosaics, Clark argues that the frequently macrophallic and otherwise non-conformist body shapes (from the perspective of the white, Italic patrician writers) of the black slaves depicted in these spaces also serve an apotropaic function (Clarke 1996: 195–8). The idea that strange or unusual images or substances may be actively sought out as a key element of magical practice is also discussed by Wilburn (2012: 87–8; see also Whitmore, this volume). According to Clarke, it is the construction of an amusing picture to illicit mirth (or the sound of laughter) and appropriate apotropaic imagery which is used in combination to provide supernatural protection to physical spaces. Whilst there are no indications that the *tintinnabula* were used in a bath-house, they clearly could have been incorporated into very similar physical spaces in order to fulfil very similar apotropaic functions. Perhaps then, as well as the sound of the bells functioning as an apotropaic device, the sound of laughter which may be associated with their unusual and fantastical features may also have served as a form of protection.

In his paper on the significance of the sound of animal bells in Early Medieval Scandinavia, Kolltveit (2008: 150)

presented a number of possible, interrelated functions of a bell in a soundscape. The functions may be practical (indicating approach of an animal or vehicle, finding missing animals, deterring predators), ritual (serving an apotropaic function, or acting as decoration within wider magico-religious rites), aesthetic (in terms of the motion, the relationship between space and time, the shaping of territories), or social (as a symbol of power or wealth). These indicators should help to assert the multi-layered complexity of a bell. In Roman terms then, a bell can be experienced visually and aurally, it may represent social concerns for the protection of space, property or an animal and is able to counter possible threats in a supernatural as well as a practical sense. These relationships between bells and spaces are important to reflect upon when considering the complex literary, linguistic, and iconographic evidence for phalli, bells, and zoomorphia.

The attribution of bells as apotropaic icons on their own remains, however, piecemeal with associations between them and elements of ritual performance for magical or religious functions being the strongest part of this argument. The exact nature and use of such bells in these situations is somewhat unclear. A tenuous association with animals in the literature is at least developed by the frequently zoomorphic nature of the *tintinnabula* figures. The idea that these wind chimes were apotropaic comes from the overt and frequent use of phallic imagery in such contexts. The discovery of bells as single finds is problematic in this light. Bells are, of course, used as individual objects and may not have been associated with a group of bells but the extent to which these individuals may have served an apotropaic function is entirely open for debate. As individual finds there are a range of associated functions which must also be considered as part of their specific function: as an indicator of movement, as a toy, or as part of a larger musical assemblage.

Spreading the net wider to consider the functions of the other noise-making objects used during the Roman period, there are several examples relevant to this discussion. The *sistrum* is a bronze rattle with an ovate, openwork head through which several hooked-rods are slotted (Figs. 6.3 and 6.4). The noise-making element arrives from the loose-fitting of these rods which may rattle *in situ* or slide through the perforations if the object was twisted towards the vertical and the rods then impact upon the side. The instrument is particularly associated with the cult of Isis (Heyob 1975: 15, 29; Swaddling 2009: 32). A second-century B.C. marble statue of Isis depicts her holding a *sistrum* raised in her right hand (Fig. 6.4) and a painted wall fresco from Herculaneum depicts a ritual dancer in front of a temple surrounded by worshippers holding *sistra* and other instruments (Museum Archaeologia Nazionale, Napoli. No. 8919). Perhaps one major difference is the prerequisite that a *sistrum* required human agency to activate its noise-making qualities, whereas a *tintinnabulum* could be activated by

Figure 6.4 Marble statue of Isis depicting her holding a sistrum, from the Villa Adriana (Tivoli), late second century B.C. Capitoline Museums MC: 744 (© Public Domain via Wikimedia Commons).

other forces. Equally, the *sistra* and allied instruments are inherently portable, whereas the wind chimes require a given level of static use in their deployment. Whilst they could be moved from space to place by human agents accordingly, there was no need for this to be the case. A *tintinnabulum* may have existed in a single physical position for its entire

operational lifespan and in this capacity it is closely related to the phallic carvings incorporated into buildings.

Also worthy of mention are *crepitacula* and *crepundia,*which are explicitly associated with children. The names both refer to a 'rattle', albeit of two different types. *Crepitacula* are physical rattles of a much more variable type: broadly in the ancient world they may be clay, wood or bronze and appear in a range of geometric or nature-inspired shapes (Horn and Martens 2009: 185) in which instances the rattling device is sealed within a container (Fig. 6.6). The *crepundia,* also known as 'amulet sets', are series of pendants/charms strung together and worn by an infant; though the imagery may be as important as the noise-making function in these devices. If the child itself moved in order to make the bells ring, this may have been an indicator of a healthy (or, at least, living) child. The noise of a rattle could also calm or distract a distressed child, realistically linking the operation of a ringing or jangling noise to the removal of a negative stimulus (a crying child). A conceptual leap from calming a child to protecting one was, perhaps, not a huge one.

Material Evidence for *Tintinnabula*

The phallic wind chimes appearing in museum collections are, predominantly, the results of antiquarian collectors or excavations in modern Western Europe. A number of examples in the Museo Archaeologico Nazionale di Napoli are explicitly from Pompeii or Herculaneum and thus provide a useful *terminus post quem* for these individual examples of A.D. 79, but the extent to which this date is applicable elsewhere is somewhat blurred by the vast majority of *tintinnabula* coming from unsecure archaeological contexts. As a case in point, of the eighteen examples encountered in the British Museum collections, only one has an attached provenance and this too is Pompeii. The use of 'Secret Cabinets' in both the Naples Museum (Fanin 1871) and the British Museum (Gaimster 2000) in the nineteenth century presented this challenging material to an antiquarian, intellectual audience; we may speculate over whether this has been a help or a hindrance in retaining contextual information (I lean towards the latter). It is not the intention of this paper to establish a complete cross-provincial catalogue of *tintinnabula*, instead it will suffice to say that beyond Italy there are *tintinnabula* from Trier (Williams 1999: pl. 9) and Merida (Blazquez 1985). The author is aware of more than thirty in public and private collections; we may speculate that the true extant number is much higher, probably more than a hundred and potentially beyond this figure.

In addition to the general stylistic properties of *tintinnabula* outlined in the above, a visual inspection of the type reveals a few additional details. Where a humanoid

Figure 6.5 Bronze sistrum of Roman Date (© The Metropolitan Museum of Art (Gift of Henry G. Marquand, 1897. No: 97.22.2)).

Figure 6.6 Ceramic rattle in the shape of a pig or boar. British Museum (© Trustees of the British Museum [CC BY-NC-SA 4.0]).

figure is ithyphallic this is, perhaps obviously, always male (there is no evidence of hermaphroditism in these examples), but female figures can be found as small riders or jockeys upon zoomorphic phalli, sitting astride the shaft. The female figures are always nude wheras the males may be partially clothed. The suspension chain above the figure is usually

singular – they are designed to be hung from one point rather than stretched or strung between multiple places; this facet inevitably improved their versatility as ornaments designed for display. A small number also included a lamp suspended beneath the figure and the bells. There is a somewhat problematic description, within modern literature at least, of zoomorphic phalli suspended on chains without bells as *tintinnabula* proper. Examples in the British Museum (e.g. BM: 1814, 0704. 1257; BM: 1865, 1118.208) feature a phallic creature suspended from a chain, but include no suspension loops beneath by which bells may be hung. We may argue that these, through lacking the noise-making element prevalent in the others, are not *tintinnabula* in the true sense but comparable figural objects. That said, there is no reason to not consider them as appropriate for the same spaces where the wind chimes may be installed.

Importantly, there are none from secure provenances in Britain. There is a single example in the collection of the Museum of Archaeology and Anthropology which may tenuously be identified as a *tintinnabulum* and, furthermore, only very tenuously related to Britain. The online catalogue entry for this object details that the collector, J. Jennings, owned several *tintinnabula*, including some from Colchester, and one example reportedly excavated from the environs of the Roman town. Unfortunately, at the time of the donation in the early twentieth century he could not be sure if this example was the one which may have been found in Colchester.[1] The figure itself is a macrophallus depicted with goat-like legs, a secondary phallus between the legs, and a pair of outstretched wings; the body is elongated as if in flight. A single suspension loop is clearly evident on the underside, beneath the glans, in a way comparable with other examples. Clearly too many question marks hang over this object for it to be considered securely Romano-British; dissapointingly though these problems with provenance and dating are somewhat endemic to the study of *tintinnabula*. If *tintinnabula* were used in Britain during the Roman period, their existence remains emphemeral to archaeological investigations.

The above object notwithstanding, *tintinnabula* either had not reached Britain during their first century predominance or were otherwise functionally or fashionably replaced here by the time it went out of fashion; it is unusual that an element of Roman material culture that existed broadly in the North Western provinces did not reach beyond these into Britain. Certainly all the relevant elements for *tintinnabula* exist in Britain – the use of the phallic image in the first century being the key. If we are unable to comment on *tintinnabula* from Britain, how about one of their component parts – specifically the bells? At the time of writing the Portable Antiquities Scheme lists over 200 copper alloy bells considered to be Roman (e.g. Figure 6.7), but none of the figural aspects of the wind chimes have been encountered.[2] The European Artefacts database lists at least fifteen individual types of Roman *clochette* (bell) with tentative dating evidence supplied from several continental European contexts (see CLT-4001 to CLT-4022).[3] In all cases the bells are copper alloy, but the form changes slightly. In general terms the bells are either hemispherical, trapezoidal, conical, squat and straight-sided or, for want of a better phrase, 'bell-shaped' (rounded at the top, narrowing slightly at the waist and flaring outwards at the foot). It is likely to have an integral suspension loop, the majority of which are lozenge-shaped (or hexagonal) with a large circular perforation in the centre, but examples without these are recorded in the typology. The earliest type listed is from the first half of the first century A.D. (CLT-4001) and the latest from A.D. 350–425 (CLT-4008) – bells were thus a perennial object throughout the Roman period and coexisted with phallic objects in Roman Britain.

It is impossible to directly associate individual bells with *tintinnabula* proper and the overt imagery they may have depicted, but we can attempt to establish their use in apotropaic ritual practices. Comparable copper alloy bells, disassociated from any chain and thus any larger 'wind chime' assemblage have been discovered in several funerary contexts in Roman Britain. At Brougham, Cumbria, the cremation of a 3–4-year-old child included such a bell (Cool 2004: 159) as do at least three graves at Colchester. Of the latter, one was of a female inhumation of a child aged 10 years (Crummy 2010: 83), one an inhumation of an infant (Crummy 2010; 47), and the third also in an inhumation grave (Crummy 2010: 46–47). Other bells from inhumations come from Guilden Morden, Chichester and London (Philpott 1991: 163, n. 7).

Dasen associates a passage from Plautus (*Mil.* 5.1, *quasi puero in collo pendeant crepundia*) with rattling devices at the necks of children (Dasen 2015: 189) and correlates this with a bell attached to a bracelet from a second century child tomb in Poitiers and a copper alloy bell from Budapest inscribed with a message of good luck (Dasen 2015: 189). She groups these together with other images suitable for the protection of children, such as the club of Hercules and phallic images. One of the above Colchester graves also contained a number of apotropaic icons including a winged phallus (Crummy 1983: 1811) and a unique carved amber head (Henig 1984: 245; Davis, this volume). Bells are also included as grave goods in at least three child inhumations in the vicinity of Arras, northern France (Jelski 1984: 277); in all cases these are also associated with phallic pendants as part of the grave assemblage. This contextual association between phalli and bells should not be dismissed as coincidental and the importance of the link between apotropaic functions of these objects in life and ritual use in funerary contexts in death should not be underestimated. Perhaps by the mid to late first century A.D., the link between phalli and bells had moved from

Figure 6.7 *Roman copper alloy pyramid-shaped bell with clapper in situ. Runhall, Norwich. (PAS: NMS-AF23E9; © Portable Antiquities Scheme [CC By-Attribution 2.0])*

physical to conceptual with both recognised as part of the same apotropaic toolkit, but lacking any requirements for physical connection.

Bells are wide-ranging in their distribution and we find them even beyond the fringes of the Roman world: five are known from Denmark and four from Sweden (Kolltveit 2008: 148). They may also be found in more 'ritualised' contexts: copper alloy bells were amongst the large metalwork assemblage from Coventina's Well in Northumberland (Allason-Jones and McKay 1985: 28, nos. 66 and 67) and from this perspective we may also consider those from assemblages in the Rivers Walbrook (Wardle 2011: 504) and Tees (PAS: BM-C82C45). Also found near the Walbrook in Roman London was an iron rod (described as a possible *sistrum* in the report) with a twisted centre and a spatulate head from an unstratified context (Rayner *et al.* 2011: 407, fig. 348). It included annular chain links on each side and may have functioned as a noise-making device through the attachment of additional chains or larger terminals onto the link, impacting upon the head when twisted.

Perhaps the underlying question in cases where we find a potentially utilitarian bell in a 'ritualised' context, such as a grave or well-deposit, is whether or not these forms of material culture carried their dual meanings with them over the course of their lives from creation to deposition (Vejby 2016: 58). There is an inherent danger of over-interpreting the material culture by assuming that the answer to this question is always 'yes.' The three possible ways of interpreting such objects highlight their material and contextual complexity (Vejby 2016: 58): that they are, in fact, strictly utilitarian and it is incorrect to assign a ritual function; that they gain a ritual significance based on their deposition at a ritual location; that these were always possessed of a dual ritual/utilitarian function. Ultimately an answer to this specific question is not yet forthcoming, but when the same question is posed for *tintinnabula* it is the latter of the three options that is most convincing.

Spatial Use of Wind Chimes

As well as the secondary use of bells in a funerary context, we must consider the primary use of a wind chime, in Roman Britain and beyond: it usually requires access to moving air to function on its own and thus must be hung in a location with access to the open air, or somewhere physically accessible if being struck by hand, or both. In reality we do not know exactly where *tintinnabula* were used but windows, doors, courtyards, and gardens all present themselves as natural candidates to fulfil these spatial criteria – though we cannot be sure if we may find them inside, outside, somewhere between or a combination of all of these. If this is the case, such boundary locations may be interpreted as the same liminal locations in the physical world which were suitable for protection by phallic carvings (see Johns 1982; Parker 2017b: 118–21). The difference is that when compared to the static, stone carvings built into a structure, the wind chimes are able to be moved occasionally, seasonally or daily to a new location if need be; establishing a functional locale for this type of object may prove impossible beyond the suggested liminal places.

Priapic statues or paintings may be found at the entranceways of houses, such as the House of the Vettii at Pompeii, in order to serve an apotropaic function (Swift 2009: 41). What better substitute avatar for Priapus than a disembodied phallus on a wind chime? Protection was not just given to doors; the common practice of hanging curtains in doorways prompts a consideration of whether fabric designs may also have included apotropaic motifs that could protect a space adorned by a curtain (Swift 2009: 42). We may speculate that a *tintinnabulum* could be activated noisily through the action of moving aside a curtain or

pushing opening a door. If the protection of liminal places within a building can be facilitated through the appropriate use of iconography, then we may certainly speculate that acoustic protection is also equally fitting. Considering doorways as entrances, a noise-making contraption which activates upon the opening of a door or pulling of a curtain serves a very simple form of protection – it identifies to those inside that another person has entered the same space. This signal could, as with modern shop bells, ensure that shop stock is not left unattended, a paying customer does not go unserved, or a guest is not left waiting. Equally it identifies to the person who has entered that their presence has been announced whether or not they intended for this to be the case. Equally, the sound of an activated *tintinnabulum* suggests the presence of people nearby. Clandestine movement around or within a structure occupied by such a wind chime could, speculatively, have been mitigated or prevented by its presence. There may well be metaphorical links between the design of the figure on the wind chime and the nuanced location in which it was intended to be put; the *tintinnabula* depicting Mercury mentioned above could have been designed for the protection of a business in this manner, perhaps guarding the entranceway to the building or a storeroom. The zoomorphic links prevalent on the other figurines could also point towards specific usage, protecting livestock or domestic pets or, in the case of the gladiatorial dwarf, a gymnasium or circus for example. The metaphorical links supplied by these images may also have provided protection *from* these subjects. As an alternative possibility, the production of laughter or mirth as an apotropaic device would have required the *tintinnabula* to be physical seen by people for this effect to occur. In such a case, maximising the number of interactions such an object may have had with people could have been desirous in order to maximise its apotropaic efficacy. Thus a very prominent and public position could be required, for example in a bar or marketplace where there was a regular footfall.

The imagery shown above shows that the phallic figures are the prominent component of the *tintinnabula* design and we have discussed the magical significance of the phallic imagery. This is not, however, the full story. Metal wind chimes – all but one of those encountered have been in a copper alloy (the anomaly is an alabaster phallus with copper alloy wings and chain, from Pompeii and now in the Wellcome Collection (no. A67895)) – were bright, brassy-coloured instruments. In direct sunlight the metal would heat up and light would be reflected, in lower temperatures the metal cools to the touch; both important considerations if they are being activated manually. Movement is an integral part of their function with the figure rotating and swinging to one side in a haphazard fashion and the bells on long chains following suit. It should be pointed out that despite the lack of evidence for the suspension of a *tintinnabulum* onto a fixing (be it a wall-bracket, door, hook, handy furniture fitting, or even a tree-branch) it is unlikely to remain completely static due to the weight distribution of the organic figural forms – the dynamic shapes are going to move. The length of chain from figure to bells is such that direct contact between bells, both between each other and with their surrounding environment, is almost ensured. The tangling of the chains must have been a problem that plagued owners. Equally a *tintinnabulum,* with its dome shaped bells, has the capacity to be activated (played) by another natural process: presuming exposure to the outside in some way, the bells may be struck and rung by rainfall. This possibility chimes nicely with the likelihood that wind, another natural force, could provide the necessary agency for the *tintinnabulum* to 'work'. These objects were, paradoxically, balanced between needing and not needing human agents to activate them and, clearly, we do not yet fully understand the complexity of relationships held between these object and the spaces which they occupied.

Conclusions

This short paper has aimed to provide an introduction to the material and apotropaic issues surrounding *tintinnabula* and to consider the various physical, literary and theoretical bases by which such wind chimes may be considered to be apotropaic and magically efficacious objects. The combination of phalli and bells were used together in, we may speculate, spatially significant locations in order to provide a form of supernatural protection to a building, its contents, it inhabitants and/or those entering or leaving it. Chaos, be it through the noise-produced by the bells, the movement the figurine takes, the action and availability of the wind or hand that chimes them, or the entrance of a stranger into a house, was an integral and efficacious element to the functionality of *tintinnabula* and this compliments the static, passive protection offered by the more prosaic phallic carvings and figurines in the Roman world. Although no extant examples are available from secure provenances in Roman Britain, its individual components (phalli and bells) are used to fulfil at least part of the same function in a variety of forms from a wide range of contexts. Looking to the future study of this specific object type, it is clearly desirous that a complete cross-provincial catalogue may be developed in order to expand on the contextual, spatial and chronological interpretation of *tintinnabula* in the Roman provinces, but for now, given the prevalence of their component parts and the existence of the same issues surrounding the supernatural protection of the self and of place, we should not be entirely surprised to discover securely stratified examples of *tintinnabula* in Roman Britain in the future.

Department of Classical Studies, Open University

Acknowledgements

With grateful thanks to my co-editor and co-conspirator Stuart McKie both for working with me on this project and for his comments on several versions of this paper, and to Alissa Whitmore for her enthusiasm, in depth discussion of an earlier version, and additional references on the topic. Thanks also to both of the anonymous reviewers for their helpful comments and to Georgia Whitney from the Wellcome Collection for information on the alabaster piece.

Notes

1   MAA online catalogue, object number: 1924.337. Available: http://collections.maa.cam.ac.uk/. [Accessed: 03/08/17]
2   It should be noted that the total number of bells known from Roman Britain is much larger than this figure, but no complete catalogues currently exist to draw upon. The author is collating evidence for bells as part of his PhD. The total number is certainly in the high hundreds.
3   Available: http://www.artefacts.mom.fr. [Accessed 01/07/07]

Bibliography

Ancient Sources

Ammianus Marcellinus (Translated by J.C. Rolfe 1935–1940). *Ammianus Marcellinus with an English Translation.* Cambridge, MA: Harvard University Press.
Apuleius (Translated by P.G. Walsh 1994). *Apuleius, The Golden Ass* (Oxford World's Classics). Oxford: Oxford University Press
Aristophanes(Translated by S.D. Olsen 2004). *Aristophanes Arcanians.* Oxford: Oxford University Press
Petronius (Translated by M. Heseltine 1913). *Poems.* London: William Heinemann.
Plautus (Translated by Riley 1912). *Psedolus. The Comedies of Plautus.* London: G. Bell and Sons.
Pliny the Elder (Translated by J. Bostock 1855). *Natural History.* London: Taylor and Francis.
Plutarch (Translated by F.C. Babbitt 1936). *Plutarch, Morals, with an English Translation.* London, London, William Heinemann.
Varro (Translated by R.G. Kent 1951). *De Lingua Latinae.* Loeb Classical Library. Revised edition. Cambridge, MA: Harvard University Press.
Virgil. (Translated by H.R. Fairclough 1916) *Eclogues, Georgics, Aeneid* (Loeb Classical Library 63). Cambridge, MS: Harvard University Press.

Modern Sources

Allason-Jones, L. and McKay, B. 1985. *Coventina's Well on Hadrian's Wall.* Chesters Roman Fort: Trustees of the Clayton Collection.
Andrews, C. 2012. *Roman Seal-Boxes in Britain* British Archaeological Report 567. Oxford: Archaeopress.
Bailey, J.B. and Haverfield, F. 1915. Catalogue of Roman inscribed and sculptured stones, coins, earthenware, etc. discovered in and near the Roman fort at Maryport and preserved at Netherhall. *Transactions of the Cumberland and Westmorland Antiquarian and Archaeological Society* (2nd Series) 152: 135–72.

Betz, H.D. (ed) 1992. *The Greek Magical Papyri in Translation(Including the Demotic Spells)*. 2nd edition. Chicago, IL, London: University of Chicago Press.

Bishop, M.C. 1988. Cavalry equipment of the Roman Army in the first century AD. In J.C. Coulston (ed) *Military Equipment and the Identity of Roman Soldiers: Proceedings of the Fourth Roman Military Equipment Conference*. British Archaeological Reports International Series 394. Oxford: British Archaeological Reports: 67–195.

Blazquez, J.M. 1985. Tintinnabula de Merida y de Sasamon (Burgos). *Zephyrus* 38: 331–5.

Clarke, J.R. 1996. Hypersexual black men in Augustan baths: ideal somatotypes and apotropaic magic. In N.B. Kampen (ed.) *Sexuality in Ancient Art*. Cambridge: Cambridge University Press: 184–98.

Clarke, J.R. 1998. *Looking at Lovemaking: Constructions of Sexuality in Roman Art, 100 BC–AD 250*. Berkeley and Los Angeles, CA: University of California Press.

Clarke, J.R. 2009. *Ars Erotica: Sexualität und ihre Bilder im anitken Rom*. Darmstadt: Primus.

Collingwood, R.G. and Wright, R.P. 1965. *Roman Inscriptions of Britain, Volume 1*. Oxford: Clarendon Press.

Cool, H.E.M. 2004. *The Roman Cemetery of Brougham, Cumbria: Excavations 1966–67*. Britannia Monograph Series 21. London: Society for the Promotion of Roman Studies.

Coulston, J.C. and Phillips, E.J. 1988. *Corpus Signorum Imperii Romani*. Volume I, Fascicule VI, Hadrian's Wall West of the North Tyne, and Carlisle. London: British Academy.

Crummy, N. 1983. *Colchester Archaeological Report 2: The Small Finds from Excavations in Colchester 1971–9*. Colchester: Colchester Archaeological Trust. Available: http://cat.essex. ac.uk/summaries/CAR-0002.html [Accessed: 01/07/17]

Crummy, N. 2010. Bears and coins: The iconography of protection in late Roman infant burials. *Britannia* 41: 37–93.

Dasen, V. 2015. Probaskania: amulets and magic in antiquity. In D. Boschung and J.N. Bremmer (eds) *The Materiality of Magic*. Morphomata 20. Paderborn: Wilhelm Fink: 177–204.

Deschler-Erb, E. and Božič, D. 2002. A late republican bone pendant from the Münsterhügel in Basel (CH). *Instrumentum Bulletin* 15: 39–40.

Fanin, S.M.C. 1871. *The Royal Museum at Naples, Being Some Account of the Erotic Paintings, Bronzes and Statues Contained in that Famous 'Cabinet Secret'*. London. Available: http:// sacred-texts.com/sex/rmn/index.htm [Accessed: 19/11/16]

Gaimster, D. 2000. Sex and sensibility in the British Museum. *History Today* 50(9). Available: http://www.historytoday.com/ david-gaimster/sex-and-sensibility-british-museum [Accessed: 19/11/16].

Greep, S. 1994. Antler roundel pendants from Britain and the North-Western Provinces. *Britannia* 25: 81–97.

Henig, M. 1984. Amber amulets. *Britannia* 15: 244–6.

Heyob, S.K. 1975. *The Cult of Isis Among Women in the Graeco-Roman World*. Leiden: Brill.

Horn, C.B. and Martens, J.W. 2009. '*Let the Little Children Come to Me': Childhood and Children in Early Christianity*. Washington DC: Catholic University of American Press.

Jelski, G. 1984. Pendentifs phallique, clochettes et peltae dans les tombs d'enfants de Gaule Belgique: une découverte à Arras. *Revue du Nord* 66: 260–79.

Johns, C. 1982. *Sex and Symbol? Erotic Images of Greece and Rome*. London: British Museum Press.

Koltveit, G. 2008. Animal bells in early Scandinavian soundscapes. In A.A. Both, R. Eichmann, E. Hickmann and L.-C. Koch (eds) *Challenges and Objectives in Music Archaeology*. Studien zue Musikarchäologie VI, Orient-Archäologie 22. Rahden: Westf: Verlag Marie Leidorf: 147–53.

Merrifield, R. 1987. *The Archaeology of Ritual and Magic*. London: Guild Publishing.

Parker, A. 2015. The fist-and-phallus pendants from Roman Catterick. *Britannia* 46: 135–49.

Parker, A. 2016. Staring at death: The jet *gorgoneia* of Roman Britain. In S. Hoss and A. Whitmore (eds) *Small Finds and Ancient Social Practices in the Northwest Provinces of the Roman Empire*. Oxford: Oxbow Books: 98–113.

Parker, A. 2017a. A new perspective on a Roman phallic carving from South Kesteven, Lincolnshire. *Lincolnshire History and Archaeology* 49: 91–98.

Parker, A. 2017b. Protecting the troops? Phallic carvings in the north of Roman Britain. In A. Parker (ed.) *Ad Vallum: Papers on the Roman Army and Frontiers in Celebration of Dr. Brian Dobson*. British Archaeological Report 631. Oxford: British Archaeological Reports: 117–30.

Parker, A. and Ross, C. 2016. A new phallic carving from Roman Catterick. *Britannia* 47: 271–9.

Philpott, R. 1991. *Burial Practices in Roman Britain: A Survey of Grave Treatment and Furnishing AD 43–410*. British Archaeological Report 219. Oxford: Tempus Reparatum.

Plouviez, J. 2005. Whose good luck? Roman phallic ornaments from Suffolk. In N. Crummy (ed.) *Image, Craft and the Classical World: Essays in Honour of Donald Bailey and Catherine Johns*. Montagnac: Éditions Monique Mergoil: 157–64.

Rayner, L., Wardle, A. and Seeley, F. 2011. Ritual and religion. In J. Hill and P. Rowsome (eds) *Roman London and the Walbrook Stream Crossing: Excavations at 1 Poultry and Vicinity, City of London*. MOLA Monograph 37. London: Museum of London Archaeology: 404–8.

Swaddling, J. 2009. Shake rattle and rôle: sistra in Etruria? In J. Swaddling and P. Perkins (eds) *Etruscan by Definition: The Cultural, Regional and Personal Identity of the Etruscans*. British Museum Research Publication 173. London: British Museum: 31–47.

Swift, E. 2009. *Style and Function in Roman Decoration: Living with Objects and Interiors*. Farnham: Ashgate.

Turner, R. 1999. *Excavations of an Iron Age Settlement and Roman Religious Complex at Ivy Chimneys, Witham, Essex 1978–83*. East Anglian Archaeology 88. Chelmsford: Essex County Council.

Turnbull, P. 1978. The phallus in the art of Roman Britain. *Bulletin of the Institute of Archaeology, University of London* 15: 199–206.

Vejby, M. 2016. Ordinary objects transformed: the compound nature of material culture. In S. Hoss and A. Whitmore (eds) *Small Finds and Ancient Social Practices in the Northwest Provinces of the Roman Empire*. Oxford: Oxbow Books: 57–67.

Versnel, H. 1991. Some reflections on the relationship magic-religion. *Numen* 38(2): 117–95.

Wardle, A. 2011. Accessioned finds. In J. Hill and P. Rowsome (eds) *Roman London and the Walbrook Stream Crossing: Excavations at 1 Poultry and Vicinity, City of London.* MOLA Monograph 37. London: Museum of London Archaeology: 495–514.

Webster, G. 1989. Deities and religious scenes on Romano-British pottery. *Journal of Roman Pottery Studies* 2: 1–28.

Williams, C.A. 1999. *Roman Homosexuality: Ideologies of Masculinity in Classical Antiquity.* Oxford and New York: Oxford University Press.

Worrell, S. and Pearce, J. 2014. II: Finds reported under the Portable Antiquities Scheme. *Britannia* 45: 397–429.

Abbreviations

PAS = Portable Antiquities Scheme Database. Available: http://www.finds.org.uk [Accessed: 10/01/17]

PGM = Papyri Graecae Magicae (see Betz 1992)

RIB = Roman Inscriptions of Britain (see Collingwood and Wright 1965)

Rubbing and Rolling, Burning and Burying:
The Magical Use of Amber in Roman London

Glynn Davis

Introduction

'Magic' is elusive in Roman Britain and, perhaps, even partially invisible to us in the archaeological record (Graf 1997; Wilburn 2012; Gordon 2015). The continuing debate surrounding defining magic – what it is, what it looked like and what it did – is compounded by a broad and complex artefactual evidence base that is difficult to interpret (cf. Gell 1977: 1). On the one hand certain singular classes of artefact are often considered magical, regardless of context, such as, for example curse tablets (McKie 2016), figurines (Bailliot 2015) and inscribed amulets (Bohak 2015). However, much artefactual evidence is considered magical through its 'oddness', 'strangeness' or 'weirdness' in regards to its context or contextual relationship with associated material remains (Thomasson 1999: 58; Aldhouse-Green 2012: 196; Wilburn 2012: 12; Chadwick 2015: 39). When ordinary or mundane objects occur in places perceived as different or liminal to their expected 'normal' use, e.g. within wells, watercourses, building foundations and cavities, they have been consigned to ritual activity (Chadwick 2012; 2015). 'Special' deposits including material remains such as articulated animal bones or foundation deposit assemblages are a good example of ritualised practice where a magical act may be theorised regarding their deposition (e.g. Merrifield 1987; Morris 2011; also Garrow 2012). Recent studies into *materia magica* have highlighted the complexity of the archaeological record and our ability in being able to comprehend this plethora of potential magic that may have been performed in the Roman world (Fulford 2001; Wilburn 2012; Chadwick 2015). Much physical material may either be lost through the magical act or its natural decay within the ground (Chadwick 2015: 38; Wilburn 2012: 89). Magic was often a discreet act, undertaken in clandestine circumstances and so we may constantly face an archaeological bias in trying to understand the full breadth of magical practice (Wilburn 2012: 21, 262). In addition, even if magical acts did leave an archaeological trace, they may go unseen during excavation and post-excavation analysis work due to the complication of not knowing precisely what to look for (Chadwick 2015: 52–5).

'Magic' itself is a highly contested term with its definition constantly being debated (e.g. Versnel 1991; Wilburn 2012; Parker 2016). Wilburn's recent synthesis perhaps offers a clearer route through our problematic archaeological record, by creating a magic 'framework' through which to look for magic in excavated remains (2012: 13–20):

1. 'Magic was firmly grounded in ritual actions, including spoken or written words and the manipulation of objects. These rituals typically are performed with the expectation of a particular result.'
2. 'Magic may draw on religious traditions for both efficacy and exoticism.'
3. 'Magic is frequently a private or personal activity, although certain practices may be undertaken in the public sphere.'

This paper will apply Wilburn's framework above in discussing a material well-known as magical throughout antiquity and especially the Roman period – amber. Amber is an ideal material to explore magical practice in Roman Britain. It was an exotic, luxury material to the province, which would have made it 'special' as either an unworked, natural material or when fashioned into objects. Secondly, it is a material that received broad commentary by ancient authors attesting its magical nature, especially preceding and during the Roman period (see e.g. Williamson 1932; Spekke 1957; Causey 2011). Theoretically, therefore, it should be an ideal candidate for assessing the magical efficacy of the objects it was made from coupled with the contexts in which it has been recovered from the province.

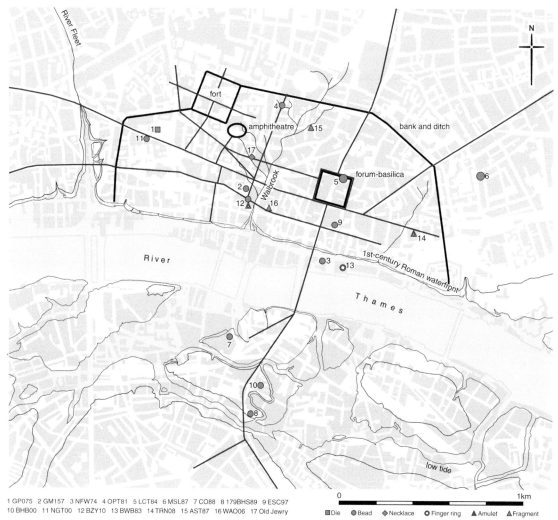

1 GP075 2 GM157 3 NFW74 4 OPT81 5 LCT84 6 MSL87 7 CO88 8 179BHS89 9 ESC97
10 BHB00 11 NGT00 12 BZY10 13 BWB83 14 TRN08 15 AST87 16 WAO06 17 Old Jewry

0   1km

■Die ●Bead ◆Necklace O Finger ring ▲Amulet △Fragment

Figure 7.1 Distribution of amber artefacts (including amulets, beads, die, finger ring, fragments and necklace) in Roman London (© Museum of London).

I will explore two case studies from one of Britain's major towns, and eventual capital, *Londinium* (Tac. *Ann.*14.32) – a relevant urban centre to study amber considering both its mercantile origins and extensive excavation history which has yielded one of largest overall assemblages of amber objects from a single Roman site (Wallace 2014: 1–2, 18–20; Davis forthcoming). The first case study discusses a rare amber die. Although bereft of archaeological context this singular object is explored in relation to its function as a practical object layered with amuletic symbolism. The second case study is a somewhat nondescript fragment of amber found as part of a complex, composite foundation deposit. Here archaeological context – ritualised deposition – is explicit in interpreting a magical act with amber being an important element of the rite. My consideration of amber within these two case studies is influenced by both a phenomenological approach to studying the 'archaeology of the senses' and materiality studies that treat objects as agents (Gell 1977: 27; Hamilakis 2011; Gordon 2015:

136–7). Such an approach will place emphasis on amber's materiality, especially the synaesthetic experience of scent when engaged with as part of a ritual (magical) act and the importance of this link to magical efficacy.

The Magic of Amber

Amber (Greek: *elektron*; Latin: *sucinum* or *succinum*) is a fossilised resin of coniferous trees such as pine, cedar and conifer formed millions of years ago, especially during the Tertiary period, through a process of hardening and deposition (Grimaldi 1996: 12; Causey 2011: 28–9). In the Roman period the prime source of amber was the Baltic (deposited during the Late Eocene–Early Oligocene) with a major centre of importation and manufacture of the raw material into luxury products located in Aquileia, on the Adriatic coast (Strong 1966: 10; Calvi 2005; Eckardt 2014: 105). Amber's popularity in Italy began in the first century A.D. reaching great demand in the second half of the century. By the late second century A.D. working of amber was coming to end in Aquileia, but another centre of production seems to have operated in the Rhineland, perhaps Cologne, during the second and third centuries A.D. (Koster 2013: 174–5; Eckardt 2014: 105). Aside from Aquileia and the Rhineland there were clearly smaller centres of amber-working and trade along the amber routes, especially coming to light in Poland, as is evidenced by artefactual finds and quantities of raw material (Koster 2013: 174). Amber in Britain, however, is extremely scarce. Morris's survey of amber from Romano-British contexts catalogued 258 objects from 57 sites (2010: 98–9, appendix 5: 168–79). Eckardt's additional survey identified only a few more individual objects (2014: 106). Recent work by the author investigating the presence of amber in Roman London has accounted for an additional 13 objects to Morris' recorded 5, from a total of 12 additional archaeological excavations (Davis forthcoming; Figure 7.1).

However, London is one of the most developed modern cities globally and with over 11,500 recorded archaeological interventions this again emphasises amber's rarity in the archaeological record (Nixon *et al.* 2002: 2–5; Wallace 2014: xiv; Francis Grew: pers. comm.). The nature of amber objects from Britain is also very different to those found elsewhere in the Empire, especially Italy. There are very few figurative pieces from Britain and highly complex pieces, such as those produced in the workshops of Aquileia, are non-existent (Eckardt 2014: 106). Those of note are well-known and include the Colchester anthropomorphic amulet (Figure 7.2a), the Carlisle Minerva finger ring and figurative handle, the Silchester fly and, most recently, the Scotch Corner figurine (Crummy 1983: 51; Henig 1984a; McCarthy *et al.* 1982: 88; 1983; Crummy 2006: 124–5; Hannah Russ: pers. comm.). Two recent discoveries from London include an amber fist-and-phallus amulet from Trinity Square and a gladiator helmet pendant from the Walbrook (MOLA TRN08[823]<57>, BZY10[3257]<1966>; Wardle *et al.* 2017; Marshall and Wardle in prep.). These again are unique in Britain although parallels can be found in Aquilea, for example, and despite being artistically and/or symbolically interesting they cannot be considered complex pieces (Calvi 2005: pl. 83, fig. 1 and pl. 73, fig. 1.; cf. Van Den Hurk 1986: 114, pl. v1.2, 391 for stylised but relevant parallels to the gladiator helmet pendant). Aside from these individualistic pieces, the majority of amber objects from Britain comprises beads (including bracelets and necklaces of multiple amber beads), making up 89% of Morris' catalogue. Beads are normally found as single objects and therefore the amber necklace from the Walbrook in London of 70 beads, incorporating two different forms, is exceptional in this regard (MOL 25869; Chapman 1974: 273–4). More detailed amber objects can be found in museum collections across Britain but these are not of Romano-British provenance (e.g. Strong 1966; Brown and Henig 1977).

Amber was an exotic import to Roman Britain and no doubt many small, highly portable objects arrived with individuals (especially soldiers) as they travelled to the province, as opposed to such objects being imported for direct sale (cf. Strabo, *Geographica*, 4.5.3; Crummy 2007: 10; Crummy 2010: 52, n. 28). Pliny the Elder is a primary source for understanding the materiality and importance of amber in the Roman period although his account may be somewhat exaggerated (Bradley 2009: 104–5; Eckardt 2014: 105). Writing during the 'amber–boom', on the one hand Pliny emphasises amber's economic value – a small amber figurine being more expensive than a number of slaves – but he equally describes the material as useless, having no *causa*, bookending his account of amber by repeating this sentiment (Plin. *HN* 37.11, 12; Bradley 2009: 105). Despite its supposed uselessness Pliny describes a multitude of medical uses for amber including beneficial effects for the throat (tonsils and pharynx), ears, eyes and stomach as well as its ability to cure disease, fever and its positive effects on strangury and mental distraction (Plin. *HN* 37.11–12). Pliny notes women's interest in amber – Nero's description of his wife, Poppaea's, hair as amber-coloured apparently setting a fashion trend for a different hair colour. Pliny also singles out the benefit of amber amulets when worn by babies (Plin. *HN* 37.12). An association with women and children made in the text is borne out through archaeological evidence. In Italy this material relationship may extend from the Pre-Roman period where amber had an especially strong gendered association with its amuletic significance, particularly relating to fertility and childbirth (Strong 1966: 11; Causey and Shepherd 2004: 74; Causey 2011: 23, 91ff.). Many of the Aquileian ambers recovered from Roman period burial contexts can be associated with women and children, for example in a rich female grave from Nijmegen (Koster 2013: 175). This association continues through the period and Swift's analysis of the consumption of 'Germanic inspired' bead strings containing amber beads is revealing. In her study of late Roman graves from the north western provinces it was clear that these objects were biased towards women and children (Swift 2003: 49). At this time, where amber is less readily available, its selection as a material and its use is more strongly associated with 'gender-specific identity' (Swift 2003: 56). A gender- and age-specific association of amber in Britain is far more difficult to identify due to the limited material and distinct lack of a contextual relationship. The anthropomorphic amulet from Colchester is likely to have been from a child's burial considering the size of the grave cut and the associated amuletic hoard it was grouped with (including pierced coins, a copper alloy bell and a horned phallus). These are objects individually paralleled in other child burials from Britain (Philpott 1991: 162; Crummy *et al.* 1993: 41; Crummy 2010). Although not a gendered artefact *per se*, finger rings of amber are referenced by Artemidorus

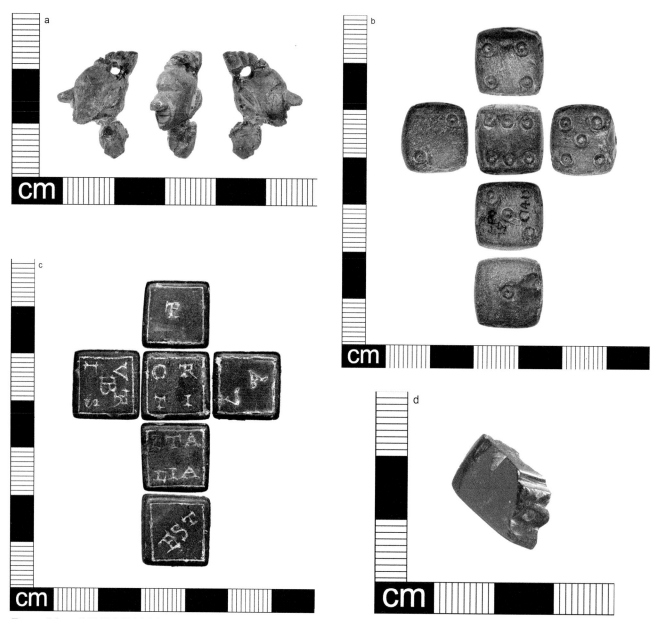

Figure 7.2 a: COLEM:1986.66.693.1 Amber anthropomorphic amulet. Colchester Museums; b: MOL GPO75[1385]<741> Amber die. Museum of London; c: MOL BHB00[2557]<880> Basalt lettered die. Museum of London; d: WAO06[1328]<529> Worked amber fragment from foundation deposit. MOLA (Museum of London Archaeology).

as being beneficial to women when dreamt about (2.5; Henig 1995: 187). Aside from beads, finger rings are the next most common type of amber artefact from Britain with seven having been recovered, including a fragment from London (MOL BWB83[184]<83>; Davis forthcoming). An amber bead appearing in a possible association with an early (pre-Boudican) male grave in London is interesting (MOL NGT00[4166]<655>; Keily 2006: 94; Watson and Heard 2006: 19): it raises questions about the indigenous Iron Age consumption of amber before and during the early Roman occupation of Britain and how this differed from the classical world (see e.g. Beck and Shennan 1991; Morris 2010: 98–9).

Amber was understood by the Romans to have an apotropaic value and this was clearly influenced by its materiality. Aside from its colour it will appear cool or warm to the touch in the cold or heat respectively due to its poor conductivity (Causey 2011: 38). It is also electrostatic, obtaining a charge when rubbed (Plin. *HN* 37.12). These material and sensual properties made it very appropriate for creating magical amulets. Of the two recent amulets discovered in London the fist-and-phallus pendant is an overtly apotropaic symbol; Varro for instance discusses young boys wearing phallic amulets around their necks as an apotropaic device (*Ling.* 7.97; Johns 1982: 63; Dickie 2003: 129; Dasen 2015: 185–7). The selection of amber for manufacturing such a device would presumably make the object more efficacious (Johns 1982: 62–4, 66). Likewise the gladiator helmet amulet, through its miniaturisation, may be made more magical (Smith 1995: 24–5; Kiernan 2009: 6–7; Wilburn 2012: 86–7), as well as gladiators being symbols of protection in their own right (Wardle 2000: 28; Bateman 2008; Marshall 2015: 3; see also Moog and Karenberg 2003). Shortly after the end of the Roman period amber still seems to have been favoured as an amulet, albeit denounced by Caesarius alongside several other 'diabolical phylacteries' (*Sermons*. 14.4; Dickie 2003: 305; Coulter 2015: 117).

Amber is often considered alongside jet as a companion 'magical' material, especially when discussed as jewellery or personal adornment (e.g. Johns 1996: 15; Swift 2009: 142; Allison 2013: 79). It is worth mentioning that although both materials are discussed by Pliny, the production and consumption of these materials through the Roman period is separated temporally. Amber, as discussed, was especially exploited during the early Empire, with trade profuse during the Flavian period. The manufacture of jet into jewellery and other portable artefacts was most popular from the third century A.D. in Britain (Allason-Jones 1996: 15). This perhaps accounts for Pliny describing the use of jet more in terms of a raw material, neglecting any mention of its use when made into decorative objects or amulets (Eckardt 2014: 112). Pliny may have been confused as to what material he was describing, as there are a number of 'black and shiny' materials that may have been employed in similar ways from different geographical sources (Allason-Jones 1996: 5, 8–9; 2005: 182). It is a much later compiler, Solinus, who specifically associates jet with Britain in the late second to third century A.D. (*Collectanea Rerum Memorabilium*. 22.2.19; Eckardt 2014: 111). It is worth emphasising the major differences between amber and jet such as their geographical sources, geological composition, and their consumption across the Empire at different points in time (Eckardt 2014: 109). In the late first century A.D., at the time Pliny was composing his Natural History, jet objects in Italy would have been as rare, if not rarer, than those of amber in Britain during the first two centuries A.D. (Allason-Jones 1996: 8; Eckardt 2014: 112). It is important not to conflate and oversimplify the meaning that objects made from these magical materials may have had to different peoples, across the Roman provinces, at different times.

Although not direct substitutes for each other, jet and amber do share great similarity in the type of artefacts they were employed to produce and the broad contexts in which they turn up across the Empire. Despite being almost polar opposites in regards to their optical qualities both amber and jet were selected for furnishing graves during the Roman period, although the rationale may, in some ways, be quite different. The selection of jet objects may be connected with its dark black colour making it a visually appropriate material, relating to the chthonic (Henig 1995: 185; Eckardt 2014: 124; Parker 2016: 107). Amber on the other hand was metaphorically associated with fire and the sun (Causey and Shepherd: 2004: 76). In recalling the myth of Phaeton's sisters, the Heliades, weeping amber after being metamorphosed into poplar trees, Diodorus Siculus states amber was 'commonly used in connection with the mourning attending the death of the young' (5.23; Causey 2011: 57). In this sense amber objects could be thought of as 'permanent tears' and as such appropriate grave gifts to accompany the deceased (Causey 2011: 55, 74). The optics of amber are much discussed but its other material qualities, especially its scent, have been perhaps somewhat overlooked in regards to magical efficacy during the Roman period.

Rubbing and Rolling: A 'Magical' Amber Die from Newgate Street

In addition to the more recent discoveries of amber amulets excavated in London (Wardle *et al.* 2017; Marshall and Wardle in prep.), a unique amber die has recently been *rediscovered* in the Museum of London's Archaeological Archive through its Arts Council England (ACE) funded programme which opens up the collections through public engagement (Davis 2014; Wardle 2017: 16–17; Figure 7.2b). This amber die is the only known example excavated from Roman Britain and was originally unearthed by the Department of Urban Archaeology in excavations at Newgate Street from 1975 to 1979 (MOL GPO75[1385]<741>; Perring and Roskams 1991) but never published. An amber die in the British Museum's collection is unlikely to be of Romano-British provenance and the largest single group of parallels are to be found in Aquileia (BM: 1772,0311.224; Strong 1966: 95; Calvi 2015).

Dice are not uncommon objects from Roman Britain but those most commonly recovered are made of bone, for example of the 81 Roman dice excavated from London 76 are manufactured from this material (Greep 1983: 242; Davis 2016; Swift 2017: 41). Aside from animal bone, dice were manufactured from a broad range of alternate materials, especially when considered across the Roman provinces. Those from Roman Britain can include metal such as copper-alloy (e.g. Niblet 1985: 124; Killock 2010: 108) and more rarely lead (e.g. Conway 1906: 112; Tyrell 2015 – although this is from an unstratified context). Less expensive versions of dice must have been commonplace: ceramic examples exist (e.g. Colchester Museum COLEM:1935.243; Allason-Jones and Miket 1984: 334) and no doubt wooden dice would have been easily produced, yet these do not survive in the archaeological record (Swift 2017: 135). More exotic, and presumably more valuable, materials can include ivory and jet (Eckardt 2014: 106) and beyond Roman Britain dice of coloured stones (such as agate and chalcedony in the British Museum's collections), as well as glass, faience and rock crystal are known (Koster 2013: 187; Swift 2017: 133).

Dice had more than a singular function within the Roman world. Most obvious would be their use in gaming, which could be used in conjunction with gaming boards or played on their own (Austin 1934: 35; Greep 1983: 235–8; Schädler 2007; Allen *et al.* 2012: 351–4; Swift 2017: 125–6). A basalt die excavated from Southwark in London is very unusual in being lettered and may have been part of a word game without the need of a board or other gaming equipment such as counters (MOL BHB00[2557]<880>; Tomlin and Hassall 2001: 397; Figure 7.2c). Another popular use of dice would have been in gambling, of which the famous painted scene from a tavern in Pompeii is testament (Ward-Perkins and Claridge 1976: no. 227; Toner 2009: 110–11; Swift 2017: 126). A more explicitly magical function of dice would have been their use in divination, although dice oracles could also employ non-cubic dice such as knuckle bones (Greek: *astragoloi*; Latin: *tali*; Martial, *Epigrams*.13.1; Graf 2005: 60; Swift 2017: 124). The archaeological evidence for dice in Britain partially supports these uses. As Swift notes it is impossible to differentiate dice used in gaming or divination, even when found in more religious contexts, such as on temple sites (Swift 2017: 125, 127). A not uncommon context in which dice are found is their purposeful inclusion in graves, sometimes in conjunction with gaming boards. An example from London was discovered in a burial from the eastern cemetery (Barber and Bowsher 2000: 135–6, 192–5). There is also evidence for their inclusion in cremations – an example from Colchester is of a ceramic cinerary urn that contained cremated remains as well as multiple bone counters and three dice (Price 1888: 37; May 1928: 275; see also Barber and Bowsher 2000: 136; Figure 7.3).

Dice of more magical materials are also found in grave contexts. Of the three jet dice known from London, two were excavated from cemetery sites and the third has no known context (MOL HOO88[788]<172>, Barber and Bowsher 2000: 225; MOLA SRP98[3254]<1816>, Wardle in prep.; MOL 1353). Jet dice are uncommon across Roman Britain with additional examples present in Canterbury (Swift 2017: 250), Gloucester (Cool 2012: 149–50) and York (Allason-Jones 1996: 49). However, jet dice were also manufactured during the medieval period and can appear very similar (Brown 1990: 694; Ottaway and Rogers 2002: 2949). Dice appearing in burial contexts have been interpreted as 'provision for the afterlife' (Barber and Bowsher 2000: 135; also Toynbee 1996: 52–3). When present in cremations they are considered to have been burnt on the funeral pyre to dispose of any malign influence the object may associate with (Barber and Bowsher 2000: 322; Atkinson *et al.* 2015: 232). Whittaker argues that the association of board games and, by extension, gaming pieces in funerary contexts held a 'deeper symbolic significance in the Roman Empire' representing transition from life to death (2004: 287–8).

Figure 7.3 Cinerary urn and contents from Colchester, including bone counters, three bone dice, fragments of fused glass and iron nails (Joslin Grave Group 81/94; © Colchester Museums).

However, considering the magical properties of jet, these dice may also be used as talismans for the dead, due to the material's apotropaic properties (Henig 1995: 185; Allason-Jones 1996; Parker 2016: 108; see also Crummy 2010 and Parker 2016 for specific imagery of objects such as jet bears and jet medusa pendants in this regard).

As well as evidence for magical and/or exotic dice there are increasing examples of bone dice being recovered from non-funerary, 'special' deposits in the Roman world. Outside of Britain a notable example is a hoard containing dice was that found embedded in the wall of a road station in Villetelle (Hérault) near the Roman site Ambrussum in Southern France (Berdeaux-Le Brazidec 2004). This cache included 43 *denarii*, two finger rings, an earring, two intaglios and four small bone dice. The interpretation of the dice is perhaps somewhat overlooked and treated as an aside in being described as objects that were easily associated with everyday activities (Berdeaux-Le Brazidec 2004: 266). These dice could well have been purposefully included as lucky talismans for the safekeeping of the cache without any previous connection to it, e.g. the result of cache being won at a game of dice. This interpretation is especially reinforced when we consider that one of two intaglios in this deposit depicts the goddess Fortuna (pers. comm. Michael Marshall).

There are now numerous examples from London of 'special' deposits, suggesting past ritual action (see Garrow

Figure 7.4 'Lyon ware' beaker deposit from Eastcheap, London (EST83), erroneously associated with a group of intaglios and a bone die (© Museum of London).

2012 for discussion). The deposition of a coin, also depicting Fortuna, beneath the mast step of the 'Blackfriars Ship' is probably the most explicit London example of a lucky talisman (Merrifield 1987: 54–7; Marsden 1994: 49; Fulford 2011: 214, n.123). Other potential 'special' deposits identified from London may not be what they seem however; for example, one discussed recently by Wallace. During excavation in 1983 a 'Lyon ware' beaker was discovered in Eastcheap associated with four intaglios and interpreted by Henig as a gem merchant's stock (1984b: 13; Figure 7.4).

Wallace's re-examination of the deposit, using Henig's original finds report, highlighted the recovery of an associated bone die, which was omitted from the eventual publication (Henig 1983: 1; 1984b: 1; Wallace 2014: 127). However, re-examination of the original site archive indicates these three types of object were not part of the same archaeological context, as previously implied and assumed. The intaglios were recovered from a separate deposit to the beaker and die, from a spatially isolated pit – context [399] (Riviere 1984: 23a). Despite the bone die and beaker fragments originating from the same pit as each other, these were deposited in separate, non-consecutive fills – contexts [508] and [520] (Riviere 1984: 25; Tim Williams: pers. comm.). The Eastcheap intaglio cache stands as an example for the need to assess primary stratigraphic data alongside the material remains themselves to identify patterning that may lead us to interpret 'material signatures' as magical acts (Chadwick 2015: 52–4).

The contexts of dice, and their contextual associations, are clearly central to our ability to interpret them as having had a special meaning and a function beyond their prosaic use (Swift 2017: 3). The amber die excavated from Newgate Street is bereft of the meaningful archaeological context that is central to Wilburn's thesis of defining magic. However, more detailed consideration of the object and its comparison against other amber dice reveals some important aspects

of its use. Although excavated from an undefined feature the context can be firmly dated to the late third to fourth century A.D. through associated material that included datable pottery and coins. This would suggest the amber die was either an heirloom, having been curated through the period, or alternatively could be a later product of German or Gaulish workshops, such as suggested for the anthropomorphic amber amulet discovered in a late grave in Colchester (Crummy 2010: 52). Although the amber die's layout of pips is standard (opposite sides of the die add up to seven) it has an unusual face arrangement. For 'standard' or 'regular' dice there are sixteen possible variant face configurations with the 'two', 'three' and 'six' faces always lying adjacent to each other (Egan 1997: 2–3). The Newgate Street amber die is of variant eight, unique amongst the assemblage of standard Roman dice excavated from London and studied by the author (Davis 2016). This is perhaps not surprising if we consider the die an imported object (Swift 2017: 208). Study of the amber die's edges reveal that these are well rounded which is in contrast to square cut amber dice from Aquileia (Calvi 2005 pl. 94, fig. 2; pl. 95, figs. 1–2; also D'Ercole 2013: 138–9 for similar worn examples). Such wear would be appropriate if it had been in use for a long time, but I suggest that this wear has also been achieved through rubbing. This rubbing may have been a purposeful act to activate the magic of the amber and bring about a desired effect on the roll. An important physical feature of amber, well-known to ancient authors, is that it elicits a pine scent when rubbed. Martial (3.65.5; 5.37.11; 11.8) and Juvenal (6.573–4) both describe the act of young girls holding or rubbing amber in the hand for its attractive scent and Fronto uses such an analogy in a letter berating his literary peers, Seneca and Lucan (*On Speeches* 4; Van den Hout 1999: 365; Casuey 2011: 66–7). The scent of amber is also mentioned by Pliny in his detailed description of the material (*HN* 37.12). This action of rubbing, of physical manipulation, may be an important step in activating the magic of the object, unlocking its agency and capacity to bring about perceived sympathetic action (cf. Parker 2016: 107; also Causey 2011: 51; Wilburn 2012: 55). If the amber die was used in gaming or gambling, activating it may be akin to the modern concept of blowing on dice to elicit a favourable outcome of the roll (see Swift 2017: 126–7 for Roman 'good and bad throws'; also Toner 2009: 38). The agency of this object, through its materiality, is interesting as Swift has argued that through the design of dice there can be a 'tension…between the desire to ensure regularity and minimise human interference, and the desire to influence the outcome to one's own profit' (Swift 2017: 123). The use of amber as a magical material may therefore be seen as different to cheating with dice that had been purposefully, physically modified (through weighting or modifying the face/s) to alter the outcome of the throw. The scent generated by rubbing the die could have had a mnemonic effect relating to a ritual function (Lodwick 2015: 56; Swift 2017: 113). This may have been a synaesthetic experience – engaging with multiple senses – in that as the amber die was physically rubbed in the hand, it would warm, produce a scent and possibly an electrostatic charge (although this would require rubbing against another material in order to generate the charge); 'sensory experience is material, it requires materiality in order to be activated' (Hamilakis 2011: 209). There is also the consideration that the amber die was used as an amulet in itself or in addition to its 'normal' use as a die for gaming etc. Traditionally amulets are thought to be objects that must be worn or tied about the body (deriving from their Greek and Latin names), as well as being highly visible objects (Dickie 2003: 304–5; Ogden 2008: 129; Wilburn 2012: 268; Dasen 2015: 185). However, we may question such an overt display of amulets. They could equally have been concealed behind or within clothing and indeed the secrecy in their secretion and possible revelation at certain times may have again been an aspect of their magical efficacy (Wilburn 2012: 262; Bohak 2015: 85, 87). This is supported by the many small carvings from Aquileia which do not have any form of suspension hole. Devoid of an attachment they would also be easier to roll and rub in the hand as suggested above, blindly feeling the contours of a figurative piece known only to the owner: a small shell, leaf, fruit or animal or indeed die for instance. Despite being un-tied and un-inscribed such magical amber objects may have acted as more than mere everyday 'passive' charms offering a 'long-term promise of well-being' (Gordon and Marco Simón 2009: 35; Causey 2011: 27; Wilburn 2012: 36). Instead they may have been serious amulets activated at specific times with explicit intent.

Burning and Burying: A 'Magical' Foundation Deposit from Canon Street

The second amber case study was excavated not far from the amber die, in Cannon Street, but some 30 years later by the archaeological unit MOLA in 2006 (Marshall 2012; 2015). Unlike the individual amber die which is bereft of archaeological context, this partially worked amber fragment was found as part of a complex assemblage inside a ceramic unguent jar (Figures 7.2d and Figure 7.5). It has been interpreted as a foundation deposit relating to a late first century A.D. building connected with industrial activity. The contents of the jar comprised of a worked fragment of amber (broken), an unset chalcedony finger ring setting (complete but unfinished/unused), the fragment of a bone military buckle (broken), a bone die (complete), an iron key with damaged head (broken), a charred fruit (burnt) and textile fragments, possibly of a bag (burnt).

Analysis of the ceramic jar by MOLA has revealed it was deliberately heated before deposition with sooting along

Figure 7.5 Unguent jar foundation deposit from Cannon Street, London (WAO06), including iron key, bone buckle, bone die, chalcedony gemstone, amber fragment and carbonised fruit (© MOLA (Museum of London Archaeology)).

one side. As argued by Marshall (2012) this assemblage is 'ritually complex' and application of Wilburn's framework can help to question and understand what it is that may be explicitly 'magical' about this deposit. Considering the many stages culminating in the act of deposition, we may wonder as to whether such a sequence and selection of objects was purely random or whether some magic formula or prescriptive spell was being adhered to (Marshall 2012). Marshall postures that 'the die was rolled into the mouth of the pot as a symbolic gamble to bring good fortune upon the new building and perhaps the start of a bold new enterprise. The iron key was then used to seal the offering in place' (2015). Even if a spell formula or instruction was not being followed, such actions suggest that the practitioner had an idea of 'what magic should look like' in order to achieve a desired result (Wilburn 2012: 63–4). The individual objects may equally all have had significance for the spell to take effect. The presence of the burnt fruit in some ways is perhaps most indicative of a magical act as organic materials are some of the most common elements of spells observed in the Greek Magical Papyri (Betz 1986; Wilburn 2012: 84, 89–90; also Gordon 2015: 142ff.). Lodwick has argued that archaeobotanical data lack integration into study of ritualised deposition and are only mentioned when obvious (2015: 56). There exist other foundation depositions in London that include limited discussion of recovered burnt ecofacts and these serve as an example of such omission (Marshall 2012). The die and key are examples of everyday, innocuous objects that find meaning through their context (Wilburn 2012: 90–4). As discussed above in regards to dice, keys can also be found in unusual contexts, such as funerary deposits, where their meaning may symbolise entry into the afterlife or protection after death (Philpott 1991: 187). Keys equally have strong iconographical associations with magic including reference in the magical papyri and their appearance on inscribed gemstones (Frere and Tomlin 1992: no. 2423.1). As well as being objects selected to engage in a specific magical rite, some may have more personal relationships to the practitioner/s of the spell. Marshall has suggested the chalcedony gemstone may have been linked to the metalworking that would take place within the building after its construction. Equally the snapped bone buckle may have been a personal object and could perhaps identify the depositor as a solider, veteran or even a craftsperson making military equipment. Unfinished militaria have since been discovered on the adjacent site at Bloomberg London (Marshall and Wardle in prep.). The ceramic pot itself may also have had a link to the intended use of the building for metalworking, as 'unguent jars' of this exact form were also used as crucibles (Marshall 2012; 2015). It is of note that many of the objects are broken or unfinished suggesting purposeful selection and manipulation as part of the magical act. Their incorporation together and subsequent burning could be interrupted as ritualised 'killing' of the objects, removing them from the 'active world in order for the magical ritual to have an effect' (Merrifield 1987: 30; Wilburn 2012: 39–40; Smith 2016: 646).

The inclusion of the amber fragment within this deposit may have additional meaning beyond its simple presence as a perceived magical material. Although all the objects excluding the fruit and possible bag were unburnt, the amber fragment may have been included in the act of heating the jar and could therefore have been selected as an intended sensory aromatic. When amber is heated or burnt it produces a pine-like, aromatic scent as is attested by Tacitus (*Germania,* 45) and Pliny (*HN* 37.11; Causey 2011: 68). The inclusion of the amber fragment may then have had an additional sensory function of producing incense necessary to the efficacy of the magical act. Causey suggests that rather than being simply destructive, the burning of amber may have 'elevated' the use of the material (2011: 69). There are numerous spells throughout the *PGM* that require purity for rituals to take effect and the heating of amber may have performed this function (Betz 1986; Smith 1995: 23). Additionally, the scent generated by this action may also have created a 'visual and olfactory bridge between the human and divine worlds' enabling engagement with the supernatural (Hamilakis 2011: 213; see also Graf 1991: 195–6; Wilburn 2012: 85, 86–7; Gordon 2015: 136).

Amber's fragrance has perhaps been somewhat omitted in regards to exploring its sensory, magical interpretation. Recent work by Brettell (2014; 2015) has explored the use of natural resins in funerary practice across Roman Britain. There are limited native British species that produce natural

exudates and so much of the resins used in high-status burials as unguents for anointing and in embalming the deceased would have been imported from the Mediterranean or Levant (Brettell *et al.* 2014: 455). Brettell's work has revealed a broader range of imported resins that were used as part of a late Roman, high status funeral 'package' than previously thought. An example from London is the late fourth century A.D. 'Spitalfields Woman' where two separate resins were found to have been applied to the body – *Pinaceae* (which includes pines, firs and larches) and *Pistacia spp* (MOL SRP98; Brettel *et al.* 2015: 643). It is of note in Britain that the Spitalfields Woman, a migrant to the province based on isotope analysis, was found with a number of jet items, emphasising consumption of a valued, local, magical material framed by an imported burial custom of body preservation (Brettell 2015: 643; see also Leach *et al.* 2010). The use of these resins in mortuary practice outside of Britain have been discovered in Italy and Greece and in some of these cases amber artefacts have been found as part of the rich ensemble of burial goods (Pearce 2013: 454; Brettell 2014: 454). Amber, as a hardened or fossilised resin, should be considered alongside these other resins and associated 'materials' as it would have produced a similar scent due to its comparative aromatic compounds (exudates) that included terpenes (Grimaldi 1996:14; Casey 2011: 29; Brettel 2014: 452; 2015: 640).

By direct association, another organic import to Britain that emitted similar odoriferous scent was the stone-pine (*Pinus pinea*). As indicated above, stone-pine was not native to Roman Britain and it is debateable as to whether it was grown and cultivated within the period (Lodwick 2017: 18). The distinctive looking cones of the stone-pine were considered 'symbols of mourning and immortality' and visually adopted into Roman material culture (Alcock 1980: 54–5). Perhaps their most obvious representation as symbols of mourning are as tombstone finials, with several having been excavated from London (Blagg 1977: 51–2; Coomb *et al.* 2015: cat no. 95, 124, 125, see also cat. no. 87 of a reclining female figure on a funerary couch possibly holding a pinecone). In regards to portable artefacts they are a not uncommon decoration for objects such as hairpins, especially in bone and metal of which there are several distinct examples from London (MOL 81.609.1, A637, BRE74[A24]<7>, LWB67[78–11]<61>). As well as being practical and decorative, such functional objects may have also served as 'indicators of social and cultural identity' (Eckardt 2014: 174). Their personal display may have shown affiliation to the eastern cults of Attis, Cybele, Bacchus, Silvanus, or Mithras of which pine cone symbolism may also allude to ideas of regeneration and rebirth amongst these 'saviour deities' (Aldhouse-Green 1976; Henig 1977: 361; Crummy 2010: 63; Lodwick 2017: 18–19).

Archaeobotanical finds of stone-pine were employed in diverse contexts and activities in Roman Britain and both pine cones and nuts have been recovered from multiple sites from Roman London in a variety of contexts (Giorgi 2000: 65–6; Bateman *et al.* 2008: 114–15; Lodwick 2015: 60–2; Lodwick 2017: 13). Within the city the remains of a single charred pine cone in the Roman Mithraeum is but one example of the use of stone-pine being burnt as part of a religious or ritual act (Shepherd 1998: 161; Lodwick 2014: 60–1). Bird has emphasised the importance of the synaesthetic experience of incenses used in such Mithraic ritual: 'in the confined space of a *mithraeum* the combination of incense with the resinous pitch from the fires would have produced a rich and intoxicating atmosphere, enhancing the spiritual experience of the initiates' (2004: 198). Another common context in which we have evidence for the consumption of stone-pine is funerary. A relevant example from London is a *bustum* burial from the southern cemetery (MOL GDV96; Mackinder 2000; see also Barber and Hall 2000). This was a rich burial containing many ceramic *tazze* and decorated lamps as well as the carbonised remains of several hundred stone-pine cones. The presence of cone scales and nuts suggested whole pine cones would have been imported and may have been consumed as part of the funerary meal at the grave side, burnt as an aromatic, or indeed both (Georgi 2000: 66; Mackinder 2010: 12). Much attention has been placed on the artefactual grave goods and their interpretation but the quantity of imported (exotic) stone-pine should not be neglected in this significant burial (Bateman 2008). These two brief examples of the consumption of stone-pine within a 'micro' and 'macro-environment' serve to highlight the convoluted, olfactory ritual smellscape that would have been experienced in Roman Britain (Derrick 2017: 76). The smellscape of a typical Roman urban centre would have been profuse with the scent of smoke generated through burning. This could have included the heating and cooking of domestic hearths, industrial workshop activity, heating of private and commercial bath buildings as well as sacrifice and incense burning in religious ceremonies. Smoke would have diffused throughout urban centres but the burning of stone-pine would have produced a distinct smell and 'sensory experience' amongst this odoriferous convergence (Morley 2015: 114; Betts 2017: 35; Derrick 2017: 77–82; Lodwick 2017: 23).

Hamilakis and Day have described the synaesthetic experience of ritual ceremony, albeit it in relation to Mycenaean and Minoan society respectively, with a mnemonic aspect to ritual occurring through intense sensory effects, especially when experienced within a restricted space (2011: 216–17; 2013: 301; see also Chadwick 2012: 296). As posited by Gell: 'we do not discover the meaning of a certain smell by distinguishing it from other smells … but by distinguishing contexts within which particular smells have a typical value' (1977: 27). Returning to our foundation deposit it is conceivable that the heating of amber appropriated an olfactory element from mainstream

religious ritual. The effluvial agency of amber was to elicit a mnemonic experience in those participating, recalling equivalent participation in religious and ritual performance – this in turn authenticated and sanctified the magical act (Hamilakis 2011: 217; Wilburn 2012: 87).

The foundation deposit from Cannon Street presents clear phenomena that afford themselves to Wilburn's criteria for defining magic within the archaeological record. First and foremost is the clear ritual action involved, through the selection and manipulation of *materia magica*, despite the absence of intangible elements such as immaterial performative acts and, especially, words. Likewise, I would argue that the manipulation of objects, such as the burning (sacrifice) of *materia magica*, and the possible use of incense draws on religious traditions to authenticate the act. Although many of the objects included in the spell are mundane, the inclusion of a fragment of magical amber lent exoticism to the efficacy of the spell. What is perhaps harder to resolve is the nature of this magical act as a private activity – a central tenet to the arguments surrounding the definition of magic (Graf 1997: 210–15; Thomassen 1999: 64–5; Versnel 1991: 178; Wilburn 2012: 18–19). Magic is often seen as being 'undertaken alone, without social approval' with negative connotations regarding 'appropriation of ritual power for personal ends' (Thomassen 1999: 65; Wilburn 2012: 18–19). There are two aspects to this magical deposit that I believe oppose such a rationale of magical practice. Firstly, the nature of the material components of the ritual suggest a number of voices or actors present in their selection and I would agree with Marshall, as discussed above, that this ritual act more likely represents the coming together of several individuals who had some relationship to the future premises. Secondly, the meaning of foundation deposits of this kind have been explained as rituals of commencement that ensure the success of the building – its safety and security for its occupants and operations (Merrifield 1987: 50–4; Smith 2016: 652). Therefore, even if we assume one individual undertook the actual act, this would be on behalf of a group of people or wider community – those sharing in the future use of the building (Thomassen 1999: 65). The preoccupation of understanding magic through the *PGM* and inscribed objects such as curse tablets would have us believe that most magic was malign, aggressive or subversive whereas 'by far the most common types of magical practice in antiquity were in a broad sense protective: medical, apotropaic or eudaemonic' (Gordon and Marco Simón 2009: 31). Wilburn's own exploration of magic across the Roman Mediterranean, with an emphasis on reviewing archaeological context, has found that despite functioning as a 'public secret' not all magical practice across the Roman world was 'marginal or viewed negatively by community members' (Wilburn 2012: 262). In light of this, when seeking to explain and define magic in Roman Britain such examples as the Cannon Street foundation deposit serve to question what 'local magic' should look like (Wilburn 2012: 256–7).

Conclusion

Hunting for magic in the western provinces of the Roman Empire is a very different exercise compared to the east with its rich heritage of *magi*, magical spells and materials. In exploring the archaeological record of Roman Britain we are perhaps looking for 'smaller-scale, worldly and mundane magical acts that emerged out of the intimate, interlinked lives and biographies of people, places, animals and different materials' (Chadwick 2015: 52). There is no doubt that amber would have been regarded as a special material in Roman Britain, however, we must be careful not to assume all amber was perceived as magical (Causey 2011: 73; Parker 2016:109 for comparison with jet). The majority of amber artefacts excavated from Britain are individual beads, often found in grave contexts, and their selection and deposition could have been purely based on amber's optical qualities, without any notion of magical meaning. However, pursuing a phenomenological appraisal of this magical material has revealed a far greater breadth to the potential meaning and agency that amber held to the Romans, or least to those on the fringe of the Empire. Such exploration is often overlooked in Roman material culture studies more generally (Eckardt 2015: 94, 125; Swift 2017: 110–13). Discussion of the magical amber die has revealed an object that would have had a well-connected, personal biography and conjures up images of a very individual expression of magic. The magical foundation deposit also demonstrates a very meaningful manifestation of magic by a small group of Roman Londoners concerned for their future and well-being. These two case studies concern two amber objects unique to the province and as such they stand in marked contrast to the normal pattern of consumption of amber artefacts. Setting amber against a broader context of *materia magica* that should include natural resins and *Pinacaea* plants has served to highlight the importance of the natural world and organic magical materials that are lost to us archaeologically. Recent studies of Roman magical practice have placed importance on perceiving what magic should *look like* in the archaeological record. By engaging with the archaeology of the senses I have not only emphasised what magic should look like, but what it should feel like and smell like too.

Department of Collections & Learning,
Colchester Museums

Acknowledgements

This paper has gestated for a long time and benefited from those who have supported my research over several years. Firstly, I would like to thank Adam Parker for originally encouraging me to speak at TRAC 2015 and for his support and patience in writing this paper. Many people have shared time and discussion with me including Nina Crummy, Hella Eckardt, Martin Henig and Stuart McKie. Ellen Swift generously provided a copy of her manuscript before publication (Swift 2017) as well as drawing my attention to additional examples of dice of unusual materials and the role of divination. I owe a special thanks to Michael Marshall (MOLA) who has shared his expertise with me. His insightful advice has greatly enriched the content of my work. I would also like to thank the following: Buxton Museum & Art Gallery: Joe Perry. Colchester Museums including the Collections & Learning team, Tom Hodgson, Emma Hogarth and Darren Stevens. The Museum of London including Helen Butler, Hazel Forsyth, Meriel Jeater, Jackie Keily, Caroline McDonald, Becky Redfern, Roy Stephenson, Richard Stroud and the Picture Library staff. Museum of London volunteers Guy Bloom, Sunny La Rose and John Walledge. The Museum of London Archaeological Archive including Adam Corsini, Kath Creed, Lucy Creighton, Francis Grew, Cath Maloney and Dan Nesbitt. MOLA (Museum of London Archaeology) including David Bowsher, Andy Chopping, Juan Jose Fuldain, Sue Hirst, Karen Thomas, Amy Thorp, Angela Wardle, Susan Wright and project managers for sharing forthcoming publications and grey literature. NAA (Northern Archaeological Associates) including Hannah Russ. PCA (Pre-Construct Archaeology) including Märit Gaimster. Institute of Archaeology, UCL: Tim Williams. Lastly, but by no means least, the London and Middlesex Archaeological Society for funding the author's research grant 'Rediscovering the Romans in the Archaeological Archive', which supported illustration and photography included in this paper.

Bibliography

Ancient Sources

Artemidorus (Translated by D. E. Harris-McCoy 2012) *Artemidorus 'Oneirocritica: Text, Translation and Commentary.* Oxford: Oxford University Press.

Diodorus Siculus (Translated by C.H. Oldfather 1952) *The Library of History Vol 3 (Books IV–V).* Cambridge, MA: Harvard University Press; London: W. Heinemann.

Fronto (Translated by C.R. Haines 1920) *The Correspondence of Marcus Cornelius Fronto Vol 2.* London: W. Heinemann; New York: G.P. Putnam's Sons.

Juvenal (Translated by S.M. Braund 2004) *Juvenal and Persius.* Cambridge, MA, London: Harvard University Press.

Martial (Translated by D.R. Shackelton Bailey 1993) *Martial: Epigrams Vol 1 (Books I–V).* Cambridge, MA, London: Harvard University Press.

Martial (Translated by D.R. Shackelton Bailey 1993) *Martial: Epigrams Vol 3 (Books XI–XIV).* Cambridge, MA, London: Harvard University Press.

Pliny the Elder (Translated by D.E. Eichholz 1962) *Natural History Vol 10 (Books XXXVI–XXXVII).* Cambridge, MA, London: Harvard University Press.

Strabo (Translated by H.L. Jones 1969) *The Geography of Strabo Vol 2 (Books III–V)*. Cambridge, MA: Harvard University Press; London: W. Heinemann Ltd.

Tacitus (Translated by J. Jackson 1962) *The Annals (Books XIII–XVI)*. Cambridge, MA: Harvard University Press; London: W. Heinemann.

Tacitus (Translated by M. Hutton, rev. by E.H. Warmington 1980) *Germania*. Cambridge, MaA: Harvard University Press; London: W. Heinemann.

Varro (Translated by R.G. Kent 1951) *On the Latin Language Vol 1 (Books 5–7)*. Cambridge, MA; London: Harvard University Press.

Modern Sources

Alcock, J.P. 1980. Classical religious belief and burial practice in Roman Britain. *Archaeological Journal* 137: 50–85.

Aldhouse-Green, M. 1976. *A Corpus of Religious Material from the Civilian Areas of Roman Britain*. British Archaeological Report 24. Oxford: British Archaeological Reports.

Aldhouse-Green, M. 2012. Cosmic dust: magic and the mundane in *Britannia Antiqua* and beyond. In M. Piranomonte and F. Marco Simón (eds) *Contesti Magici-Contextos Mágicos. Atti del Convegno Internazionale*. Roma: De Luca editori d'arte: 195–210.

Allason-Jones, L. 1996. *Roman Jet in the Yorkshire Museum*. York: Yorkshire Museum.

Allason-Jones, L. 2005. Coals from Newcastle. In N. Crummy (ed.) *Image, Craft and the Classical World: Essays in Honour of Donald Bailey and Catherine Johns*. Montagnac: M. Mergoil: 181–6.

Allason-Jones, L. and Miket, R. 1984. *The Catalogue of Small Finds from South Shields Roman Fort*. Newcastle upon Tyne: Society of Antiquaries of Newcastle upon Tyne.

Allen, T., Donnelly, M., Hardy, A., Hayden, C. and Powell, K. 2012. *A Road through the Past: Archaeological Discoveries on the A2 Pepperhill to Cobham Road-Scheme in Kent*. Oxford: Oxford Archaeology.

Allison, P.M. 2013. *People and Spaces in Roman Military Bases*. Cambridge: Cambridge University Press.

Atkinson, M. Allot, L., Doherty, A., Sibun, L. and Raemen, E. 2015. An early Roman cremation cemetery at Haslers Lane, Great Dunmow. *Transactions of the Essex Society for Archaeology and History* 6: 189–234.

Austin, R.G. 1934. Roman board games I. *Greece & Rome* 4(10): 24–34.

Bailliot, M. 2015. Roman magic figurines from the western provinces of the Roman Empire: an archaeological survey. *Britannia* 46: 93–110.

Barber, B. and Bowsher, D. 2000. *The Eastern Cemetery of Roman London: Excavations 1983–1990*. London: Museum of London Archaeology Service.

Barber, B. and Hall, J. 2000. Digging up the people of Roman London: interpreting evidence from Roman London's cemeteries. In I. Haynes, H. Sheldon and L. Hannigan (eds) *London Under Ground: The Archaeology of a City*. Oxford: Oxbow Books: 102–20.

Bateman, N. 2008. Death, women, and the afterlife: some thoughts on a burial in Southwark. In J. Clarke, J. Cotton, J. Hall, R. Sherris and H. Swain (eds) *Londinium and Beyond: Essays on Roman London and its Hinterland for Harvey Sheldon*. York: Council for British Archaeology: 162–6.

Bateman, N., Cowan, C. and Wroe-Brown, R. 2008. *London's Roman Amphitheatre: Guildhall Yard, City of London*. London: Museum of London Archaeology Service.

Beck, C. and Shennan, S. 1991. *Amber in Prehistoric Britain*. Oxford: Oxbow Books.

Berdeaux-Le Brazidec, M.L. 2004. Un dépôt de deniers découvert dans la station routière d›Ambrussum (Villetelle, Hérault). *Revue Archéologique de Narbonnaise* Tome 37: 259–75.

Betts, E. 2017. The multivalency of sensory artefacts in the city of Rome. In E. Betts (ed.) *Senses of the Empire: Multisensory Approaches to Roman Culture*. Oxford and New York: Routledge: 23–38.

Betz, H.D. 1986. (ed.) *The Greek Magical Papyri in Translation: Including the Demotic Spells*. Chicago, IL, London: University of Chicago Press.

Bird, J. 2004. Incense in Mithraic ritual: the evidence of the finds. In M. Martens and G. De Boe (eds) *Roman Mithraism: The Evidence of the Small Finds*. Brussel: Instituut voor het Archeologisch Patrimonium: 191–9.

Blagg, T.F.C. 1977. Schools of stonemasons in Roman Britain. In J. Munby and M. Henig (eds) *Roman Life and Art in Britain: A Celebration in Honour of the Eightieth Birthday of Jocelyn Toynbee*. British Archaeological Report 41. Oxford: British Archaeological Reports: 51–73.

Bohak, G. 2015. Amulets. In R. Raja and J. Rüpke (eds) *A Companion to the Archaeology of Religion in the Ancient World*. Chichester: Wiley Blackwell: 84–95.

Bradley, M. 2009. *Colour and Meaning in Ancient Rome*. Cambridge: Cambridge University Press.

Bradley, M. 2015. Introduction: smell and the ancient senses. In M. Bradley (ed.) *Smell and the Ancient Senses*. London, New York: Routledge: 1–16.

Brettell, R.C., Stern, B., Reifarth, N. and Heron, C. 2014. The 'semblance of immortality'? Resinous materials and mortuary rites in Roman Britain. *Archaeometry* 56(3): 444–59.

Brettell, R.C., Schotsmans, E.M.J.,Walton Rogers, P., Reifarth, N., Redfern, R.C., Stern, B. and Heron, C.P. 2015. 'Choicest unguents': molecular evidence of the use of resinous plant exudates in the late Roman mortuary rites in Britain. *Journal of Archaeological Sciences* 53: 639–48.

Brown, D. 1990. Dice, a games-board, and playing pieces. In M. Biddle (ed.) *Object and Economy in Medieval Winchester: Artefacts from Medieval Winchester*. Oxford: Clarendon Press: 692–706.

Brown, D. and Henig, M. 1977. Figured amber in the Ashmolean Museum, Oxford. In J. Munby and M. Henig (eds) *Roman Life and Art in Britain: A Celebration in Honour of the Eightieth Birthday of Jocelyn Toynbee*. British Archaeological Report 41. Oxford: British Archaeological Reports: 21–34.

Calvi, M.C. 2005. *Le Ambre Romane di Aquileia*. Aquileia: Associazione nazionale per Aquileia.

Causey, F. and Shepherd, J. 2004. Amber. In L. Cleland and K. Stears (eds) *Colour in the Ancient Mediterranean World*. British Archaeological Reports International Series 1267. Oxford: John and Erica Hedges: 74–7.

Causey, F. 2011. *Amber and the Ancient world*. Los Angeles, CA: J. Paul Getty Museum.

Chadwick, A.M. 2012. Routine magic, mundane ritual: towards a unified notion of depositional practice. *Oxford Journal of Archaeology* 31.3: 283–315.

Chadwick, A.M. 2015. Doorways, ditches and dead dogs – excavating and recording material manifestations of practical magic amongst later prehistoric and Roman-British communities. In C. Houlbrook and N. Armitage (eds) *The Materiality of Magic: An Artefactual Investigation into Ritual Practices and Popular Beliefs*. Oxford: Oxbow Books: 37–64.

Chapman, H. 1974. Three Roman objects from the City of London. *Transactions of the London and Middlesex Archaeological Society* 25: 273–7.

Conway, R.S. 1906 (ed.) *Melandra Castle: Being the Report of the Manchester and District Branch of the Classical Association for 1905*. Manchester: Manchester University Press.

Cool, H.E.M. 2012. Other small finds. In R. Jackson. (ed) *Ariconium, Herefordshire: An Iron Age Settlement and the Romano-British 'Small Town'*. Oxford: Oxbow Books: 134–57.

Coombe, P., Grew, F., Hayward, K. and Henig, M. 2015. *Roman Sculpture from London and the South-East*. Oxford: Oxford University Press.

Coulter, C. 2015. Consumers and artisans. Marketing amber and jet in the early medieval British Isles. In G. Hansen, S.P. Ashby and I. Baug (eds) *Everyday Products in the Middle Ages: Crafts, Consumption and the Individual in Northern Europe c. AD 800–1600*. Oxford: Oxbow Books: 110–24.

Crummy, N. 1983. *The Roman Small Finds from Excavations in Colchester 1971–9*. Colchester: Colchester Archaeological Trust.

Crummy, N. 2006. The small finds. In M. Fulford, A. Clarke and H. Eckardt (eds) *Life and Labour in Late Roman Silchester: Excavations in Insula IX*. London: Society for the Promotion of Roman Studies: 120–32.

Crummy, N. 2007. Grave goods from grave 115. In R. Casa Hatton and W. Wall (eds) A late Roman cemetery at *Durobrivae*, Chesterton. *Proceedings of the Cambridge Antiquarian Society* 95: 5–24.

Crummy, N. 2010. Bears and coins: the iconography of protection in Late Roman infant burials. *Britannia* 41: 37–93.

Crummy, N., Crummy, P. and Crossan, C. 1993. *Excavations of Roman and Later Cemeteries, Churches and Monastic Sites in Colchester, 1971–1988*. Colchester: Colchester Archaeological Trust and English Heritage.

Dasen, V. 2015. Probaskania: amulets and magic in antiquity. In D. Boschung and J.N. Bremmer (eds) *The Materiality of Magic*. Paderborn: Wilhelm Fink: 177–203.

Day, J. 2013: Imagined aromas and artificial flowers in Minoan society. In J. Day (ed) *Making Senses of the Past: Toward a Sensory Archaeology*. Center for Archaeological Investigations, Occasional Paper 40. Carbondale, IL: Southern Illinois University Press: 286–309.

Davis, G.J.C. 2014. Opening up to archaeology – the VIP way. *Museum Archaeologist* 35: 47–61.

Davis, G.J.C. 2016. Collections in focus: dice. *Museum of London Online Catalogue Group.* Available: http://collections.museumoflondon.org.uk/online/group/25454.html [Accessed: 10/01/17].

Davis, G.J.C. forthcoming. The tears of the Heliades: a catalogue of amber from Roman London. *Transactions of the London and Middlesex Archaeological Society*.

D'Ercole, M.C. 2013. *Ambres gravés: La Collection du Département des Antiquités Grecques, Étrusques et Romaines du Musée du Louvre*. Paris: Somogy: Louvre.

Derrick, T.J. 2017. Sensory archaeologies: a Vindolanda smellscape. In E. Betts (ed.) *Senses of the Empire: Multisensory Approaches to Roman Culture*. London, New York: Routledge: 71–85.

Dickie, M.W. 2003. *Magic and Magicians in the Greco-Roman World*. London: Routledge.

Eckardt, H. 2014. *Objects and Identities: Roman Britain and the North-Western Provinces*. Oxford: Oxford University Press.

Egan, G. 1997. Dice. *Finds Research Group Datasheet* 23, London: Roman Finds Research Group.

Frere, S.S. and Tomlin, R.S.O. (eds) 1992. *The Roman Inscriptions of Britain, Volume II, Fascicule 4*. Stroud: Administrators of the Haverfield Bequest.

Fulford, M. 2001. Links with the past: pervasive 'ritual' behaviour in Roman Britain. *Britannia* 32: 199–218.

Garrow, D. 2012. Odd deposits and average practice. A critical history of the concept of structured deposition. *Archaeological Dialogues* 19(2): 85–115.

Gell, A. 1977. Magic, perfume, dream … In I. Lewis (ed.) *Symbols and Sentiments: Cross-cultural Studies in Symbolism*. London: Academic Press: 25–38.

Giorgi, J. 2000. The plant remains – a summary. In A. MacKinder (ed.) *A Romano-British Cemetery on Watling Street: Excavations at 165 Great Dover Street, Southwark, London*. London: Museum of London Archaeology Service: 65–6.

Gordon, R.L. 2015. From substances to texts: three materialities of 'magic' in the Roman imperial period. In D. Boschung, and J.N. Bremmer (eds) *The Materiality of Magic*. Paderborn: Wilhelm Fink: 133–76.

Gordon, R.L. and Marco Simón, F. (eds) 2009. *Magical Practice in the Latin West: Papers from the International Conference Held at the University of Zaragoza, 30 Sept.–1 Oct. 2005*. Leiden: Brill.

Graf, F. 1991. Prayer in magic and religious ritual. In C. A. Faraone and D. Obbink (eds) *Magika Hiera: Ancient Greek Magic and Religion*. New York, Oxford: Oxford University Press: 188–213.

Graf, F. 1997. *Magic in the Ancient World* (Translated by Philip Franklin). Cambridge, MA, London: Harvard University Press.

Graf, F. 2005. Rolling the dice for an answer. In S.I. Johnson and S.T. Struck (eds) *Mantikê: Studies in Ancient Divination*. Leiden: Brill: 52–97.

Greep, S. 1983. *Objects of Animal Bone, Antler, Ivory and Teeth from Roman Britain*. Unpublished PhD Thesis: University of Cardiff.

Grimaldi, D.A. 1996. *Amber: Window to the Past*. New York: Harry N. Abrams, Publishers, in association with the American Museum of Natural History.

Hamilakis, Y. 2011. Archaeologies of the senses. In T. Insoll (ed) *The Oxford Handbook of the Archaeology of Ritual and Religion*. Oxford: Oxford University Press: 208–25.

Henig, M. 1977. Death and the maiden: funerary symbolism in daily life. In J. Munby and M. Henig (eds) *Roman Life and Art in Britain: A Celebration in Honour of the Eightieth Birthday of Jocelyn Toynbee.* British Archaeological Report 41. Oxford: British Archaeological Reports: 347–66.

Henig, M. 1983. *A Cache of Roman Intaglios from Eastcheap, City of London.* Unpublished Department of Urban Archaeology Report: Museum of London: 1–9.

Henig, M. 1984a. Amber amulets. *Britannia* 15: 244–6.

Henig, M. 1984b. A cache of Roman intaglios from Eastcheap, City of London. *Transactions of the London and Middlesex Archaeological Society* 35: 11–15.

Henig, M. 1995. *Religion in Roman Britain.* London: Batsford.

Johns, C. 1982. *Sex or Symbol: Erotic Images of Greece and Rome.* London: British Museum.

Johns, C. 1996. *The Jewellery of Roman Britain: Celtic and Classical Traditions.* London: UCL Press.

Keily, J. 2006. The accessioned finds. In S. Watson and K. Heard (eds) *Development on Roman London's Western Hill: Excavations at Paternoster Square, City of London.* London: Museum of London. Archaeology Service: 92–107.

Kiernan, P. 2009. *Miniature Votive Offerings in the North-west Provinces of the Roman Empire.* Mainz: Franz Philipp Rutzen.

Killock, D. 2010. *An Assessment of an Archaeological Excavation at 28–30 Trinity Street, London SE1, London Borough of Southwark.* Unpublished Pre-Construct Archaeology Report.

Koster, A. 2013. *The Cemetery of Noviomagus and the Wealthy Burials of the Municipal Elite.* Nijmegen: Museum Het Valkhof.

Leach, S., Eckardt, H., Chenery, C., Muldner, G. and Lewis, M. 2010. A Lady of York: migration, ethnicity and identity in Roman Britain. *Antiquity* 84(323): 131–45.

Lodwick, L. 2015. Identifying ritual deposition of plant remains: a case study of pine cones in Roman Britain. In T. Brindle, M. Allen, E. Durham and A. Smith (eds) *TRAC 2014: Proceedings of the Twenty-Fourth Annual Theoretical Roman Archaeology Conference.* Oxford: Oxbow Books: 54–69.

Lodwick, L. 2017. Evergreen plants in Roman Britain and beyond: movement, meaning and materiality. *Britannia* 48: 1–39.

Mackinder, A. 2000. *A Romano-British Cemetery on Watling Street: Excavations at 165 Great Dover Street, Southwark, London.* London: Museum of London Archaeology Service.

Marsden, P. 1994. *Ships of the Port of London: First to Eleventh Centuries AD.* London: English Heritage.

Marshall, M. 2012. *Analysis Report of the Roman Registered Small Finds from The Walbrook Building (WAO06) – St. Swithin's House, Walbrook House and Granite House, London EC4.* Unpublished MOLA report.

Marshall, M. 2015. *Artefacts and the Study of Life in Roman London* (Gresham College Lecture Transcript). London: Museum of London. Available: https://www.gresham.ac.uk/lectures-and-events/artefacts-and-the-study-of-life-in-roman-london [Accessed: 09/01/17].

Marshall, M. and Wardle, A. forthcoming. *The Roman Small Finds, Coins, Glass and Textiles from the Bloomberg Excavations 2010–14.* London: MOLA (Museum of London Archaeology).

May, T. 1928. *Catalogue of Roman Pottery in the Colchester and Essex Museum.* Cambridge: Printed on behalf of the Colchester Corporation at the University Press.

McCarthy, M.R., Padley, T.G. and Henig, M. 1982. Excavations and finds from The Lanes, Carlisle. *Britannia* 13: 79–89.

McCarthy, M.R., Padley, T.G. and Henig, M. 1983. An amber knife handle from Carlisle. *Britannia* 14: 267–9.

McKie, S. 2016. Distraught, drained, devoured, or damned? The importance of individual creativity in Roman cursing. In M.J. Mandich, T. Derrick, S. González-Sánchez, G. Savani and E. Zamperini (eds) *TRAC 2015: Proceedings of the Twenty-Fifth Annual Theoretical Roman Archaeology Conference, Leicester 2015.* Oxford: Oxbow Books: 15–27.

Merrifield, R. 1987. *The Archaeology of Ritual and Magic.* London: Batsford.

Moog, F.P. and Karenberg, A. 2003. Between horror and hope: gladiator's blood as a cure for epileptics in ancient medicine. *Journal of the History of the Neurosciences* 12.2: 137–43.

Morely, N. 2015. Urban smells and Roman noses. In M. Bradley (ed) *Smell and the Ancient Senses.* London, New York: Routledge: 110–19.

Morris, F.M. 2010. *North Sea and Channel Connectivity During the Late Iron Age and Roman Period (175/150 BC–AD 409.* British Archaeological Reports International Series 2157. Oxford: Archaeopress.

Morris, J. 2011. *Investigating Animal Burials: Ritual, Mundane and Beyond.* British Archaeological Report 535). Oxford: Archaeopress.

Niblett, R. 1985. *Sheepen: An Early Roman Industrial Site at Camulodunum.* Council for British Archaeology R esearch Report 51. London: Council for British Archaeology.

Nixon, T., McAdam, E., Tomber, R. and Swain, H. (eds) 2002. *A Research Framework for London Archaeology 2002.* London: Museum of London Archaeology Service.

Ogden, D. 2008. *Night's Black Agents: Witches, Wizards and the Dead in the Ancient World.* London, New York: Hambledon Continuum.

Ottaway, P. and Rogers, N. 2002. *Craft, Industry and Everyday Life: Finds from Medieval York.* Archaeology of York Fascicule 17/15. York: York Archaeological Trust and Council for British Archaeology.

Parker, A. 2016. Staring at death: the jet *gorgoneia* of Roman Britain. In S. Hoss and A. Whitmore (eds) *Small Finds and Ancient Social Practices in the Northwest Provinces of the Roman Empire.* Oxford: Oxbow Books: 98–113.

Pearce, J. 2013. Beyond the grave: excavating the dead in the late Roman provinces. In L. Lavan and M. Mulryan (eds) *Field Methods and Post-Excavation Techniques in Late Antique Archaeology.* Late Antique Archaeology 9. Leiden: Brill: 441–82.

Perring, D. and Roskams, S. 1991. *The Archaeology of Roman London Volume 2. Early Development of Roman London West of the Walbrook.* Council for British Archaeology Research Report 70. London: Museum of London and the Council for British Archaeology.

Philpott, R.A. 1991. *Burial Practices in Roman Britain: A Survey of Grave Treatment and Furnishing, A.D. 43–410.* British Archaeological Report 219. Oxford: Tempus Reparatum.

Price, J.E. 1888. *Contents of the Private Museum of Anglo-Roman Antiquities Collected by Mr George Joslin at Colchester, Essex.* Colchester: W. Wiles & Son.

Riviere, S.J. 1984. *Excavations at 27–29 Eastcheap (Sitecode EST83) Archive Report.* Unpublished Department of Urban Archaeology Report: Museum of London.

Schädler, U. 2007. The doctor's game – new light on the history of ancient board games. In P. Crummy, S. Benfield, N. Crummy, V. Rigby and D. Shimmin (eds) *Stanway: An Élite Burial Site at Camulodunum*. London: Society for the Promotion of Roman Studies: 359–75.

Shepherd, J.D. 1998. *The Temple of Mithras, London: Excavations by W. F. Grimes and A. Williams at the Walbrook*. London: English Heritage.

Smith, A. 2016. Ritual deposition. In M. Millett, L. Revell and A. Moore (eds) *The Oxford Handbook of Roman Britain*. Oxford: Oxford University Press: 641–59.

Smith, J.Z. 1995. Trading places. In M. Meyer and P. Mirecki (eds) *Ancient Magic and Ritual Power*. Leiden, New York: E.J. Brill: 13–27.

Spekke, A. 1957. *The Ancient Amber Routes and the Geographical Discovery of the Eastern Baltic*. Stockholm: Goppers.

Strong, D. 1966. *Catalogue of the Carved Amber in the Department of Greek and Roman Antiquities*. London: British Museum.

Swift, E. 2003. Transformations in meaning: amber and glass beads across the Roman frontier. In G. Carr, E. Swift and J. Weekes (eds) *TRAC 2002: Proceedings of the Twelfth Annual Theoretical Roman Archaeology Conference*. Oxford: Oxbow Books: 48–57.

Swift, E. 2009. *Style and Function in Roman Decoration: Living with Objects and Interiors*. Farnham: Ashgate.

Swift, E. 2017. *Roman Artefacts and Society: Design, Behaviour and Experience*. Oxford: Oxford University Press.

Thomassen, E. 1999. Is magic a subclass of ritual? In D.R. Jordan, H. Montgomery and E. Thomassen (eds) *The World of Ancient Magic: Papers from the First International Samson Eitrem Seminar at the Norwegian Institute at Athens, 4–8 May 1997*. Bergen: Norwegian Institute at Athens: 55–66.

Tomlin, R.S.O. and Hassel, M.W.C. 2001. Roman Britain in 2000: II Inscriptions. *Britannia* 32: 388–400.

Toner, J. 2009. *Popular Culture in Ancient Rome*. Cambridge: Polity.

Toynbee, J.M.C. 1996. *Death and Burial in the Ancient World*. Baltimore, ML, London: Johns Hopkins University Press.

Tyrell, R. 2015. Dice. In M. Atkinson and S. Preston. Heybridge: A late Iron Age and Roman settlement. Excavations at Elms Farm 1993–5. Volume 2. *Internet Archaeology 40*. Available: http://dx.doi.org/10.11141/ia.40.1 [Accessed: 16/01/17].

Van den Hout, M. P. J. 1999. *A Commentary on the Letters of M. Cornelius Fronto*. Leiden: Brill.

Van den Hurk, L.J.A.M. 1986. *The Tumuli from the Roman Period of Esch, Province of North Brabant*. Nijmegen: Katholieke Universiteit te Nijmegen.

Versnel, H.S. 1991. Some reflections on the relationship magic-religion. *Numen* 38(2): 177–97.

Wallace, L. 2014. *The Origin of Roman London*. Cambridge: Cambridge University Press.

Ward-Perkins, J.B. and Claridge, A. 1976. *Pompeii AD79*. Bristol: Imperial Tobacco.

Wardle, A. 2000. Funerary rites, burial practices and belief. In A. MacKinder (ed.) *A Romano-British Cemetery on Watling Street: Excavations at 165 Great Dover Street, Southwark, London*. London: Museum of London Archaeology Service: 27–30.

Wardle, A. 2017. The Roman finds group autumn conference: town and country in southern Britain reviews. Section Three – Finds from Roman London. *Lucerna* 52: 16–17.

Wardle, A., Richardson, B. and Cubit, R. 2017. The registered finds (excluding coins). In MOLA *10 Trinity Square London EC3: Post-excavation Assessment and Updated Project Design*. Unpublished MOLA report.

Wardle, A. forthcoming. The accessioned finds. In M. McKenzie and C. Thomas (eds) *The Northern Cemetery of Roman London: Excavations at Spitalfields Market, London E1, 1991–2007*. London: Museum of London Archaeology.

Watson, S. and Heard, K. 2006. *Development on Roman London's Western Hill: Excavations at Paternoster Square, City of London*. London: Museum of London. Archaeology Service.

Whittaker, H. 2004. Board games and funerary symbolism in Greek and Roman contexts. *Papers and Monographs from the Norwegian Institute at Athens 7*. Bergen: Norwegian Institute at Athens: 279–302.

Wilburn, A.T. 2012. *Materia Magica: The Archaeology of Magic in Roman Spain, Egypt, Cyprus and Spain*. Ann Arbor, MI: University of Michigan Press.

Williamson, G.C. 1932. *The Book of Amber*. London: Ernest Benn.

Abbreviations

PGM = Papyri Grecae Magicae (see Betz 1986)
MOL = Museum of London

Linking Magic and Medicine in Early Roman Britain:
The 'Doctor's' Burial, Stanway, Camulodunum

Nicky Garland

Introduction

In the study of ancient healing there is a conceptual divide between a wholly 'scientific' understanding of medicine and the ritual and/or mystic comprehension of magic. Influenced by our modern understanding and definition of these practices (Baker 2002), 'magic' is considered mystical, symbolic or irrational, while medicine is viewed as scientific, functional or logical. Currently viewed as a dichotomy, this division originates from the application of post-Enlightenment and Western thought, which disregards the archaeological evidence and is projected onto the past. These deep-set and erroneous divisions are nowhere more apparent than in the understanding of transition periods. Previous research has argued that Iron Age Britain was occupied by informal spiritual healers (e.g. druids), while the Roman Empire brought a superior form of medicine that usurped previous indigenous tradition (Carr 2002: 58–9; Baker 2016: 555). In recent years, research into other cultures, such as Ancient Egypt, has demonstrated the overlap between magical rites and a variety of medical treatments (e.g. Draycott 2012; Forshaw 2014). In Roman studies, the complex relationship between magic and medicine has also begun to be revealed, including in the influence of religious experience as part of the healing process (e.g. Jackson 1988: 138–69; 2011: 245–8; Cruse 2004: 107–39; 2013) or the votive deposition of medical instruments within liminal contexts, such as rivers or graves (e.g. Baker 2002; 2004). This paper argues that it is anachronistic in current scholarship to separate magical and medical practices in the Roman Empire and that a modern comprehension of these practices only masks a deeper understanding of healing in the past.

The Doctor's Burial at Stanway (Figure 8.1) provides a unique opportunity to explore our current understanding of the relationship between ancient magical and medical practice. Dating to some point between just before or after the Claudian invasion of Britain, the grave contained a series of objects interpreted as having either a 'magical' or 'medical' function. This research focuses on examining the specific archaeological context of these items, the materials from which they were constructed and their use in burial rites and reveals the diversity of the function and significance of these grave goods. By challenging past interpretations and exploring new understandings this paper allows us to deepen our knowledge of the interaction between medical and magical practice in Late Iron Age/Early Roman Britain.

Medicine is defined here as the understanding, treating and healing of disease, while magic is characterised (in this context) as the attempt to influence events using supernatural forces, in part for the purpose of healing. In a recent TRAC session on magic and medicine, in which an early version of this paper was first presented, the organisers argued that medicine and magic may 'have fulfilled a very similar function … [as] both aim to improve an individual's situation through the application of specialist, learned, or arcane knowledge and often required the use of specialist equipment pertinent to specific situations' (Derrick and Parker 2016). In the present study 'healing' is used to refer to the overall process of improving a person's situation, whether referred to as specially 'magical' or 'medical' in past research. Ultimately it is the goal of this paper to illustrate how magic and medicine were not competing or parallel entities but in fact formed part of the same system of past behaviour. However, it is somewhat necessary to follow these distinctions here to allow the incorporation of past research within the framework of this paper and to illustrate how modern assumptions may have influenced our interpretations of the Late Iron Age and early Roman periods.

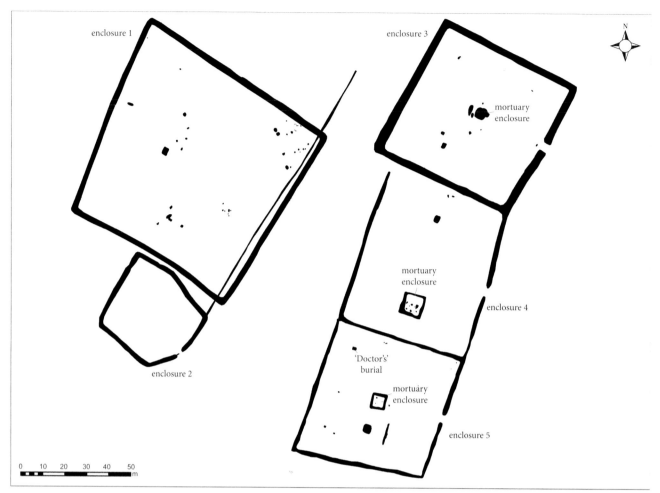

Figure 8.1 The Stanway enclosures in the mid-first century A.D. (After Crummy et al. 2007: 11, fig. 8).

Iron Age 'Magic' vs Roman 'Medicine'

The interpretation of 'healing' in Iron Age and Roman studies have traditionally followed two different trajectories. Whilst Iron Age archaeology in Britain has concentrated more on shamanistic practices, divination and 'magic', within a wider sphere of ritual activities (Carr 2002; Creighton 2000), Roman studies has focused on what might be considered traditional forms of 'medicine' that have been paralleled closely to modern medical practices (Baker 2002; 2004; 2016). This divergence has developed somewhat due to a lack of physical evidence for healing in the prehistoric period, in comparison to the wealth of material culture and literary texts associated with studies of Romano-British 'medicine' (see below). Ethnographic data, however, suggests that ritual or magic acts in some societies may leave little trace in the archaeological record (Chadwick 2015: 38). This disparity in evidence likely reflects the ephemeral nature of magical or medical practices in the Iron Age, rather than to suggest that these activities were not present at all. Moreover, this split in understanding is also heavily influenced by what we, as a modern society, may consider familiar or unusual.

'Magic', for example, is often used as a general term to encompass a wide range of past practices that remain unexplained or are peculiar to modern interpretation, while more recognisable evidence, such as the appearance of surgical instruments in the Roman period, are immediately recognised and interpreted as serving a similar purpose to modern tools without an appropriate level of evidence to support this claim (e.g. Baker 2002: 23–6). These divisions endure despite the realisation by Carr (2003: 58–9) among others, that Iron Age and Roman medical practices were both very much unlike their modern counterpart.

The division between how healing is perceived in the Iron Age and Roman periods has partly led to the assumption that Roman medicine was in some way superior to what had preceded it in Late Iron Age. However, in Britain several recent osteological studies have suggested that the results of 'healing' practices were not as clear-cut as previously understood (Redfern 2010; Redfern *et al.* 2011; 2012). Regional studies of human remains in Dorset have suggested that in both periods 'highly skilled practitioners were able to successfully treat a range of fractures and by doing so, minimised the patient's risk of impairment'

(Redfern 2010: 465). Moreover, an examination of sub-adult dietary practices, suggests that dental health decreased from the Late Iron Age to early Roman period and that cases of specific metabolic diseases, such as scurvy and rickets, rose in number (Redfern *et al.* 2012). These changes have been attributed to changes following the Roman invasion of Britain including the introduction of urban living, new diets from the Continent and the migration of populations from elsewhere in the Empire (Redfern *et al.* 2012: 1257). Although regionally specific, these studies demonstrate the pitfalls of assuming the primacy of Roman medicine and that an increase in health and well-being did not simply correlate to the introduction of new technologies. What follows is an examination of current research for 'healing' in both the Iron Age and Roman periods, to recognise possible modern prejudices in our understanding and recognise the wider context in which 'magical' and 'medical' practices were carried out.

The investigation of healing in the Iron Age is less concerned with identifying medical procedures or activities and concentrates mainly on magical or ritual activity during this period. The examination of shamanism was, and continues to be, a strong theme for understanding magic and healing in prehistoric contexts (e.g. Reynolds 2014) and in Iron Age studies, shamanic practices have been linked to the creation of trance-like states to conjure imagery later inscribed onto Late Iron Age coinage (Creighton 1995; 2000). Where attempts are made to identify specific 'healers' in the Iron Age, the presence and role of 'druids' are frequently discussed. Little is known about this social or religious group, as testified by the mere two pages dedicated to the subject in Cunliffe's (2005: 573–4) *Iron Age Communities in Britain*. Much of the evidence for *druides* comes from descriptions given in contemporary and later Roman historical sources. Druids were described by Julius Caesar, for example as overseeing religion, acting as judges or arbitrators in disputes, and teachers and keepers of knowledge, potentially of a medical nature (Julius Caesar, *Gallic Wars*, 4.13).

However, detailed examination of the historical sources suggests that the role of druids was likely complex and may have shifted over time (Webster 1999). Webster (1999: 10) argues that by the mid-first century A.D., druids were not 'philosophers, supra-tribal judges and arbiters, but magicians and seers' (*contra* Creighton 1995). Iron Age scholars continue to find it uncomfortable to identify and interpret the *druides* from the archaeological record. This is in part due to the controversial relationship between archaeologists and modern druidism (e.g. Pluskowski 2011) but also because of the wider complexity surrounding so-called 'Celtic' origin myths (often referred to as the 'Celtic controversy'), to which druidism is often connected (e.g. Hingley 2011). Despite this hesitance, recent research by some archaeologists (Carr 2002; Fitzpatrick 2007) has

attempted to classify the types of material remains that could be associated with these religious specialists. The evidence includes objects associated with divination and sacrifice, whether human, animal or the deliberate breakage of objects (Carr 2002: 60–4), the presence of spoons, the appearance of lunar symbols on short swords or headdresses within burials (Fitzpatrick 2007: 290–305). Concerning evidence specifically related to 'healing', Fitzpatrick (2007: 305–6) highlights the presence of surgical instruments within a small number of burials on the Continent (e.g. Bavaria, see de Navarro 1955), as well as the surgical kit found in the 'Doctor's' Burial at Stanway. Furthermore, Iron Age studies have been particularly useful in the recognition that healing and magical practices fell within a wider network of ritual activity and belief in this period (Carr 2002; Chadwick 2015: 38–40). This includes evidence for structured deposition (Brück 1999; Hill 1995), metalwork production (Budd and Taylor 1005; Giles 2007) and the deposition of animal remains (Merrifield 1987). It is through examining the evidence for these practices where a greater understanding of magic and/or medicine in the Iron Age will be established.

The study of Roman medicine draws upon a wealth of historical sources, epigraphy, and material remains, represented either by evidence for possible hospital type structures (usually within military contexts) or, more frequently, the identification and examination of 'Roman-style' medical tools (Baker 2002: 16). The evidence for surgical instruments, which is of direct relevance to the Doctor's burial at Stanway, has received a great deal of attention over the last 30 years, particularly by experts such as Ernst Künzl (1996) and Ralph Jackson (1988; 2007). While past research has made comparisons between Roman and modern medicine and suggested the homogeneity of medical practice across the Roman Empire, the ground-breaking research of Patty Baker, among others, has done much to dispel these notions and highlight the complexity and diversity of medicine across the Roman world. The idea of homogeneity across the Empire comes, in part, from the assumption that local societies would have adopted more 'civilised' and 'effective' Roman medical practices once drawn into the Empire (Baker 2016: 555), but also due to the similarity between medical evidence, particularly surgical instruments, found from contexts across Europe.

Surgical instruments, for example, have been found in as stray finds from Lauriacum in Austria (Gostencnik 2013), in graves from Viminiacum, Serbia (Spasić-Djurić 2005), from a shipwreck off the coast of Sicily (Gibbins 1988) and mostly recently, during the excavation of a grave in Ljubljana, Slovenia (RT Slovenia 2017). In Britain, a number of isolated medical instruments have been uncovered (including by the Portable Antiquities Scheme, e.g. a spoon probe from Hampshire (PAS: HAMP-59BD53), a ligula from Milton Keynes (PAS: CAM-44E605), and a scoop from Darlington (PAS: NCL-DB00F3)), however, the original context of many of these items is unknown and consequently there is little information as to their origin or deposition in the archaeological record. In a small number of cases single instruments have been found within burials (Baker 2016: 559), while the only extensive surgical kit was recovered from the Doctor's burial at Stanway (Jackson 1997). Baker's (2011; 2016) identification of regional distinctions within the available evidence has led her to argue that that the practices and beliefs surrounding 'Roman' medicine were adapted and imported into existing traditions in different provinces.

This merging of practices is apparent in part by the multifunctional nature of so-called 'medical' items in the provinces during the Roman period. This is evident in the ritual deposition of surgical instruments in Gaul, the Rhineland and the Upper Danube (Baker 2004) or the (re)use of collyrium stamps in Gaul as amulets or votive offerings across Gaul (Baker 2011), which each reflecting earlier traditions. This diversity should partly be expected, as contemporary Roman scholars held variant philosophies about the body, illness and treatment during this period (Baker 2016: 556). Studies of Roman medicine have also gone some way to explore the context of religious belief as part of the healing process. Gods with specific healing powers, such as Asclepius, were worshipped throughout the Greek and Roman world and evidence for religious dedication suggests that these deities formed part of the wider remit of healing practices during this period.

In Britain, a number of stone altars and dedications to Asclepiushave been uncovered from military sites in the north (e.g. *RIB* 609, Burrow in Lonsdale; *RIB* 1052, South Shields; *RIB* 1072, Lanchester) and, in more rare instances, in areas in the south (Jackson 2011: 246). Baker (2013: 563–4) argues that the worship of these deities may suggest that people placed more trust in the gods rather than medical procedures or alternatively that they felt that medical practitioners needed divine assistance to heal effectively. Despite the acceptance of ritual and religious practice as part of the healing process, the division between 'medical' and 'magical' in Roman studies is still paramount. This is apparent in the separation in these texts between the discussion of 'traditional' forms of medicine, typified by surgical instruments, and religious intervention (e.g. Jackson 2011 – 'Divine medicine' vs 'Mortal medicine'). Cruse's (2004) research into Roman medicine, further typifies this division. From the outset Cruse (2004: 13) defines "rational medicine' [as a] type of medical practice which looks for the cause of a disease before prescribing its treatment', while "irrational' is used to describe magic and superstition'. Despite the growing evidence for complexity, our modern perception of these topics continues to be projected onto Roman practices of magic and medicine.

Table 8.1. Oppositions in modern social constructs

Medicine	Magic
Logical	Illogical
Domestic	Ritual
Scientific	Mystical
Functional	Symbolic
Rational	Irrational

Dichotomies and Dualities

The relationship between magic and medicine is problematised by the equation of the former with the mystical and/or illogical, and the latter with the rational and/or scientific (Table 8.1). This dichotomy may be compared directly to the debate surrounding the separation of 'domestic' and 'ritual' practices in prehistoric contexts (Brück 1999; Bradley 2005). Brück (1999: 314) has argued that the separation of activities into 'ritual' or 'non-ritual' categories has been shaped by western post-Enlightenment thought; a distinction that may not have held any validity in the prehistoric past. Although it is tempting to label archaeological material as either 'ritual' or 'domestic' in nature, by assuming these practices are placed in direct opposition to one another, both physically and conceptually (Bradley 2005: 28). Bradley has shown that these facets were in fact closely linked in many elements of prehistoric life including the interconnection between mortality and agriculture, the construction of domestic buildings and cosmology and the evidence for feasting as a commemorative or ritual act, among others. Similar ideas have been shown to be paralleled in the Roman world, both in consideration that ritual activity associated with temple sites formed part of daily 'domestic' life (Ghey 2005: 111–2) or that magic in Roman Britain was exhibited partly by structured deposition of so-called 'rubbish' within domestic contexts (Chadwick 2015). An interpretive framework that distinguishes the ritual from the secular poses a significant set of problems in understanding the past (Brück 1999: 336–7) and reinforces the assumption that domestic or secular activities are usually assumed to have functionality, while ritual practice implies strictly the non-functional or symbolic (Brück 1999: 314–6). Furthermore, by compartmentalising these oppositions, our interpretation of the archaeological evidence is also often separated, both chronologically, as different phases of activity within a single site, and spatially, as discrete zones of activity where different activities took place (Bradley 2005: 28–30).

Chronological distinctions between so-called 'rational' and 'non-rational' acts are exacerbated by transition periods. For example, while it has been argued that magic and religion played a key role in medicine in Ancient

Egypt, medical advances in these areas have usually been attributed to 'rational' Greek medical practitioners, with little understanding of how they related to ritual practice during this period (David 2004). Past research into the Late Iron Age–Early Roman transition in Britain led to the association of called 'rational' and 'non-rational' acts with simplistic identity categories, such as 'Romans' and 'natives'. Post-colonial critique of basic identity groups has been prevalent in Roman studies since the late 1990s and, due to the complexity of the archaeological evidence, has been thoroughly rejected by British scholars (e.g. Freeman 1993; Mattingly 1997: 2004; Woolf 1997). The comfortable dichotomy between 'Romans' and 'Natives' continues to be present in some debates surrounding transitional periods and/ or areas on the edge of the Empire, where society is easily separated between the invading and dominant 'Roman' Empire and indigenous and suppressed 'native' groups. Recent exploration of this dichotomy along frontier zones has begun to break down these aggregate categories and unmask the complex interactions within and between social groups, both before and during the early Roman period (e.g. González Sánchez and Guglielmi 2017). The 'Doctor's' burial forms an important example of this dichotomy. Interred in Britain at some point across the Late Iron Age/ Early Roman transition period, much of the discussion of the burial and the associated grave goods has fallen into one of two comfortable categories; reflecting either 'indigenous' or 'Roman' culture (see discussion in Jackson 2007). This simplicity is reflected in the interpretation of the material culture; 'magical' items often associated with 'indigenous' traditions, while 'medical' objects, such as the surgical instruments are associated with imported Roman culture, despite limited archaeological parallels.

As discussed above, the available evidence suggests a greater complexity in health and wellbeing than has been previously understood. Our separation of domestic from ritual has become impractical in our understanding of social spheres of the past (Moore and Armada 2012: 32) and our interpretations should move away from the belief that past actions were simply either 'domestic' or 'ritual'/'functional' or 'symbolic' and towards one which sees these practices as part of a continuum of activity that combine each in a single framework (Chadwick 2012: 303). This paper asserts that the concepts of magic and medicine represent a duality in the Late Iron Age/early Roman Britain; i.e. that those practices were intimately entwined in both their conception and application. Despite this complexity, understanding the relationship between magic and medicine should not be viewed as a problem to be overcome but instead an opportunity to examine clues as to the origin and nature of these activities in Britain and, in turn, the wider Roman world (e.g. Bradley 2005: 37).

Approach

Understanding the complexity of magic and medicine within the Late Iron Age/Early Roman transition period requires an explicit and precise approach. This paper aims to explore, both theoretically and methodologically, how we may better address the overlapping nature of these two concepts in a nuanced and detailed manner. Part of this approach reflects the individual nature of religious and ritual action. McKie (2016: 15) argues that religion is a personal experience, subject to specific circumstances and differing interpretations as to how its practiced. The use of magic and/or medicine in the past would have equally been subject to changing conditions and was situated to meet an individual's specific needs in times of crisis. As such, this research focuses on the deep analysis of a single instance where evidence for magical and medical practice are uncovered together (the 'Doctor's' burial), but with a view to consider closely the specific context of this material culture, as well as the site in general.

The examination of cremation burials often relies on evidence of grave goods to examine and understand the status of the deceased. This is, in part, due to the small quantities and poor quality of the human remains found within these burials, which make it extremely difficult to determine age, sex or pathology. There is a danger in these instances that we view grave goods purely as personal items, whereas the meanings behind these objects were diverse and reflect specific motives and individual approaches to burial sites (Parker-Pearson 2003: 94). At Stanway, the consequences of this approach are seen in assignment of monikers such as the 'Doctor' or 'Warrior' to some of the burials which contain specific grave goods. Grave goods likely reflected the actions and motivations of those who participated in the mortuary rites (such as family members, officiants), perhaps to emphasise the distinctiveness of the deceased (Giles 2012, 171), or as a form of symbolic communication to those who witnessed the funeral (Ekengren 2013, 175). However, this does not mean that the interpretations of such objects are not useful for understanding the deceased and their role in wider society. Garrow and Gosden (2012: 196) suggest that when objects were deposited in burial contexts 'their meanings and association were actually more visible than usual' and thus reflect a desire to construct an appropriate image after death. Moreover, in his discussion of warrior burials, Hunter (2005: 43) has argued that the creation of a desired image may have 'intended to appeal to or influence contemporary audiences'. Moreover, in burial contexts the individual biographies of grave goods themselves must also be considered. While a coin may be viewed purely as currency during its lifetime, it takes on a different meaning and purpose when deposited in a hoard or in a watery context. In addition, similar items may be interpreted in different ways by different societies in different contexts. Iron Age coinage, for example, may have been viewed as a ceremonial or ritual object rather than as currency (e.g. Haselgrove and Wigg-Wolf 2005). We must not assume that the function and/or meaning behind magical and/or medical items as used during their 'lifetime' directly reflect their importance within a burial or in fact that this importance was viewed by different groups in the same way.

Two themes strongly link our understanding of the concepts of magic and medicine and allow us to explore connections between the practice of each: materiality and performance. Materiality is defined in this research as the physical manifestation of beliefs or customs through artefacts and monuments (after Houlbrook and Armitage 2015: 3–5). The detailed examination of medical/magical objects allows us to interpret how they may have been used in the past and how this interpretation can aid in understanding belief structures, rituals or ways of thinking. The context of these 'things' is key to considering how similar material culture, from an isolated perspective, could be used in different ways and with separate intentions. Furthermore, we should consider not just what these objects were used for, but also what the composition and properties of these materials may tell us about their significance in the past (Ingold 2007). The examination of performance has, in the past, been undertaken in order to reconstruct mortuary rituals associated with Late Iron Age burial contexts (e.g. Fitzpatrick 1997; 2000; Giles 2012) and through an understanding of material culture and context, has the ability to understand the choreography of death and the wider social implications of these actions (Giles 2012: 175–213). The archaeology of performance encompasses both human action and the 'things' of the material world (DeMarrais 2014: 161) and explores how each interacted with and inhabited spaces and places. Practice based approaches (e.g. Bourdieu 1977; Giddens 1984) can help to understand the agency of past objects and how, through performance, they formed part of a wider social and physical structure. Performance also has the ability, on the large-scale, to transform and alter the social and political status quo (e.g. Johnston *et al.* 2014: 206–7) and on an individual or small-scale, to understand the meaning behind specific actions, such as those associated with ritual and belief systems (e.g. Hull 2014: 166). Exploring performance on multiple scales allows us, in part, to understand how material culture was interpreted and used by multiple scales of society (Garland 2016).

The Stanway Burial Site

Excavated between 1987–97, the burial and ritual site at Stanway lay on the western edge of the town of Colchester (For summary see Crummy *et al.* 2007: 7–14). The mortuary site consisted of two phases (see Figure 8.1); initially a large

enclosure (1), erected in the second half of the mid-first century B.C., followed by three enclosures constructed in a row (3–5). Enclosure 3 was built at some point between *c.* A.D. 35–45, while Enclosures 4 and 5 were constructed as a pair between *c.* A.D. 40–50, coinciding with the Claudian invasion of Britain in A.D. 43. The Late Iron Age mortuary enclosure (1) was preceded by a Middle Iron Age farmstead and droveway (Enclosure 2), occupied between 200–50 B.C. Of note were two currency bars, which were purposefully placed along the edge of the Middle Iron Age enclosure ditch (Crummy *et al.* 2007: 26–68).

A number of cremation burials were uncovered within each of the Late Iron Age and Early Roman enclosures. Each of the burials contained a similar range of deposited grave goods (e.g. locally made and imported food and drink containers), but were varied in the number of distinct items present (e.g. gaming boards) and the ways in which these goods were deposited in the burial, suggesting diverse and complex mortuary activities. An underground burial chamber was present in several of the enclosures, in addition to several small pits that contained pyre-related debris and broken grave goods but no cremated human remains. Areas of burning and small enclosed areas within Enclosures 3–5 also possibly denoted pyre sites. A number of the cremation burials contained significant graves goods, which have been argued to 'signify something about the occupation of the dead person: a 'doctor' (with surgical instruments), a presumed 'warrior' (with spear and shield) and a literate person (with an inkwell)'(Crummy *et al.* 2007: 12).

The 'Doctor's' Burial

The focus of this research is one of the so-called 'significant' burials; the 'Doctor's' Burial (CF47. For full details see Crummy *et al.* 2007: 201–53). Located in the northwestern corner of Enclosure 5, the burial pit measured 2.1 m long, 1.75 m wide and between 0.5–0.7 m deep. Small quantities of cremated human remains (158.1 g) were discovered along the western edge of the grave (Figure 8.2). The base of the grave was divided into two levels, possibly with a wooden suspended floor, to accommodate a full amphora found standing along the western edge. An unusual assemblage of items, interpreted as 'medical' or 'magical' objects were uncovered as grave goods including a surgical kit, items used for divination and a gaming board (Crummy 2002). The excavators suggest that the grave goods as a whole were divided spatially within the grave into three main groups; a dining service in the southeast, vessels for the preparation of food and drink in the northeast and personal items to the west (Crummy *et al.* 2007: 202). While some of the goods were stacked on top of each other in the grave, eleven cups and platters were found upright and separate from one another, as if purposefully placed to hold food and drink. The importance of these items and their placement within the

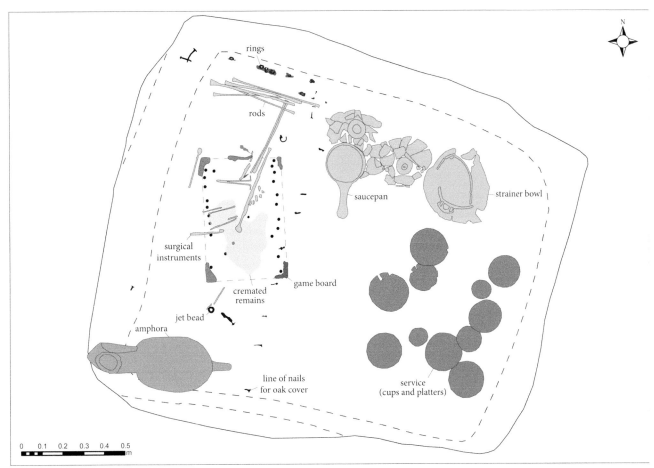

Figure 8.2 The 'Doctor's' Burial (After Crummy et al. *2007: 203, fig. 98).*

grave will be discussed in greater detail below. The burial was dated to between A.D. 40–50 based on the presence of two brooches and Gallo-Belgic pottery, including a Samian bowl, recovered from the grave (Crummy *et al.* 2007: 212). The deceased therefore may have been interred immediately before, during or after the Claudian invasion of Britain.

Materiality

The following section focuses on elements of the material culture recovered from the 'Doctor's' burial and, through comparison and the interpretation of function and meaning, attempts to understand the belief system or customs associated with these objects. A critical analysis of the original interpretations for the material culture is forwarded to demonstrate the multiple meanings and functions for the recovered items. These sections are necessarily divided between magical and medical 'things' to reflect the original interpretation of these grave goods and discuss each objectively in turn, however, it is apparent that there is a convincing overlap between the functional and ritual use of these objects.

Magical 'things'

The foremost evidence for 'magical' practice within the 'Doctor's' burial is represented by the discovery of a set of eight iron and brass rods. Found in close proximity to one another in the western part of the grave, the rods formed an intriguing set of four long, four short and differentially four brass and four iron implements (Table 8.2). Although the objects themselves tell us little about how they were used in the past, the excavators argue that the potential for grouping suggests their role as divination rods, used to call for 'divine assistance' possibly as part of a suite of medical practices (Crummy *et al.* 2007: 228). The excavation volume cites a passage by Tacitus, which describes how the Germani practised divination by slicing a branch into strips (representing the rods), each marked with different signs, which are then thrown 'completely at random onto a white cloth' (Tac. *Germ.* 10). Although there were no obvious markings on the rods themselves, it was argued that the difference in their composition (i.e. long, short, iron, bronze) and elements that may have not survived in the archaeological record (e.g. different coloured tags), may have provided the 'signs' alluded to by Tacitus (Crummy

Table 8.2. Typological groupings of rods in the 'Doctors' Burial (Crummy et al. 2007: 224, table 35)

	Four iron	Four brass	Four long	Four short	Two long iron	Two short iron	Two long brass	Two short brass
Iron short (CF47.23a)	X			X		X		
Iron short (CF47.23b)	X			X		X		
Iron long (CF47.23b)	X		X		X			
Iron long (CF47.23b)	X		X		X			
Brass short (CF47.23b)		X		X				X
Brass short (CF47.23b)		X		X				X
Brass long (CF47.23b)		X	X				X	
Brass long (CF47.23b)		X	X				X	

et al. 2007: 229). This interpretation relies on few direct comparisons for these items and a single ancient source discussing rites undertaken in a completely different part of the world. Moreover, while the grouping of the items is intriguing, this analysis assumes that they form a single set, rather than multiple sets, perhaps collected over a lifetime and deposited in the same context. The specific context of the rods may be key to their interpretation. Similar wooden rods, sometimes described as wands, also appear as grave goods in Christian medieval burials and are argued to symbolise pilgrimage or acts as protective symbols (Gilchrist 2008: 126–7). Crucially, Gilchrist (2008: 127) has suggested that their origins lie with earlier burial customs and shamanistic practices, visible in the recovery of iron, bronze and wooden rods from Viking burials of the ninth and tenth centuries. In the context of the Doctor's burial, these rods may reflect symbols of earlier traditions, reformulated in light of contact with the Roman world.

The rods were recognised as resembling the form of a *stylus* (i.e. a blunt rounded terminal at one end with a spatula eraser at the other). It was suggested that the size of the rods (307–402mm), in comparison to Roman examples, made them too large to be used as such, but they may have been used to make marks on the ground (Crummy *et al.* 2007: 224). Considering the date of the burial and the wider context of the site, the link between these items and literacy is perhaps overlooked in the original excavation volume. In a pre-literate society the use of a writing object may have been considered a particularly unusual, powerful and/or magical skill. Creighton (2000: 165–6) has argued that the use of lettering in Late Iron Age Britain, particularly in the context of inscribed coinage, would have been viewed as 'profoundly disturbing, magical, awesome'. Where evidence for literacy does exist in Late Iron Age Britain, including in the production of inscribed Iron Age coinage, it is usually associated with *oppida* (Fitzpatrick 2007: 305–6), which are interpreted as centres of social change and the emergence of elite society (Garland 2017). At Stanway, the importance of writing as an emerging skill is apparent in an adjacent

and contemporary burial containing an inkwell and the presence of graffiti on pottery from one of the chamber burials. These writing implements could have been afforded a certain importance as magical items in their own right and perhaps were used to write on the ground by ritual specialists following the creation of trance like states to conjure images inscribed into 'Celtic' artwork (Creighton 1995: 2000). The inclusion of such powerful implements in the burial may have reflected the power of the individual buried and/or may have been used by others as protective symbol for the journey of the deceased.

Eight copper alloy rings, stacked on top of one another, were found in the western part of the grave. The rings were of two different forms (plain – three; terret-form – five) and measured approximately 31–34.5mm in diameter. The lack of consistency in the rings, in contrast to the neat pattern found for the rods, may suggest that they were not originally part of the same set and have been used, lost and added to over time (Crummy *et al.* 2007: 229). Few parallels are known for the rings, apart from perhaps Late Iron Age horse fittings (Crummy *et al.* 2007: 231). It is feasible that these objects were intentionally created for such a function and later repurposed and deposited in the grave. A recent study of Iron Age and Roman terrets (Lewis 2015: 272–5) suggests that while these objects frequently appear as part of hoards and votive assemblages on both wet and dry ground, they rarely appear in graves, apart from in the chariot burial tradition of North Yorkshire. While the inclusion of these objects within this grave is likely tied to their reuse rather than original function, this does not negate their initial importance. The imagery of chariots and horses, particularly on coinage, has been linked to emerging power structures in the Late Iron Age Britain (Creighton 2000: 101–5) and it may be that this original function was imbued into its later importance. Although evidence is sparse, three interesting interpretations for the rings were presented; to hold specific magical or medicinal compounds, as 'divining' rings forming a set with the eight rods or as part of a wooden rattle (Crummy *et al.* 2007: 231). The surviving evidence indicates that the rings were each attached to a narrow leather thong and in turn a larger wooden object, of which only trace elements survived. Although we should proceed with some caution due to the fragmentary nature of the evidence and the lack of contemporary parallels, this may suggest the rings were attached to a central shaft as a rattle. Some evidence for musical instruments, albeit in rare instances, have been recovered from Iron Age contexts, although these are usually blown instruments (e.g. the Carnyx, see Hunter 2001). In Roman contexts, 'noise making objects' such as bells, have been associated with religious ceremony and included as votive items within burials possibly to ward off evil spirits (Crummy 2010: 53–54; Parker, this volume). This function would be appropriate within this burial context, where ensuring the undisturbed passage of the deceased to the afterlife may have been a key goal.

The final implement found within the grave that may have been used in magical practice is a single jet bead. The bead, which measured 35mm in diameter, had a central hole and appeared to be similar in size and shape to the iron rings discussed above. Jet beads are rare in Iron Age and early Roman context in Britain and mostly date to the fourth century A.D. (Eckardt 2014: 117). These beads have, in different contexts, been used as a dress accessory, a healing object or possibly an item for divination (Allason-Jones 1996: 15). Pliny the Elder records both the mystical nature but also the healing power of jet as a material. Pliny (*HN* 36.142) suggests that it was 'ignited by water and quenched by oil', but used to drive off snakes, relieve 'suffocation of the uterus', toothache or tumours and detect fake illness. Although based on a small number of examples, the association between jet and funerary contexts has been highlighted in a number of studies (e.g. Crummy 2010) and led to the interpretation in some contexts that jet was an apotropaic material that served as a 'form of protection against physical and supernatural malignant influences interfering with the deceased' (Parker 2016: 108). Eckardt (2014: 116) also argues that there is a strong link between jet and women, visible in the ancient sources but also the types of personal adornment that were made from this material (beads, bracelets, hairpins). Within the context of the Doctor's burial this item was unusual and rare, however, the examples above demonstrate the multi-faceted nature of jet and that the bead likely served more than a single purpose. This valuable item held more than one role, linking personal adornment and status with the ability to call divine assistance and perform acts of healing.

In isolation, the understanding of these magical objects within the 'Doctor's' Burial conjures familiar interpretations. However, through comparison to similar items in different contexts it has been shown that these 'things' may have served more than one purpose; simultaneously or sequentially used for both magical and medical practices in the ancient world. The multi-faceted nature of these objects also demonstrates the complexity in understanding their life cycles (construction, use, disuse) and how they may have 'functioned' over time.

'Materia Medica'

Initial and continued attention on the 'Doctor's' burial has stemmed from the discovery of an impressive surgical kit (e.g. Johnson 2008), which thus far represents the earliest known set of medical instruments found in Britain and 'one of the earliest *instrumentaria* found anywhere in the Roman world'(Crummy *et al.* 2007: 245). The details of the kit have been discussed in great detail by Ralph Jackson (1997; 2007) and are summarised in the table below. In addition to these metallic items, Jackson (2007: 246) argues that 'implements of wood, bone, leather, reed and feather, as well as an assortment of bandages, dressings, pads, plugs, ligatures, threads and sutures' may have also been present but have not have survived in the archaeological record. Although usually discussed as a single kit, the medical instruments show great diversity in composition, size, construction style and decoration (Table 8.3). Most known Roman *instrumentaria* are composed of copper alloy or an amalgam of copper alloy and copper, however, there are eight single piece iron instruments from Stanway, which are found only rarely in Roman contexts (Jackson 2007: 246–7). Jackson (2007: 247–9) parallels these iron objects, as well as other items (e.g. a saw), with 'Celtic' examples and consequently it is acknowledged that many of the tools may represent the use of local technology and preferences for material (Baker 2012: 559). Jackson (1997; 2007) and Crummy (2002) argue that this overlap of local technology and Roman form suggests that medical ideas were exchanged following the Roman invasion, although there is some disagreement whether these ideas were adapted rather than adopted in full (Baker 2013: 102–3).

Although the excavation volume provides a detailed analysis of the medical instruments, the life cycle (production, use, disuse) of these objects is somewhat overlooked, leading to several assumptions that may affect our interpretation of these objects. Firstly, the construction of these items was likely undertaken by a highly knowledgeable and skilled craftsperson, which as stated above, were likely using local technologies. There has previously been little examination of how local traditions may alter our interpretations of these objects. Although the instruments were found in a Roman-period grave, the 'Doctor's' burial represents the culmination of 100 years of funerary occupation. For Iron Age contexts, it has been argued that the production of iron would have been associated with a violent and destructive transformation of one material (ore) to another (metal), which may have been considered a magical or alchemistic practice (Budd and Taylor 1995; Giles 2007: 396). Furthermore, it has

Table 8.3. Summary of surgical kit from the 'Doctor's Burial (after Crummy et al. 2007: 250–2)

Instrument	Composition	Length (mm)	Weight (g)	Comments
Scalpel (CF47.26)	Iron	169	26.8	Heavily corroded
Scalpel (CF47.27)	Iron	188	25.4	Heavily corroded
Saw (CF47.28) – broken into 4 pieces	Iron (blade), composite (handle)	112	6.7	Handle comprised of iron with flanking plates of wood/bone sandwiched between bronze outer platers.
Combined sharp & blunt hook (CF47.29)	Bronze	144	10.0	Double ended retractor
Combined sharp & blunt hook (CF47.30)	Iron	140	12.3	Double ended retractor. Degraded wood remains & textiles attached to instrument
Retractor? (CF47.31)	Bronze	166	21.2	Single piece instrument
Fixation forceps (CF47.32)	Bronze	133	22.3	Spring forceps with looped head
Forceps/tweezers (CF47.33)	Iron	81	5.7	Tweezers or small forceps, possible pointed jaws
Needle? (CF47.34)	Iron	127	27.4	Single piece instrument with stout handle. Textile found adhered to handle
Needle? (CF47.35)	Iron	109	9.6	Textile found adhered to handle.
Needle? (CF47.36)	Iron	55.4	3.5	
Scoop probe (CF47.37)	Bronze	132	3.7	'Drawing' lines on grip
Handle (CF47.38)	Bronze	91.3	7.9	Thin sheet of iron component affixed with rivet to 1 end – possibly composite instrument
Knife (CF47.39)	Iron	97.7	19	Short solid handle & acutely angled blade

been suggested that the production and use of iron acted as wider metaphor for life and death during this period (Giles 2007), which may link this material directly to the burial context in which it was found. If the creation of the medical instruments were representative of a belief system stemming from the Late Iron Age, then they may have been viewed as particularly important and/or magical items. Duplicating Roman forms of medical instruments in iron may have involved the use of foreign knowledge and accordingly amplified these magical properties.

The unique collection of these instruments in one context has led to their interpretation as representing a single kit of a medical practitioner, however, the idiosyncratic nature of the kit may suggest that these objects were never intended to represent a single group but were collected over a lifetime. Individual objects may have commissioned by local craftspeople, were exchanged with incomers to Britain or collected during travels across the Continent. Jackson (2007: 245) admits that if the 'saw, ?handled needles, ?retractor or iron forceps/tweezers been casually found, or even excavated, as single unassociated finds, it is most unlikely that any medical function would have been ascribed to them'. Baker (2002: 23–4; 2004: 4–5) has argued that modern assumptions are sometimes used to interpret the function of Roman medical instruments and that some items usually attributed as medical tools could have served multiple purposes such as craft tools or

toilet instruments. A spatula probe, for example, could be used as a 'cautery, blunt dissector, tongue depressor, probe and pharmaceutical tool' (Baker 2004: 5). By viewing the medical instruments as individual items we begin to comprehend that they may have been multi-functional in nature, holding both practical and symbolic functions that may have changed over time.

The deposition of the metal instruments, as well as other metal objects, within the grave may have also held a particularly significance within this context. The ritual deposition of metal objects is common in both Iron Age and Roman contexts (e.g. Hingley 2006), however, the deposition of iron was also a pre-established tradition at Stanway, visible in the deliberate placement of two iron currency bars within the Middle Iron Age enclosure ditch (Crummy *et al.* 2007: 33). Similar practices involving medical instruments have also been identified in Roman period sites. Baker (2001: 57–8; 2002: 25) has shown that medical instruments, along with other objects associated with the body (shoes, armour), were ritually deposited by soldiers in certain contexts and may have been viewed as having magical powers. The importance of the instruments in this context, potentially both as metal items and medical objects, is demonstrated somewhat by their specific positioning on the board game within the grave. The location of the objects suggests that they were individually and purposefully placed as part of the mortuary ritual (Crummy *et al.* 2007: 250) and formed part of a wider performative element to the funerary practice (discussed below).

Although much previous research has focused on the surgical instruments, there was another object within the grave that was interpreted as being of medical use; the strainer bowl. Typically, a Late Iron Age vessel, the copper alloy bowl had a spouted strainer and a spill plate and measured *c*. 210mm in diameter (Crummy *et al.* 2007: 221). A small piece of vegetal matter that survived in the spout of the bowl was identified as a tea-like drink made with Artemisia (common name mugwort/wormwood) and sweetened with honey (suggested by the presence of bee pollen), to counteract the bitter taste of *Artemisia* species. It has been argued, based on the presence of the surgical instruments, that the *Artemisia* held a predominantly medicinal purpose, possibly as a herbal remedy, which required specialist knowledge in its preparation (Wiltshire 2007: 395–7). Some ancient and more recent texts discuss the uses of Artemisia as a medicinal compound. Pliny the Elder (*HN* 25.36) states that it was 'used for the cure of female complaints', while a number of ailments are listed by Grieve (1931) for its use, including as an emmenagogue (a substance that stimulates or increase menstrual flow), a diaphoretic (to induce perspiration), a nervice (to calm nerves) or a diuretic (to induce the passing of urine). The use of the strainer bowl to prepare a curative beverage may suggest that it was linked to the placement of the dinner service in the eastern part of the grave. A number of ancient sources recommended the consumption of certain foods to improve overall health including honey and sugar, wholemeal bread and bone marrow (Cool 2009: 67–8, 77, 91). Set upright as if to hold food and drink, the service may serve as a metaphor for the benefits of nutrition to greater health.

While it is tempting to interpret the strainer bowl as of purely medical value, to reflect the inclusion of the surgical instruments, alternative interpretations of these items may be of more relevance to this specific context. Sealey (1999: 121–2), for example, has argued that, due to the dating of excavated examples, 'spouted strainer bowls were used to serve a native drink, Celtic beer'. Pliny (*HN* 14.109) states that Artemisia and honey, among other garden plants, were also used to flavour wine. Together these interpretations suggest consumption for pleasure rather than health and suggest a close connection to the funerary rites themselves. The consumption of food and drink as funerary feasts has been long recognised in Late Iron Age Britain, particularly in East Anglia (e.g. Ralph 2007). The presence of the dinner service within the burial may also suggest the presence of a funerary feast and if placed within the grave containing food and drink, likely represented an offering to the deceased rather than reflecting medical knowledge. Likewise, in examining the specific deposition of the strainer bowl it should be noted that, in contrast to the dinner service, the

bowl was stacked with a number of items in the north-eastern part of the grave (Crummy *et al.* 2007: 202). While the use of the bowl did not form part of burial rites, perhaps instead its overall symbolic value was the reason for its deposition.

Although interpreted above as either for medical use or ritual feasting, the understanding of the strainer bowl may be a reflection of personal perspective. To the uneducated the preparation of such drinks could be construed as the creation of a 'potion' within an unfamiliar vessel (akin to a cauldron) and viewed as a magical practice designed to cure ailments. Alternatively, while the preparation of food, such as meat or bread, is comprehended by all as a simple act of cooking, the understanding that these items were of health benefit is also a reflection of specific knowledge.

Other Practice: the Game Board

Although the discussion above has focused on the material culture attributed specifically to 'magical' or 'medicinal' practice, the variety of grave goods implies a complex picture of activity connected to this burial. One particular addition, the game board, requires some specific consideration as it forms a particularly unusual item in Iron Age and Romano-British burials. The importance of the game board as part of the burial is demonstrated by the placement of cremated remains directly on its surface followed by the rods and surgical instruments. This sequence of events will be discussed in greater detail below. The board game was a wooden object measuring approximately 38 × 56cm and constructed using two pieces of maple, joined by brass hinges and reinforced by copper alloy sheets at the corners (Crummy *et al.* 2007: 217). The game, as shown in similar examples, appears to have folded in half, presumably reflecting its portability. Only small sections of original wood surface of the board survived *in situ*, particularly those parts held within the metal fixtures. The surviving wood did illustrate that the edge of board game had been painted in a chevron pattern and that the playing surface was recessed in order to create a raised lip around the edge of the board (Crummy 2007: 352). Twenty-six glass counters (13 white, 13 blue) were found arranged as if placed on the surface of the board (Crummy *et al.* 2007: 217).

Unusually, and despite the relative rarity of these items, this was not the only board game found within the Stanway mortuary site. Similar boards were found within a chamber burial (Crummy *et al.* 2007: 126, BF6.26) and the Warrior's burial (Crummy *et al.* 2007: 186–90, BF64.28–29), both located within Enclosure 3. A number of Claudio-Neronian examples are also known from the surrounding area including the cemetery at King Harry Lane, Verulamium (Stead and Rigby 1989: 109, Grave 117) and Baldock (Stead and Rigby 1986: 68–9, Burial 6). Later instances, including the discovery of a board game found within a second- to third-century burial at Trentholme Drive, York (Wenham 1968), suggest that these ideas may have continued beyond early Roman Britain and became, in some areas at least, a more pronounced and prolonged tradition. There is extensive debate as to the origins of gaming boards in Britain, namely whether they came from prehistoric/indigenous origins or if they arrived through contact with the Roman world (e.g. Hall and Forsyth 2011). In this instance, there is disagreement whether this was a 'Celtic' board game (Schädler 2007) or one, which in the 'possession of Romanised Britons provides strong evidence in favour of the playing of a Roman game of some sort' (Crummy *et al.* 2007: 359). Within the context of the Doctor's burial a more nuanced approach, one which does not classify the makers, players or owners of this game as either 'Romanised' or 'Celtic', is more useful.

The association with game boards and gaming pieces with burial contexts is well established in Iron Age and Romano-British contexts, as well as other cultures including the Scandinavian Iron Age and the wider Graeco-Roman world (Whittaker 2004; 2006). Although the inclusion of game boards, as well as other grave goods (e.g. weapons), in burials was in part attributed to their general value as objects, the symbolic association between the progression of a game and progression through life and death may suggest that they held a wider meaning in mortuary beliefs of the period (Whittaker 2006, 106–8). In the 'Doctor's' burial this association is somewhat reinforced by the purposeful laying out of the board (from its unused/folded state) and the positioning of the counters in in preparation for the start of the game. Detailed examination of the post-depositional movement of the board and counters has led to the (albeit tentative) argument that some early moves may have been played while the board lay in the burial, including purposefully inverting a single counter (Crummy 2007: 356–8, B13). These moves may represent the abrupt way the deceased departed the community and the unfinished business of a life not fully lived, or the start of a journey to the afterlife that only the deceased could complete. The fact the game was played by at least two people suggests that part of this journey was not undertaken alone but required outside assistance. The purposeful actions, which each contributed to the performance of the burial, operated in conjunction with the items discussed above and represent the intertwining of magical and medical agency.

Performance

The following section focuses on examining the performance of specific mortuary practices undertaken for the 'Doctor's' burial. Due to a nuanced understanding of the deposition and movement of many of the grave goods, it is possible to undertake a detailed analysis of the performance of burial and suggest the specific roles that magical and medical objects played in those actions. The following section focus initially on the activities associated with the deposition of the cremated human remains and grave goods within the

burial and explores how magic and medicine were deeply intertwined within this context. This discussion is followed by an understanding of these practices as part of our wider knowledge of mortuary rituals and societal beliefs during the Late Iron Age and Early Roman periods.

The Doctor's Burial

In some instances, it is possible to reconstruct the sequence of deposition in certain parts of the grave due to the physical association between certain objects. It is uncertain, however, in what order the three groups of grave goods (service, vessels for food and drink, personal items) were interred, however, it is surmised that the groupings of these artefact represent three different stages of mortuary activity. Following the preparation of the grave for burial (see below), a specific order of actions was undertaken.

The laying out of the dinner service, each placed upright and capable of holding food/drink, suggests that ritual feasting may have formed a component of this burial rite. The items in the grave may have represented a feast prepared and consumed by the mourners (either physically or symbolically) or contained items to sustain and aid the deceased in their journey into the afterlife. This evidence links to the presence of similar services uncovered in other graves at Stanway (Crummy *et al.* 2007: 431–2) and the deposition of broken pottery in the enclosure ditches, which may also result from feasting associated with burial events and later commemorative acts (Biddulph 2015). The sequence associated with the 'personal' items' in the west of the grave, including the magical and medical objects, presents the most interesting sequence of activities. The purposeful acts undertaken at the graveside suggests that healing, and generally improving the situation of the deceased, was a major motivator in the burial rites and the use of certain implements. The placement and setting out of the game board, onto which the cremated remains were placed, implies a deep connection between this item and the deceased. By playing a series of opening moves, a participant in the funeral may have acted as a surrogate or intermediary for the departed to start their journey into the afterlife. The presence of game boards in other burials at Stanway may suggest that the placement of the board was a sign of familial connection to others buried in this area or that it was generally a signifier of power and status within the wider community. Directly on top of the cremated remains, a rod (stylus?) was placed, followed by the laying out of surgical instruments and subsequently two more rods. If we are to accept that the action of placing the rods implies a protective symbol, then it must be assumed that least one of the participants had specific knowledge of the use and interpretation of these items.

The positioning of the rods and surgical instruments, as well as their similar composition, suggests a close connection between the two and that perhaps, in this context at least, the surgical instrument formed part of the protective power instilled during the mortuary rites. The ability of the surgical instruments to heal, potentially due to the 'magical' processes that resulted in their creation (from ore to iron), may have contributed to the symbolic significance of these items and aided in improving the situation of the deceased.

Other items of healing, including the jet bead, possibly some compounds (including *Artemisia*?) and the objects used to prepare them (strainer bowl, saucepan), all suggest that the participants were eager to provide some supernatural assistance for the deceased, perhaps to heal whatever malady caused their death, or more likely to help them transfer from one state of being (life) to another (death). Chanting and the use of a rattle(?), which was also deposited in the grave, may have been used to ward off evil spirits and protect the passage of the deceased into the afterlife. At the end of the funeral the grave was closed by placing an oak cover over the grave goods. It is probable that earth was heaped on the oak cover, resulting in the collapse of the strainer bowl and Samian bowl and the breaking apart of the flagon (Crummy *et al.* 2007: 212). With the final acts of burial complete, the collected assembly of mourners retreated from the eastern entrance of the enclosure.

MICRO-LEVEL EVENTS IN THE 'DOCTOR'S' BURIAL
Grave excavated and prepared for final deposition of human remains and grave goods

WEST
Game board unfolded and placed in the western part of the grave.
The white and blue counters laid out on the game board.
A series of opening moves are made on the game board.
The cremated human remains (mixed with some ash) placed on the game board and over some of the counters.
One of the long iron rods (styli?) placed on the cremated remains.
The surgical instruments are carefully laid out one by one.
Two small rods positioned over surgical instruments (one iron, one brass).
Remainder of the rods laid in a bundle across the outer ends of the two short rods.
The eight rings (rattle?) are deposited to east of the bundle of rods.
A garment was spread over the board game and the deposited items.

CENTRAL/SOUTHERN
Eleven cups and platters containing food and drink placed in the central and southern part of the grave.

NORTH-EASTERN
Flagon, strainer bowl, copper alloy pan, and samian bowl stacked in one another in the north-eastern corner of the grave.

Last Actions
Oak cover placed on top of the grave goods.
Amphora placed in western end of grave

It is important to consider the deposition of the human remains and grave goods as part of a wider funerary process. These actions required the movement of the deceased's body to the site, possibly its storage in a central mortuary enclosure (for an unspecified period) and finally its cremation on a funeral pyre. The relative heat required to efficiently and overwhelmingly cremate a human body requires temperatures greater than 800°C (McKinley 2013). This process would have rivalled the temperatures and heat produced during metal production and may have destroyed any material (e.g. *Artemsia*, jet etc) placed on the pyre with the body. In a similar vein this intense burning may have been considered a dramatic and transformative process of the deceased into a new state of being. Following this change, and ultimately the cooling of the pyre, a small selection of the cremated remains (156 g of possible 2 kg produced, approx. 8% of total) were identified, collected and ultimately deposited within the grave along with the other grave goods. The remaining cremated remains may have been discarded or taken as a memento by the mourners back to their homes. The placement of the medical and magical items may have, through their significance and healing power, formed part of this specific and transformative process that started with the removal of the body from the settlement and led to its cremation and burial. Each of these events aided in the transition of the deceased from life to the afterlife.

MACRO-LEVEL EVENTS IN ENCLOSURE 5
Body transported to the enclosure and displayed and/or stored in mortuary enclosure.
Pyre material gathered from surrounding area and constructed within mortuary enclosure.
Body placed on pyre and lit.
Six to seven hours of burning to fully cremate the body.
Leave pyre to cool (perhaps overnight).
Collection of selected cremated remains from funeral pyre.
Excavation of grave and placement of cremated remains and grave goods (see above).
The marking of the burial (in some cases with a mound).
Commemorative feasting and deliberate deposition of broken pottery in the enclosure ditches/mortuary enclosures.

The Stanway Enclosures and the Surrounding Landscape

Although the above analysis tells us much about the use of magical and medical items in the context of the burial, we must situate the performance within a wider understanding of the site and the surrounding landscape. The construction of the Stanway mortuary enclosures represented a significant investment, in both time and energy, by the community and marked a repeated tradition, stemming originally from the construction of Enclosure 1 almost 100 years prior to the 'Doctor's' burial. A number of high status and important burials have been uncovered at Stanway, including a number of large chamber burials and other significant burials, such

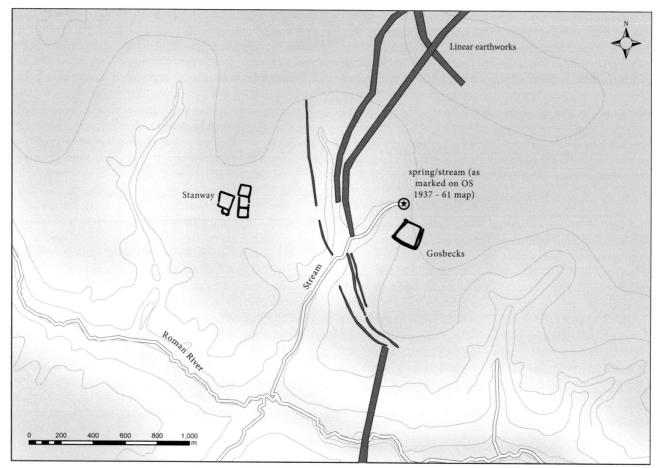

Figure 8.3 Stanway and the surrounding landscape (© Lesley Davidson).

as the 'Warrior' burial and 'Inkwell' burial. The mortuary activities undertaken at Stanway were likely not isolated in themselves but built within, and formed part of, a wider set of belief structures. This is demonstrated by the presence of 'non-burial' features within each enclosure, which were similar to the central burials but contained no human remains (Crummy *et al*. 2007: 157–62). These features suggest that structured deposition was occurring in parallel to existing funerals and burial rites, while the deposition of deliberately broken pottery within the ditches of Enclosure 4 (88 vessels) and Enclosure 5 (ten vessels including two amphorae), also suggest repeated commemorative events at the site.

While there is insufficient space here to consider the complexity of the landscape surrounding Stanway in any great detail, it may be useful to consider how people moved from the east, where the evidence for settlement lies at Gosbecks (Hawkes and Crummy 1995), to the enclosures themselves. Linear earthwork systems, established in the Late Iron Age to define the territorial *oppidum*, continued to lay between Stanway and Gosbecks, following the Claudian conquest, and directed the movement of people in specific ways (Figure 8.3). Originating from a spring adjacent to the Gosbecks enclosure, people may have followed the route of

the stream, (a low-lying position) and through the entrance to the earthworks, represented by 2–3m high banks that flanked the slopes of either side of the river valley (Creighton 2006; Davidson and Garland 2017). Water was an important part of other Late Iron Age and Roman ritual action (e.g. metalwork deposition) and formed a key element in the route towards Stanway through a monumental entrance/exit to the main area of settlement. The processional route towards Stanway may have been followed by those who undertook commemorative events at the site as well as those who carried the dead to be transformed within the Stanway enclosures (Esmonde Cleary 2005).

In considering the performance of the cremation and burial described above, it is striking that this process (as well as the events that preceded and followed it) required the participation of a large number of people, whether they be family, associates, or the wider community. Many of these people may have participated in at least some aspects of the funeral and likely had an interest in its outcome. After all, in the context of the burial, it should not be assumed that success was inevitable. Stress may have been placed on the participants and the wider community, to ensure the deceased completed their journey to the afterlife and were consequently favourable to the living in reaching the afterlife (Giles 2012: 213). The placing of apotropaic gifts in the grave may have been a reaction to appease the deceased following a particularly 'bad' death (Giles 2012: 120–1). This need to ensure the support of the deceased may have been exacerbated by the significance of this individual to the community at large, whether that be in a personal, political or professional capacity. Furthermore, the process of burial was just as important to the mourners themselves as it was for the deceased. Giles (2015: 546) argues that the performance created a controlled structure for grief and mourning and formed a substitute for the loss of the individual through death. While the role of magic/medicine, together representing healing and transformation, may have formed an important component in ensuring the success of the burial, it also facilitated closure and emotional healing for those who participated in the burial and knew the deceased. The heightened stress and concern caused by social upheaval surrounding the Claudian invasion of Britain, would have made the outcome of burials such as these more important than ever.

Conclusion

This paper has shown that medicine and magic in early Roman Britain were interlinked, operating as parallel and overlapping social practices to improve a person's situation through specialist knowledge and equipment. Although in the past the understanding of magic and medicine fell into two distinct categories, this division has been created by following modern social classifications and arbitrarily projecting this understanding onto the past. This division has been aggravated by those existing boundaries that exist within archaeological studies, which separate the 'practical' and 'symbolic', 'domestic' and 'ritual', and 'prehistoric' and 'Roman'. This research has shown that looking beyond these groupings allows the formation of a more nuanced understanding of the complexities of medical and magical social practices. Detailed analysis and cross comparison of the material remains from the 'Doctor's' burial demonstrate that rather than being labelled as either 'magical' or 'medicinal', these objects likely served multiple purposes with numerous meanings. The surgical instruments, for example, could be viewed purely as a single medicinal kit, however, the individual instruments were constructed in different ways, potentially by different people, and reflect the symbolic and/or magical properties of their materials and the context in which they were deposited. Moreover, the substance of the jet bead may have held importance in undertaking divination and performed acts of healing, however, this decorative object also reflected personal adornment and status in the Late Iron Age/Early Roman transition period.

Understanding the archaeological context of these items is paramount to understanding their 'magic/medicinal' use in specific situations. By understanding the context of the 'Doctor's burial', this research has explored beyond the identity of the deceased (i.e. the Doctor), which may mask a deeper understanding of the rites associated with the burial and why these specific objects were placed in the grave. The unusualness of these items may reflect their relative rarity in this period (cf. Gilchrist 2008: 124), however, the evidence for activities that leave no material trace, such as performance, is vital for understanding what role 'magical/medicinal' objects held in specific contexts. The context of the burial has helped to embrace the multiplicity of meanings behind these objects, which may have changed through their life-cycles, but also focus on specific attributes that held importance within particular situations. Within a burial context, for example, 'magical/medicinal' practices were transformed to suit new situations and provide assistance and healing, both in life and death. By exploring how 'magical/medicinal' practices effected, and were affected by, the sociological variances between different scales of society, it is possible to understand how such concepts and practices may have been incorporated into wider belief structures. At Stanway, the use of 'magical/medical' practices improved the situation of the deceased and aided in their delivery to the afterlife, however, it also helped to alleviate the grief of the immediate family or close social group. The importance of these practices to the community may be seen in the integration of specific performances within the wider landscape and in relation to domestic space. As part of the series of burials undertaken at Stanway, the 'Doctor's' burial formed part of a series of rites that assisted in the continuation of local beliefs in light of Imperial control.

This research has demonstrated the theoretical and methodological avenues that can be explored in understanding magic and medicine in the Roman world. Further research into comparable sites in Britain and the Continent, particularly those that have been interpreted as evidence for magic *or* medicine, may allow us to continue to build a greater understanding of this complex relationship.

School of History, Classics and Archaeology,
Newcastle University

Acknowledgements

The author would like to thank the editors of the volume for the invitation to write this paper and for their valuable ideas and comparable references. Their input, and that of the anonymous referee, has much improved the content of this paper. I would also like to thank Tom Derrick and Adam Parker for accepting an early version of this paper to the 'Material approaches to Medicine and Magic' session at TRAC 2017 in Durham and the participants of that session for their feedback. I would also like to thank Stefanie Hoss for providing a number of useful comparisons from the Continent, which have been referred to in this paper. Lastly, I would like to thank my partner Lesley, for all her encouragement, ideas and help. It would not have been possible to complete this, or any of my research, without her support. All remaining errors are my own.

Bibliography

Ancient Sources

Julius Caesar. (Translated by W.A. McDevitte and W. S. Bohn). *Gallic War*. Available: http://classics.mit.edu/Caesar/gallic.html [Accessed: 05/11/17].

Pliny the Elder. (Translated by J. Bostock 1855). *Natural History*. London: Taylor and Francis.

Tacitus (Translated by J.B. Rivers 1999). *Germania*. Oxford: Oxford University Press.

Modern Sources

Allason-Jones, L. 1996. *Roman Jet in the Yorkshire Museum*. York: Yorkshire Museum.

Baker, P. 2001. Medicine, culture and military identity. In G. Davies, A. Gardner and K. Lockyear (eds) *TRAC 2000: Proceedings of the Tenth Annual Theoretical Roman Archaeology Conference, London 2000*. Oxford: Oxbow Books: 48–68.

Baker, P. 2002. Diagnosing some ills: the archaeology, literature and history of Roman medicine. In P. Baker and G. Carr (eds) *Practitioners, Practices and Patients: New Approaches to Medical Archaeology and Anthropology*. Oxford: Oxbow Books, 16–29.

Baker, P. 2004. Roman medical instruments: archaeological interpretations of their possible 'non-functional' uses. *Social History of Medicine* 17(1): 3–21.

Baker, P. 2013. *The Archaeology of Medicine in the Greco-Roman World*. New York: Cambridge University Press.

Baker, P. 2016. Medicine. In M. Millett, L. Revell, and A. Moore (eds) *Oxford Handbook of Roman Britain*. Oxford: Oxford University Press: 555–72.

Biddulph, E. 2015. Residual or ritual? Pottery from the backfill of graves and other features in Roman cemeteries. In T. Brindle, M. Allen, E. Durham and A. Smith (eds) *TRAC 2014 Proceedings of the Twenty-Fourth Annual Theoretical Roman Archaeology Conference*. Oxford: Oxbow Books: 41–53.

Bourdieu, P. 1977. *Outline of a Theory of Practice*. Cambridge: Cambridge University Press.

Bradley, R. 2005. *Ritual and Domestic Life in Prehistoric Europe*. London: Routledge.

Brück, J. 1999. Ritual and rationality: some problems of interpretation in European Archaeology. *European Journal of Archaeology* 2(3): 313–44.

Budd, P. and Taylor, T. 1995. The faerie smith meets the bronze industry: magic versus science in the interpretation of prehistoric metal-making. *World Archaeology* 27(1): 133–43.

Carr, G. 2002. A time to live, a time to heal and a time to die: healing and divination in later Iron Age and early Roman Britain. In P. Baker and G. Carr (eds) *Practitioners, Practices and Patients: New Approaches to Medical Archaeology and Anthropology*. Oxford: Oxbow Books: 58–73.

Chadwick, A. 2012. Routine magic, mundane ritual: towards a unified notion of depositional practice. *Oxford Journal of Archaeology* 31(3): 283–315.

Chadwick, A. 2015. Doorways, ditches and dead dogs: excavating and recording material manifestations of practical magic amongst later prehistoric and Romano-British communities. In C. Houlbrook and N. Armitage (eds) *The Materiality of Magic: An Artefactual Investigation into Ritual Practices and Popular Belief*. Oxford: Oxbow Books: 37–64.

Cool, H.E.M. 2009. *Eating and Drinking in Roman Britain*. Cambridge: Cambridge University Press.

Creighton, J. 1995. Visions of power: imagery and symbols in late Iron Age Britain. *Britannia* 26: 285–301.

Creighton, J. 2000. *Coins and Power in Late Iron Age Britain*. Cambridge: Cambridge University Press.

Creighton, J. 2006. *Britannia: The Creation of a Roman Province*. London: Routledge.

Crummy, N. 2010. Bears and coins: the iconography of protection in late Roman infant burials. *Britannia* 41: 37–93.

Crummy, P. 2002. A preliminary account of the doctor's grave at Stanway, Colchester, England. In P. Baker and G. Carr (eds) *Practitioners, Practices and Patients: New Approaches to Medical Archaeology and Anthropology: Conference Proceedings*. Oxford: Oxbow Books: 1–9.

Crummy, P. 2007. The gaming board in CF47: the remains as found, possible reconstructions and post-depositional movements. In P. Crummy, S. Benfield, N. Crummy, V. Rigby and D. Shimmin (eds) *Stanway: An Elite Burial Site at Camulodunum*. London: Society for the Promotion of Roman Studies: 352–9.

Crummy, P., Benfield, S., Crummy, N., Rigby, V. and Shimmin, D. (eds) 2007. *Stanway: An Elite Burial Site at Camulodunum*. London: Society for the Promotion of Roman Studies.

Cruse, A. 2004. *Roman Medicine*. Stroud: Tempus Publishing.

Cruse, A. 2013. Roman medicine: science or religion? *Bulletin of the John Rylands Library* 89(1): 223–52.

David, R. 2004. Rationality versus irrationality in Egyptian medicine in the Pharonic and Graeco-Roman periods. In H.F.J. Horstmanshoff and M. Stol (eds) *Magic and Rationality in Ancient Near Eastern and Graeco-Roman Medicine*. Studies in Ancient Medicine 27. Leiden: Brill: 133–51.

Davidson, L. and Garland, N. 2017. *Experiencing Oppida: Understanding Linear Earthwork Systems at Camulodunum*. [Poster]. Exhibited at Iron Age Oppida conference, 22nd April 2017, University of Reading.

DeMarrais, E. 2014. Introduction: the archaeology of performance. *World Archaeology* 46(2): 155–63.

Derrick, T.J. and Parker, A. 2016. 'Take two of these for what ails you' – Material approaches to Medicine and Magic: Session Abstract for the 2017 Theoretical Roman Archaeology Conference, University of Durham [online]. Theoretical Roman Archaeology Conference. Available: http://trac.org.uk/take-two-of-these-for-what-ails-you-material-approaches-to-medicine-and-magic/ [Accessed: 25/06/17].

Draycott, J. 2012. *Approaches to Healing in Roman Egypt*. British Archaeological Reports International Series 2416. Oxford: Archaeopress.

Eckardt, H. 2014. *Objects and Identities: Roman Britain and the North-western Provinces*. Oxford: Oxford University Press.

Ekrengren, F. 2013. Contextualiszing grave goods: theoretical perspectives and methodological implications. In L.N. Stutz and S. Tarlow (eds) *The Oxford Handbook of the Archaeology of Death and Burial*. Oxford: Oxford University Press: 174–92.

Esmonde Cleary, A.S. 2005. Beating the bounds: ritual and the articulation of urban space in Roman Britain. In A. MacMahon and J. Price (eds) *Roman Working Lives and Urban Living*. Oxford: Oxbow Books: 1–17.

Fitzpatrick, A.P. 1997. *Archaeological Excavations on the Route of the A27 Westhampnett Bypass, West Sussex, 1992: Volume 1: Late Upper Palaeolithic-Anglo-Saxon*. Salisbury: Trust for Wessex Archaeology.

Fitzpatrick, A.P. 2000. Ritual, sequence and structure in late Iron Age mortuary practices in North-West Europe. In J. Pearce, M. Millett and M. Struck (eds) *Burial, Society and Context in the Roman World*. Oxford: Oxbow Books: 15–29.

Fitzpatrick, A.P. 2007. Druids: towards an archaeology. In C. Gosden, H. Hamerow, P. de Jersey and G. Lock (eds) *Communities and Connections: Essays in Honour of Barry Cunliffe*. Oxford: Oxford University Press: 287–315.

Forshaw, R. 2012. Before Hippocrates: healing practices in ancient Egypt. In E. Gemi-Iordanou, S. Gordon, R. Matthew, E. McInnes and R. Pettitt (eds) *Medicine, Healing and Performance*. Oxford: Oxbow Books: 25–41.

Freeman, P. 1993. 'Romanisation' and Roman material culture. *Journal of Roman Archaeology* 6: 438–45.

Garland, N. 2016. Agency, structure and place: finds in the landscape in the late Iron Age/early Roman transition. In M. Mandich, T.J. Derrick, S. González-Sánchez, G. Savani, and E. Zampieri, (eds) *TRAC 2015: Proceedings of the 25th Annual Theoretical Roman Archaeology Conference*. Oxford: Oxbow Books: 76–91.

Garland, N. 2017. *Territorial Oppida and the Transformation of Landscape and Society in South-eastern Britain from BC 300 to 100 AD*. Unpublished PhD thesis, University College London.

Garrow, D. and Gosden, C. 2012. *Technologies of Enchantment: Exploring Celtic Art 400 BC to AD 100*. Oxford. Oxford University Press.

Ghey, E. 2005. Beyond the temple: blurring the boundaries of sacred space. In J. Bruhn, B. Croxford and D. Grigoropoulos, (eds) *TRAC 2004: Proceedings of the Fourteenth Annual Theoretical Roman Archaeology Conference, Durham 2004*. Oxford: Oxbow Books: 109–18.

Gibbins, D. 1988. Surgical instruments from a Roman shipwreck off Sicily. *Antiquity* 63: 294–7.

Giddens, A. 1984. *The Constitution of Society: Outline of the Theory of Structuration*. Cambridge: Polity Press.

Giles, M. 2007. Making metal and forging relations: ironworking in the British Iron Age. *Cambridge Archaeological Journal* 25(3): 539–50.

Giles, M. 2012. *A Forged Glamour: Landscape, Identity and Material Culture in the Iron Age*. Oxford: Windgather Press.

Giles, M. 2015. Performing pain, performing beauty: dealing with difficult death in the Iron Age. *Oxford Journal of Archaeology* 26(4): 395–413.

González Sánchez, S. and Guglielmi, A. (eds) 2017. *Romans and Barbarians Beyond the Frontiers: Archaeology, Ideology and Identities in the North*. Oxford: Oxbow Books.

Gostencnik, K. 2013. Medizinische Instrumente aus Lauriacum in den Sammlungen der Oberösterreichischen Landesmuseen. *Römisches Österreich* 36: 95–107.

Grieve, M. 1931. *A Modern Herbal* [online]. Available: http://www.botanical.com/botanical/mgmh/mgmh.html [Accessed: 10/07/17].

Hall, M.A. and Forsyth, K. 2011. Roman rules? The introduction of board games to Britain and Ireland. *Antiquity* 85(330): 1325–38.

Haselgrove, C. and Wigg-Wolf, D. 2005. Introduction: Iron Age coinage and ritual practices. In C. Haselgrove and D. Wigg-Wolf (eds) *Iron Age Coinage and Ritual Practices*. Mainz am Rhein: Von Zabern: 9–22.

Hawkes, C.F.C. and Crummy, P. 1995. *Camulodunum 2*. Colchester: Colchester Archaeological Trust.

Hill. J.D. 1995. *Ritual and Rubbish in the Iron Age of Wessex: a Study on the Formation of a Specific Archaeological Record*. British Archaeological Report 242). Oxford: Tempus Reparatum

Hingley, R. 2006. The deposition of iron objects in Britain during the later Prehistoric and Roman Periods: contextual analysis and the significance of iron. *Britannia* 37: 213–57.

Hingley, R. 2011. Iron Age knowledge: Pre-Roman peoples and myths of origin In T. Moore and X. Armada (eds) *Atlantic Europe in the First Millennium BC: Crossing the Divide*. Oxford: Oxford University Press: 617–37.

Houlbrook, C. and Armitage, N. 2015. Introduction: the materiality of the materiality of magic. In C. Houlbrook and N. Armitage (eds) *The Materiality of Magic: An Artefactual Investigation into Ritual Practices and Popular Beliefs*. Oxford: Oxbow Books: 1–14.

Hull, K.L. 2014. Ritual as performance in small-scale societies. *World Archaeology* 46(2): 164–77.

Hunter, F. 2001. The carnyx in Iron Age Europe. *Antiquity* 81: 77–108.

Hunter, F. 2005. The image of the warrior in the British Iron Age: coin iconography in context. In C. Haselgrove and D. Wigg-Wolf (eds) *Iron Age Coinage and Ritual Practices*. Mainz am Rhein: Von Zabern: 43–68.

Ingold, T. 2007. Materials against materiality. *Archaeological Dialogues* 14(1): 1–16.

Jackson, R. 1988. *Doctors and Diseases in the Roman Empire*. London: British Museum Press.

Jackson, R. 1997. An ancient British medical kit from Stanway, Essex. *The Lancet* 350(9089): 1471–3.

Jackson, R. 2007. The surgical instruments. In P. Crummy, S. Benfield, N. Crummy, V. Rigby and D. Shimmin (eds) *Stanway: An Elite Burial Site at Camulodunum*. London: Society for the Promotion of Roman Studies: 236–52.

Jackson, R. 2011. Medicine and hygiene. In L. Allason-Jones (ed.) *Artefacts in Roman Britain: Their Purpose and Use*. Cambridge: Cambridge University Press: 243–68.

Johnson, A. 2008. Iron Age mystery of the 'Essex druid' [online]. Available: http://www.independent.co.uk/news/uk/this-britain/iron-age-mystery-of-the-essex-druid-812194.html [Accessed:21/07/17].

Johnston, S., Crabtree, P. and Campana, D. 2014. Performance, place and power at Dún Ailinne, a ceremonial site of the Irish Iron Age. *World Archaeology* 46(2): 206–23.

Künzl, E. 1996. Forschungsbericht zu den antiken medizinischen Instrumenten. *Aufstieg und Niedergang der römischen Welt* II 37(3): 2433–639.

Lewis, A. 2015. *Iron Age and Roman-era Terrets from Western and Central Britain: An Interpretive Study*. Unpublished PhD thesis, University of Leicester.

Mattingly, D. 1997. Dialogues of power and experience in the Roman Empire. In D. Mattingly (ed) *Dialogues in Roman Imperialism: Power, Discourse, and Discrepant Experience in the Roman Empire*. Journal of Roman Archaeology Supplementary Series 23. Portsmouth, RI: Journal of Roman Archaeology: 7–26.

Mattingly, D. 2004. Being Roman: expressing identity in a provincial setting. *Journal of Roman Archaeology* 17: 5–25.

Merrifield, R. 1986. *The Archaeology of Ritual and Magic*. London: B.T. Batsford

McKie, S. 2016. Distraught, drained, devoured, or damned? The Importance of Individual Creativity in Roman Cursing. In M. Mandich, T.J. Derrick, S. González-Sánchez, G. Savani, and E. Zampieri (eds) *TRAC 2015: Proceedings of the 25th annual Theoretical Roman Archaeology Conference*. Oxford: Oxbow Books: 15–27.

McKinley, J. I. 2013. Cremation. In L. Nilsson Stutz and S. Tarlow (eds) *The Oxford Handbook of the Archaeology of Death and Burial*. Oxford: Oxford University Press, 147–172.

Moore, T. and Armada, X. 2011. Crossing the divide: opening a dialogue on approaches to Western Europe First Millennium BC Studies. In T. Moore and X. Armada (eds) *Atlantic Europe in the First Millennium BC: Crossing the Divide*. Oxford: Oxford University Press: 3–77.

Navarro, J.-M., de. 1955. A Doctor's grave of the Middle La Tène period from Bavaria. *Proceedings of the Prehistoric Society* 21: 231–48.

Parker, A. 2016. 'Staring at death: the jet gorgoneia of Roman Britain'. In S. Hoss and A. Whitmore. *Small Finds and Ancient Social Practices in the North-west Provinces of the Roman Empire*. Oxford: Oxbow Books: 99–113.

Parker-Pearson, M. 2003. *The Archaeology of Death and Burial*. Stroud: Sutton Publishing.

Pluskowski, A. 2011. Druidism and Neo-Paganism. In T. Insoll (ed.) *The Oxford Handbook of the Archaeology of Ritual and Religion*. Oxford: Oxford University Press: 1032–42.

Ralph, S. 2007. *Feasting and Social Complexity in Later Iron Age East Anglia*. British Archaeological Report 451. Oxford: Archaeopress.

Redfern, R. 2010. A regional examination of surgery and fracture treatment in Iron Age and Roman Britain. *International Journal of Osteoarchaeology* 20: 443–71.

Redfern, R. and DeWitte, S.N. 2011 A new approach to the study of Romanization in Britain: a regional perspective of cultural change in Late Iron Age and Roman Dorset Using the Siler and Gompertz–Makeham models of mortality. *American Journal of Physical Anthropology* 144: 269–85.

Redfern, R., Millard, A.R. and Hamlin, C. 2012. A regional investigation of subadult dietary patterns and health in late Iron Age and Roman Dorset, England. *Journal of Archaeological Science* 39: 1249–9.

Reynolds, F. 2014. Early Neolithic Shamans? Performance, Healing and the Power of Skulls at Hambledon Hill, Dorset. In E. Gemi-Iordanou, S. Gordon, R. Matthew, E. McInnes and R. Pettitt (eds) *Medicine, Healing and Performance*. Oxford: Oxbow Books: 6–24.

RT Slovenia. 2017. Tomb of doctor from Emona from below Slovenska street displayed in City Museum. [online] Available: http://www.rtvslo.si/news-in-english/tomb-of-doctor-from-emona-from-below-slovenska-street-displayed-in-city-museum/395615 [Accessed:05/11/17].

Schädler, U. 2007. The doctor's game – new light on the history of ancient board games. In P. Crummy, S. Benfield, N. Crummy, V. Rigby and D. Shimmin, *Stanway: An Elite Burial Site at Camulodunum*. London: Society for the Promotion of Roman Studies, 359–75.

Sealey, P. 1999. Finds from the Cauldron Pit. In N.R. Brown. *The Archaeology of Ardleigh, Essex, Excavations 1955–1980*. East Anglian Archaeology 90. Chelmsford: Essex County Council: 117–24.

Spasić-Djurić, D. 2005. Grob lekara iz Viminacijuma. *Glasnik Srpskog Arheološlog Društva* 21: 281–92.

Stead, I. and Rigby, V. 1986. *Baldock: the Excavation of a Roman and pre-Roman Settlement, 1968–72*. Oxford: Oxbow Books.

Stead, I. and Rigby, V. 1989. *Verulamium: The King Harry Lane site*. London: English Heritage.

Webster, J. 1999. At the end of the world: Druidic and other revitalization movements in post-conquest Gaul and Britain. *Britannia* 30: 1–20.

Wenham, L.P. 1968. *The Romano-British Cemetery at Trentholme Drive, York*. London: HMSO.

West, S. 2015. 'Out of town and on the edge?': evaluating recent evidence for Romanization within the *Verulamium* region. In K. Lockyear (ed.) *Archaeology in Hertfordshire: Recent Research: A Festschrift for Tony Rook*. Hatfield: University Hertfordshire Press: 197–221.

Whittaker, H. 2004. Board games and funerary symbolism in Greek and Roman contexts. In S. des Bouvie (ed.) *Myth and Symbol II. Symbolic Phenomena in Ancient Greek Culture. Papers from the Second and Third International Symposia on Symbolism at the Norwegian Institute at Athens, September 21–24, 2000 and September 19–22, 2002*. Papers of the Norweigan Institute at Athens 7. Bergen: Norweigan Institute at Athens: 279–302.

Whittaker, H. 2006. Game boards and gaming pieces in the Northern European Iron Age. *Nordlit. Tidsskrift i kultur og litteratur* 24: 103–12

Woolf, G. 1997. Beyond Romans and natives. *World Archaeology* 28(3): 339–50.

Abbreviations

PAS = Portable Antiquities Scheme. Available: https://finds.org.uk/database [Accessed: 20/11/17]

RIB = S. Vanderbilt & University of Oxford. *Roman Inscriptions of Britain Online*. Available: https://romaninscriptionsofbritain.org/inscriptions/searchnumber [Accessed: 20/11/17]

The Archaeology of Ritual in the Domestic Sphere: Case Studies from Karanis and Pompeii

Andrew Wilburn

Introduction: The Home as a Locus for Magic and Ritual Performance

In the Greek and Demotic Magical Papyri, a corpus of ritual texts preserved from Roman, Byzantine, and, to a lesser degree, Ptolemaic Egypt, instructional texts occasionally specify a place for the practitioner to undertake a ritual. The house is named more often than any other location, and sometimes, the ritual recipes even stipulate a space in the home such as 'a room where you reside' (*PGM* 1.83), 'your bedchamber' (*PGM* 2.148) or 'your housetop' (*PGM* 4.2711) (Smith 1995: 23). In one example, instructions are provided for the manufacture and consecration of a small iron lamella that has been inscribed with three Homeric verses. The resulting amulet can serve a variety of purposes, including spells to divine the future, restrain enemies, induce affection, or wreck a chariot. The practitioner is told:

> Go, I say, into a clean room. Set up a table, on which you are to place a clean linen cloth and flowers of the season. Then sacrifice a white cock, placing beside it 7 cakes, 7 wafers, 7 lamps; pour a libation of milk, honey, wine and olive oil (*PGM* .4.2187–2190, trans. Betz 1992).

This text provides precise instructions for the performance of a specific rite that involves a variety of materials: a textile, vegetation, an animal, prepared foodstuffs, lamps, and liquids. We must understand rituals such as this as rich in material components, speech acts, and gestures. For Roman and Late Roman Egypt, this and similar spell texts can be employed to flesh out our conception of the sorts of rites that were appropriate for domestic performance, and suggest that types of artefacts and materials that may have been employed. The sketch that can be derived from the magical papyri, however, is by its very nature fragmentary,

as it is dependent on the written records of ritual instructions that survive from a limited range of geographic locations. Literary evidence from other regions of the Mediterranean attest to the variety of rites that may have occurred in houses elsewhere in the Roman world, but in all cases, it is necessary to consider the role of the local environment in ritual enactment.

In this paper, I employ the term 'ritual', as it can be used to encompass a variety of performative activities that might be categorised as 'religion', 'magic', or 'domestic cult' (Merrifield 1987: 5–9; Versnel 1991; Wilburn 2012: 12–20). These terms – religion, magic, and domestic cult – are fluid, and often describe activities that may fit into one or more category. My goal is to investigate the archaeological evidence with an eye to identifying ritual practices in the domestic sphere. I define ritual practices as performances employing language, gesture, and material culture to bring about change in the world through mechanistic methods. In the conclusion, I will return to these terms to reassess their application for the archaeological material under consideration.

Archaeological evidence can reveal ritual activity through the investigation of material remains. As the actor moves through and creates space, his or her speech acts and gestures are aimed at the pursuit of a goal, whether sacred or profane (Bell 1992; Rappaport 1999: 24; Bell 2007: 405). Rituals occur within a place, such as a built structure or in the landscape, and alter that space in some fashion, even if this change occurs only with the minds of the participants. Studies of the archaeological remains of ritual have focused on the formality and repetition of ritual acts, as these features are more likely to leave physical evidence (Kyrkiadies 2007: 291; Barrett 2015b: 403). Many parts of a ritual performance, such as gestures or spoken words, are ephemeral, and leave few archaeological traces. Other rituals possess distinct material components that are reified through gesture, including the attire worn by the celebrant; plants or animals that are offered, consumed, or manipulated; and artefacts that are created, employed, or destroyed (Frankfurter 2015). As ritual directs agency (such as that of a god or the community) toward the achievement of a specific goal, objects can serve to harness or focus this agency (Rappaport 1999: 48).

Analyses of the domestic sphere offer opportunities to investigate the ways in which private individuals engaged with ritual practices. The home is identifiable both spatially and through the presence of movable material culture (Nevett 2010: 9–16). Literary and artistic evidence records the variety of cultic activities that were centred on the household and the built structure of the home. Locating ritual events in domestic spaces must focus on identifying and interpreting the results of ritual processes through the contextual analysis of architecture, objects and assemblages. The performance of rituals within the home employ domestic space as a critical element of in the efficacy of the rite. This paper will first posit that the home can be used as a distinct archaeological unit to investigate ritual performances related to its occupants and residents. Next, I will use this framework to explore two different ritual contexts that relate to the house: an assemblage intended to compel the affection of a victim, and a floor mosaic meant to protect the residents from the evil eye. In the first case study from the site of Karanis, analysis of finds from beneath a house permits us to sketch a rite that employed a small figurine to compel the erotic desire of a victim. Archaeological context suggests the performance of a rite that employed the house as a key component of an aggressive act. The second case study uses the famous *cave canem* mosaic from the House of the Tragic Poet at Pompeii to explore the processes by which apotropaic magic may have functioned. While it is possible to suggest that the artistic representation of a fierce dog was intended to protect the home from the evil eye, it is more difficult to articulate the ritual processes that may have either initiated, actualised, or reified the protective power of the mosaic. In each of the two case studies, images or representations were employed to bring about change in the world, but our ability to reconstruct ritual actions and actors varies significantly, largely due to the depositional processes through which the archaeological record was formed.

Houses and Rituals

As an architectural unit that differentiated interior and exterior spaces while providing protection for its occupants, the house is central to a family, society, and culture. Humans often are conceived and reared within a home, and customarily retreat to its confines after engaging with the

dangers and stresses of 'outside' (Bachelard 1964, 38–9; Alston, 2002: 44). Domestic spaces are focused inwards on the residents, providing for the family through the production of food and clothing, while also sheltering and socialising the products of the family unit: children.

Built structures – the floor, the roof and the walls – provide a physical demarcation between inside and outside (Rykwert 1972: 191–2; Semper 1989: 102). The physical boundaries of the house, however, were porous, and domestic activities passed through and around the doors and windows, moving beyond thresholds to streets, below ground to basements, and upstairs to roofs that faced the sky. For example, the courtyard, which could be adjacent to the home, was considered part of the living space, even if it was simultaneously outside. The conceptual house, therefore, must be defined as both the built structure of a domicile and its adjacent and proximate spaces. Beyond the physical structure, the 'house' may refer to its residents, that is, not only the immediate family related by blood, but also the household slaves, animals and ancestors (Bodel 2008: 248). The house extends outwards both spatially and temporally, reaching into the past and future.

Within a house, individual rooms served multiple purposes during the day and night. Usage was determined both by fixed and moveable objects (Wallace-Hadrill 1988; 1994: 117; Berry 1997: 185; Allison 1999: 70). A raised platform on which couches were placed might indicate that a room was used for dining; similarly, the orientation of a mosaic might suggest the ideal placement for furniture. Often, in the archaeological record, architectural details that would aid in identifying the function of a room are absent. A more productive approach may lie in the analysis of artefact assemblages coupled with an assessment of architectural space, but it is also important to note that objects might have been used for a variety of purposes (Berry 1997: 193–5; Allison 2006: 398).

Literary evidence speaks to the variety of cultic activities that accompanied daily life, many of which occurred in the home. Rituals that intersected with points of transition – births, weddings, and funerals – regularly took place in the house and involved the participation of householders. The architecture of the house may have some marked places in which certain rituals occurred. Shrines or niches could be built into the walls, or may have been freestanding but relatively permanent fixtures. Images of the Lares and Penates, the Roman household gods, typically were housed in a *lararium*, a small shrine or niche, creating a space set aside for offerings (Bakker 1994: 8–12; Foss 1997; Flower 2017). Votive figurines intended for dedication at a shrine or kept as a memento many have found various places within the home (Barrett 2015b: 406–7; Frankfurter 2015). Ritual paraphernalia, such as vessels or lamps, libations, and offerings of plants or animals, may have been brought out for the duration of the rite, and at its conclusion, returned to storage or to normal, non-ritual use (Wilburn 2012: 90–3).

Many activities undertaken in the house may have been infused with ritual significance. Actions taken by an individual or by a collective group may have involved religion, maintaining a right relationship with the gods (Beard *et al.* 1998: 1: 43; Rupke 2007: 9). The ancients did distinguish special rites, which were marked by specific requirements or preparation. The Roman author Festus, for example, tells us that ritual sweeping used to occur after a death (Festus, s.v. *Everriator*), although it is likely that such rituals no longer occurred by the author's time. Augustine records that sweeping protected a new mother from the evil eye (Augustine *De civ. D.* 6.9). Ritual sweeping may have differed from the act of cleaning the home through the actors or their attire; in Augustine's telling, freeborn men or the head of the household, rather than slaves, swept. Even in non-ritual time, sweeping with the goal of house cleaning may have recalled the ritualised version, or may have served a conceptual function of ridding the house of both dirt and unwelcome spiritual visitants. The materials used within each rite were likely indistinguishable; the same broom may have been used for both mundane and ritual sweeping.

Collective, polis-based rites as well as household rituals existed in the same cultural continuum as magical ones (Smith 1995: 13–27; Kindt 2012: 92–102; Hamori 2015: 21–2). Some ritual acts were vilified as foreign, criminal, or 'magic,' as they were viewed as contrary to the traditional religious activities of the local polis or state (Smith 1978: 429; Kindt 2012: 115). This does not mean, however, that such rites were not performed, or even that those performing the rites viewed them as anti-social or forbidden.

Rituals in which domestic performance is mandated may have been situated in these contexts because of the intended result. In the Greek and Demotic Magical Papyri, we find rites to ensure a divine visitation, perhaps as part of a dream; others called down celestial powers to aid the practitioner. In these contexts, a sleeping room or a rooftop would have facilitated the encounter with the divine. The private dwelling offered an opportunity for concealment, where rites could occur without notice, or, perhaps more importantly, interruption. Reading ritual into the evidence requires us to reconstruct performance not as a snapshot of activity but rather as a motion picture, where ritual actors moved about through space, employing objects, enacting gestures and speaking words – generating both ephemeral and material traces in the world around them. By analysing the artefacts employed in rituals, archaeology can permit an investigation of performance, and can suggest the points at which such analyses are productive or deficient. In the sections that follow, I present two disparate case studies to explore how ritual activities intersect with domestic space.

Case Study: Karanis

The University of Michigan excavations at the site of Karanis, in Egypt, undertaken between 1924 and 1935, unearthed more than 100,000 individual artefacts, largely discovered in what appear to have been private houses. Beneath the floor of one of these houses on the eastern side of the settlement, Structure 165, in context 165*, the excavators discovered a small, roughly-made mud figurine (Figure 9.1, Kelsey Museum of Archaeology accession number 7525; on the archaeological context: Wilburn 2012: 129–40). The figurine depicts a woman with spiky hair, a slight indentation marking the neck, and two hand-moulded protrusions for breasts. Details, including the eyes, nose, mouth, nipples, genitals and a necklace, have been picked out using a tool. The object is broken off just below the genitals, perhaps because of an intentional act. The back of the figurine was blackened, indicating that it had been placed into a fire. As no other artefacts in the deposit show similar signs of burning, it is likely that the small figurine was treated in a specific and perhaps significant way, and then deposited in this location. The same context yielded other artefacts, including a bone pin (Figure 9.2, Kelsey Museum of Archaeology accession number 21776), the end of which is the same size as the proper right eye of the figurine (3.9mm), suggesting that this was the tool used to decorate the artefact. Although another object may have been used to create the decoration, the discovery of these objects in the same archaeological context allows us to associate the two artefacts with one another and suggest a possible ritual function.

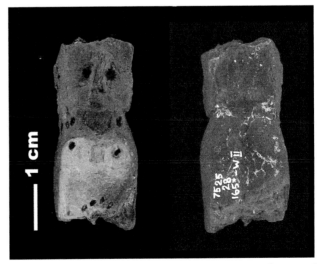

Figure 9.1 Mud figurine of a woman from Karanis, discovered beneath structure 165. Kelsey Museum of Archaeology Inventory Number 7525 (courtesy Kelsey Museum of Archaeology, Ann Arbor, Michigan).

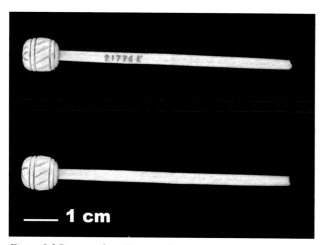

Figure 9.2 Bone pin from Karanis, discovered beneath structure 165. Kelsey Museum of Archaeology Inventory Number 21776 (courtesy Kelsey Museum of Archaeology, Ann Arbor, Michigan).

In the case of the Karanis figurine, its function may be understood through comparison with other, similar representations from Egypt. Several roughly made figurines are preserved from the Pharaonic period, identifiable as female through the presence of a pubic triangle. These objects have been discovered in both funerary and domestic contexts. Pinch has suggested that the domestic figurines may have been employed to encourage fertility, used by individuals who wished to conceive children (1993: 211–25). Such objects were effective because of proximity to spaces in which sexual activity occurred. Domestic figurines that were broken may have been damaged to eliminate the power of the charm and prevent conception. In contrast, the figurines discovered in male graves may have been intended to promote male virility and potency in the next world, suggesting that the function of these objects may have differed according to where they were employed (Ritner 2002: 291–2). Figurines used for binding rituals have been discovered throughout the Mediterranean (Faraone 1991; Bailliot 2015). Most often, binding figurines show clear indications of restraint, such as the use of moulded manacles or other restraints, or the figurine may have been twisted or otherwise manipulated to bring about the goals of the rite. Such binding figurines are related conceptually to curse tablets, which seek to prevent the victim from engaging in a specific activity (Gordon 2015). While the small Karanis figurine lacks features that would indicate an intention to restrain, the lower part of the legs appear to have been broken off, an action that may suggest ritual activity to prevent movement. Breaking or otherwise damaging an artefact, particularly a representation of a human, may have formed part of a ritual act. Similar breaking is common in Egypt (Ritner 1993: 148–52) and is apparent in one of the recently discovered figurines from Mainz (Witteyer 2005: 111–14; Bailliot 2015: F3, 100–1).

Objects allow human beings to articulate complex ideas that may not be easily expressed, and the meaning of such artefacts is not always readily apparent (Miller 1998: 28). Representations employed in ritual performances embody the desires of the practitioner, who might view the object as an extension of his or her personhood (Gell 1998: 96–8; Miller 2010: 60). The process of creating or manipulating the image allowed the practitioner to mime a desired reality into being (Taussig 1993: 30, 106–8; 2009: 271). The small size of the figurine necessitated choices on the part of the practitioner, who determined which features of the original (the victim) should be emphasised (Stewart 1984: 44, 54). Such features are significant, as they were viewed as the elements of the representation that were critical to its efficacy. In the case of the Karanis figurine, the modelling of the breasts and pudenda suggest that the figurine was intended to reference a female victim; the practitioner likely was focused on controlling the sexual activity of the target.

The assemblage can be identified as the product of an erotic spell through comparison with instructional texts that record ritual recipes and with similar artefacts from other locations.[1] In the spell manuals from Graeco-Roman Egypt, rituals use fire, metaphorically and in reality, to compel erotic desire (e.g. *PGM* 36.69–101; *PGM* 19a; Faraone 1999: 26 n. 115, 58–9 and n. 81). Heat may have also been employed as a method of torture, intended to compel the target of the spell to be with the commissioner (Faraone 1993). Other recipes require the creation of figurines that are manipulated and sometimes pierced with nails to achieve a similar effect. In *PGM* 4.296–466, which states its purpose as a 'wondrous spell for binding a lover,' the practitioner is instructed to create two images: one of a bound woman, and the other of the god Ares. He or she must pierce the figurine of the woman with copper needles in its brain, eyes, ears, mouth, midriff (the heart?), hands, genitals and feet. The love spell was doubly efficacious, both because Ares is shown threatening the female victim, and the practitioner has pierced the female victim with pins, binding her body and preventing her from coupling with another man. The spell instructions are similar to artefacts discovered in three different archaeological assemblages from Graeco-Roman Egypt. In the best-known example, clandestine excavation uncovered a clay figurine of a bound woman, pierced with needles, that was discovered with an inscribed lead tablet in an earthenware pot (du Bourguet 1975; Kambitsis 1976; Martinez 1991; Ritner 1993: 112–13; Faraone 1999; 2002; Wilburn 2012: 28–34). The bone tool may have been used in a similar way, to pierce the figurine and cause its double – the victim – to be transfixed or to feel pain. The ritual celebrant at Karanis may have synthesised disparate ritual techniques, recombining them for the commissioner of the spell, or the practitioner may have drawn upon a generalised knowledge of effective techniques for erotic magic. The ritual assemblage also had the potential

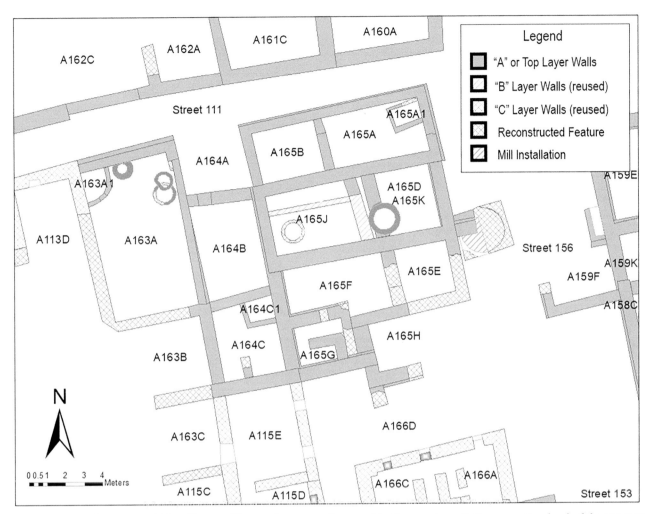

Figure 9.3 Plan of structure A165 at Karanis. The artefacts were discovered in the area beneath the occupation level of the structure (digital reconstruction by the author).

to alter how the practitioner viewed the world or believed that he or she was viewed by friends, neighbours, and the victim of the spell (Brown 2001: 4; Barrett 2015a: 123).

The archaeological context designated as 165* (Figure 9.3, the '*' indicates an archaeological context below the floor level) includes the soil beneath structure A165, as well as the adjacent structure 166, and street AS156. Like many other domestic structures at Karanis, structure A165 included underground spaces that were used for storage (Husselman 1979: 37). This context included grain, presumably used in the domestic structure above where there is evidence for a milling installation. The placement of the artefacts in this space may have been intended to draw the target to the house. The context and the other associated finds suggest intentional deposition, rather than loss or abandonment (Schiffer 1987: 58–64). Elsewhere in the magical recipes, power objects are utilised by the commissioner to entice or attract the victim to a specific space, or as a means of localising the effect of a rite. In *PGM* 46.134–160, for

example, the practitioner is told to mix myrrh, frankincense, and vinegar in a cup, and then to place the vessel in the door socket of his own house. Most often, however, the house and its constituent parts are used to direct the focus of a magical rite at a resident. Deposition at the threshold or around the door of a victim's home appears to have been especially important for love spells. In Jerome's *Life of Saint Hilarion the Hermit*, a virgin is driven mad by a love spell placed underneath the threshold of her door by an amorous pagan suitor (Migne *PL* vol 23, col 38). Tacitus (*Annals* 2.69) associates the burial of ritual material beneath the temporary residence of Germanicus with magical practice, and this technique is echoed in the magical papyri, where, in *PDM* 61.112–127, the practitioner is told to bury an image of Osiris made of wax along with the hair and wool of a donkey and the bone of a lizard beneath the doorsill of the desired woman (Faraone 1999: 56). Although it is not possible to determine with surety whether the commissioner or target was a resident of Structure A165, the house is used to activate ritual practice, and functions as a focal point for the intended result of the spell. Once the figurine had been deposited in this space, it was activated, and continued to operate upon the target indefinitely. Papyrological and literary evidence suggest that the assemblage would have been rendered inactive only by removing it from this space (Wilburn 2012: 47). The space of deposition is critical to understanding how the ritual functioned.

This image and an associated pin were deposited with the intent that the victim would be attracted to the commissioner. The Karanis figurine is quite small, and measures only about three and a half centimetres in height; its miniature size highlights the sexual characteristics of its double, the victim of the spell, reinforcing its erotic purpose. The object served as a manifestation of the will of the practitioner, allowing him or her to act out, or mime, his or her desire on the representation. The object should not be understood as connected sympathetically to the victim, but rather as an agent, permitting the practitioner to have an effect on the world (Frankfurter forthcoming) The mud figurine was invisible, both to the commissioner and to the victim of the spell, but it was 'hidden' in view (Ruppel 2003; Manning 2014). Archaeological evidence allows us to partially reconstruct the ritual process that resulted in these artefacts: the practitioner moulded the mud, pierced it with the pin, burned the figurine, and finally deposited it in this space. In this instance, the domestic sphere is critical for the performance of the rite, as the deposition of the object beneath the home utilises the house as a beacon for attracting the victim.

Case Study: Pompeii

At Pompeii, the remarkable preservation permits an unparalleled investigation of a city and its residents from one particular moment in time: August, A.D. 79. The residents of Pompeii, however, were not instantly buried by the lapilli, ash, and pyroclastic flows emanating from Vesuvius; the archaeological record reflects their responses to the natural disaster that would encapsulate the city (Berry 2007: 293). Locating ritual activity in the archaeological record has proven elusive, as the investigation of the Pompeiian evidence cannot provide snapshots of ritual performances that were frozen in time.

One of the most famous images from Pompeii is a mosaic of a ferocious dog, placed at the entryway to the House of the Tragic Poet, VI.viii.5 (Figure 9.4). Below the figure of the dog, closer to the threshold, the mosaicist has inscribed the words *CAVE CANEM*, 'Beware of the dog,' a phrase that resonates with modern viewers due to its seeming similarity with contemporary warnings posted at the entryways to houses or businesses. The assemblage, in this case, consists of the mosaic and its surrounding architectural elements; its context is defined as the building and the street outside. Although the

Figure 9.4 Mosaic of a chained dog with the inscription cave canem from VI.8.3, the House of the Tragic Poet at Pompeii (photo: Scala/ Art Resource, New York).

inscription was composed for a literate audience, analysis of the representation and its context suggests that it was intended to ward off a variety of unseen threats to the family that may have included the evil eye, demons, and ghosts. Like the figurine from Karanis discussed above, its efficacy lay in its ability to act as an agent in the world.

A drain, set into the floor, suggests that the exterior doors to the house may have stood open with some regularity (Proudfoot 2013: 103). The '*Cave Canem*' mosaic is located just within the threshold of the House of the Tragic Poet. The axial view into the house is one of the most commonly reproduced in artistic depictions (Bergmann 1994: 228–32). The house lies on the western side of the town, along the Via della Terme, an east–west thoroughfare that branched off of the Via del Mercurio/Via del Foro. The street would have seen a significant amount of traffic, as individuals from various social strata would have passed by the House of the Tragic Poet on their way to the forum or the public baths. The dog, mostly black with two white patches on its right foreleg and right rear flank, and a white stripe between its eyes onto its muzzle, crouches or lunges towards the right.

Scholars are in relative agreement that the image and its accompanying inscription served an apotropaic function. Such objects 'worked' either by inducing fear in the viewer, or by causing laughter through the use of obscene and often humorous images (Levi 1941: 3.225; Barton 1993: 168–72; Clarke 1998: 130–1). Clarke has suggested that the image induced laughter. The humour lies in the juxtaposition of the image and the inscription, which 'unmask(s) the humor of the artifice' (Clarke 2007: 54–7). In his review of Clarke's work, Ling disagrees sharply, suggesting that the image of the dog alluded to a real creature that waited inside (Ling 2009: 510). In analysing the same image, Beard is sceptical of both assessments for their reliance on the idea of apotropaia, suggesting that scholars too readily rely on this concept to explain the unusual (Beard 2007: 248; 2014: 58–9 and 234 n.25).

Images of dogs were believed to provide protection that was comparable to that of their flesh and blood counterparts. Statuettes of dogs were deposited at the entrances to Neo-Babylonian palaces, inscribed with spells intended to repel hostile forces or to let 'enter the good ones' (Feldt 2015: 73–5, 83). Odysseus encounters statues of dogs made of gold and silver outside of the palace of Alcinous; Homer (*Od.* 7.108) tells us that Hephaestus had made these automatons to 'protect the home of Alcinous.' Later, Medieval and Post-Medieval traditions may connect protection with the burial of dogs or cats within a house, particularly when the animal has been deposited near the entrance (Merrifield 1987: 119, 125, 128–30; Davies 2015: 390–1). Details of the mosaic suggest that the dog was intended to convey this sense: the dog's ears are pitched forward, and its mouth is open, baring its teeth and gums, which have been picked out in red. The animal's claws have been outlined in black tessserae, drawing attention to these as prominent features in the depiction.

At the House of the Tragic Poet, the image of a dog likely was believed efficacious against the evil eye as well as other threats. The evil eye was an outward expression of envy, *phthoneros* or *invidia*, sent invisibly through the air. The most common idea of sight, shared by a number of medical writers, held that the eye transmitted a substance to the thing perceived, which existed outside the person (Thibodeau 2016: 131–2). The envious, according to Heliodorus (*Aeth.* 3.7), on seeing the object of envy, sends forth particles from the eye that infuse the air; the victim absorbs the particles through the eyes, nose, or pores. Plutarch's explanation is similar: envious individuals send forth poisoned darts from the eye to attack the target (*Quaest. conv.* 5.7.4). In either case, the organ of sight produced the threat to the victim; it was necessary to evade or deflect these malicious particles.

The evil eye was dangerous because the particles that it transmitted could cause illness. Folk belief in the evil eye could co-exist with medical views espoused by doctors, who viewed disease as a result of humoral imbalance or environmental factors (Harris 2016: 3–4). An image of Phthonos, preserved from Kephallenia, depicts the personification as an emaciated figure that clutches his throat (Dunbabin and Dickie 1983: 8–9); the inscription suggests that he shows the signs of wasting that affect those who have suffered an attack of the evil eye. In the Kephallenia mosaic, the figure's rib cage is clearly visible, stressing the wasting nature of his ailment; the choking motion may indicate respiratory distress, or the inability to breathe. The mosaic seems likely to show an individual suffering from disease. Those who spent most of their time within the home – wives and matrons, especially those who were pregnant with reduced immunity, young children, and the elderly – manifested the symptoms of these invisible attacks, and unexplained disease or death could be attributed to hostile

Figure 9.5 Mosaic from the House of the Evil Eye Mosaic at Antioch on the Orontes (© Public Domain via Wikimedia Commons).

forces (Johnston 1999: 198–9). Demography points to the high incidence of childhood death through disease. As a precaution, children and pregnant women wore a variety of bells and amulets, including the bulla, to absorb the threat of the evil eye and protect against illness (Dasen 2015: 181).

Most often, the eye of the envious one was considered the source of the attack, and as such, it could be liable to counterattack as a defensive measure. Apotropaic images such as the phallus may have been believed to strike or penetrate the eye, rendering it powerless (Bartsch 2006: 147–9; on the phallus, Johns 1982: 62–75; Bailliot 2010: 32–41). The phallus even may be shown ejaculating into the evil eye, as at Leptis Magna, as well as on three examples from Roman Britain (Parker and Ross 2016; Parker 2017: 115, 119; on obscene bodily activities, Bailliot 2010: 44–8). Although not always depicted, the dog was one of several creatures that might be shown attacking a depiction of the evil eye in artistic representations. In the vestibule leading into the peristyle court at a house at Late Antique Antioch, a large eye (the evil eye) that is being attacked by a variety of figures: a raven, a trident, a scorpion, a snake, a dog, and a centipede (Figure 9.5). To the left of the eye, a dwarf strides away; his large phallus points backwards between his legs, as if it too, is attacking the evil eye (Levi 1941: 220–5; Trentin 2015: 56–7). An inscription above the eye (καὶ σύ, 'kai su') can be read in different ways, either directing the gaze (malign or beneficial) back at the viewer, or as a protective warning that the threatening force should suffer ill (Trentin 2015: 55). The same motifs could be miniaturised to be worn on the body for transportable protection. On a magical gem from the Capitoline Museum, an image of the evil eye is surrounded by, moving clockwise from top, thunderbolts, a pair of birds, a pair of dogs, a turtle, a lizard, a scorpion, another dog, a griffin, another bird, and a final dog (Mastrocinque 2007: 128 RoC 4; Bélyácz *et al.* nd). The amulet would protect the bearer from the *phthoneros*, as the dogs and other animals could threaten and ward off his or her dangerous gaze. A similar aim is likely behind a bone plaque discovered in the construction levels of a house a Butrint. On this object, a hunting dog is depicted leaping over a representation of the evil eye, presumably holding it at bay or bringing it down (Mitchell, 2007: 294–6).

The choice of the dog as an image for protection may have been significant, as Pliny praises the canine blood for its ability to ward off dangerous ghosts and relates that the genitals of a black dog, buried beneath the threshold, repel sorcery (*HN* 30.82; Ogle 1911: 254). The House of the Tragic Poet is positioned directly across from the Forum Baths, with its potential for supernatural threats. Demons of the bath might cause physical harm or suffocation, and a variety of Jewish and Christian authors associate bathing facilities with unclean spirits that could cause seizures (Bonner 1932; Dunbabin 1989: 35–6). Other spirits were believed to wander the streets. Gello or Mormo was held responsible for diseases and conditions such as pre-eclampsia that threatened pregnant women and babies, especially near that time of childbirth (Johnston, 1995: 364; 1999: 165–9). Unexplained misfortune was often blamed on *daimones* and the restless dead, so that the illness and death of a young child was symptomatic not of disease but of a spiritual or supernatural attack.

The mosaic is a placed at a position that would be highly visible to passers-by, effectively controlling or framing the view into the house whenever the door was open. This boundary marked the space of the property owner, and would have been culturally significant to the residents of Pompeii (Berry 2016: 127, 134). Decoration can highlight transitional places where ambiguities in social order are in play (Parker Pearson 1994: 27–8). The house façade, and the door set within it, encouraged looking, as certain owners, by stressing the size and scale of a house, drew the gaze of passersby (Laurence 1994: 88–9; Hartnett 2017: 158–61, 169). Supernatural threats, or – perhaps more importantly – the physical particles that comprise the gaze might slip in unseen. Movable screens or curtains may have limited this view, but it seems that owners constructed the interior of the house with the view from the entryway in mind (Hartnett 2017: 188–92). As clients crowded around the open door, waiting to step into the vestibule or enter the house, the entryway permitted invited guests as well as those on the street – strangers – a view into the house. Inside the house, susceptible residents might inadvertently pass within the gaze of the envious.

The deep fauces of the house would have limited the view into the atrium. For many of those who passed by the house, the mosaic would have been the dominant or even only visible feature of the house (Figure 9.6). The eyes of the dog would have tracked the viewer as he or she moved along the street; when the viewer reached the position from which the atrium might be seen, the interior of the

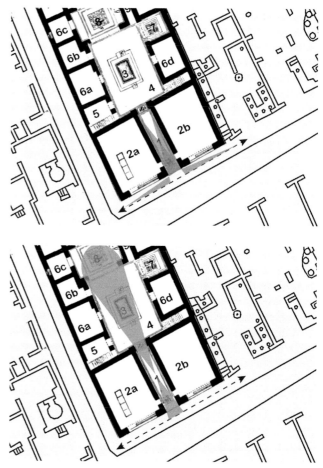

Figure 9.6 Plan of VI.8.3, the House of the Tragic Poet, showing viewshed along the street outside of the building. The upper image shows the viewshed in grey, where the gaze of the passerby is largely confined to the interior walls of the fauces (1). In the lower image, the interior of the house would have been visible from only a limited number of positions along the street (figure adapted from Mau 1899).

house was protected from below by the mosaic decoration. The mosaic should be understood in the context of other prophylactic measures employed at the entryway to the house. Brides would smear the doorposts of the house with the fat of a wolf to ward off malign spells (Pliny *HN* 28.142; 28.135). Diogenes Sinopensis Epistulae informs us that the lintels of homes could be inscribed with an invocation to Heracles Kallinikos (resplendent in victory): 'the son of Zeus, Herakles Kallinikos lives within; let no evil enter!' (ὁ τοῦ Διὸς παῖς καλλίνικος Ἡρακλῆς ἐνθάδε κατοικεῖ· μηδὲν εἰσίτω κακόν. Weinrich 1915: 8–9; Faraone 1992: 13 n. 5, 58, 69 n. 39; 2009: 228–34). The inscription appears with few modifications at sites in various areas of the Roman Empire, from Thasos to Kurdistan; a painted inscription, in Greek, was discovered in Pompeii at V.2.7 (Weinrich 1915: 13–14; Robert 1965). According to Diogenes Laertius newlyweds typically inscribed the text above their doorways. The prohibition is directed against a general evil, κακόν, which may refer to demonic spirits or the dead, dangers that would represent a special threat for the newly married, who hoped for a successful pregnancy and childbirth.

Apotropaia were viewed as efficacious because they could act against seen and unseen threats: intruders, humans who, through envy, wished harm, witchcraft, malicious spirits, and the restless dead. These dangers, though secret or even unseen, had tangible results that were easily recognised: the theft of goods, disease, infant mortality, or mental illness. Like the mud figurine from Karanis, the image of the dog may have been endowed with agency to protect the occupants from spiritual or supernatural danger. As a protective measure against the *phthonos* or *invidia* the phallus was believed to pierce the eye, which was comparable to a vagina. In a similar way, the dog was endowed with agency to attack and dispel the threats that faced the occupants. The processes by which this image was activated or set in motion are obscure. The mosaicist or homeowner, or maybe a separate ritual specialist perhaps performed a rite that involved the image. The god Hephaestus was said to have placed *pharmaka*, some sort of magical substances, inside of an image of a bronze lion given to Makar to animate it; the bronze lion then functioned as a phylactery (*P. Oxy.* 3711; Faraone 1992: 21). In the Near East, ritual activity endowed buried guardian statues with magical power, so that they might protect entrances and doorways (Nakamura 2005). The magical papyri from Egypt suggest that rituals were undertaken to endow magical amulets with protective powers, as exemplified by the text quoted at the beginning of this article (Moyer and Dielemann 2003). The mosaic may also have been made efficacious through repeated actions that took place at the threshold. During the day, members of the household would have encountered and touched the mosaic in different ways – sweeping dirt across its surface, or treading upon the image of the dog as they exited and entered the house. As we noted above, sweeping, could be invested with a ritual function aimed at ridding the house of malign spirits or the threat of the restless dead. These tactile experiences may have been understood as animating or activating the image.

The use of dog mosaics for protection appears to be limited to the Vesuvian cities, although comparable protective measures can be attested from other sites in the Mediterranean. At Pompeii, four other mosaics and paintings of dogs positioned at the entrances to houses and shops, although the others lack the fierceness of the House of the Tragic Poet (Clarke 1979 10–14; mosaics: I.viii.1; V.i.26; painting of a dog: IX.2.26n). Some of these images likely functioned in a similar way. At the Casa di Paquius Proculus (I.viii.1), positioned along the Via Abbondanza, just inside the threshold, the viewer encountered a mosaic pavement of a chained dog, lying prone before a set of double doors. Martial images are affixed to each door: a spear and shield on one and an axe other, perhaps heightening the threat against potential intruders. At the House of L. Caecilius Jucundus (V.1.26), a mosaic of a dog appears just within the threshold of the house. The dog is curled up, seemingly

asleep, but one watchful eye is open; the animal is poised to spring into action, should it be required.

Conclusion

The small figurine from Karanis, deposited beneath the house of a desired lover, and the mosaic of the ferocious dog, positioned in the fauces of the House of the Tragic Poet at Pompeii can each be categorised as powerful objects or artefacts that were endowed with magical force. For the modern investigator, like the ancient observer, 'magic' is an etic category. The term can be applied to illegal or illicit ritual actions that are undertaken in secret with the intent to harm another, or to subvert their agency to that of the practitioner. Alternatively, 'magic' is appropriate for a wide range of objects reliant on pre–modern ideas of the world, including amulets or apotropaic representations, that were believed to bring about change by harnessing divine power. If both are power objects, a crucial question lies in the relationship between these two artefacts, and how they might be used to mutually illuminate the process by which ritual power was harnessed in the world.

In each case, archaeological context permits us to identify the artefacts as power objects, able to act upon the world. The small figurine and the hairpin were both discovered beneath structure 165 at Karanis; the forensic connection between the decoration of the figurine and the size of the hairpin solidifies this depositional association. Analysis of the objects can permit us to construct elements of the ritual. The objects were found in this space because deposition was a critical part of the ritual act. At the House of the Tragic Poet in Pompeii, the physical architecture of the building informs our reading of the artefact, largely through the arrangement of the mosaic, the long entryway into the house, and the internal space of the domicile.

The desired result – whether the love of the victim, or protection from unseen threats – was achieved through the agency of a representation. In neither case was the image intended as a duplicate or even a substitute of the thing depicted. Rather, the form of representation is determined by the choices made by the practitioner; the features that are present may be significant to the efficacy of the representation. At Karanis, the practitioner, by creating and manipulating the small figurine, believed that he or she could impose his or her will upon the target of the spell. Placing the figurine into a fire and piercing it with the hairpin enacted the desire of the practitioner, that the victim would be tortured until she came to the commissioner of the spell. In contrast, the ritual that activated the mosaic – if it occurred – remains obscure, as its enactment have left no identifiable traces within the archaeological record. Evidence may exist beneath the A.D. 79 layer, but it is not possible to access this archaeological context. The apotropaic image was created for the benefit of the residents of the house, and it was presumably intended to function in perpetuity, as different individuals occupied the domicile. It is possible, however, that mundane actions undertaken during the day, such as sweeping or walking over or around the mosaic, may have activated or empowered the image.

The house provides a discrete environment within which to explore and engage with archaeological evidence, as the space suggests both the performers and beneficiaries of ritual activity. The material from Karanis indicates that rituals intended to disrupt the house and undermine domestic tranquillity could also intrude upon living space. The ritual deposited beneath structure 165 draws upon the larger religious and magical corpus of Graeco-Roman Egypt, focusing a composite ritual action on the goals of a single commissioner. In contrast, the evidence from Pompeii conveys different messages depending on the viewer and their spatial and social position relative to the household. The placement of the mosaic speaks to the importance of the house as a space that required both separation and protection from the public sphere. Situated in a liminal area, at the boundary between home and exterior world the mosaic is both inside and outside, and engages simultaneously with residents, guests, and passers-by. The mosaic also prompts us to interrogate its ritual function, and to consider whether it obscures ritual behaviours and events that may be invisible to us. In each case, archaeological context is vital for interpreting the role of artefacts and assemblages within the domestic sphere. The house focused the force of the power objects, permitting them to act upon the world.

Department of Classics, Oberlin College

Acknowledgements

This paper had its genesis at the conference 'Self and Space: Household Identity and Domestic Cult in the Ancient Mediterranean and Near East,' held at Yale University in April 2014. I am grateful to the organisers of that conference, Sara E. Cole and Elizabeth Lang, for the invitation to present a keynote for the panel 'Ritual and Performativity in Domestic Cult Practice.' Portions of this paper were presented at the conference Symposium Campanum 2017: Recent Work in Vesuvian Lands: New Projects, Practices, and Approaches. I am grateful to the thoughtful suggestions provided by the other speakers at the symposium, especially Joanne Berry. I also wish to express my thanks to the organiser of this volume, Adam Parker, for the invitation to contribute to this timely and important collection. I am grateful to the anonymous reviewers of this paper, and to Adam Parker and Stuart Mckie for comments and suggestions. Research for this paper was carried out through an Oberlin College Powers Grant, with additional funding provided by the Thomas F. Cooper Fund for Faculty Development of the Department of Classics. I have benefitted immensely from the support and suggestions of colleagues at Oberlin and beyond, including Christopher Trinacty, Kirk Ormand, and John Harwood (University of Toronto Faculty of Architecture, Landscape and Design).

Note

1   Figurines used for binding are collected in Faraone 1991 and Bailliot 2015.

Bibliography

Allison, P.M. 1999. Labels for ladles: interpeting the material culture of Roman households. In P.M. Allison (ed.) *The Archaeology of Household Activities.* New York: Routledge: 57–77.

Allison, P.M. 2006. *The Insula of the Menander at Pompeii, Volume III: The Finds, a Contextual Study.* Oxford: Clarendon Press.

Bachelard, G. 1964. *The Poetics of Space.* New York: Orion Press.

Bailliot, M. 2010. *Magie et Sortilèges dans l'Antiquité Romaine.* Paris: Hermann éditeurs.

Bailliot, M. 2015. Roman magic figurines from the western provinces of the Roman Empire: an archaeological survey. *Brittania* 46: 93–110.

Bakker, J.T. 1994. *Living and Working with the Gods: Studies of Evidence for Private Religion and Its Material Environment in the City of Ostia (100–500 AD).* Amsterdam: J.C. Gieben.

Barrett, C. 2015a. Material evidence. In E. Eidinow and J. Kindt (eds) *The Oxford Handbook of Ancient Greek Religion.* New York: Oxford University Press: 113–30.

Barrett, C. 2015b. Terracotta figurines and the archaeology of ritual: domestic cult in Greco-Roman Egypt. In S. Huysecom-Haxhi and A. Muller. (eds) *Figurines Grecques en Contexte: Présence Muette dans le Sanctuaire, la Tombe et la Maison.* Villeneuve d'Ascq: Presses Universitaires du Septentrion: 401–19.

Barton, C.A. 1993. *The Sorrows of the Ancient Romans: The Gladiator and the Monster.* Princeton, NJ: Princeton University Press.

Bartsch, S. 2006. *The Mirror of the Self: Sexuality, Self-Knowledge, and the Gaze in the Early Roman Empire.* Chicago, IL: University of Chicago Press.

Beard, M. 2014. *Laughter in Ancient Rome: On Joking, Tickling, and Cracking Up.* Berkeley, CA: University of California Press.

Beard, M., North, J.A. and Price, S.R.F. 1998. *Religions of Rome.* New York: Cambridge University Press.

Bell, C. 2007. Response: defining the need for a definition. In E. Kyriakidis (ed.) *The Archaeology of Ritual.* Los Angeles, CA: Cotsen Institute of Archaeology, University of California, Los Angeles: 277–308.

Bell, C.M. 1992. *Ritual Theory, Ritual Practice.* New York: Oxford University Press.

Bélyácz, K., Endreffy, K. and Nagy, Á.M. (nd) *The Campbell Bonner Magical Gems Database.* Available: http://www2.szepmuveszeti.hu/talismans/. [Accessed: 25/10/17].

Bergmann, B. 1994. The Roman house as memory theater: the house of the tragic poet at Pompeii. *The Art Bulletin* 76: 225–56.

Berry, J. 1997. Household artefacts: towards a reinterpretation of Roman domestic space. In R. Lawrence and A. Wallace-Hadrill (eds) *Domestic Space in Roman World: Pompeii and Beyond.* Supplementary Series 22. Portsmouth, RI: Journal of Roman Archaeology, 183–195.

Berry, J. 2007. *Instrumentum domesticum* – a case study. In J. Dobbins and P.W. Foss (eds) *The World of Pompeii.* New York: Routledge: 292–301.

Berry, J. 2016. Boundaries and control in the Roman house. *Journal of Roman Archaeology* 29: 125–41.

Betz, H.D. 1992. *The Greek Magical Papyri in Translation.* Chicago, IL: University of Chicago Press.

Bodel, J. 2008. Cicero's Minerva, Penates, and the mother of the Lares: an outline of Roman domestic religion. In J. Bodel and S.M. Olyan (eds) *Household and Family Religion in Antiquity.* Malden, MA: Blackwell: 248–75.

Boedeker, D. 2008. Family matters: domestic religion in Classical Greece. In J. Bodel and S.M. Olyan (eds) *Household and Family Religion in Antiquity.* Malden, MA: Blackwell: 229–47.

Bonner, C.A. 1932. Demons of the bath. In Egypt Exploration Society and S.R.K. Glanville (eds) *Studies Presented to F. Ll. Griffith.* London: Egypt Exploration Society: 203–8.

Brown, B. 2001. Thing Theory. *Critical Inquiry* 28: 22.

Bryen, A.Z. and Wypustek, A. 2009. Gemellus' evil eyes (*P.Mich.* VI 423–424). *Greek, Roman and Byzantine Studies* 49: 535–55.

Clarke, J.R. 1979. *Roman Black-and-White Figural Mosaic.*, New York: New York University Press.

Clarke, J.R. 1998. *Looking at Lovemaking: Constructions of Sexuality in Roman Art, 100 B.C.–A.D. 250.* Berkeley, CA: University of California Press.

Clarke, J.R. 2007. *Looking at Laughter: Humor, Power, and Transgression in Roman Visual Culture, 100 B.C.–A.D. 250.* Berkeley, CA: University of California Press.

Collins, D. 2008. *Magic in the Ancient Greek World.* Malden, MA: Blackwell.

Dasen, V. 2015. Probaskania: amulets and magic in antiquity. In D. Boschung and J.N. Bremmer (eds) *The Materiality of Magic.* Paderborn: Wilhelm Fink: 177–203.

Davies, O. 2015. The material culture of post-medieval domestic magic in Europe: evidence, comparisons and interpretations. In D. Boschung and J.N. Bremmer (eds) *The Materiality of Magic.* Paderborn: Wilhelm Fink: 379–417.

Donderer, M. 1984. Münzen als Bauopfer in Römischen Privathäusern. *Bonner Jahrbücher des Rheinischen Landesmuseum in Bonn und des Vereins von Altertumsfreunden im Rheinlande* 184: 177–87.

Du Bourguet, P. 1975. Ensemble magique de la période Romaine en Égypte. *Revue du Louvre* 25: 255–7.

Dunbabin, K.M.D. 1999. *Mosaics of the Greek and Roman World.* New York: Cambridge University Press.

Dunbabin, K.M.D. and Dickie, M.W. 1983. *Invidia rumpantur pectora*: the iconography of Phthonos/Invidia in Graeco-Roman art. *Jahrbuch für Antike und Christentum* 26: 7–37.

Dunbabin, K. 1989. *Baiarum grata voluptas*: pleasures and dangers of the baths. *Papers of the British School at Rome,* 57: 6–46.

Faraone, C.A. 1991. Binding and burying the forces of evil: the defensive use of 'voodoo dolls' in ancient Greece. *Classical Antiquity* 10: 165–220.

Faraone, C.A. 1992. *Talismans and Trojan Horses: Guardian Statues in Ancient Greek Myth and Ritual.* New York: Oxford University Press.

Faraone, C.A. 1993. The wheel, the whip and other implements of torture: erotic magic in Pindar *Pythian* 4.213–19. *Classical Journal* 89: 1–19.

Faraone, C.A. 1999. *Ancient Greek Love Magic.* Cambridge, MA: Harvard University Press.

Faraone, C.A. 2002. The ethnic origins of a Roman-era *Philtrokatadesmos* (*PGM* IV. 296–434). In P.A. Mirecki and M. Meyer (eds) *Magic and Ritual in the Ancient World.* Leiden: Brill. 319–43.

Faraone, C.A. 2009. Stopping evil, pain, anger, and blood: the ancient Greek tradition of protective iambic incantations. *Greek Roman and Byzantine Studies* 29: 227–55.

Faraone, C.A. 2013. The amuletic design of the Mithraic bull-wounding scene. *Journal of Roman Studies* 103: 96–116.

Feldt, L. 2015. Monstrous figurines from Mesopotamia: texuality, spatiality and materiality in rituals and incantations for the protection of houses in first millenium Aššur. In D. Boschung and J.N. Bremmer (eds) *The Materiality of Magic.* Paderborn: Wilhelm Fink: 59–95.

Flower, H.I. 2017. *The Dancing Lares and the Serpent in the Garden: Religion at the Roman Street Corner.* Princeton, NJ, Princeton University Press.

Foss, P.W. 1997. Watchful Lares: Roman household organization and the rituals of cooking and dining. In R. Laurence and A. Wallace-Hadrill (eds) *Domestic Space in the Roman World: Pompeii and Beyond.* Supplementary Series 22. Portsmouth, RI: Journal of Roman Archaeology: 196–218.

Frankfurter, D. 2015. Female figurines in early Christian Egypt: reconstructing lost practices and meanings. *Material Religion* 11: 190–223.

Frankfurter, D. forthcoming. Magic and the forces of materiality. In D. Frankfurter (ed.) *Guide to the Study of Ancient Magic.* Leiden: Brill.

Gell, A. 1998. *Art and Agency: An Anthropological Theory.* New York: Oxford University Press.

Gordon, R.L. 2015. Showing the gods the way: curse tablets as deictic persuasion. *Religion in the Roman Empire* 1: 148–80.

Hales, S. 2003. *The Roman House and Social Identity.* New York: Cambridge University Press.

Hamori, E.J. 2015. *Women's Divination in Biblical Literature: Prophecy, Necromancy, and Other Arts of Knowledge.* New Haven, CO: Yale University Press.

Hartnett, J. 2017. *The Roman Street: Urban Life and Society in Pompeii, Herculaneum, and Rome.* New York: Cambridge University Press.

Husselman, E.M. 1979. *Karanis Excavations of the University of Michigan in Egypt 1928–1935: Topography and Architecture: A Summary of the Reports of the Director, Enoch E. Peterson.* Ann Arbor, MI: University of Michigan Press.

Johns, C. 1982. *Sex or Symbol: Erotic Images of Greece and Rome.* London: British Museum.

Johnston, S.I. 1995. Defining the dreadful: remarks on the Greek child-killing demon. In M.W. Meyer and P.A. Mirecki (eds) *Ancient Magic and Ritual Power.* New York: E.J. Brill: 361–87.

Johnston, S.I. 1999. *Restless Dead: Encounters Between the Living and the Dead in Ancient Greece.* Berkeley, CA, University of California Press.

Kambitsis, S. 1976. Une nouvelle tablette magique d'égypte, Musée du Louvre Inv. E27145, 3e/4e Siècle. *Bulletin de l'Institut Francais d'archeologie orientale* 76: 213–23.

Kindt, J. 2012. *Rethinking Greek Religion.* New York: Cambridge University Press.

Kyriakidis, E. 2007. Archaeologies of ritual. In E. Kyriakidis (ed.) *The Archaeology of Ritual.* Los Angeles: Cotsen Institute of Archaeology, University of California, Los Angeles: 289–308.

Laurence, R. 1994. *Roman Pompeii: Space and Society.* New York: Routledge.

Levi, D. 1941. The evil eye and the lucky hunchback. In R. Stillwell (ed.) *Antioch on the Orontes III: The Excavations 1937–1939*. Princeton, NJ: Princeton University Press: 220–32.

Ling, R. 2009. Roman laughter: Review of J.R. Clarke 2007. *Journal of Roman Archaeology* 22: 508–10.

Manning, M.C. 2014. Material culture of ritual concealments in the United States. *Historical Archaeology* 48: 52–83.

Martinez, D.G. 1991. *Michigan Papyri XVI: A Greek Love Charm from Egypt (P.Mich. 757)*. Atlanta, GI: Scholars Press.

Mastrocinque, A. 2007. *Sylloge Gemmarum Gnosticarum II*. Rome: Istituto Poligrafico e Zecca dello Stato.

Mau, A. 1988. *Pompeii, Its Life and Art*. New York: Macmillan.

Merrifield, R. 1987. *The Archaeology of Ritual and Magic*. London: B.T. Batsford.

Miller, D. 1998. *Material Cultures: Why Some Things Matter*. Chicago, IL: University of Chicago Press.

Miller, D. 2010. *Stuff*. Cambridge: Polity Press.

Mitchell, J. 2007. Keeping the demons out of the house: the archaeology of apotropaic strategy and practice in late antique Butrint and Antigoneia. In L. Lavan, E. Swift and T. Putzeys (eds) *Objects in Context, Objects in Use: Material Spatiality in Late Antiquity*. Leiden: Brill: 313–62.

Moyer, I. and Dieleman, J. 2003. Miniaturization and the opening of the mouth in a Greek magical text (*PGM* XII.270–350). *Journal of Ancient Near Eastern Religions* 3: 47–72.

Nakamura, C. 2005. Mastering matters: magical sense and apotropaic figurine worlds of Neo-Assyria. In L. Meskell (ed.) *Archaeologies of Materiality*. Malden, MA: Blackwell: 18–45.

Nevett, L.C. 2010. *Domestic Space in Classical Antiquity*. New York: Cambridge University Press.

Ogle, M.B. 1911. The house-door in Greek and Roman religion and folk-lore. *American Journal of Philology* 32: 251–71.

Parker, A. 2017. Protecting the troops? Phallic carvings in the north of Britain. In A. Parker (ed) *Ad Vallum: Papers on the Roman Army and Frontiers in Celebration of Dr. Brian Dobson*. British Archaeological Report 631. Oxford: British Archaeological Reports, 117–30.

Parker, A. and Ross, C. 2016. A new phallic carving from Roman Catterick. *Britannia* 47: 271–9.

Parker Pearson, M. and Richards, C. 1994. Ordering the world: perceptions of architecture, space and time. In M. Parker Pearson and C. Richards (eds) *Architecture and Order: Approaches to Social Space*. London, New York: Routledge: 1–37.

Pinch, G. 1993. *Votive Offerings to Hathor*. Oxford: Griffith Institute, Ashmolean Museum.

Proudfoot, E. 2013. Secondary doors in entranceways in Pompeii: reconsidering access and the 'view from the street'. In A. Bokern, M. Bolder-Boos, S. Krmnicek, D. Maschek and S. Page (eds) *TRAC 2012: Proceedings of the Twenty-Second Annual Theoretical Roman Archaeology Conference Which Took Place at Goethe University in Frankfurt 29 March–1 April 2012*. Oxford: Oxbow Books: 91–116.

Praz, M. 1982. *An Illustrated History of Interior Decoration: From Pompeii to Art Nouvea*. New York: Thames and Hudson.

Rappaport, R.A. 1999. *Ritual and Religion in the Making of Humanity*, New York: Cambridge University Press.

Ritner, R.K. 1993. *The Mechanics of Ancient Egyptian Magical Practice*. Chicago, IL: Oriental Institute of the University of Chicago.

Ritner, R.K. 2002. Necromancy in ancient Egypt. In L.J. Ciraolo and J.L. Seidel (eds) *Magic and Divination in the Ancient World*. Leiden: Brill, Styx: 89–96.

Robert, L. 1965. Échec au Mal. *Hellenica* 13: 265–71.

Rüpke, J. and Gordon. R.L. 2007. *Religion of the Romans*. Cambridge: Polity.

Ruppel, T., Neuwirth, J., Leone, M.P. and Fry, G.-M. 2003. Hidden in view: African spiritual spaces in North American landscapes. *Antiquity* 77: 321–35.

Rykwert, J. 1972. *On Adam's House in Paradise: The Idea of the Primitive Hut in Architectural History*. New York: Museum of Modern Art.

Schiffer, M.B. 1987. *Formation Processes of the Archaeological Record*. Albuquerque, NM: University of New Mexico Press.

Semper, G. 1989. *The Four Elements of Architecture and Other Writings*. New York: Cambridge University Press.

Smith, J.Z. 1978. Towards interpreting demonic powers in Hellenic and Roman Antiquity. In W. Haase (ed.) *Austieg Und Niergang Der Römischen Welt*. New York: Walter de Gruyter: 423–39.

Smith, J.Z. 1995. Trading places. In M.W. Meyer and P.A. Mirecki (eds) *Ancient Magic and Ritual Power*. New York: E. J. Brill: 13–27.

Stewart, S. 1984. *On Longing: Narratives of the Miniature, the Gigantic, the Souvenir, the Collection*. Baltimore, ML: Johns Hopkins University Press.

Taussig, M. 1993. *Mimesis and Alterity: A Particular History of the Senses*. New York: Routledge.

Taussig, M. 2009. What do drawings want? *Culture, Theory and Critique* 50: 263–74.

Thibodeau, P. 2016. Ancient optics: theories and problems of vision. In G.L. Irby (ed.) *A Companton to Science, Technology and Medicine in Ancient Greece and Rome*. Malden, MA: Wiley: 130–44.

Trentin, L. 2015. *The Hunchback in Hellenistic and Roman Art*. London: Bloomsbury Academic.

Versnel, H. S. 1991. Some reflections on the relationship magic-religion. *Numen* 38: 177–97.

Wallace-Hadrill, A. 1988. The social structure of the Roman house. *Papers of the British School at Rome* 56: 43–97.

Wallace-Hadrill, A. 1994. *Houses and Society in Pompeii and Herculaneum*. Princeton, NJ: Princeton University Press.

Weinrich, O. 1915. De dis ignotis quaestiones selectae. *Archiv für Religionwissenschaft* 18: 1–52.

Wilburn, A.T. 2012. *Materia Magica: The Archaeology of Magic in Roman Egypt, Cyprus and Spain*. Ann Arbor, MI: University of Michigan Press.

Witteyer, M. 2005. Curse tablets and voodoo Dolls from Mainz: the archaeological evidence for magical practices in the sanctuary of Isis and Magna Mater. *MHNH: revista internacional de investigación sobre magia y astrología antiguas* 5: 105–23.

Abbreviations

PGM = *Papyri Graecae Magicae* (see Betz 1992).

10

The Legs, Hands, Head and Arms Race:
The Human Body as a Magical Weapon in the Roman World

Stuart McKie

Introduction

This chapter aims to show that alongside the gems, tablets, amulets and other materials that were of central importance to Roman magical practices, the physical bodies of those who used them could also be viewed as powerful magical objects, able to influence the world around them through certain movements and gestures. The focus here will be on gestures of binding and unbinding, which usually involved crossing or intertwining body parts such as the fingers, arms or legs, or tying or binding a body part or another material object with metal or fabric. The chapter will examine the literary and material evidence for such gestures, and will set them within the wider social and cultural contexts of Italy and the western Roman provinces.

Although the study of the material nature of ancient magical practices is still in its infancy, it has made significant contributions to our understanding of the topic. The 'material turn' has arrived in the world of ancient magic, and so in recent years there has been a greater recognition of the importance of objects in magical rituals, the significance of the materials that were used in their creation and the ways in which these objects were altered and manipulated for magical effect (Wilburn 2012; papers in Boschung and Bremmer 2015). As Brown (1970: 18) once noted, scholars of Roman magic have an embarrassment of riches when it comes to the material evidence available for study, so this growing field of material studies has considerable potential when applied to ancient magic.

However, amid the sustained excitement for material studies of ancient magic, two important facets of the wider 'material turn' debate are at risk of being overlooked: embodied experience and the materiality of the body. Recent studies of material magic have often taken the bodies of those who produced magical objects or engaged in magical

rituals for granted, overlooking the role of, for example, sensory perception, gender and age in these processes. In contrast, archaeologists and anthropologists engaged in wider material culture studies have not examined objects in isolation, but have conceptualised them as part of the lived experience of embodied human beings (Hicks 2010: 71–3). Embodied archaeology, which has been firmly grounded in the phenomenology of Heidegger and Merleau-Ponty, suggests that objects are revealed to humans through their sensory perceptions of the world around them (Thomas 1996: 79–80; 2006: 46–8). Such sensory perception varies widely based on class, race, gender and ethnicity, and involves not only the classic five senses (sight, hearing, smell, taste and touch), but a wider sensorium including balance, memory, movement, intoxication and so on (Hamilakis 2014: 2–3, 113; Betts 2017: xiv–xv). Furthermore, it has been argued that the form, meaning, and understanding of objects, places, and people around the individual are changed by the actions of the individual, who is active in the creation of their life-world (Ingold 2000).

A related area of study to these phenomenological interpretations is the scholarship on the power and importance of gesture and movement. Psychologists such as McNeill (1992; 2005) have argued that such non-verbal forms of communication are inseparable from speech, and are just as important for conveying meaning and intention. Anthropologists have recognised that, in similar ways to spoken language, movements and gestures of the human body are not universal, but are culturally determined and have changing importance based on the contexts in which they are performed (Farnell 1999: 345, 359; Noland 2009: 2).

The creative, transformative and destructive power invested in magical rituals would seem to be an obvious arena for testing these theories, but such practices have been relatively ignored by both phenomenological archaeologists and anthropologists who have studied the body. When scholars of the Roman world have approached the subject of gesture and movement it has most often been through representations in ancient art (Brilliant 1963), use on the dramatic stage (Panayotakis 2005) or in the guides to rhetorical delivery written by the likes of Cicero and Quintilian (Gleason 1995; O'Sullivan 2011). Corbeill (2004) is the only recent scholar to consider the movements of the body in Roman religious or magical rituals in terms of embodied experience.

This paper seeks to address these gaps by considering the importance of the moving human body in Roman magical rituals. The range of gestures and movements that could be included in this study is vast and incredibly varied across time and space. As a result, this chapter focuses on two related and relatively well-defined types of gesture – binding and unbinding – and, where possible, restricts the study to evidence from Italy and the western provinces in the imperial period. As will be demonstrated throughout this chapter, Romans considered a range of movements and gestures to be related to binding or unbinding, including tying or untying fabrics, crossing or interlacing body parts, piercing dolls and folding metal sheets. These movements and gestures were predominantly used in rituals aimed at stopping or preventing something from happening, or enhancing the power of a more complex ritual by fixing it to the victim more securely. Such gestures received some attention from scholars in the nineteenth and twentieth centuries (Sittl 1890; Heckenbach 1911; Eitrem 1953) but, although their collections of sources are still incredibly valuable, the conclusions of these scholars that only women and lower-class men were given to practicing such superstitious rituals is in need of revision. These scholars, especially Heckenbach, uncritically accepted elite Roman male divisions of ritual practice into acceptable religion and unacceptable superstition, a position that has been convincingly deconstructed over subsequent decades (see, in particular, Beard *et al.* 1998: 211ff; Gordon 2008).

Some comment needs to be made on the structure of the main argument of this chapter, which analyses the literary and material evidence separately. Although other divisions were no doubt possible, this seemed the most sensible, owing to the nature of the evidence for the gestures and movements discussed here. The movements of the human body are ephemeral and transient, leaving traces in the archaeological record only when they interact with durable material objects such as metal sheets. As such, finding evidence for them is incredibly hard, especially for those movements and gestures that did not involve the use of other objects. Rituals of this kind are discussed in the written sources that have survived from the Roman world, but often only in passing and with little further explanation. As will be seen, the ways in which

magical gestures were talked about in the literary sources, however briefly, were part of wider Roman cultural debates over normative behaviour in society, and as such cannot be accepted at face value. There is, therefore, something of a disconnect between the material and literary evidence for gestures of binding and unbinding, which makes it appropriate to explore them separately. In the conclusion at the end of the chapter I will bring both forms of evidence together.

The Unbound Body in Roman Literature

As has already been mentioned, there is a good deal of recent scholarship on the importance of gesture and bodily comportment in Roman culture. Through this work it is clear that, at least among elite Roman men, there was a culture of 'unremitting scrutiny… on deportment' (Gleason 1995: 57), in which every movement of their bodies was analysed for signs of conformity or deviance from normative standards. This was especially true in terms of gender roles, as tiny movements of the hands, eyes or limbs of men could be interpreted as evidence for effeminacy or sexual deviance (for one example see Plut. *Caes.* 4.8–9. See Edwards 1993: 63–97 for detailed discussion). Orators and other public figures were scrutinised particularly harshly, and guidebooks were written to help these individuals to navigate their way through this behavioural minefield (examples include Cicero, *De or.* and Quint. *Inst.* 11.3). On the other side, the discipline of physiognomy was developed to aid in the decoding of the movements and gestures of others (Gleason 1995). Actions involved in religious worship were as much part of this codification as any other facet of public life, and to act improperly in these contexts could open the individual to derision or more serious accusations of impiety (Corbeill 2004: 26). Debates over correct religious practice are also evident in more imaginative literature, particularly poetry written around the time of Augustus (Phillips 1992; Feeney 1998: 115–35), when religious imagery was a central part of the Golden Age narrative constructed around the ascent of the first emperor. From at least the late republican period, correct bodily comportment in religious worship and all other walks of life became a central part of the construction of elite Roman identity. It is in this context that the literary evidence for binding and unbinding gestures should be interpreted.

Roman writers often conceptualised gestures of binding as impediments to standard, acceptable communications with the gods, or as symbols of impurity or uncleanliness. When depicting someone in the act of worshipping, numerous authors make the explicit point that certain parts of the worshipper's body were unbound. A standard trope in such depictions, especially of women, is that they addressed the gods with hair unbound, with bare feet and wearing no rings (Petron. *Sat.* 44; Verg. *Aen.* 3.62; Ov. *Fast.* 4.318). This state of dress seems to have suggested purity, honesty, and at times desperation in communication with the gods, particularly as these tropes were often connected to times of crisis such as drought or warfare. Women with bare feet and unbound hair also suggested a natural, primordial or fertile state, opposed to the bound or covered hair and feet normally worn by Roman wives, which has been interpreted as a symbol of their submission to a husband's control (Myerowitz Levine 1995: 102–5). This state of dress could arouse suspicion rather than praise, depending on the circumstances and intentions of the women themselves. Powerful women were a perennial concern for elite Roman men, who were paranoid about feminine challenges to their masculine authority (Stratton 2007: 72ff). Unbound, wild hair and bare feet were familiar aspects of the standard image of the witch in Roman literature, who became the archetypal powerful women, with the ability to control the natural world and to attack male sexuality (Luc. 6.607–18; Verg. *Aen.* 4.509–10). In the Roman literary imagination then, the act of unbinding hair, as well as feet and other body parts, had the effect of releasing women from their symbolic bindings to their husbands or fathers, and allowing them to act independently. Unbound from this state, women could act either for communal good, as in the case of traditional matrons responding to civic crises, or, in the case of witches, to satisfy their own selfish desires.

Although women were more commonly depicted as engaging in religious rituals without bindings, the image could be applied to men too. Among the many restrictions reportedly placed on the behaviour of the *flamen Dialis*, the high priest of Jupiter, were bans on him having a knot in any part of his dress or to be in the presence of anyone in fetters (Gell. *NA* 10.15). It was also considered improper for him to wear a ring, unless it was perforated and without a gem. Whether these restrictions were followed in reality is unclear: Beard, North and Price (1998: 28) suggest they may have been gradually relaxed over the course of the republican period. Even still, the image of the priest they create is one of unbound purity, open and ready to communicate with the gods, much like the women discussed above. It is significant that, when reporting these restrictions, Gellius claims to have read about them in Fabius Pictor, an association which gives them authority through an appeal to hallowed ancestral practice. Pliny the Elder (*HN* 28.17) does something similar in this passage discussing binding gestures, not just in religious performances but also at military and political meetings, and even in the presence of pregnant women:

> To sit in the presence of pregnant women, or when medicine is being given to patients, with the fingers interlaced comb-wise, is to be guilty of sorcery (*veneficium*), a discovery made, it is said, when Alcmena was giving birth to Hercules. The sorcery is worse if the hands are clasped round one knee or both, and also to cross the knees first in one way and then in the other. For this reason our ancestors forbade such postures at councils of war or of officials, on the ground that they were an obstacle to the transaction of all business. They also forbade them, indeed, to those attending sacred rites and prayers. (trans. Jones).

As with the *flamen Dialis*, it is unclear how scrupulously these proscriptions were adhered to in reality, but the emphasis on open, honest comportment is striking nevertheless. Across all of the literary evidence discussed in this section, there is a strong suggestion that gestures of binding, no matter how abstract or subtle, could be interpreted as an impediment to normal communications with the gods and, by extension, to normal running of the whole state. The image of a good Roman appearing in these specific public contexts, as taught by ancestral custom, was without rings, knotted clothing, tied hair or interlaced hands, and therefore fully invested in the smooth running of the state. The conclusions of Edwards (1993), Gleason (1995) and O'Sullivan (2011) on the intense scrutiny of public figures' bodily comportment can be applied here to suggest that these images of correct, traditional Roman comportment could have exerted pressure on people performing such rituals in the real world. When individuals were involved in religious, military or political business they may have been keenly aware of their posture, as they attempted to adhere to ancestral standards by keeping their fingers, hands and legs uncrossed. However, Pliny's suggestion that performing such gestures meant that the individual could be accused of intentionally trying to impede medical cures or public business takes these gestures beyond cultural constructions of correct behaviour. All of the literary descriptions of binding and unbinding rituals discussed here show that the Romans understood the human body as a potentially powerful object, the movements of which could have an impact on the outcome of events. In these depictions, activities such as successful communications with the gods or councils of war are predicated upon the movements and positions of the bodies of those involved. Behaving incorrectly in these situations did not only invite public censure, but could actively compromise the outcome.

It would be tempting to argue from these images of open, unbound worshippers that some individuals reversed the norm, and performed gestures of binding in order to achieve a negative outcome in these specific circumstances. Can we take Pliny at his word, and suggest that individuals performed gestures of binding at meetings of generals or politicians, with the explicit intention of blocking them from being completed successfully? Caution is needed when trying to use literary sources to reconstruct ritual actions as they were practiced in real life, especially on the subject of practices that could be interpreted as malign or magical. A number of scholars have demonstrated that literary depictions of magical practices rely heavily on stock imagery, which has more relevance to the construction of archetypal witch-figures than descriptions of real magical practices (Gordon 1987: 235–9; Dickie 2001: 176; Stratton

2007: 86; Paule 2014: 756). This is a symptom of the elite Roman concern over challenges to their dominance of both political and religious power structures, particularly from women. Any practice deemed to threaten male superiority in these arenas was denigrated as *superstitio* (Martin 2004; Gordon 2008), and the images of those who practiced them were often stereotyped and exaggerated for the greatest effect. Pliny's description of binding gestures at war councils would certainly fall into this category, and should therefore be treated with some suspicion. However, there is a ritual found in the *Greek Magical Papyri* (*PGM* 13.251–4) which indicates that binding gestures were promoted as being powerful and effective, and which resonates particularly strongly with the above quote from Pliny:

> To restrain anger: enter the presence of a king or magnate, and while you have your hands inside your garment say the name of the sun disk while tying a knot in your *pallium* or shawl. You will marvel at the results. (trans. Morton Smith)

Again, caution needs to be applied here. Comparing two sources produced at different times in very different cultural contexts cannot be done lightly or uncritically. The *PGM* are products of very specific Egyptian religious and cultural contexts, and scholars have long debated their purpose and the extent of their wider circulation (Frankfurter 1998: 228–33; Dieleman 2005: 285–94). There is very little evidence for their influence in the western Mediterranean before the mid-second century (Gordon *et al.* 2010: 518–19), and so it is unlikely that the Graeco-Egyptian magical tradition had any direct relationship with Pliny's binding gestures. Nevertheless, the similarities between the two are hard to ignore: in both, the hands are used to perform a binding gesture in the presence of a political or religious leader, with the intention of influencing the actions of others. By taking these two examples together, the importance of context becomes even more apparent. It would seem that, if they were practiced in reality, binding gestures such as these could only have the desired effect if performed at the right time and place, which in these cases meant the presence of magistrates, generals or priests.

There is an issue of subjectivity at work, not just here but throughout the binding and unbinding gestures discussed in this section. From the perspective of an official in the process of performing his duties – either a general in a war council, a magistrate passing judgement, or the magnate mentioned in the *PGM* charm – any attempt to impede him might seem like a serious challenge to the normal running of society, and therefore a practice to be vilified as a form of dangerous sorcery. From the other side, perhaps a person at the mercy of an official judgement or a group on the receiving end of Roman military action, these decisions might seem corrupt or cruel, and could have had serious consequences for their lives and livelihoods. It might seem reasonable for them to take any and all precautions against unfavourable outcomes, including the performing of magical rituals. The subjectivity of moral judgements against magical rituals is a serious issue with older scholarly divisions between 'religion' and 'magic', and something of which modern scholars are increasingly aware (Gordon 2013: 269). In terms of the binding and unbinding rituals that I am discussing here, it would be easy to slip unthinkingly into making an absolute division between negative/magical/binding on the one hand and positive/religious/unbinding on the other. This might have been how some elite Romans saw it, as demonstrated by the prevalent image of the unbound worshipping body in Latin literature, but the spell from the *PGM* should be a warning against assuming that it was a universally held division.

This brief analysis of the Roman literary sources has shown that the movements and gestures of human bodies were indeed thought of as being able to influence the world around them. Postures of openness and freedom from bindings were a common part of images of worshippers in literature, not only representing purity and independence of action, but directly aiding in successful communications with the gods. The close interrelationship between religion and politics in the Roman world meant that these associations between unbinding gestures and honest intent affected other aspects of public life, and may have had a role in the comportment of people attending the meetings of military and state leaders. From a certain perspective, these gestures were just one part of the ongoing debates within the Roman elite about the correct ways to behave in society. However, as the next section will demonstrate, belief in the power of bodily movements extended beyond the elite to have a much wider significance.

Binding Gestures and Curse Tablets

Curse tablets – inscribed pieces of lead intended to influence the actions or welfare of persons against their will (Jordan 1985: 151) – are perhaps the best-known form of binding magic from the ancient world. Thousands of these texts have been found, and they come from almost every province of the Roman Empire (Ogden 1999: 4). The focus of much modern scholarship on curses has been on the texts written on the tablets, and these have been extensively mined for their linguistic and literary value (see Kropp 2008 and Adams 2007 for two of many examples). Only recently has their materiality been discussed by scholars (Wilburn 2012; Curbera 2015; Sánchez Natalías, this volume), and I have argued elsewhere for a greater appreciation of the embodied realities of creating curse tablets in the northwestern provinces (McKie 2016). For the purposes of this chapter, curses provide evidence for ritual actions that were performed by individuals in the Roman world with the explicit intention of binding their victims in some way. Reconstructing the movements and gestures that went into making a curse tablet is not a simple task, as many of the actions that were involved in their creation were not recorded in the curse text. However, the physical state of the tablet itself can be seen as a record of the actions of the petitioner up to the point of deposition. By working backwards from that point, through the process of ritual creation of the curse, the series of actions that led to the final object can be reconstructed. To demonstrate the importance of binding gestures in the creation of curse tablets, this section will analyse those found in Italy and the wider western Empire. Recent scholarship has emphasised the continuity of practice in cursing across this region (Kropp 2008) and, although local variations do exist (especially in Britain), there are enough similarities in the form of the ritual to consider them together. This is not to claim, however, that cursing in the western parts of the Empire was totally divorced from Greek antecedents. Influences from Greece and other parts of the eastern Mediterranean are clearly visible in cursing rituals as practiced in the west (argued emphatically by Versnel 2010: 283), in both the texts of the curses and the material forms of the objects themselves. These influences are important, and have been a central feature of past scholarship on ancient cursing, but they are not necessarily my focus here. Large-scale cultural shifts were arguably less important for individuals making curse tablets, who were concerned with creating the most effective curse possible, using whatever knowledge they had at their disposal. To examine the embodied experience of binding gestures in cursing rituals it is necessary to reduce the analysis to the smallest scale possible: that of the individual.

Movements and gestures were crucial parts of the ritual creation of all curse tablets, and I would go so far as to argue that they were impossible to make without them. Apart from the action of writing, itself a significant ritual activity (Ingold 2000: 401–2), the people who made curse tablets also manipulated or mutilated the tablet in a variety of ways that symbolised and enhanced the binding power of the written curse. Folding and rolling the tablet were the most common of these movements, and were mostly done in such a way that the inscribed words would be hidden from view. Where a curse was written on both sides, as with *DTM* 4 from Mainz, it was usually the first side that was hidden. Patterns in the direction and number of folds within caches of curses are difficult to draw, and it seems that in each individual instance the petitioners themselves made decisions about how the ritual should be performed. These decisions might not have been premeditated, and could have been based on a variety of factors including the size and shape of the tablet itself, their own understandings of cursing and advice or information gained from other people, as well as perhaps previous experience of making curses or writing on other materials. Lead is a soft and malleable metal, and so folding or rolling a tablet would have been relatively easy to achieve by hand for

most able-bodied people, although not without some exertion. This would have been even more pronounced with thicker tablets such as *Tab. Sulis* 16 or *DTM* 3. Multiple folds of the metal become progressively more difficult to perform, which might account for the high proportion of tablets folded only once or twice. By folding or rolling their tablets, the people making them would not only have been obscuring their curse from public view, making it the sole concern of the gods or spirits involved, but were also symbolically fixing the curse (Ogden 1999: 13). Folds or rolls envelop the words written on the tablet, keeping them in place. They also mimic the binding and fixing formulas which could have been included in the written or spoken curse (Kropp 2010: 270–2). The action of folding a sheet of lead involves closing the hands together with some force, and this exertion of energy could have had an element of catharsis for the person performing it.

Some individuals sought to enhance the binding power of their curse by driving a nail through the tablet. Usually these hit the text, and so in these cases nailing must have occurred after inscribing (examples include *Tab. Sulis* 10 and *DTM* 16). Driving a nail through a single, thin sheet of lead is possible by hand, but requires much more exertion than the action of folding, and would therefore not have been possible for all petitioners. To pierce thicker tablets, such as *Tab. Sulis* 115, or after folding, as was done to one of the curses from Hockwold-cum-Wilton (Tomlin 2008: 130–1), would have required either considerable strength or a tool such as a hammer. In either case, the action of hammering or pushing a nail through something has strong connotations of fixing and binding, which would have enhanced the intentions of the written or spoken curse. The downward motion of the action was especially important, in that it reified the downward binding or fixing inherent in some cursing formulas. An example of this would be *RIB* 7, a curse from London on which the petitioner 'fixes down' (*defigo*) a woman called Trentia Maria. The tablet was pierced seven times after the words were written on it, a dramatic and unmistakably aggressive action that turned the symbolic fixing of the curse formula into an action with physical consequences in the real world.

A brief excursus on nailing is necessary here, to deal with other, more mundane possibilities behind the action. Some scholars have wondered whether curse tablets were nailed for the purpose of display, with the intention of communicating to the wider community the fact that the curse had been placed (Dungworth 1998: 155; Kiernan 2004a: 108–10; 2004b: 131). Although this is technically possible, it makes less sense when the ritual of cursing is considered from the perspective of those who practiced it. These individuals would have trusted the power of the gods to enact the curse, and in fact keeping the curse between themselves and the gods could have enhanced the possibility of success, because without knowledge that the curse had been placed there was no chance of the victim attempting to protect themselves with amulets, warding gestures or counter-curses (Ogden 1999: 51–2; Gager 1992: 219–22; Corbeill 2004: 32). Evidence from modern contexts reveals that this is a common concern for people engaging in magical practices, to the point where few anthropologists have ever recorded witnessing them being enacted. To take one example, in the Sri Lankan coastal village of Seenigama, the cursing shrine is located behind a wall on a small island off-shore, making it very difficult to see what is happening from the mainland (Feddema 1997: 204). The anthropologist who studied the shrine was only able to record the rituals after obtaining special permission to enter the shrine and witness the cursing procedure himself (Feddema 1997: 212). In other contexts, some anthropologists have even gone so far as to wonder if magical practices only exist in the fears of the general population, never actually being practiced in reality (Evans-Pritchard 1937: 404; Marwick 1965: 82). Whether these modern comparisons are directly relatable to the Roman material is far from certain, but they should at least make us consider more seriously the importance of secrecy in ancient cursing rituals. On balance, I argue that nailing is more likely to have been used as a symbolic gesture of binding, rather than for purposes of display. This is certainly the case for those tablets pierced multiple times, including the above curse from London.

Folding, rolling and nailing are all binding gestures that are visible on tablets found in the archaeological record. However, it is possible that other gestures were performed during the creation of curse tablets of which no trace has survived, either because they involved the use of perishable materials or only the movements of the performer's body. Instructions preserved in the *PGM* provide some possible examples, although, as has already been discussed, they should only be applied to cultural contexts outside Graeco-Roman Egypt with great care. Two of the recipes for curses in the papyri involve the petitioner binding the tablet with threads tied with 365 knots (4.330–4; 7.453). This number is clearly symbolic for the number of days in a year, but has connotations of binding too.[1] To emphasise this, both of these recipes instruct the petitioner to speak a specific phrase aloud while tying the knots ('Abrasax, hold her fast' and 'keep him who is held' respectively), which, when repeated over 300 times, would certainly have reinforced the intention behind the action in their mind. In the second of these two instructions (7.429–58), the string can be tied around the tablet in another way, which allows the curse to be broken in the future if necessary. To do so the petitioner should forgo the 365 knots (which otherwise make the curse unbreakable), and must have attached the string to the bank of the stream or drain before throwing it in, allowing it to be recovered and untied should the need arise. Whether these spells were ever performed exactly as written is debatable, but nevertheless it is clear that there was a connection between binding spells and physical gestures of tying or binding.

When the creation of curse tablets is considered alongside the literary evidence for binding gestures discussed earlier, some connections can be made. Folding a curse tablet could perhaps have been seen as conceptually similar to folding the legs or arms, and tying threads around tablets could easily be connected to the other rituals of binding using fabrics. There is certainly a connection to be made here between the image of the unbound body, which stood for openness and independent action, and the bound curse tablet, which restricted and controlled its victim. Although it is the material objects that are the focus of attention here, we should not forget the necessity of bodily engagement for the performance of these gestures. When they were performed by real, living human beings these gestures of binding would have influenced and been influenced by a whole range of sensations: the texture, temperature and weight of the materials, the ease or difficulty of moving the parts of body in the proscribed ways, physical exertion and so on.

Binding Gestures and Magical Dolls

There is another category of material object that has close associations with binding magic, not to mention the power attributed to human bodies and their movements: magical dolls, sometimes known as poppets or (erroneously) voodoo dolls (see Armitage 2015 for a detailed history of this term). Models of human bodies, usually made of clay, wax or metal, featured in the ritual practices of a number of ancient civilisations in the Near East (Faraone 1991: 172–89), but their use in binding spells is a particular feature of Graeco-Roman practice (Armitage 2015: 87), and during the imperial period seems to have been especially connected to erotic binding spells (Ogden 1999: 71–9). Their production seems not to have been exceptionally common, certainly less so than cursing with lead tablets: Curbera and Giannobile (2015: 124) note only 90 dolls from the whole Graeco-Roman period, a figure dwarfed by the 2000 curses now known. However, this is almost certainly due to the perishable nature of the materials from which they were usually made, which only rarely survive in the archaeological record. As with many other aspects of magical practice, the processes by which they were created grew more complex over the course of the Roman imperial period, and some of the latest examples from the western Empire, such as the fourth- or fifth-century dolls from the Fountain of Anna Perenna in Rome (Blänsdorf 2010; Piranomonte 2010; 2012), show clear influences from complicated Graeco-Egyptian magical traditions, including inscriptions of magical words and *charakteres*. Other scholars have discussed these influences in detail (most notably Faraone 1991, but see Bailliot 2015 for more recent work), and it is not my intention to repeat their conclusions here. Instead, I will analyse the movements and gestures that went into their creation, continuing the embodied perspective that I have used throughout this chapter. As with curse tablets, few scholars have examined magical dolls from such an approach, which enables us to view them as the end product of a series of ritual actions performed by a human actor, rather than privileging their final form. There are two ways in which magical dolls show the power of human bodies: (1) as objects produced by the movements and gestures of human hands and (2) as magical objects that represent bodies and that were believed to influence the real bodies of their victims.

With perhaps one exception (a terracotta bust of a couple and child, which was perhaps a reused ex-voto, see Faraone 1991: 203, n. 22), all of the magical dolls known from the western provinces of the Roman Empire were made by hand, either from clay, lead or a combination of perishable materials including wax. The figures are only roughly human-shaped, and are never accurate portraits of the victim (Faraone 1991: 190; Graf 1997: 139; Ogden 1999: 75). The figurines made of lead tend to have longer limbs, which were then bent or twisted as part of the binding ritual (Faraone 1991: nos. 21, 25, 26). The clay figurines almost all have more stunted arms and legs protruding from the torso, shaped with finger pressure (Bailliot 2015: 99). The seven figurines from the fountain of Anna Perenna were made of complicated mixtures of materials, including wax, flour, sugar, herbs and liquids such as milk, which have only survived because they were all sealed in lead containers (Piranomonte 2010: 205–6; 2012: 171–2). In most cases, for dolls made from any material, some pointed tool has been used to create eyes and a mouth, and many have prominent male genitalia. There is very little evidence in the western provinces for the entwined-couple type (except for one from Morocco, Faraone 1991: n.25), which seems to have been specific to Egypt and other eastern provinces. On one hand, the male genitalia on many of the dolls from the west could mean that their victims were all men, or, on the other hand the phallus could be performing some apotropaic function (Ogden 1999: 73. For the significance of phalli in Roman magic see papers by Parker and Whitmore in this volume). The specific motives behind the creation and deposition of the dolls are rarely, if ever spelled out, so ultimately the function of most of them is unknown. One of the Anna Perenna dolls (inv. 475542, see Blänsdorf 2012: 156), was inscribed with the name Petronius Cornigus, presumably the name of the victim, but gives no further clue to the motive behind the ritual. Some scholars (particularly Graf 1997: 137–46) have assumed an erotic motive, drawing on the complex recipe for dolls in the *PGM* (4.296–466) as evidence, but Faraone (1991: 193) has discussed the possibility that they could have been used defensively, to restrain enemies in any aspect of life.

The embodied experience of making one of these dolls will have varied considerably depending on the materials being used. Lead is dryer, harder and more difficult to manipulate than wet clay, for example, and producing a doll from lead may have involved a preliminary step of cutting a shape from a larger sheet of the metal, which may have required specialist tools or help from a skilled individual (for an example see Bailliot 2015: F12). The figurines deposited in the Fountain of Anna Perenna may also have required specialist input to ensure that the correct ingredients were used in the mixture. As the mixture was worked, the texture would have changed, from sticky and wet to drier and more solid, perhaps not unlike the making of bread or pastry dough. Most of the Anna Perenna dolls were formed around an inscribed piece of animal bone, again something that may have required specific knowledge to produce (Piranomonte 2010: 206).

Whether any of the dolls from Italy and the western provinces were made by professional magical practitioners is contested among scholars, but would have had an impact on the experience of the ritual. A professional making a doll for another person would have much less of an emotional stake in the outcome of the spell than someone producing one for their own intentions, and they might also be more familiar with the process if they had made more dolls previously. Many of the magical figurines, especially those from the north-western provinces in the first two centuries A.D. (Bailliot 2015), are very simple, with only faint echoes of the complex rituals preserved in sources such as the *PGM*. This might suggest that they were made by non-professionals, who perhaps had some idea that making dolls in these ways could enhance a binding spell (on the different levels of magical knowledge in the Roman Empire see Gordon 1987: 235–7). The Anna Perenna dolls are perhaps more likely to have been produced by a specialist, as they are made from a complicated mixture of ingredients and were deposited in a very specific manner. Each of the seven dolls from the spring was sealed in three lead containers, one inside the other, all of which were inscribed with magical symbols, drawings and formulas, including depictions of the Gnostic demon Abraxas (Blänsdorf 2012b: 155; Piranomonte 2012: 169–70. Abraxas was a popular figure in later Graeco-Egyptian magic, and is regularly invoked in the *PGM*. See Betz 1992: 331 for discussion and bibliography). Whether produced by a specialist or not, the ritual creation of magical dolls demonstrates the power invested in the movements and gestures of the human body, as the hands of whoever made the doll were able to transform an inert material into a powerful magical object, able to influence the minds and bodies of others. This power could have been gained through the study of written spell books, but that was certainly not essential.

Once made, a variety of binding gestures could be performed on the figurines. Many of the dolls from across the imperial period have been pierced, often multiple times (examples include Faraone 1991: n. 21; Bailliot 2015: F3, F4, F10). As with the curse tablets discussed above, piercing dolls is an unmistakably aggressive act that requires at least some physical exertion, something which can also be said for the twisting and bending of the dolls' limbs (Faraone 1991: ns. 25, 26: Bailliot 2015: F12). Again, the Anna Perenna dolls are at the more complex end of the ritual spectrum. One example from the spring (inv. 475550) shows repeated symbolism of binding, as it was bound with a model snake, wrapped in a lead sheet (on which magical symbols had been drawn), nailed, sealed in three separate inscribed containers and then deposited in the water of the fountain (Piranomonte 2010: 207–8; Sánchez Natalías 2015: 199–200). All of these movements, simple or complicated, were probably intended to amplify the binding power of the ritual, making them more effective at controlling the actions and intentions of their victims. Again, the material of the doll has an impact on the embodied experience, as well as which actions were actually possible. Piercing wax or wet clay is much easier than lead, but the limbs of lead dolls are perhaps more suited to bending or twisting. Graf (1997: 146) has cautioned against seeing spontaneous discharges of emotion or frustration in these actions, arguing that there is no place for such feelings in the complex rituals outlined for making the dolls in the *PGM*. While I agree that there would be an element of emotional detachment involved when the figurines were produced by professionals, it is clear that this is not the case for all of them. Cathartic release or transfer of emotion is much more likely in cases where individuals made dolls for their own intentions, as they would have had a more personal connection to the victim being represented by the doll, and would have had more emotional investment in the outcome of the ritual.

This brings the discussion onto the second of the two ways in which magical dolls show the power of human bodies in Roman magic that I outlined above. These figurines are an unambiguous demonstration of the potential for human bodies to be powerful magical objects, in that they are direct representations of them. Through the movements and gestures outlined above, inert materials were transformed into representations of the bodies of the victims, which were then available to be manipulated or mutilated as part of the binding spell. In effect, the dolls made the absent bodies of the victims symbolically present, and put them under the power of the person who made the doll. However, although the actions of piercing and twisting damaged the physical object of the doll, they were not intended to kill or physically harm the victim, something that a number of scholars have pointed out (Faraone 1991: 193; Graf 1997: 140, 145; Ogden 1999: 73). Instead, these gestures of binding were aimed at restraining or containing the victim, making the overall intention of the binding spell impossible to resist. Piranomonte (2010: 206) has argued that the binding and containing of the dolls in the Fountain of Anna Perenna isolated the victim, cutting them off from their social relationships. The figurines did not only represent the

physical body of the victim then, but symbolically stood for their whole person, including their emotional state, their mental capacities and their place in society. By piercing, binding or twisting the dolls, the person conducting the ritual attempted to directly influence all of these aspects of their victim's lives. Here we can see a conceptualisation of binding rituals similar to those explored in the first section of this chapter. If the image of unbound bodies symbolised openness and the proper running of society, then these magical dolls, pierced through with nails and with their limbs bound and twisted, were opposing symbols of isolation and hindrance.

Conclusions

As I mentioned in the introduction, the range of potential gestures and movements that could have been studied in this paper is vast. What I have included here is only a small sample, and is of course not intended as the final word on the subject. There is considerable scope for future research on the embodied experience of practicing magical rituals in the Roman world, and I hope that this paper will provoke discussion and thought. Nevertheless, a few brief conclusions can be made at this point.

The materiality of magical practices in the Roman world has become a welcome staple of scholarly debate in recent years. This paper has argued that, alongside tablets, amulets, gems and books, the physical bodies of the practitioners themselves could also be potent magical objects, and that by considering magical practices from an embodied perspective we can gain a much more developed understanding of their impact in the lives of those who practiced them. Gestures of binding and unbinding, no matter how simple or complicated, had the potential to be interpreted as powerful rituals intended to influence the outcome of real-world. These gestures could be made in conjunction with material objects, but not necessarily, and even when other objects were involved it was the ways in which they were manipulated by the movements and gestures of the body that mattered. To attempt to alter the outcome of a particular situation it was enough to just move or position parts of the body in certain ways, and it seems that people in the Roman world were always alive to the possibility that the people around them could be trying to do just that. As a result, binding and unbinding gestures formed part of the wider discussions among the Roman elite, not only about proper bodily comportment but also about correct, acceptable religious practice. The image of the unbound worshipping body is exceptionally common in Roman literature, as a powerful symbol of traditional communications with the gods. Unbinding a body, especially a female body, through letting hair down, or removing rings or shoes, removed social constraints and gave the individual the ability to act independently. Conversely, binding a body restricted their capacity to act in society, as seen in the twisted, nailed figures of the magical dolls.

Homogeneity of understanding, practice or experience should not be assumed for any of the gestures and movements that have been explored in this paper, and the types of bodies involved clearly made a difference. In terms of gender, it played a significant role in the literary images of binding gestures, with unbound female bodies being thought of as potentially dangerous for wider society, at least by elite male writers. Codifications of bodily comportment and action, including gestures of binding and unbinding, were an important part of gender identity among the Roman elite, with correct behaviour seen as an essential part of public life for men and women. Prominent male genitalia are a common feature on magical dolls from Italy and the west, either to identify their victims as men, or to make use of the magical power of phallic imagery. In terms of the actual practicing of binding and unbinding gestures, there would have been a whole range of possible experiences and responses, depending on age, experience and ability. As was discussed, professional practitioners making dolls or curses would have had a much lower emotional connection to the ritual than someone conducting the same ritual for their own personal intentions. Removing hairbands or forcing a nail through a sheet of lead might be relatively easy things to achieve for young, able-bodied adults, but might present much greater challenges for the elderly or infirm. These insights are only possible when rituals are considered from an embodied perspective, the importance of which I have demonstrated throughout this paper.

Department of Classics and Ancient History,
University of Manchester

Acknowledgements

I would like to thank Adam Parker for organising the panel from which the motivation for this volume originally came, and for the many stimulating conversations on Roman magic since. Thanks also go to Véronique Dasen, conference audiences in Milton Keynes, Canterbury and Manchester, and the two anonymous reviewers; their comments and suggestions have greatly improved various aspects of this paper.

Note

1   Using Gematria – the system of assigning numerical values to letters of the alphabet – 'Abrasax' adds up to 365, further strengthening the connection between the demon and the number (Bonner 1950: 133–4).

Bibliography

Ancient Sources

Aulus Gellius (Translated by J. Rolfe 1927). *Attic Nights.* Cambridge, MA: Harvard University Press.

Cicero (Translated by E. Sutton 1942). *On The Orator.* Cambridge, MA: Harvard University Press.
Lucan (Translated by J. Duff 1928). *Pharsalia.* Cambridge, MA: Harvard University Press.
Ovid (Translated by J. Frazer 1931). *Fasti.* Cambridge, MA: Harvard University Press.
Petronius (Translated by M. Heseltine and W. Rouse, revised by E. Warmington 1913). *Satyricon.* Cambridge, MA: Harvard University Press.
Pliny the Elder (Translated by W. Jones 1963) *Natural History.* Cambridge, MA: Harvard University Press.
Plutarch (Translated by B. Perrin 1919). *The Life of Caesar.* Cambridge, MA: Harvard University Press.
Quintilian (Translated by D. Russell). *Institutio Oratoria.* Cambridge, MA: Harvard University Press.
Virgil (Translated by H. Rushton Fairclough, revised by G. Goold 1916) *Aeneid.* Cambridge, MA: Harvard University Press.

Modern Sources

Adams, J. 2007. *The Regional Diversification of Latin, 200 BC–AD 600.* Cambridge: Cambridge University Press.
Armitage, N. 2015. European and African figural ritual magic: the beginnings of the voodoo doll myth. In C. Houlbrook and N. Armitage (eds) *The Materiality of Magic: An Artefactual Investigation into Ritual Practices and Popular Beliefs.* Oxford: Oxbow Books: 85–101.
Bailliot, M. 2015. Roman magic figurines from the western provinces of the Roman Empire: an archaeological survey. *Britannia* 46: 93–110.
Beard, M., North, J. and Price, S. 1998. *Religions of Rome.* Cambridge: Cambridge University Press.
Betts, E. 2017. Introduction: senses of empire. In E. Betts (ed.) *Senses of the Empire: Multisensory Approaches to Roman Culture.* London, New York: Routledge: xiv–xxiv.
Betz, H. (ed.) 1992. *The Greek Magical Papyri in Translation Including the Demotic Spells.* 2nd edition. Chicago, IL: University of Chicago Press.
Blänsdorf, J. 2010. The texts from the *Fons Anna Perenna.* In R. Gordon and F. Marco Simón (eds) *Magical Practice in the Latin West: Papers from the International Conference Held at the University of Zaragoza, 30 Sept.–1 Oct. 2005.* Leiden: Brill: 215–44.
Blänsdorf, J. 2012a. *Die Defixionum Tabellae des Mainzer Isis- und Mater Magna-Heiligtums: Defixionum Tabellae Mogontiacenses (DTM).* Mainz: Generaldirektion Kulturelles Erbe (GDKE), Direktion Landesarchäologie.
Blänsdorf, J. 2012b. The social background of the defixion texts of Mater Magna at Mainz and Anna Perenna at Rome. In M. Piranomonte and F. Marco Simón (eds) *Contesti Magici/ Contextos Magicos.* Rome: De Luca Editori D'Arte: 147–60.
Bonner, C. 1950. *Studies in Magical Amulets: Chiefly Graeco-Egyptian.* Ann Arbor, MI: University of Michigan Press.
Boschung, D. and Bremmer, J. (eds) 2015. *The Materiality of Magic.* Paderborn: Wilhelm Fink.
Brilliant, R. 1963. *Gesture and Rank in Roman Art: the Use of Gestures to Denote Statue in Roman Sculpture and Coinage.* New Haven, CO: The Academy.
Brown, P. 1970. Sorcery, demons, and the rise of Christianity from Late Antiquity to the Middle Ages. In M. Douglas (ed.)

Witchcraft Confessions and Accusations. London: Routledge: 17–46.

Collingwood, R. and Wright, R. 1965. *The Roman Inscriptions of Britain*. Oxford: Clarendon Press.

Corbeill, A. 2004. *Nature Embodied: Gesture in Ancient Rome*. Princeton, NJ, Oxford: Princeton University Press.

Curbera, J. 2015. From the magician's workshop: notes on the materiality of Greek curse tablets. In D. Boschung and J. Bremmer (eds) *The Materiality of Magic*. Paderborn: Wilhelm Fink: 97–122.

Curbera, J. and Giannobile, S. 2015. A 'voodoo doll' from Keos in Berlin's Antikensammlung. In D. Boschung and J. Bremmer (eds). *The Materiality of Magic*. Paderborn: Wilhelm Fink: 123–6.

Dickie, M. 2001. *Magic and Magicians in the Graeco-Roman World*. London, New York: Routledge.

Dieleman, J. 2005. *Priests, Tongues, and Rites: The London-Leiden Magical Manuscripts and Translation in Egyptian Ritual (100–300 CE)*. Leiden: Brill.

Dungworth, D. 1998. Mystifying Roman nails: *clavus annalis, defixiones* and *minkisi*. In C.H. Forcey, J. Hawthorne and R. Witcher (eds) *TRAC 97: Proceedings of the Seventh Annual Theoretical Roman Archaeology Conference*. Oxford: Oxbow Books: 148–59.

Edwards, C. 1993. *The Politics of Immorality in Ancient Rome*. Cambridge: Cambridge University Press.

Eitrem, S. 1953. Die Gestensprache Abwehr oder Kontakt. *Geras Antoniou Keramopoullou*. Athens: Typographeion Myrtide: 598–608.

Evans-Pritchard, E. E. 1937. *Witchcraft, Oracles and Magic Among the Azande*. Oxford: Clarendon Press.

Faraone, C. 1991. Binding and burying the forces of evil: the defensive use of "voodoo dolls" in ancient Greece. *Classical Antiquity* 10: 165–205, 207–20.

Farnell, B. 1999. Moving bodies, acting selves. *Annual Review of Anthropology* 28: 341–73.

Feddema, J. 1997. The cursing practice in Sri Lanka as a religious channel for keeping physical violence in control: the case of Seenigama. *Journal of Asian and African Studies* 32: 202–22.

Feeney, D. 1998. *Literature and Religion at Rome*. Cambridge: Cambridge University Press.

Frankfurter, D. 1998. *Religion in Roman Egypt: Assimilation and Resistance*. Princeton, NJ: Princeton University Press.

Gager, J. 1992. *Curse Tablets and Binding Spells from the Ancient World*. Oxford: Oxford University Press.

Gleason, M. 1995. *Making Men: Sophists and Self-Presentation in Ancient Rome*. Princeton, NJ: Princeton University Press.

Gordon, R. 1987. Lucan's Erictho. In M. Whitby, P. Hardie and M. Whitby (eds) *Homo Viator: Classical Essays for John Bramble*. Bristol: Bristol Classical Press: 231–41.

Gordon, R. 2008. *Superstitio*, superstition and religious repression in the late Roman republic and early principate. In S. Smith and A. Knight (eds) *The Religion of Fools? Superstition Past and Present*. Oxford: Oxford Journals: 72–94.

Gordon, R. 2013. Gods, guilt and suffering: psychological aspects of cursing in the north-western provinces of the Roman Empire. *Acta Classica Universitatis Scientiarum Debreceniensis* 49: 255–81.

Gordon, R., Joly, D. and Van Andringa, W. 2010. A prayer for blessings on three ritual objects discovered at Chartres-*Autricum* (France/Eure-et Loir). In R. Gordon and F. Marco-Simón (eds) *Magical Practice in the Latin West: Papers from the International Conference Held at the University of Zaragoza, 30 Sept.–1 Oct. 2005*. Leiden: Brill: 487–518.

Graf, F. 1997. *Magic in the Ancient World* (Translated by F. Philip). Cambridge, MA, London: Harvard University Press.

Hamilakis, Y. 2014. *Archaeology and the Senses: Human Experience, Memory and Affect*. Cambridge: Cambridge University Press.

Heckenbach, J. 1911. *De nuditate sacra sacrisque vinculis*. Giessen: A. Töpelmann.

Hicks, D. 2010. The material-cultural turn: event and effect. In D. Hicks and M. Beaudry (eds) *The Oxford Handbook of Material Culture Studies*. Oxford: Oxford University Press: 25–98.

Ingold, T. 2000. *The Perception of the Environment: Essays on Livelihood, Dwelling and Skill*. London, New York: Routledge.

Jordan, D. 1985. A survey of Greek *defixiones* not included in the special corpora. *Greek, Roman and Byzantine Studies* 26: 151–97.

Kiernan, P. 2004a. Britische Fluchtafeln und 'Gebete um Gerechtigkeit' als öffentliche Magie und Votivritual. In K. Brodersen and A. Kropp (eds) *Fluchtafeln: Neue Funde und neue Deutungen zum antiken Schadenzauber*. Frankfurt: Antike Verlag: 99–114.

Kiernan, P. 2004b. Did curse tablets work? In B. Croxford, H. Eckardt, J. Meade and J. Weekes (eds) *TRAC 2003: Proceedings of the 13th Annual Theoretical Roman Archaeology Conference*. Oxford: Oxbow Books: 123–134.

Kropp, A. 2008. *Magische Sprachverwendung in vulgärlateinischen Fluchtafeln (defixiones)*. Tübingen: G. Narr.

Kropp, A. 2010. How does magical language work? The spells and *formulae* of the Latin *defixionum tabellae*. In R. Gordon and F. Marco Simón (eds) *Magical Practice in the Latin West: Papers from the International Conference Held at the University of Zaragoza, 30 Sept.–1 Oct. 2005*. Leiden: Brill: 357–80.

Martin, D. 2004. *Inventing Superstition: From the Hippocratics to the Christians*. Cambridge, MA: Harvard University Press.

Marwick, M. 1965. *Sorcery in its Social Setting: a Study of the Northern Rhodesian Ceŵa*. Manchester: Manchester University Press.

McKie, S. 2016. Distraught, drained, devoured, or damned? The importance of individual creativity in Roman cursing. In M. Mandich, T. Derrick, S. González-Sánchez, G. Savani and E. Zampieri (eds) *TRAC 2015: Proceedings of the 25th Annual Theoretical Roman Archaeology Conference 2015*. Oxford: Oxbow Books: 15–27.

McNeill, D. 1992. *Hand and Mind: What Gestures Reveal About Thought*. Chicago, IL, London: University of Chicago Press.

McNeill, D. 2005. *Gesture and Thought*. Chicago, IL, London: University of Chicago Press.

Myerowitz Levine, M. 1995. The gendered grammar of ancient Mediterranean hair. In H. Eilberg-Schwarz and W. Doniger (eds) *Off with Her Head! The Denial of Women's Identity in Myth, Religion, and Culture*. Berkeley, CA: University of California Press: 76–130.

Noland, C. 2009. *Agency and Embodiment*. Harvard, NJ: Harvard University Press.

Ogden, D. 1999. Binding spells: curse tablets and voodoo dolls in the Greek and Roman worlds. In B. Ankarloo and S. Clark (eds) *Witchcraft and Magic in Europe: Ancient Greece and Rome*. Philadelphia, PA: University of Philadelphia Press: 3–90.

O' Sullivan, T. 2011. *Walking in Roman Culture*. Cambridge: Cambridge University Press.

Panayotakis, C. 2005. Nonverbal behaviour on the Roman comic stage. In D. Cairns (ed.) *Body Language in the Greek and Roman Worlds*. Swansea: Classical Press of Wales: 175–94.

Paule, M. 2014. *Quae saga, quis magus:* on the vocabulary of the Roman witch. *Classical Quarterly* 64: 745–57.

Phillips, R. 1992. Roman religion and literary studies of Ovid's *Fasti. Arethusa* 25: 55–80.

Piranomonte, M. 2010. Religion and magic at Rome: the fountain of Anna Perenna. In R. Gordon and F. Marco Simón (eds) *Magical Practice in the Latin West: Papers from the International Conference Held at the University of Zaragoza, 30 Sept.–1 Oct. 2005*. Leiden: Brill: 191–214.

Piranomonte, M. 2012. Anna Perenna: un contesto magico straordinario. In M. Piranomonte and F. Marco Simón (eds) *Contesti Magici/Contextos Magicos*. Rome: De Luca Editori D'Arte: 161–74.

Sánchez Natalías, C. 2015. Magical poppets in the western Roman Empire: a case study from the fountain of Anna Perenna. In T. Minniyakhmetova and K. Velkoborska (eds) *The Ritual Year 10: Magic in Rituals and Rituals in Magic*. Innsbruck, Tartu: ELM Scholarly Press: 194–202.

Sittl, C. 1890. *Die Gebärden der Griechen und Römer*. Leipzig: Teubner.

Stratton, K. 2007. *Naming the Witch: Magic, Discourse and Ideology*. New York: Columbia University Press.

Tomlin, R. 1988. The curse tablets. In B. Cunliffe (ed.) *The Temple of Sulis Minerva and Bath: Volume 2 The Finds from the Sacred Spring*. Monograph 16. Oxford: Oxford University Committee for Archaeology: 59–278.

Tomlin, R. 2008. Inscriptions. *Britannia* 39: 369–90.

Thomas, J. 1996. *Time, Culture and Identity: An Interpretative Archaeology*. London, New York: Routledge.

Thomas, J. 2006. Phenomenology and material culture. In C. Tilley, W. Keane, S. Küchler, M. Rowlands and P. Spyer (eds) *Handbook of Material Culture*. London: SAGE Publications: 43–59.

Versnel, H. 2010. Prayers for justice in east and west: recent finds and publications. In R. Gordon and F. Marco Simón (eds) *Magical Practice in the Latin West: Papers from the International Conference Held at the University of Zaragoza, 30 Sept.–1 Oct. 2005*. Leiden: Brill: 275–354.

Wilburn, A. 2012. *Materia Magica: The Archaeology of Magic in Roman Egypt, Cyprus and Spain*. Ann Arbor, MI: University of Michigan Press.

Abbreviations

DTM = Defixionum Tabellae Mogontiacenses (see Blänsdorf 2012a).

PGM = Papyri Graecae Magicae (see Betz 1992).

RIB = Roman Inscriptions of Britain (see Collingwood and Wright 1965).

Tab. Sulis = Tabellae Sulis (see Tomlin 1988).

Amulets, the Body and Personal Agency

Véronique Dasen

Magic and the History of the Body

The contribution of ancient magic to the history of the body has undergone a shift in the past decade thanks to an increased attention to the materiality of magical practices, as well as to magic as an embodied experience. This turn contributes to a renewed assessment of the place of magical knowledge in past societies, no more seen as marginal, a-historical, and opposed to religion. As McKie and Parker underscore in the introduction to this volume, ancient magic is now addressed as a cultural phenomenon, with varying forms in time and space, that reflects the beliefs, norms, and expectations of a specific society (see also Gordon and Marco Simon 2010; Dasen and Spieser 2014; Boschung and Bremmer 2015; Frankfurter in press; Endreffy *et al.* in press).

A number of scholars have now demonstrated the porosity of the boundaries between magic, medicine, and religion. Each field represents a specific knowledge, *technê*, or *ars*, that aims to act on the body, its health and integrity for different purposes, but with a similar cultural way of apprehending it, from head to toes, *a capite ad calcem*, with binary oppositions (up/down, right/left, feminine/masculine). In common they share a similar semiology of the body taking into account physical features, gestures, behaviours. Each *technê* has its autonomy, interpreting the same signs with different means and objectives, but all similarly postulate the existence of correspondences between the human body, animals, plants and stones, according to the principle of sympathies and antipathies, and its corollary, the notion of providential nature. These contiguities also appear in the use of instruments or containers of symbolic shape or with unusual contents, for medicine, ritual or poisoning (on glass *unguentaria*, see Derrick, this volume. On an enigmatic container in the shape of a hippopotamus from a doctor's tomb in Bingen see Martini 2015. For comparisons between medicine, physiognomony and magic see Bonnard *et al.* 2015. See also Garland, this volume, on the 'doctor's' burial in Stanway).

The study of medico-magical recipes and of *defixiones* or curse tablets has yielded significant results. Close investigations of the logic of medical incantations and amulets, as listed for example in the *Natural History* of Pliny the Elder, unveil subtle networks of associations and symbolic linkages between the human body and remedies. The choice of the substances, such as a green lizard for eye diseases or a swallow for angina, conforms to a hidden coherent system (e.g. Gaillard-Seux 1998; 2012; 2014; 2017; Totelin 2009; Galoppin 2015). Thus the use of medico-magical recipes often follows mimetic principles that operate by transferring the disease onto a substance or an animal by various processes (desiccation, burial, destruction by fire etc.). The transformation of the product reflects the evolution of the disease. The pioneering work of Heinrich von Staden (1991; 2008) also represents a benchmark. In 1991 he showed how the use of human or animal excrements (*Dreckapotheke*) in ancient gynecology participated in the cultural construction of the otherness of the female body, which must be purified and fertilised, like earth. Similar symbolic networks between nature, cosmos, and the body are at play in amulets.

Researches on aggressive magic also deliver important outcomes for the history of the body. As Sanchez Natalias demonstrates in this volume, lead *defixiones* or curse tablets (lat. *defigere*, 'to nail', gr. *katadesmoi*, 'tied down') also operate by mimetic action, based on the properties attributed to lead, regarded as cold and inert. The tablet is pierced with a nail materialising the will to paralyse the victim and fixing the imprecation formulas. The revival of interest for this material is partly due to new discoveries. Since the publication of Audollent in 1904, listing 300 *Defixionum tabellae*, the finds have multiplied. Nearly 2,000 tablets are currently known, of which about two-thirds are written in Greek, the rest in Latin (*c.* 600, see Sanchez Natalias, this volume), more rarely in other languages, such as Gaulish. Several databases provide access to the material (e.g. Dreher, project in progress; Curbera 2018; Eidinow 2007), and work is being done to better define their place of production and their circulation thanks to archaeometric analysis. Their production extends over a very broad chronological period, from the end of the sixth century B.C. to the sixth century A.D. In the Roman imperial period their diffusion in an extended space, from the provinces of the Orient to territories of the Germania, reflects the globalisation of magical knowledge also visible in magical gems and amulets.

Curse tablets are still classified as defined by Audollent (1904), following their aims: erotic contest, lawsuit, commercial or agonistic rivalry. In addition, some are 'judicial prayers' for the repair of a wrong committed by a thief or defamer. The curses list the body parts of the victim according to the conventional order from head to toe, *a capite ad calcem,* to immobilise and make helpless, without necessarily trying to kill. The body sites have several analogies with physiognomic practices and divination. In judicial *defixiones*, the speech, the soul (*psychê*) and the spirit (*nous*) are particularly targeted, in agonistic context, hands and feet when the rival is an athlete or a gladiator. The list can reach up to 35 anatomical terms, associating the outside (head, teeth, eyes, flesh) and inside of the body (*kardia, uenter, pulmones, stomachos, gastros, intestine, splanchna, cor, medulla*e), including the '365 muscles' of the body. As in physiognomy, the eyes are not just sense organs but they constitute the identity of the person. On a curse tablet found in Mainz, the whole body is hit, except the eyes, perhaps so that the victim attends his or her own death. Gordon notes that in general the magician must provoke psychosomatic type of pain, fatigue, loss of sleep, internal pain, especially abdominal (Gordon 2000; 2015). In judicial *defixiones*, the use of a legal terminology to demand revenge does not extend to the means to execute it. The tortures of divine justice, fevers and consumption, do not correspond to the sentences of human justice (Versnel 1998).

The logic of erotic *defixiones*, and love magic in general, reflects social dynamics. As Winkler (1990) has demonstrated, ritual erotic constraints develop in societies where women are closely controlled. Magical action can save face when the girl escapes the control of her family. The *agogai* do not deny female desire and pleasure, but integrate it. Bad effects are temporary (insomnia, loss of appetite, dizziness) and should motivate action 'until she comes to me'. Ties and nails are the projection of the torments felt by both the agent and the victim in societies where love is synonymous

of dependence and suffering. The mode of action is visible on lead figurines, bronze or clay (see the first comprehensive study of Faraone 1991; see also McKie, this volume). The head is turned, the limbs shackled, the eyes and ears missing, showing that the victim must lose orientation and be deprived of senses. Traces of the ritual performed may leave archaeological traces, like the miniature mud figurine found under the floor of a house in Karanis, burnt into a fire and pierced with a hairpin (see Wilburn, this volume). The power of these performative gestures (engraving, binding, firing, piercing) enact the incantations in order to master the entire body in a chthonian space.

Amulets

The publication of extensive *corpora* of material, as well as the creation of databases, have significantly contributed to the development of the research. The Campbell Bonner Database (CBd) created in 2012 by Nagy in Budapest soon will contain over 4000 magical gems, kept in public and private collection, allowing ground breaking outcomes. A corpus of Greek and Roman amulets, however, remains to be compiled. Their shapes and material belong to long-lived traditions, in a continuing process of transmission and transformation, some going back to ancient Egypt, such as the *lunula* or the shell, but in a continuing process of transmission and adaptation to new religious and social contexts (Herrmann and Staubli 2010; Bohak 2015).

The modern term 'amulet' involves a large range of objects, made of various materials, modest and cheap, like bone or shell, or very costly, like semi-precious stones and gold jewellery (for a preliminary typology, Dasen 2003, 2015a: 281–318 and 2015b). All are designated by generic Greek and Latin words expressing the idea of ties and protection: in Latin *ligatura* or *amuletum*, in Greek *periapton* or *periamma,* meaning 'what is tied, attached or suspended on a person', whereas *phylaktêrion* derives from *phylassô*, 'to guard, defend'. An amulet is thus basically an object or a substance that one has attached (Jouanna 2011), *habere secum*, to various parts of the body, according to a specific coporeal geography, around the neck, the thigh, the ankle, or the wrist, depending of the aim. Physical contact was essential in order to transmit the properties of the charm to its wearer. Some aimed at protecting in a generic way by warding off malevolent influences and ensuring success, others at preserving or healing a specific part of the body. Their characteristic is also to be transportable, moving with their owners in and outside the house, but retaining their private and personal value. Some terms refer to their medico-magical qualities. In Latin, for example, *remedia* means 'remedies', *praebia*, 'providing protection', as Varro (*On the Latin Language,* 7.107) explains: '*Praebia,* 'amulets', from *praebere* 'providing', that he may be safe, because they are prophylactics to be hung on boys' necks, *in collo pueris*'. Other terms refer to the shape of the amulet, such as *fascinum* for the phallus, *lunula* for the moon-shaped pendant, or *bulla* for the famous Roman gold container. *Phylaktêrion* or *phylacterium* also designate the metallic case containing a sheet with a magical formula or the medicine itself.

These small objects were ubiquitous in Roman daily life. They deliver a visual and material discourse on the body, life cycle and sexuality, varying according to age, sex, and social status. The crescent-shaped pendant, *lunula,* was thus reserved to women, young and adults; no man seems to have worn it. Social strategies were at work too, as for the gold *bulla*, allegedly reserved to freeborn boys (Dasen 2015a: 309–13; 2015b). Their growing visibility in the Roman period participates to the development of concern for the self, 'le soin de soi' (Foucault 1994; Rüpke 2013: 3–38). They evidence an embodied religious experience implying a personal communication with the divine. A large range was worn as charms by individuals at risk, especially children and women, the most fragile members of the society. Two examples will show how they can be used to analyse a cultural discourse on the body and on personal agency. The first one concerns amulets associated to the growing up process, physiological changes, and transition rites of children. The second one is based on gems, and concerns lithotherapy as evidence of cultural focuses on specific or 'societal' diseases, in particular gynecological. The use of protections implies awareness of the vulnerability, but also the search for command. I will thus argue that amulets can be interpreted as evidence of the intensive care that surrounded Roman-period children despite the high mortality, and of the mastery that Roman-period women aimed at having of their own body.

Coming of Age and Teething

Funerary archaeology may help identify traces of rituals surrounding the child's physiological development, associated with social integration. Some avenues for reflection can be opened on the basis of the abundant documentation gathered in recent years for the Roman period. The imposition of the name at the *dies lustricus* did not imply a modification of funerary rites (Dasen 2015a: 223–47), but another milestone can be identified by the changes in the location of the tomb and its material according to the age of the child. A first important threshold seems to take place around the age of six months, corresponding with teething. The transition period ends towards two or three years, when weaning occurs. Changes in feeding practices thus seem to have induced shifts in the social integration of the child. As they grow older, they are increasingly included in the community cemeteries, and their tombs are characterised by the deposit of a significant amount of amuletic devices between 6 months and 3 years (on this process in protohistoric southern France, see Dedet 2008:

323–7; for distribution table of amulets in children's tombs in Roman Gaul, see Bel 2012: 205, fig. 9).

Teething occupies an important place in ancient medical treatises relating to children. An entire Hippocratic treatise of the Roman period was devoted to the subject (*On Dentition*). Hippocratic *Aphorisms* (3.24–25) identify the main dangers of this transition period. It was dreaded as are all changes in diet and lifestyle that disrupt the fragile humoral balance of children:

> 24. In the different ages the following complaints occur: to little children and babies, aphthae, vomiting, coughs, sleeplessness, terrors, inflammation of the navel, watery discharges from the ears.
> 25. At the approach of dentition, irritation of the gums, fevers, convulsions, diarrhea, especially when cutting the canine teeth, and in the case of very fat children, and if the bowels are hard.

Gum pain, fevers, convulsions, and diarrhea are also listed by Celsus *(On medicine* 6.11.3). They occur in critical periods: around the fortieth day, in the seventh month, at the seventh year, then approaching puberty. Harmless ailments in adults can cause the death of the child, such as canker sores that are lethal for sucklings when they hamper proper feeding. Gaillard-Seux collected about 23 amulets for the teething of infants in Greek and Latin authors of the Roman imperial period (Gaillard-Seux 2013: 196). The belief that 'teeth can kill' belongs to the *longue durée*. Until the nineteenth century the high rate of infant mortality was regarded as partly due to teething, and the actual diseases, unrelated to dentition, were not treated (Dasen 2014b).

Amulets may represent gifts that marked this developmental phase, expected and apprehended at the same time. A detailed examination of the funerary material suggests their relation to health care. A burial in Nîmes (France) thus contained a child who died at the age of about 6 months. A set of amulets was found in the southeast corner of the pit (Figure 11.1).

Next to glass beads, a series of pierced charms includes three cattle teeth and three amber objects, in the shape of animals (rabbit, fish) and a stylised artificial tooth (Bel 2012: 209, fig. 14). The shape and the material of these charms can be associated with health problems specific to the age of the deceased, especially those of the dentition.

The set can be related to the animal substances recorded by Pliny the Elder. Many recipes are based on the principle of sympathetic magic, that 'the same heals the same'. The teeth of animals, dolphin, wolf, horse, or dog are thus believed to help the teething process: 'the first teeth of horses to fall out make the cutting of teeth easy for babies who wear them as an amulet, a more efficacious one if the teeth have not touched the ground' (*HN* 28.258–9).

This principle could explain the presence of animal teeth of different kinds, perforated or mounted as a pendant, in children's tombs, such as the horse molar of an infant burial

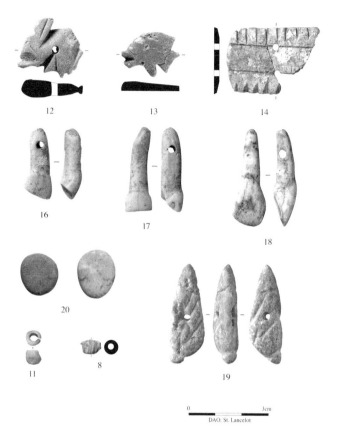

Figure 11.1 Set of teeth and amber amulets from tomb SP 1362, 78 av. Jean Jaurès, Nîmes (France) second century A.D (photo: Stéphane Lancelot, Inrap).

at Argentomagus. Pliny mentions other ways to use these protective teeth, such as doing a mouthwash with dog's teeth boiled in wine, or using ashes of dog's teeth, mixed with honey, as toothpaste (*HN* 30.22). The animal shape of amber pendants may be related to the same concern. Several therapeutic products are also derived from the hare, such as hare brains to rub the gums (*HN* 28.258–9). Dolphin tooth ashes mixed with honey are also good for children's gums. As an amulet (*adalligatus*) a proper dolphin tooth calms sudden fears (*HN* 32.137).

The material of the amulets adds its beneficial power. Amber, a resin of mysterious origin was believed to have multiple therapeutic qualities, especially for children. It preserved them from fevers, jaundice and bladder stones (on the qualities of amber, see Davies, this volume). Amulets are also made of bone, an animal substance that could have regenerative properties similar to those attributed to antler (Dasen 2003: 287–8; Alonso 2006). In the necropolis of Ste-Barbe in Marseille, a young child of about one year was thus buried with four glass beads, two bronze and amber phallic amulets, a bone-shaped tooth amulet (Figure 11.2a), and an actual dog canine (Figure 11.2b; Feugère 2003: 172).

The presence of a bottle that contained some drink could signal that the child was in the weaning process. The presence of dogs in the form of teeth may also have been

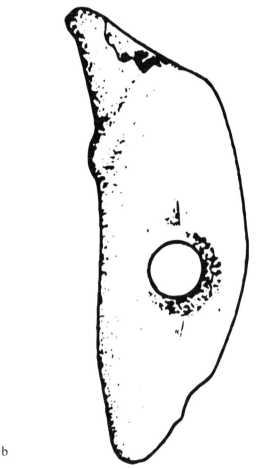

Figure 11.2 a: Marseille, Ste-Barbe cemetery, tomb 169. Set of bone objects First half of the second century A.D (photo Fr. Cognard); b: Dog canine, from the same tomb as in Fig. 11.2a (drawing Ph. Chapon).

meant to ward off hostile forces, as they did in other contexts, such as the mosaic pavements at the entrance of houses and shops in Vesuvian cities (see Wilburn, this volume).

The collection of this small material in funerary context still needs to be completed. A precise age at death is often unknown, as is the sex of the young deceased. In the sample gathered here, the objects are mainly associated with children under three years. Their high number evidence that the awareness of children's fragility did not generate indifference but, on the contrary, anxiety and constant care enacted by an uninterrupted 'votive cover', *pro salute*, and magical practices (on votive rites, see Cazanove 2008; Derks 2014; Carroll and Graham 2014).

Could amulets also represent traces of ritual acts? A first rite of passage was performed the day of birth by the midwife under the gaze of the Parcae or other divine entities patronising the entry into life. The first vows could be pronounced on the *dies lustricus,* eight or nine days after birth (Dasen 2015a: 243–7). No written source allows us to identify if the teething process was carried out under the patronage of a specialised deity. Many Latin entities listed in the *Indigitamenta* watch over the child, cradle (Cunina), growth (Carna, Ossipagina) and first steps (Statina) (e.g. Varro, *Antiquitates rerum humanarum et divinarum, apud* Augustine, *City of God,* 4.11.2–3; Bonnard *et al.* 2017: 381–2). Did a hypothetical Dentata or Dentina exist, or was the teething process ensured by Educa and Rumina?

Amulets and Lithotherapy: Societal Diseases

Magical gems are part of *physika,* natural remedies as minerals with a therapeutic value according to the principle of sympathetic magic, augmented by the engraving of divine images and magical texts (*uox magica, logoi, charaktêres*) carved to be read directly on the stone, not printed as seals. Most of them were produced in the second or third century A.D. (Dasen and Nagy in press).

The study of these objects has recently developed thanks to the publication of collections in Great Britain (Michel 2001; 2004), Italy and Germany, supported by the creation of the CBd in Budapest. Nagy (2012) traced the first Greek testimonies of the medical action of stones and rings. Materials, images and texts work metaphorically. The influence of astrological melothesia, where each sign governs a part of the body, is found on the gems in the figure of Chnoubis, a snake with a radiant lion head, from the Egyptian decans, which controls the stomach and belly area (Dasen and Nagy 2012; Spadini in press). Mimetic action can take different forms. Attilio Mastrocinque looked for the correspondences between the colours of minerals and corporal fluids (Mastrocinque 2011). A *historiola* often stages the pursuit of the personified illness, such as Heracles and the bile (cf. Sagiv, this volume), or Perseus and gout (Nagy 2015: 220–33), sometimes creating new myths (Ares and Tantalus, Athena and the snake). These stories also stage personal agency. The owner of the gem could identify himself with the hero depicted, engaging in the fight against the disease. The author of the Hippocratic

Epidemics (1.2.12) thus expects that the patient actively participates in the healing process described as a fight: 'the art has three factors, the disease, the patient, the physician. The physician is the servant of the art. The patient must cooperate with the physician in combating the disease.' Evil can also be hunted according to the principle of *deletio morbis* represented by a text or a image disappearing in the shape of wing or triangle (Faraone 2012).

It must be noted that gems do not cure all diseases equally. Ordinary ailments such as tooth aches or fractures are totally absent. No gem alludes to the care for limbs whereas anatomical offerings of arms, hands, legs, and feet abound in Greek, Etrusco-Roman and Gallo-Roman sanctuaries of healing deities. The largest series of medical gems instead focus on the belly region, and more specifically the uterus and the stomach. This selection may reflect the anxiety of internal and hence mysterious process. It also corresponds to what might be called 'societal diseases', partly because of the frequency of food poisoning and intestinal parasites, partly because procreation was central in a woman's life, and pregnancy very dangerous. In Greek and Latin literature, womb and belly ailments are thus common *topos* (Dasen 2014a; Dasen and Nagy 2012).

The study of haematite stones shows how mimetic action and sympathetic correspondences operate. Haematites, a type of iron ore, thus regulate human procreation (Figure 11.3).

When crushed and added to water or oil, the mineral turns the liquid blood red. This 'blood stone' was thus believed to control flows of blood, especially of women, by sympathetic magic. The stone does not represent just any blood. According to the Orphic Lapidary (21.658–663), it was produced by the drops of blood of the god Ouranos emasculated by Kronos. The blood falling to the earth hardened into haematite. Giants and the avenging Erinyes were also born from this blood. The story thus connects the power of the stone to both blood and reproductive organs, adding symbolically a strong male generative power to a stone beneficial to fecundity.

The image usually carved on stone depicts a medical cupping device that represents the womb. The metaphor occurs in Greek medical texts. Ancient authors compare the organ with different types of pots, such as the generic *angos* (a jar or jug). Soranus of Ephesus (*Gynecology*, 1.9) thus explains that the uterus is similar to a cupping vessel. The metaphor explains the sucking up action of the uterus: sperm ascends in the uterus because it is drawn up by heat. The cupping device thus can represent the attractive capacity of the womb, reflecting the idea that it is living being, and even a wilful and dangerous creature, as mentioned in magical papyri. Oribasius (*Medical collections,* 22.3) reports that 'often men feel their virile member attracted into the womb as if it were a cupping device'. This idea is reinforced by the use of haematite, resembling a magnet, called Heraclean stone, with an attractive power (Dasen 2015a: 34–41).

Figure 11.4 Red jasper (12 × 10.4 mm) second or third century A.D. Hamburg, coll. W. Skoluda M090. CBd-1631. Photo W. Skoluda.

Figure 11.3 Haematite stone (15 × 10mm), second or third century A.D. Private collection (photo: M. Depowska).

The representation of demonic entities, such as the god Seth-Typhon, refers to the notion of female body inhabited by a migrating uterus. Exorcism procedures put it in its place in the lower abdomen, a region of the body that Faraone (2011) associates with the desolate areas where the demons are expelled. Health and order are maintained as long as the organ remains anchored in the upper part of the body where the faculties of thought and judgement reside.

Women's Vulnerability or Power?

A series of gems throws an unexpected light on women's capacities, far from the victimised image reflected by the literary discourse on hysterical diseases; they reveal the presence of a strong divine feminine champion in the form of a 'magical' Omphale, endowed with special competences, substituting for her powerful lover, Heracles (Dasen 2015a: 87–108).

On uterine stones, Heracles controls the evils of the belly region, because he has a reputation as a glutton who gorges without falling ill. As an indefatigable lover and a father of a hundred children, Heracles also protects the uterus and its ills. His powers are translated visually and metaphorically. On a red jasper (Figure 11.4) Heracles fights against a lion

that he smothers with his bare hands. He is standing on a cupping device surrounded by the ouroboros snake and three K letters that could be an abbreviation for the word *Kolike*, colic. The scene shows that Heracles masters an undisciplined organ, subject to dangers whose violence evokes that of a wild animal.

A variant represents a naked woman, seen in front, squatting, her legs apart, in a delivery position, but wearing a lion's skin and waiving a club which designate her as Omphale, queen of Lydia (Figure 11.5).

Heracles served as her slave, before falling in such passionate love that they interchange roles. He dresses like a woman, and spins the wool whereas Omphale gets his club and the skin of the lion of Nemea. On the gems, Heracles still fights a lion, while Omphale struggles against a donkey with an erect phallus. The animal personifies the Egyptian god Seth who was believed to cause abortion or injure delivery to the embryo by inoculating his seed, compared to the poison of the scorpion. This evil power is here mastered; the gesture of Omphale implements a play of words: she waves a *skutalè* that means in Greek 'the club', as well as metaphorically 'the phallus' (on the phallus as a weapon against the evil eye, see also Whitmore, and Parker, this volume). The woman and the donkey thus fight with the same weapons, but the donkey is defeated, the spine curved or lying on its back. The dual competence of Omphale, mother and seducer, is included in her name, derived from *omphalos*, the navel, which evokes

Figure 11.5 Red jasper (12 × 16mm) second or third century A.D. The J. Paul Getty Museum 82.AN.162.80.CBd-2338 (© The J. Paul Getty Museum, Villa Collection, Malibu, California).

Figure 11.6 Gold pendant (H: c. 2cm) Hellenistic period? Collection Derek J. Content (photo C. Wagner).

the protection of the foetus as well as her sexual power. This combative Omphale also exists in the form of small pendants and protective statuettes long mistakenly named *Baubô* (Figure 11.6). In magical practice Omphale actively watches over the health, sexuality and fertility of women. She represents more than the female doublet of Heracles, a woman who controls her body and knows how to defend herself against the malignant influences.

Conclusion

The collection of papers in this volume demonstrates the wealth of information that material evidence can provide about the anthropology of the body. They open up a range of perspectives, for example on the study of the corporeal geography of amulets, or on the use of the body itself for protection. As McKie (this volume) convincingly argues, body language, such as binding and unbinding fingers, arms, or legs, was a significant part of religious experience (cf. Corbeill 2004). This still neglected field is contiguous with the divinatory dimension of bodily signs that yields original outcomes (Dasen 2008; Costanza 2009; Chandezon *et al.* 2013). The profile of the clients as well as the identity of the purveyors of amulets and magical devices in general (specialist or not? citizen or foreign? man or woman?) is getting slowly clearer thanks to archaeological approaches. Several papers also involve reflections on the *longue durée*, allowing little by little the reconstruction of the modes of transmission and transformation of magical knowledge as

a lived religious experience (see also Faraone 2010; Dasen and Spieser 2014).

University of Fribourg

Bibliography

Ancient Sources

Hippocrates (Translated by W. H. S. Jones). *Aphorisms*. Loeb Classical Library. Cambridge, MA: Harvard University Press.
Pliny the Elder (Translated by H. Rackham). *Natural History*. Loeb Classical Library. Cambridge, MA: Harvard University Press.
Orphic Lapidary (Translated by R. Halleux and J. Schamp 1985). Paris: Les Belles Lettres.
Soranus of Ephesus (Translated by O. Temkin). *Gynecology*. Baltimore, ML: Johns Hopkins University Press.
Varro (Translated by R. G. Kent). *On the Latin Language*. Loeb Classical Library. Cambridge, MA: Harvard University Press.

Corpora and Databases

CBd: Bélyácz, K., Endreffy, K. and Nagy, Á.M. (nd) *The Campbell Bonner Magical Gems Database*. Available: http://www2.szepmuveszeti.hu/talismans/. [Accessed: 25/10/17].
Campbell Bonner Database, Budapest. Available:http://classics.mfab.hu/talismans/.
Thesaurus Defixionum Magdeburgensis. (M. Dreher) Available: http://www.iges.ovgu.de/Lehrstühle+und+Fachgebiete/Altertum/Forschung+und+Projekte/TheDeMa.html

Modern Sources

Alonso, É. 2006. Les médaillons en bois de cerf de l'est et du centre-est de la Gaule romaine: étude d'après l'ensemble d'Alésia. *Revue archéologique de l'Est* 55: 197–223.
Audollent, A. 1904. *DefixionumTabellae. Quotquot innotuerunt tam in graecis orientis quem in totius occidentis partibus praeter atticas*. Paris: Fontemoing.
Bel, V. 2012. Les dépôts de mobilier dans les tombes d'enfants et d'adolescents en Gaule Narbonnaise au Haut-Empire. In A.

Hermary and C. Dubois (eds) *L'enfant et la mort dans l'Antiquité III, Le matériel associé aux tombes d'enfants.* Paris: Editions Errance; Aix-en-Provence: Centre Camille Jullian: 193–216.

Bodiou, L. and Mehl, V. in press. *Dictionnaire anthropologique du corps antique.* Rennes: Presses universitaires de Rennes.

Bohak, G. 2015. Amulets. In R. Raja and J. Rüpke (eds) *A Companion to the Archaeology of Religion in the Ancient World.* Blackwell Companions to the Ancient World. Chichester, Malden, MA, Oxford: Wiley Blackwell: 83–94.

Bonnard, J.-B., Dasen V. and Wilgaux J. 2017. *Famille et société dans le monde grec et en Italie du Vᵉ siècle au IIe siècle av. J.-C.* Rennes: Presses universitaires de Rennes.

Boschung, D. and Bremmer, J. (eds) 2015. *The Materiality of Magic.* Paderborn: Wilhelm Fink.

de Cazanove, O. 2008. Enfants en langes: pour quels vœux? In G. Greco and B. Ferrara (eds) *Doni agli dei. Il sistema dei doni votivi nei santuari.* Pozzuoli: Naus Editoria: 271–84.

Carroll, M. and Graham, E.-J. (eds). 2014. *Infant Health and Death in Roman Italy and Beyond.* Supplementary Series 96. Portsmouth, RI: Journal of Roman Archaeology.

Chandezon, C. Dasen, V. and Wilgaux, J. 2013. Dream interpretation, physiognomy, body divination. In Th. K. Hubbard (ed.) *A Companion to Greek and Roman Sexualities.* Malden, MA, Oxford, Chichester: Wiley-Blackwell: 297–313.

Corbeill, A. 2004. *Nature Embodied: Gesture in Ancient Rome.* Princeton, NJ, Oxford: Princeton University Press.

Costanza, S. 2009. *Corpus palmomanticum Graecum.* Papyrologica Florentina 39. Florence: Edizioni Gonnelli.

Curbera, J. 2018. Einblicke in die Arbeit eines Magiers. Wiederentdeckte Bleistücke erzählen über eine unbekannte Seite Athens. *Antike Welt* 1.18: 33–35.

Dasen, V. 2003. Amulettes d'enfants dans le monde grec et romain. *Latomus* 62: 275–89.

Dasen, V. 2008. Le langage divinatoire du corps. In V. Dasen and J. Wigaux (eds) *Langages et métaphores du corps dans le monde antique.* Rennes: Presses universitaires de Rennes: 223–42.

Dasen, V. 2014a. Healing images. Gems and medicine. *Oxford Journal of Archaeology* 33: 177–91.

Dasen, V. 2014b. Iconographie et archéologie des rites de passage de la petite enfance dans le monde romain. Questions méthodologiques. In A. Mouton and J. Patrier (eds) *Life, Death, and Coming of Age in Antiquity: Individual Rites of Passage in the Ancient Near East.* Leiden: Nederlands Instituut voor het Nabije Oosten: 231–52.

Dasen, V. 2015a. *Le sourire d'Omphale. Maternité et petite enfance dans l'Antiquité.* Rennes: Presses universitaires de Rennes.

Dasen, V. 2015b. Probaskania: amulets and magic in antiquity. In D. Boschung and J. N. Bremmer (eds) *The Materiality of Magic.* Paderborn: Wilhelm Fink: 177–203.

Dasen V. In press. Magical games. In A. Mastrocinque, J. Sanzo and M. Scapini (eds) *Ancient Magic, then and now.* Nordhausen: Verlag Traugott Bautz.

Dasen V. and Nagy, A.M. 2012. Le serpent léontocéphale Chnoubis et la magie de l'époque romaine impériale. *Anthropozoologica* 47: 291–314.

Dasen, V. and Nagy, Á.M. in press. Magical gems. In D. Frankfurter (ed) *Guide to the Study of Ancient Magic.* Leiden: Brill.

Dasen, V. and Spieser, J.-M. (eds) 2014. *Les savoirs magiques et leur transmission de l'Antiquité à la Renaissance.* Florence: Sismel.

Dasen, V. and Wilgaux, J. 2013. De la palmomantique à l'éternuement, lectures divinatoires des mouvements du corps. *Kernos* 26: 111–22.

Dedet, B. 2008. *Les enfants dans la société protohistorique. L'exemple du Sud de la France.* Rome: École française de Rome.

Derks, T. 2014. Seeking divine protection against untimely death: infant votives from Roman Gaul and Germany. In M. Carroll and E.-J. Graham (eds) *Infant Health and Death in Roman Italy.* Supplementary Series 96. Portsmouth, RI: Journal of Roman Archaeology: 47–68.

Eidinow, E. 2007. *Oracles, Curses, and Risk among the Ancient Greeks.* Oxford: Oxford University Press: 352–454.

Endreffy, K. Nagy, Á.M. and Spier, J. (eds) in press. *Magical Gems in their Context.* Rome: L'Erma Breitschneider.

Faraone, C.A. 1991. Binding and burying the forces of evil: the defensive use of 'voodoo-dolls' in Ancient Greece. *Classical Antiquity* 10: 165–220.

Faraone, C.A. 2010. A Greek magical gemstone from the Black Sea: amulet or miniature handbook? *Kernos* 23: 79–102.

Faraone, C.A. 2011. Magical and medical approaches to the wandering womb in the ancient Greek world. *Classical Antiquity* 30: 1–32.

Faraone, C.A. 2012. *Vanishing Acts on Ancient Greek Amulets: From Oral Performance to Visual Design.* London: Institute of Classical Studies.

Feugère, M. 2003. Le petit mobilier d'époque romaine. In M. Moliner, P. Mellinand, L. Naggiar, A. Richier and I. Villemeur *La nécropole de Sainte-Barbe à Marseille (IVᵉ s. av. J.-C. – IIᵉ s. ap. J.-C.).* Etudes Massaliètes 8. Aix-en-Provence: Édisud: 166–81.

Foucault, M. 1994. *Histoire de la sexualité*, III, *Le souci de soi.* Paris: Gallimard.

Frankfurter, D. (ed.) in press. *Guide to the Study of Ancient Magic.* Leiden: Brill.

Gaillard-Seux, P. 1998. Les maladies des yeux et le lézard vert. In G. Sabbah (ed.) *Nommer la maladie. Recherches sur le lexique gréco-latin de la pathologie.* Saint-Etienne: Publications de l'université de Saint-Etienne: 93–105.

Gaillard-Seux, P. 2012. Traitement magique des maux de dents à l'époque impériale romaine (Iᵉʳ-Vᵉ siècles). In E. Samama and F. Collard (eds) *Dents, dentistes et art dentaire. Histoire, pratiques et représentations, Antiquité, Moyen Âge, Ancien Régime.* Paris: L'Harmattan: 191–210.

Gaillard-Seux P. 2014. De l'Orient à l'Occident: les recettes médico-magiques tirées de l'hirondelle. In V. Dasen and J.-M. Spieser (eds) *Les savoirs magiques et leur transmission de l'Antiquité à la Renaissance.* Florence: Sismel: 169–94.

Gaillard-Seux, P. 2017. L'épilepsie de l'enfant dans l'Antiquité (Iᵉʳ-Vᵉ siècles): prévention et traitement. In V. Dasen and P. Gaillard-Seux (eds) *Accueil et soin de l'enfant (Antiquité, Moyen Âge, Annales de Bretagne et des Pays de l'Ouest)* 124(3): 175–202.

Galloppin, T. 2015. *Animaux et pouvoir rituel dans les pratiques magiques du monde romain.* PhD thesis. Paris: École Pratique des Hautes Études.

Gordon R. L. 2000. 'What's in a list?': Listing in Greek and Graeco-Roman malign magical texts. In D. Jordan, H. Montgomery and E. Thomasson (eds) *The World of Ancient Magic. Proceedings of the First International Eitrem Seminar, Athens May 1997.* Bergen: Norwegian Institute at Athens: 239–77.

Gordon, R. and Marco Simón, F. (eds) 2010. *Magical Practice in the Latin West: Papers from the International Conference Held at the University of Zaragoza, 30 Sept.–1 Oct. 2005.* Leiden: Brill.

Gordon, R. 2015a. Temporary deprivation. In R. Raja and J. Rüpke (eds) *A Companion to Archaeology of Religion in the Ancient World.* Malden MA, Oxford: Wiley Blackwell: 194–206.

Herrmann, C. and Staubli, T. 2010. *1001 Amulett. Altägyptischer Zauber, monotheisierte Talismane, säkulare Magie.* Freiburg: Bibel and Orient Museum.

Jouanna, J. 2011. Médecine rationnelle et magie: le statut des amulettes et des incantations chez Galien. *Revue des études grecques* 124: 44–77.

Martini, V. 2015. Du Nil au Rhin. L'imaginaire égyptien du médecin de Bingen. In V. Dasen (ed.) *Agir. Identité(s) des médecins antiques. Histoire, médecine et santé* 8: 115–33.

Mastrocinque, A. 2011. The colours of magical gems. In C. Entwistle and N. Adams (eds) *'Gems of Heaven'. Recent Research on Engraved Gemstones in Late Antiquity* c. *AD 200–600.* London: British Museum: 62–68.

Nagy, Á.M. 2012. *Daktylios pharmakites.* Magical healing gems and rings in the Graeco-Roman World. In C. Burnett and I. Csepregi-Vardabasso (eds) *Ritual Healing. Magic, Ritual and Medical Therapy from Antiquity until the Early Modern Period.* Florence: Edizioni del Galluzzo: 71–106.

Nagy, Á.M. 2015. Engeneering ancient amulets: magical gems of the Roman imperial period. In D. Boschung and J. N.

Bremmer (eds) *The Materiality of Magic.* Paderborn: Wilhelm Fink: 205–40.

Rüpke, J. (ed.) 2013. *The Individual in the Religions of the Ancient Mediterranean.* Oxford: Oxford University Press.

Spadini, F. in press, Astrologie et mélothésie. In L. Bodiou and V. Mehl (eds) *Dictionnaire anthropologique du corps antique.* Rennes: Rennes: Presses universitaires de Rennes.

von Staden, H. 1991. Matière et signification, Rituel, sexe et pharmacologie dans le corpus hippocratique. *L'Antiquité classique* 60: 42–61.

von Staden, H., 2008. Animals, women, and *Pharmaka* in the Hippocratic Corpus: beaver's testicle and the care of the womb. In V. Boudon-Millot, V. Dasen and B. Maire (eds) *Femmes en médecine. En l'honneur de D. Gourevitch.* Paris: Medica: 171–204.

Totelin, L.V. 2009. *Hippocratic Recipes: Oral and Written Transmission of Pharmacological Knowledge in Fifth-and Fourth-Century Greece.* Leiden; Boston: Brill.

Versnel, H.S. 1998. '... and any other part of the entire body there may be ...' An essay on anatomical curses. In F. Graf (ed.) *Ansichten griechischer Rituale. Geburtstags-Symposium für Walter Burkert.* Stuttgart, Leipzig: Teubner: 216–67.

Winkler, J.J. 1990. *The Constraints of Desire: the Anthropology of Sex and Gender in Ancient Greece.* London: Routledge.